CW01654736

Generative AI System Design Interview

Ali Aminian | Hao Sheng

ByteByteGo

Generative AI System Design Interview

Additional Resources

This book contains many references at the end of each chapter. The following GitHub repository contains all the clickable links.

https://bit.ly/genai-bytebytego

Other Books By ByteByteGo

The following books are available in paperback on Amazon:

To Niloufar.

Ali Aminian

To Jingyi, Keke, and my parents.

Hao Sheng

Acknowledgment

We wish we could say that every design in this book is entirely original. The reality is that most of the ideas presented here are drawn from various resources: engineering blogs, research papers, open-source code, and presentations on platforms like YouTube. We've gathered these valuable insights, reflected on them, and infused them with our own experiences and interpretations to create a guide that's easy to understand and accessible.

This book wouldn't have been possible without the thoughtful contributions and critical reviews from engineers and leaders in the field. A heartfelt thank you to Jayant Kumar (Adobe), Siavash Khodadadeh (Google DeepMind), Xinyue Liu (Google), Jingyi Su (Google), David Qiaojing Yan (Amazon), and Akhilesh Kumar (Meta). Your input has been invaluable, and we deeply appreciate your support.

Contents

1

Introduction and Overview

This book is designed to help machine learning (ML) engineers and data scientists succeed in ML system design interviews, with a focus on generative AI (GenAI). It complements the earlier book, "*ML System Design Interview*" [1], which covers conventional yet fundamental topics, such as search and recommendation systems. This book, however, explores GenAI applications and the unique challenges of designing such systems. It's also intended to serve as a guide for those who want to understand how GenAI is applied in practical scenarios.

This chapter explores two key topics. First, it provides an overview of GenAI, delving into its fundamental concepts and applications. Then, it introduces a comprehensive framework for building ML systems, which is essential for real-world applications and interview preparation. This framework will serve as the foundation for developing popular GenAI systems in the following chapters.

Let's dive in.

GenAI overview

Artificial intelligence (AI) is a branch of computer science focused on creating systems that can perform tasks that typically require human intelligence, such as reasoning, planning, and problem-solving. ML is a subset of AI that uses algorithms to learn from data rather than relying on predefined rules. These algorithms analyze data, identify patterns, and make predictions or generate new content based on the learned patterns. Applications such as recommendation systems, fraud detection, autonomous vehicles, and chatbots are generally powered by ML models.

ML models generally fall into two categories:

- Discriminative
- Generative

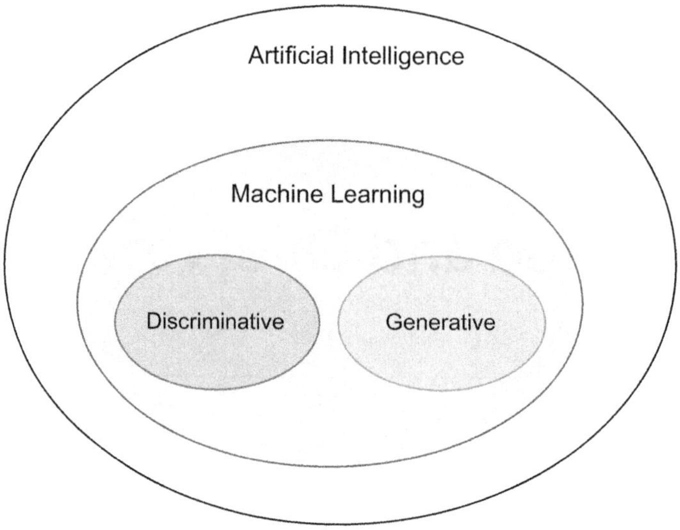

Figure 1.1: The relationship between AI and ML

Discriminative

Discriminative models classify data by learning the differences between classes based on input features. Formally, they learn the conditional probabilities, $P(Y \mid X)$, where Y represents the target variable and X represents the input features.

Discriminative models can be used for both classification, where the goal is to determine the class to which an input belongs, and regression, where the goal is to predict a continuous value. For example, in fraud detection, a discriminative model might classify transactions as either legitimate or fraudulent by analyzing features such as transaction amount and purchase history. Similarly, in movie recommendations, a model predicts a user's rating for a movie based on the user's historical interactions.

Common algorithms for developing discriminative models include:

- **Logistic regression:** A linear model that predicts the probability of a binary outcome based on input features.
- **Support vector machines (SVMs):** SVMs find the hyperplanes that best separate classes in the feature space. They can be extended to learn non-linear boundaries using kernel functions [2].
- **Decision trees:** These models and their variations, such as random forests, recursively split the data into subgroups based on the target variable.
- **K-nearest neighbors (KNN):** A non-parametric method that classifies a sample based on the majority label among its nearest neighbors in the feature space.
- **Neural networks:** These models consist of layers of interconnected neurons. They use weighted inputs, activation functions, and backpropagation to learn and approximate complex functions for tasks such as classification and regression.

While these algorithms can predict a target variable from input features, most of them lack the capability to learn the underlying data distribution needed to generate new data instances. For that, we turn to generative models.

Generative models

Generative models aim to understand and replicate the underlying distribution of data. Formally, they model the distribution $P(X)$ when focusing solely on the input data (e.g., image generation), or the joint probability distribution $P(X,Y)$ when considering both the input data and the target variable (e.g., text-to-image generation). This allows them to generate new data instances by sampling from these learned distributions.

Unlike discriminative models, which focus on distinguishing data instances, generative models can create new data samples that closely resemble the original data. For instance, a generative model trained on images of human faces can generate entirely new faces. These models are applied in various tasks such as text generation, image generation, and speech synthesis.

Generative algorithms can be divided into two categories: classical and modern. Classical algorithms are good at learning patterns from structured data. However, they can struggle to learn from more complex or unstructured data. Common classical generative algorithms include:

- **Naive Bayes:** A probabilistic model based on Bayes' theorem [3].
- **Gaussian mixture models (GMMs):** GMMs [4] represent data as a mixture of Gaussian distributions.
- **Hidden Markov models (HMMs):** HMMs [5] model the joint probability of observed sequences and the hidden states generating those sequences.
- **Boltzmann machines:** Energy-based models used for feature learning or dimensionality reduction [6].

On the other hand, modern generative algorithms learn from complex data distributions and are well suited for tasks such as generating realistic images and producing accurate textual outputs in response to queries. Common modern generative algorithms include:

- **Variational autoencoders (VAEs):** A type of autoencoder that models the distribution of data by encoding it to a latent space and then reconstructing the original data using a decoder.
- **Generative adversarial networks (GANs):** A class of neural networks in which a generator and discriminator are trained simultaneously. The generator creates realistic data, and the discriminator tries to distinguish between real and generated data.
- **Diffusion models:** Models that learn complex data distributions through a reverse diffusion process. They are commonly used for image and video generation.
- **Autoregressive models:** Models that generate data by predicting each element in a se-

quence based on the preceding elements. They are commonly used in text generation and time series forecasting.

Discriminative and generative models are used for different purposes. Discriminative models are typically used when the goal is to classify or predict; generative models are used to generate new samples. Figure 1.2 shows popular tasks powered by generative and discriminative models.

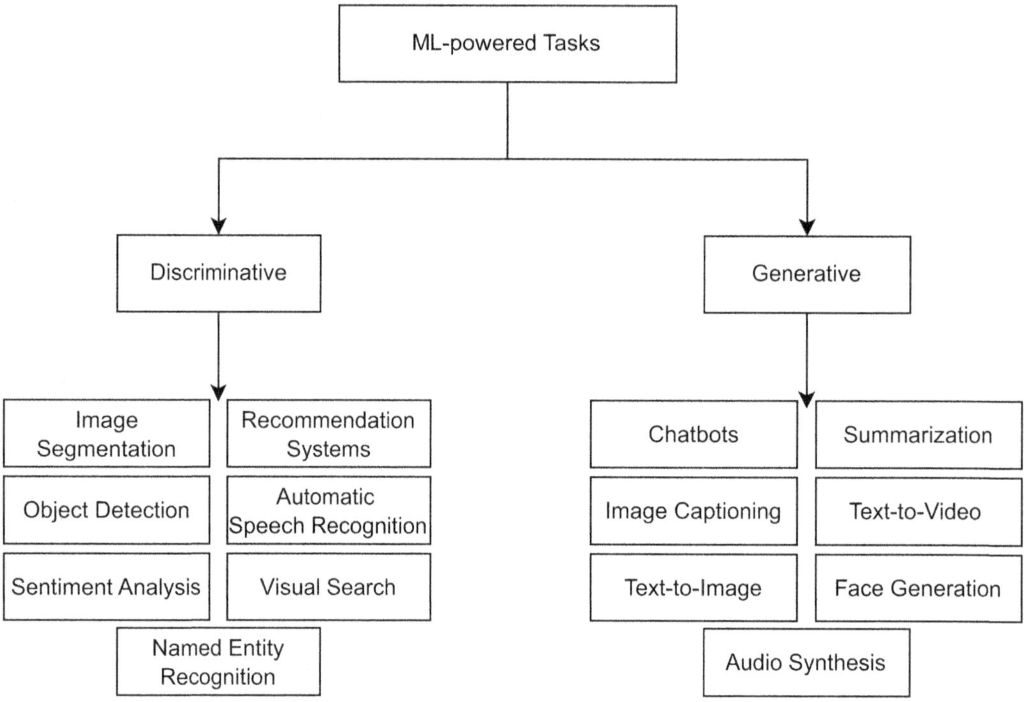

Figure 1.2: Popular ML-powered tasks

What is GenAI and why is it gaining popularity?

GenAI involves using modern generative algorithms to train models capable of producing new data samples such as images, videos, text, and audio.

GenAI has gained a lot of popularity recently for two main reasons. First, these models can perform various tasks across different domains such as generating text, creating realistic images, and composing music. This multitasking capability makes them valuable across industries, from creative arts and entertainment to healthcare and software development.

Second, GenAI applications significantly enhance productivity. For instance, in content creation, these models can generate drafts, suggest improvements, or even produce final outputs, saving considerable time and resources. Another example is the use of large language models (LLMs) such as ChatGPT [7], which can assist in tasks like answering complex questions and engaging in meaningful conversations. In a recent report by McKinsey [8], GenAI is predicted to enable labor productivity growth of 0.1 to 0.6 percent annually through 2040.

Why GenAI is becoming so powerful?

GenAI models have recently demonstrated impressive capability and are becoming very powerful. Three key factors driving this advancement are:

1. Data
2. Model capacity
3. Compute

Data

An ML model's effectiveness depends on its training data. For example, if a model has not been trained on extensive medical data, it might struggle to diagnose diseases accurately. Improving a model for a specific task requires large datasets with labels, but collecting this data can be challenging and expensive.

One key driver behind the success of GenAI is self-supervised learning. Unlike classical models that typically work well when trained on labeled data, GenAI models can learn from unlabeled data. This approach lets them use vast datasets from the internet without the need for costly and time-consuming labeling processes.

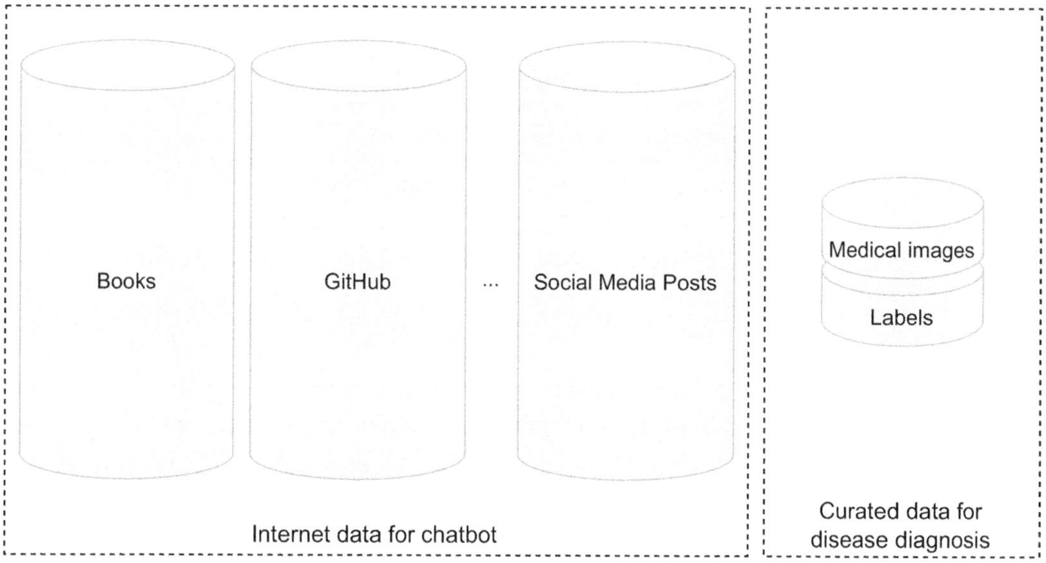

Figure 1.3: Data scale comparison between training a chatbot and disease diagnosis

Because of easy access to very large datasets from the internet, modern GenAI models can be trained on massive datasets, sometimes exceeding billions of text documents or images. For example, Meta's Llama 3 model [9] was trained on 15 trillion tokens—roughly 50 terabytes of data; Google's Flamingo model [10] was trained on 1.8 billion (image, text) pairs. Being trained on this massive amount of data helps these models learn complex patterns and nuances, resulting in high-quality outputs.

Model capacity

Another key factor in the effectiveness of ML models is their capacity to learn. Model capacity is measured in two ways:

- Number of parameters
- FLOP count

Number of parameters

Parameters are the values within a model that are learned during the training process. The number of parameters is a key indicator of a model's capacity to learn from data.

A model with more parameters generally has a greater capacity to learn the complex patterns and relationships that exist within the data. This often translates to better performance, assuming the model has been trained on a large dataset. Table 1.1 shows five popular models and their number of parameters.

Model Name	Parameters
Google's PaLM [11]	540B
OpenAI's GPT-3 [12]	175B
Google's Flamingo [10]	80B
Meta's Llama 3 [9]	405B
Google's Imagen [13]	2B

Table 1.1: Popular GenAI models and their number of parameters

FLOP count

FLOP (Floating Point Operations) measures the computational complexity of a model by counting the floating-point operations required to complete a forward pass. This includes basic arithmetic operations like addition, multiplication, and others that happen as data moves through the model's layers.

To better understand FLOP count, let's walk through a simple example.

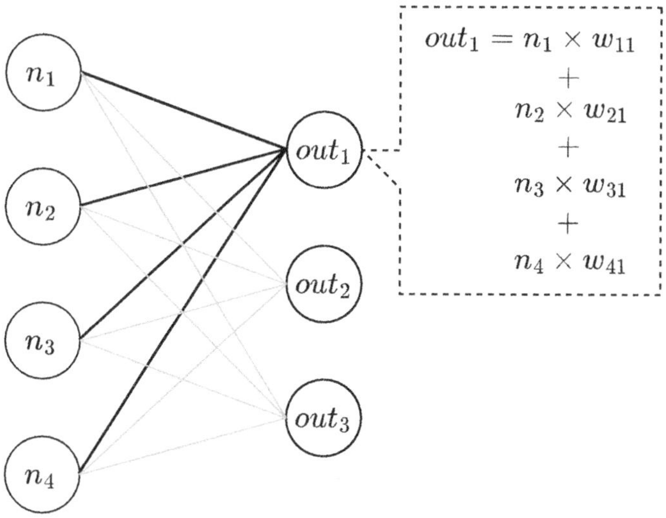

Figure 1.4: A simple fully connected layer and arithmetic calculations for a single output neuron

Consider a fully connected layer with 4 input neurons and 3 output neurons. Each output neuron is computed by multiplying the input neurons with their corresponding weight and summing them up. This results in 4 multiplications and 3 additions for each output neuron, as shown in Figure 1.4. Therefore, total FLOPs are $3 \times (4 + 3) = 21$.

While the number of parameters measures a model's size, FLOP indicates the number of arithmetic computations and provides insight into the model's computational complexity. Although a model with more parameters often has a higher FLOP count, this isn't always the case. The architecture plays a crucial role. For example, dense layers typically require more FLOPs than sparse connections, even if the parameter count is the same. Understanding this distinction is crucial when optimizing a model, as it helps us design models that are both accurate and computationally efficient.

Compute

As models increase in capacity, their performance tends to improve, but training these large models requires enormous amounts of computational resources. The compute required during model training is often measured in FLOP, representing the total number of operations performed. For example, Google's PaLM-2 model was trained using 10^{22} FLOPs [14].

Compute power is typically provided by hardware like CPUs, GPUs (Graphics Processing Units), and TPUs (Tensor Processing Units). Nvidia, for instance, offers advanced GPUs such as the H100, A100, and A10, each with different costs and processing capabilities. The performance of these machines is often measured in FLOP/S (Floating Point Operations Per Second). For example, Nvidia's H100 can deliver up to 60 teraflops per second (60 TFLOP/S) [15].

Training advanced GenAI models is expensive, requiring thousands of GPUs over weeks-long periods. To grasp the computational demands for models such as PaLM-2, let's calculate the required number of H100 GPUs. Assuming the H100 has a peak performance of 60 TFLOP/S, it can complete approximately 5.18×10^{18} FLOPs per day. Given that PaLM-2 required 10^{22} FLOPs, it would take around 5.5 years for a single H100 GPU to complete the necessary computations. Therefore, the cost of training large models is extremely high, often exceeding tens of millions of dollars. For example, Sam Altman, OpenAI's CEO, has stated that the cost of training GPT-4 was more than $100 million [16].

Training a model with billions of parameters (e.g., GPT-4, Llama 3) was not possible just a few years ago. The shift in capability has been mainly due to hardware advancements, particularly with specialized hardwares like GPUs and TPUs, designed for deep learning tasks. Distributed training has also been crucial, allowing the workload to be shared across thousands of machines in parallel. This significantly speeds up the process, making it feasible to train very large models on huge datasets. These infrastructure improvements and training techniques have made it possible to train GenAI models at unprecedented scales.

Scaling law

Within the constraints of a compute budget (measured in FLOPs), what is the optimal combination of model size and training data (measured by the number of tokens) that yields the lowest loss? This is the fundamental question researchers aim to answer through scaling laws.

In 2020, OpenAI researchers conducted extensive LLM training experiments, exploring various factors such as model sizes (N), dataset sizes (D), computational resources (C), model architectures, and context lengths [17]. Their findings revealed two key insights. First, the impact of scaling on model performance is significantly more pronounced than the influence of architectural variations. Second, as model size, dataset size, or computational resources are increased, there is a corresponding and predictable improvement in performance, which follows a power-law trend.

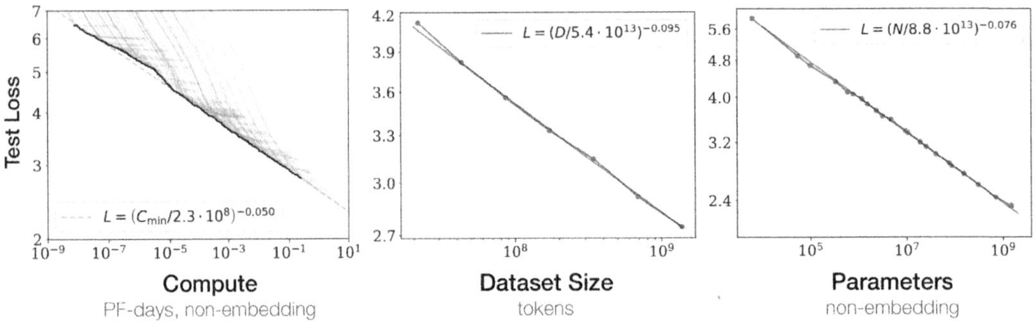

Figure 1.5: OpenAI's scaling law (Credit: [17])

In 2022, DeepMind researchers extended this understanding by highlighting that many existing LLMs were undertrained, meaning the models were not large enough for the amount of data on which they were trained [18]. They found that the amount of data should scale linearly with model size to achieve optimal performance.

With the recent release of OpenAI's o1 model [19], researchers have begun to speculate about the existence of a scaling law during inference, as well [20].

GenAI risks and limitations

GenAI has evolved quickly, driving advancements across many industries by creating realistic text, images, and videos. However, it also brings critical risks and limitations that need careful consideration. Addressing these issues is key to ensuring responsible and sustainable development. Common challenges include:

- **Ethical concerns:** Issues relating to bias, intellectual property (IP), misinformation, and misuse of generated content can have harmful societal impacts.
- **Environmental impact:** The high computational power required to train large models contributes to substantial energy consumption and carbon emissions.
- **Model limitations:** GenAI models may lack true understanding, leading to inaccuracies and limitations in complex reasoning tasks, and hallucination.
- **Security risks:** There are threats posed by the use of GenAI to create deepfakes used for blackmail, political manipulation, automated phishing attacks, and adversarial exploits that manipulate model outputs in critical systems such as healthcare and finance.

Each of these areas represents a significant challenge in the development of GenAI applications. Addressing these risks requires a multidisciplinary approach involving not just technical solutions but also ethical frameworks, legal regulations, and societal awareness.

A framework for ML system design interviews

Many engineers think of ML algorithms—for instance, autoregressive Transformers or diffusion models—as the entirety of an ML system. However, building and deploying GenAI systems involves much more than just training a model. These systems are complex, with components such as data pipelines to handle and preprocess large datasets, evaluation mechanisms to assess output quality and safety, infrastructure to deliver AI-generated content at scale, and monitoring to ensure consistent performance over time.

In an ML system design interview, particularly those focused on GenAI, you'll often face open-ended questions. For example, you might be asked to design a chatbot for customer service or an AI-powered image-editing tool for creatives. There isn't a single "correct" answer. The interviewer is interested in how you approach complex problems, your understanding of GenAI concepts, your system design process, and the reasoning behind your design choices.

To succeed in a GenAI system design interview, it is crucial to follow a structured framework. Disorganized responses can obscure your thought process and reduce clarity. This book introduces a framework to guide you through GenAI system design interviews. The framework includes the following key steps:

1. Clarifying requirements
2. Framing the problem as an ML task
3. Data preparation
4. Model development
5. Evaluation
6. Overall ML system design
7. Deployment and monitoring

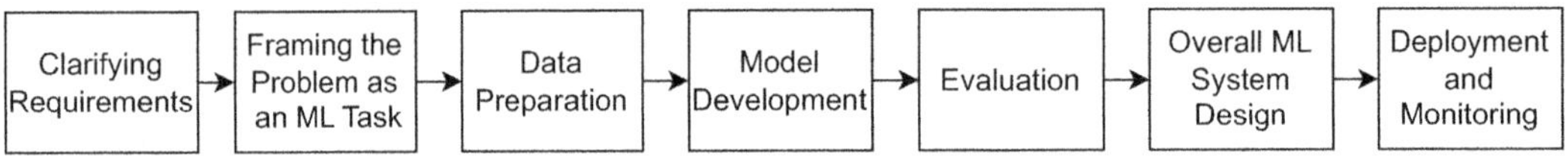

Figure 1.6: ML system design steps

Let's dive into each step to examine the key considerations and talking points when designing a GenAI system.

Clarifying Requirements

When you start to develop an ML system to solve a particular task, you often have minimal information to begin with. Similarly, in interviews, ML system design questions are often vague, providing minimal details. For instance, an interview might ask you to "design an image generation system." The first step is to ask clarifying questions. But what questions should you ask?

Your questions should help in understanding the problem space and the specific goals the system needs to achieve. They fall into two types:

- Functional requirements
- Non-functional requirements

Functional requirements

Functional requirements describe what the system should do—the core capabilities of the system. For example, "generate an image and customize its style based on the user's prompt" is a functional requirement for a text-to-image system. In the context of designing a GenAI system, functional requirements are crucial because they shape the high-level architecture of the system. They guide the development of essential components and functionalities that the system needs to deliver to meet user needs.

Non-functional requirements

Non-functional requirements focus on how the system performs, not what it does. These include performance metrics such as latency and throughput, along with considerations for fairness, security, and scalability. In an image generation system, for example, non-functional requirements might define the acceptable speed for generating images and the quality standards they must meet. While these requirements are usually advanced topics in GenAI system design and may not significantly alter the initial architecture, it's crucial to identify and understand them early, as they will often shape the later stages of design, especially during performance tuning and system improvements.

Here are some questions to help you get started:

- **Business objective:** What is the primary goal of this system? What specific purpose will it serve? For example, when designing an image captioning system, it's essential to know if it will be used for generating detailed product descriptions on an e-commerce platform or for suggesting short captions for photos on social media.
- **System features:** What features should the system support that might influence the ML design? For instance, when designing an image generation system, it's important to know if users can provide feedback or rate the generated images, as these interactions could enhance the model. Similarly, when designing an LLM, it's crucial to know which languages should be supported.
- **Data:** What are the data sources? How large is the dataset? Is the data labeled? These questions are crucial because the quality and quantity of the data might influence the design.
- **Constraints:** What are the available computational resources? Will the system be cloud-based or designed to run on-device?
- **System scale:** How many users are expected to use the system? How many images need to be generated, and what is the expected growth in demand? These questions are important to clarify because a system designed to generate images for a small group of users will not require the same level of scalability as one expected to serve millions of users.
- **Performance:** How quickly should the content be generated? Is real-time generation required? Is there a higher priority on content quality or generation speed?

This list isn't comprehensive, but it provides a good starting point. Other topics, such as privacy, ethics, and data security, can also be important.

By the end of this step, you should be aligned with the interviewer on the system's scope and requirements. It's generally a good idea to clarify these details to ensure you're addressing the interviewer's expectations.

Framing the problem as an ML task

If an interviewer asks you to design a feature that automatically summarizes emails for users, you have a problem to solve. But you can't simply ask AI to summarize emails. Instead, you need to frame the problem so that AI techniques can address it. Framing a problem as an ML task is a key step in designing ML systems, as doing this shapes the rest of your design.

When tackling a problem, you first need to determine whether ML is even necessary. However, with GenAI systems, you can typically assume ML will be required since it's the main tool for developing these systems.

The following two steps are useful for framing your problem as an ML task:

- Specify the system's input and output
- Choose a suitable ML approach

Specify the system's input and output

To frame the problem, you first define the system's input and output. This involves identifying the input data modality (text, image, audio, video) and the expected output. For instance, in a chatbot system, the input is the user's text query, and the output is the system's response.

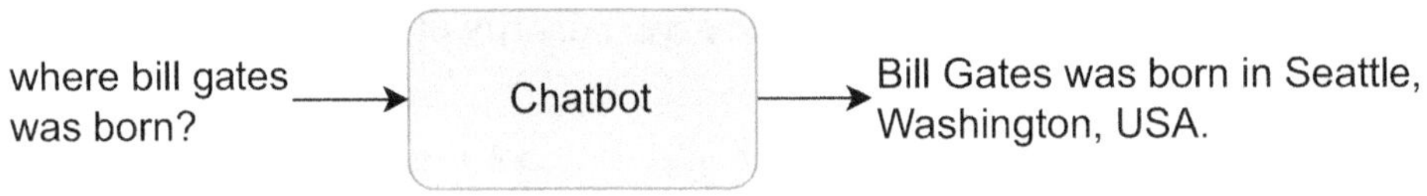

Figure 1.7: Input and output of a chatbot

Choose a suitable ML approach

After defining the input and output of the system, the next step is to choose the most suitable ML approach. This involves identifying key components of your system and selecting an algorithm that aligns with the specific needs of the problem. As illustrated in Figure 1.8, there are numerous ML algorithms to choose from, each with its own strengths and weaknesses. It is crucial to compare them, discuss the trade-offs, and choose the one that is most suitable for your task.

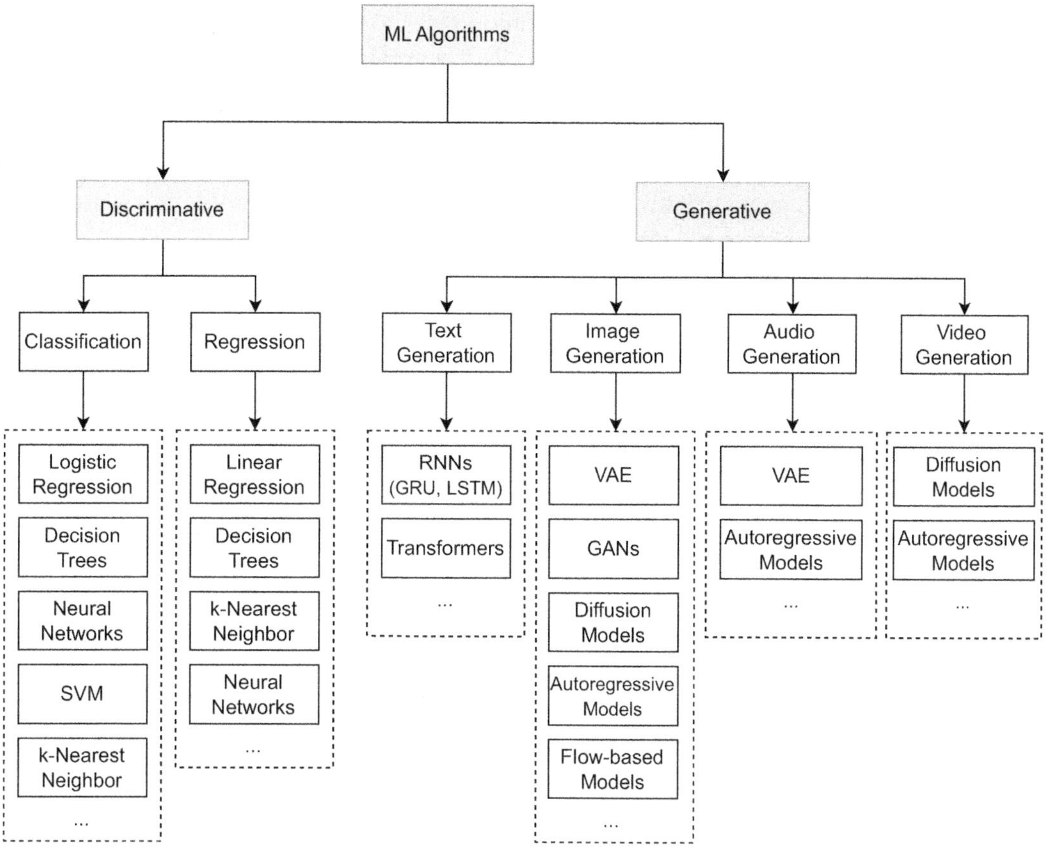

Figure 1.8: Common ML algorithms

There are different ways to select an appropriate ML algorithm, and the criteria for selection vary from application to application. The following steps can help you narrow down your options when choosing the most suitable algorithm:

1. **Discriminative vs. generative:** First, determine whether the problem requires a discriminative or generative model. This can be easily determined based on the system's output. For example, in an object detection problem, where the output is the class of the input image, the task is discriminative. In contrast, designing a chatbot that produces text as output is a generative task.

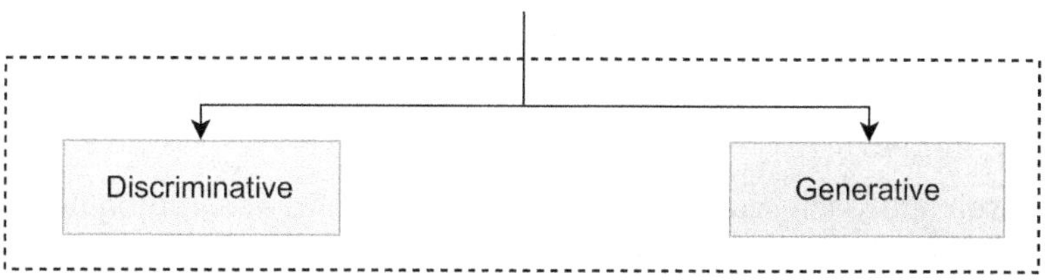

Figure 1.9: Step one for choosing a suitable ML approach

2. **Identify the task type:** Next, identify the specific task type to further narrow the

choice of algorithms. The two most common tasks for discriminative models are classification and regression. Generative models commonly undertake tasks such as text, image, audio, and video generation.
The system's output can help identify the task type. For instance, an image captioning system generates text, making it a text generation task; a face generation system produces images, making it an image generation task; an object detection system that outputs an object class is a classification task.

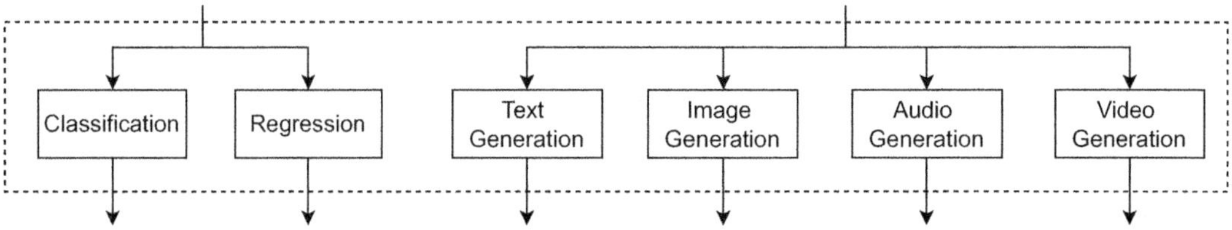

Figure 1.10: Step two for choosing a suitable ML approach

3. **Choose a suitable algorithm:** Finally, select an algorithm that is most suitable based on the requirements. Consider factors such as the ability to handle different input modalities, efficiency, and quality expectations. For example, in a text-to-image system, the algorithm must process text as input and generate an image as output; therefore, VAEs or GANs might not be ideal despite their abilities to generate images. This step is the ideal time to evaluate the various options and discuss their trade-offs.

In the upcoming chapters, we will examine various ML approaches used in popular GenAI applications.

Talking points

- What are the system's inputs and outputs based on the requirements?
- Which data modalities (text, image, audio, video) does the model need to understand and process? How will the model handle different modalities?
- Should a single model handle all input modalities, or is it more effective to use multiple models for different modalities? What are the benefits and drawbacks of using a unified model versus specialized models for each modality?
- Which generative algorithm (e.g., diffusion models, VAEs, GANs) is best suited for the task at hand, and why? What are the specific trade-offs between different algorithms in terms of quality, efficiency, and ease of use?
- What are the performance, stability, and resource implications of choosing one algorithm over another?
- Is the chosen approach scalable and flexible enough to accommodate future changes or additions to the system's capabilities? How easily can the system adapt if new input modalities or outputs are introduced later?

Data Preparation

ML models learn directly from data; therefore, high-quality data is crucial for effective training. This section explains different data types and key considerations when preparing them for ML models.

Data types

In ML, data is generally categorized into two types: structured and unstructured.

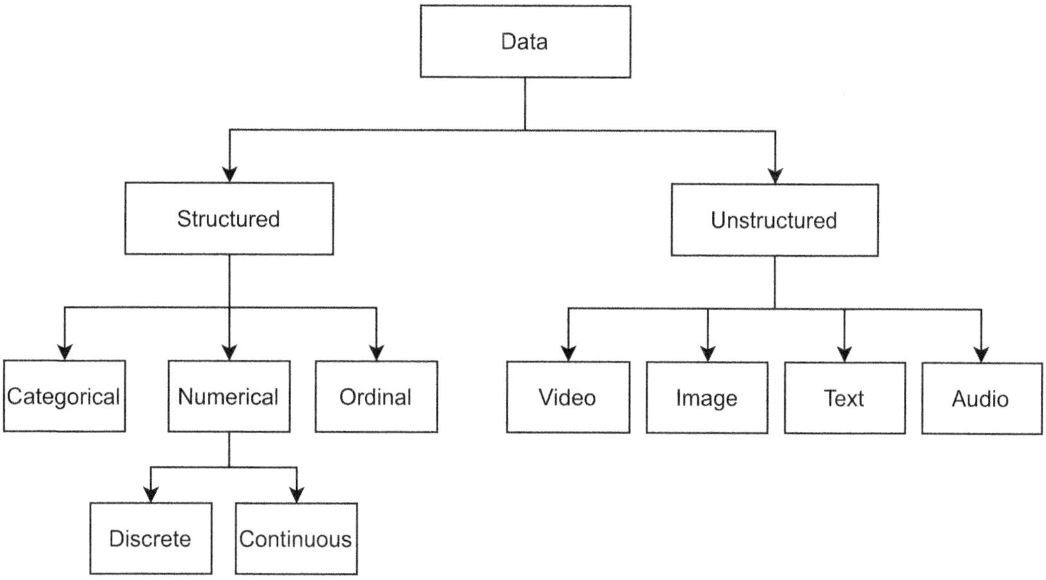

Figure 1.11: Data categories

Structured data: This type of data can be organized into tables with rows and columns. Financial records and customer data are examples of structured data. Structured data can be further divided into the following categories:

- **Categorical data:** Data that represent distinct groups or categories (e.g., gender, color).
- **Numerical data:** Data that represent measurable quantities (e.g., number of items sold, house price).
- **Ordinal data:** Data with a predetermined order (e.g., satisfaction ratings).

Unstructured data: Unstructured data refers to data with no underlying data schema or structure, such as text, images, videos, audio files, or a combination of them. For example, social media posts or emails are examples of unstructured data.

Traditional ML models are typically trained on structured data. In contrast, models that power GenAI applications primarily deal with unstructured data. As a result, the focus of data preparation differs significantly between traditional models handling structured data and generative models working with unstructured data. Let's explore each in more detail.

Data preparation in traditional ML

Preparing structured data for traditional models typically involves two key steps: data engineering and feature engineering.

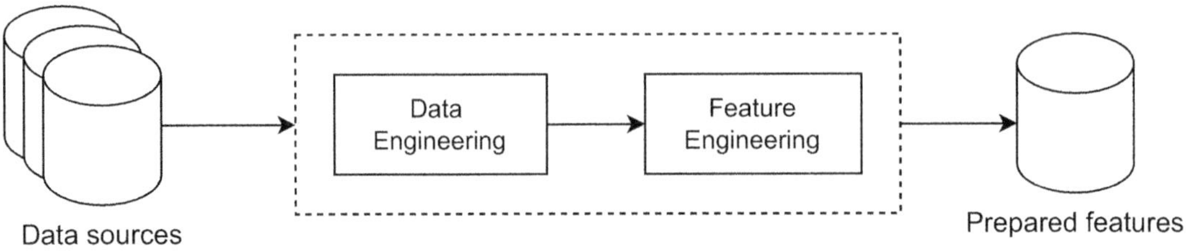

Figure 1.12: Data preparation process for structured data

Data Engineering

Data engineering involves building and maintaining systems for collecting, storing, retrieving, and processing data. A core component of this is ETL (Extract, Transform, Load) [21], which refers to the process of extracting data from various sources, transforming it into a usable format, and loading it into a data warehouse or other storage system. Data engineering ensures that data is clean, reliable, and accessible.

Feature Engineering

Feature engineering involves selecting and extracting predictive features from raw data and transforming them into a format usable by ML models. This process often utilizes feature stores, such as Tecton [22] or Amazon SageMaker [23], which offer a centralized platform for managing and serving features at scale.

Selecting the right features is crucial when developing and training ML models. It's important to choose features that provide the most information. The feature engineering process requires subject matter expertise and is highly task-specific. It includes techniques such as handling missing values, representing categorical features, and bucketing.

Since this book focuses on GenAI, we concentrate primarily on data preparation specific to GenAI models. For a deeper dive into data engineering and feature engineering techniques, refer to [24].

Data preparation in GenAI

When preparing unstructured data for generative models, the focus shifts from feature engineering to collecting vast amounts of data; ensuring the data is of high quality and safe; and utilizing tools to store and retrieve the data efficiently and at scale.

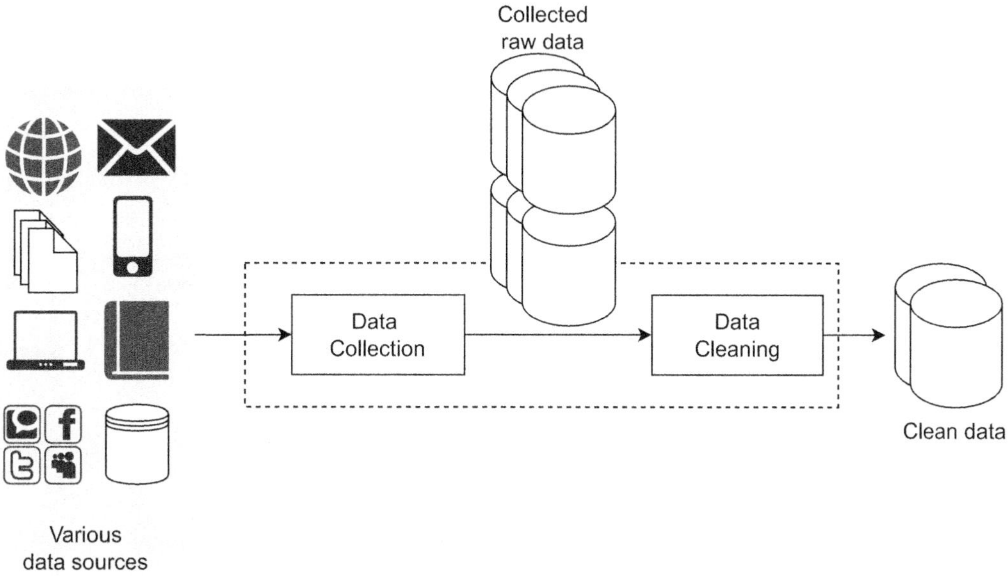

Figure 1.13: Data preparation process in GenAI

Let's examine the following key steps in data preparation:

- Data collection
- Data cleaning
- Data efficiency

Data collection

Advanced GenAI models have billions of parameters that enable them to learn and generalize from data. Due to their size, these models require vast amount of training data to capture complex patterns. For instance, Llama 3 was trained on 15 trillion tokens from various internet sources—equivalent to 50 terabytes of data. To put this into perspective, a person reading nonstop at the typical rate of 250 words per minute would take around 85,000 years to read that amount of text. The data collection process gathers large datasets by scraping text from different sources (e.g., websites, social media, and forums).

As models grow larger, there's a trend toward enhancing training datasets with AI-generated content. This involves using existing models to create synthetic data, which is then used to train another GenAI model.

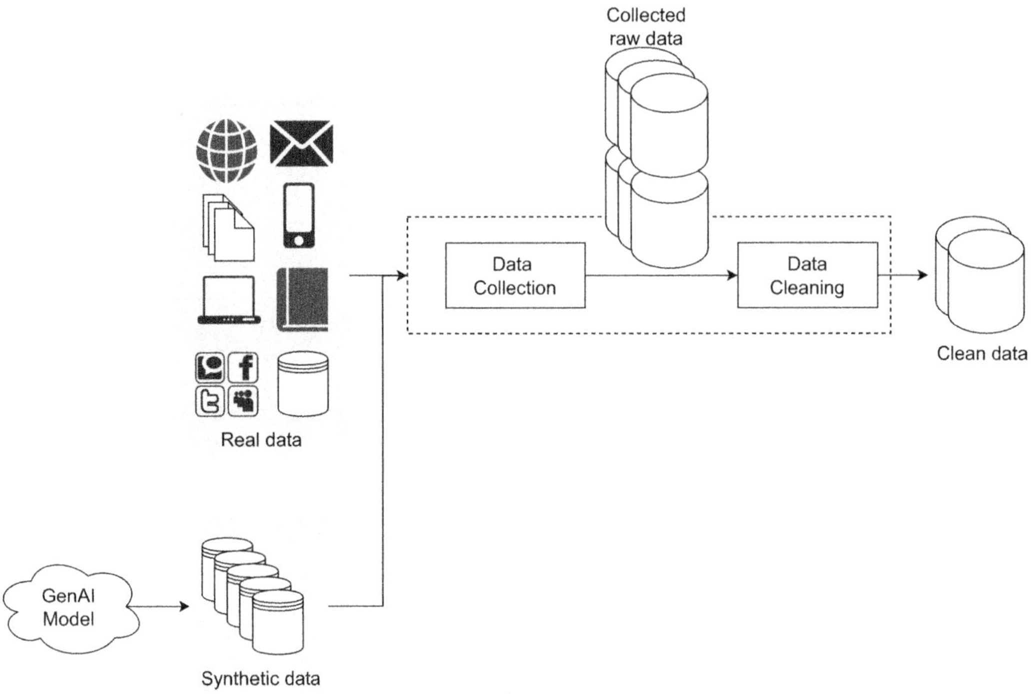

Figure 1.14: Augmenting training data with AI-generated data

Training GenAI models with AI-generated content has several pros and cons.

Pros:

- **Improving data diversity:** AI-generated content adds variety to existing data, thus enhancing the model's ability to generalize, especially when the original data is limited or imbalanced.
- **Scalability:** As demand for data grows, AI-generated content provides a scalable way to create large datasets that are difficult to gather manually.

Cons:

- **Quality concerns:** The quality of synthetic data depends on the original model. Poor-quality data can lead to the spread of biases or errors.
- **Representation issues:** The synthetic data might not represent the original data well. Ensuring the synthetic data is diverse and representative can be challenging.
- **Real-world distribution gaps:** AI-generated data may not fully capture the complexity of real-world scenarios, thereby risking the omission of important details.

Using AI-generated data to train GenAI models is a rapidly evolving area of research. New techniques are constantly being developed to improve the quality and relevance of synthetic data. For more information, refer to [25].

Data cleaning

Very large datasets from the internet are often noisy, and they may contain low-quality or inappropriate content. We must clean the data carefully to avoid introducing biases, misinformation, or harmful material into the model, which can affect its performance. In addition, it is crucial to have data that is representative. This requires removing duplicate content and ensuring it is diverse and balanced.

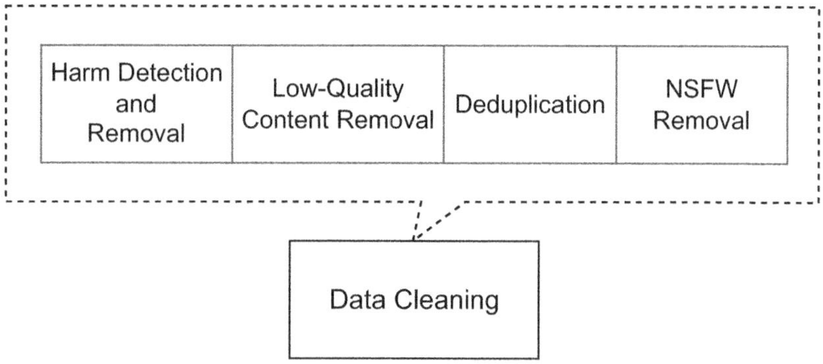

Figure 1.15: Common data cleaning steps

Throughout this book, we will explore key data-cleaning techniques including filtering harmful content, detecting NSFW (Not Safe For Work), assigning quality scores, and removing duplicates.

Data efficiency

Managing large datasets requires efficient tools and techniques for storage and retrieval. Let's look at each in detail.

Efficient storage

Storing massive amounts of data with traditional tools can be expensive and slow. Distributed storage systems such as Hadoop Distributed File System (HDFS) [26] and Amazon S3 [27] are built to store massive amounts of data across multiple machines. These systems are particularly suited for managing large volumes of unstructured data. In addition, columnar storage formats such as Parquet [28] and ORC [29] are ideal for structured data or unstructured data that has been converted to structured form. These formats, optimized for analytics, offer better compression and faster query performance.

Efficient retrieval

Training an ML model requires fast data retrieval. Common techniques to retrieve data efficiently from large datasets include:

- **Sharding:** Splitting data across multiple devices allows parallel access and speeds up retrieval and processing.
- **Indexing:** Technologies such as Apache Lucene [30] or Elasticsearch [31] are used to

index data, making it easy and quick to locate specific pieces of information.

- **Pre-loading or caching:** Frequently accessed data is pre-loaded into memory to reduce I/O delays during retrieval.

Talking points

- **Data sources:** What data is available, and where do you collect it from? How diverse are they? How large is the dataset?
- **Data sensitivity:** How sensitive is the data (e.g., personal, financial, medical)? Is anonymization necessary to protect sensitive information?
- **Bias:** Are there inherent biases in the data (e.g., demographic, geographical)? How do you detect and mitigate these biases to ensure fair representation?
- **Data quality:** How do you filter low-quality, irrelevant, or noisy data? Are there any outliers or anomalies in the dataset? How do you handle them?
- **Inappropriate data:** Are there inappropriate, harmful, or NSFW content in the dataset? What processes are in place to detect and remove such data?
- **Data preprocessing:** How is the data represented in a format the model can understand? If using text data, how is it tokenized and transformed into numerical format (e.g., embeddings)? If dealing with multimodal data (e.g., images, text, audio), how do you preprocess them for the model to consume?

Model development

Model development is a critical step in building ML systems. It involves selecting the appropriate architecture, training the model, and finally, generating new data from the trained model. Let's dive into each of these components in more detail.

Model architecture

In this step, you should talk about the architecture of the model in detail. There might be several viable architectures for different ML algorithms. For instance, diffusion models can be built using either the U-Net or DiT architectures. In an interview, it's important to explore different architectural options and weigh their advantages and disadvantages.

Once an architecture is selected, it's helpful to analyze its specific layers and examine how the input is transformed into the output. For example, in a U-Net architecture, the output should be the same size as the input image; therefore, reviewing the layers to ensure they meet this requirement is beneficial.

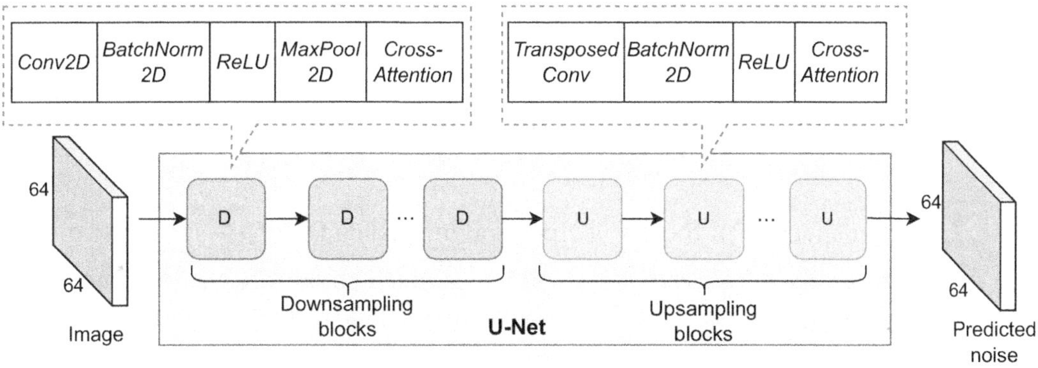

Figure 1.16: U-Net architecture

You might be asked follow-up questions and have to modify the architecture to support a new feature. For example, in an image generation model, you might need to modify the architecture to let users control the style of generated images. Similarly, in a text-to-video model, you might be asked to control the direction of motion (e.g., left to right) during generation. These features could require adding or modifying components in the architecture to integrate style vectors or motion information.

Let's dive into a real example—the Transformer's self-attention—to show what it means to discuss architecture in an interview.

Transformer's self-attention architecture

Transformers are a cornerstone of modern GenAI, especially in natural language processing and image generation. Since their introduction in 2017 [32], they have rapidly taken over the AI community, becoming the dominant architecture for a wide range of tasks across natural language processing (NLP) [33, 12], computer vision [34], and even multimodal learning [35, 36].

At the core of Transformers is the attention mechanism. Initially introduced in the context of machine translation [37], the attention mechanism has become a fundamental component of various neural network architectures, particularly in the Transformer model. It addresses the limitations of traditional sequence models such as RNNs and LSTMs by enabling the model to more effectively capture long-range dependencies and contextual information.

Self-attention, also known as scaled dot-product attention, is the most common form of the attention mechanism used in modern models. It enables each element in the input sequence to focus on every other element. This is done by converting the input embeddings for each token into three vectors: the query (Q), key (K), and value (V) vectors. These vectors are computed using learnable weight matrices W_Q, W_K, and W_V:

$$Q = XW_Q,\ K = XW_K,\ V = XW_V$$

where X represents the input sequence of embeddings.

The attention scores are computed by taking the dot product of the query vector, Q, with all the key vectors, K, followed by a scaling operation and a softmax function. This can be represented as:

$$\text{Attention}(Q, K, V) = \text{softmax}\left(\frac{QK^T}{\sqrt{d_K}}\right)V$$

Here, d_K is the dimension of the key vectors, and the scaling factor $\frac{1}{\sqrt{d_K}}$ is used to prevent the dot-product values from becoming too large, which could result in extremely small gradients during backpropagation. The softmax function is applied to ensure that the attention scores are normalized, summing to 1. This produces a weighted sum of the value vectors, V, where the weights are determined by the relevance of each input token as indicated by the attention scores.

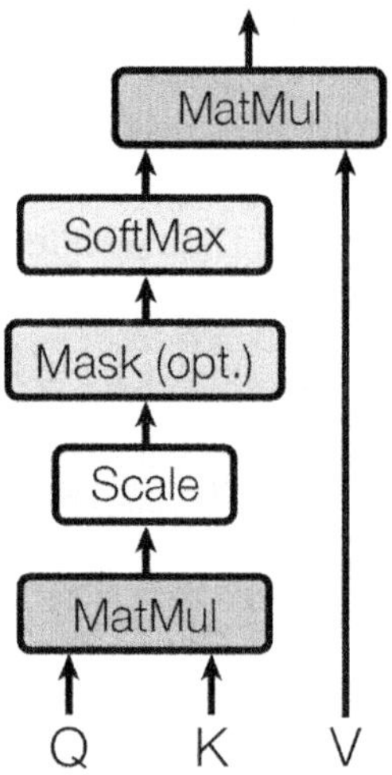

Figure 1.17: Scaled dot-product attention (Credit: [32])

Multi-Head Attention

To capture different types of relationships and contextual dependencies, the self-attention mechanism is often extended to multi-head attention. Instead of computing a single set of Q, K, and V vectors, the input is projected into multiple sets, or "heads," each with its own learnable weight matrices:

$$\text{MultiHead}(Q, K, V) = \text{Concat}(\text{head}_1, \text{head}_2, \cdots, \text{head}_h)W_O$$

where each attention head is computed independently as:

$$\text{head}_i = \text{Attention}(QW_Q^i, KW_K^i, VW_V^i)$$

The results of the different heads are concatenated and then linearly transformed using the output weight matrix, W_O. This allows the model to jointly attend to information from different representation subspaces and capture richer dependencies.

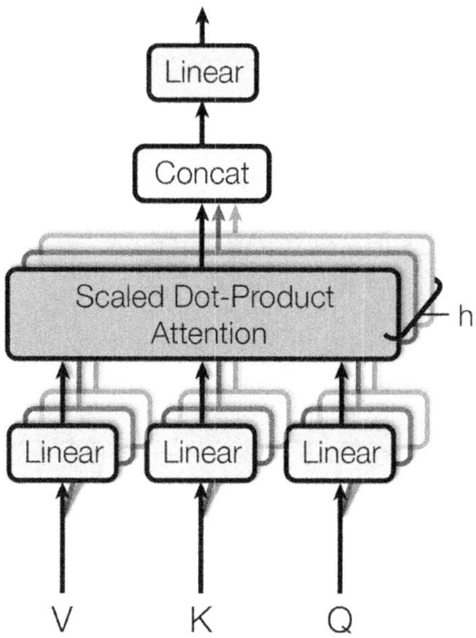

Figure 1.18: Multi-head attention (Credit: [32])

There is no one-size-fits-all architecture for every problem. Interviewers want to assess your understanding of different ML architectures, their strengths and weaknesses, and your ability to choose the right one based on specific requirements and constraints. In this book, we introduce various Transformer-based models through GenAI applications and explain their necessity.

Model training

Model training is the process of adjusting the model's parameters (weights) to produce the desired output. Key aspects to discuss during model training include:

- Training methodology
- Training data
- ML objective and loss function
- Task-specific challenges and mitigations

Let's examine each in more detail.

Training methodology

Each model follows a distinct training process suited to its architecture and purpose. For example, diffusion models gradually denoise data to generate high-quality samples from noise. In contrast, GANs rely on adversarial training, where a generator and a discriminator compete to improve over time.

Many models also undergo multi-stage training for better performance. LLMs, for instance, typically follow three stages: pretraining on large datasets to learn general patterns; supervised finetuning to adapt to the specific task; and an alignment stage to ensure outputs align with human values or intended behaviors. This approach helps models perform well across various applications.

Having an in-depth understanding of these training methodologies for different GenAI applications is crucial, especially when discussing them in an interview.

Training data

Understanding the training data is essential for successful model development. The data used can vary across different GenAI applications and may also differ in multi-stage training approaches. For instance, when training an LLM, publicly available datasets such as Common Crawl [38] might be used during the pretraining stage, while expert-annotated, carefully curated data would be used for the alignment stage.

It's important to discuss the datasets, including how they are sourced, why they are valuable for model training, and an estimate of their size for effective training.

ML objective and loss function

ML objective is the goal of the ML task during training. For example, in an LLM, it might be to accurately predict the next token (e.g., next-token prediction). In contrast, in VAE, the ML objective is to reconstruct the original image.

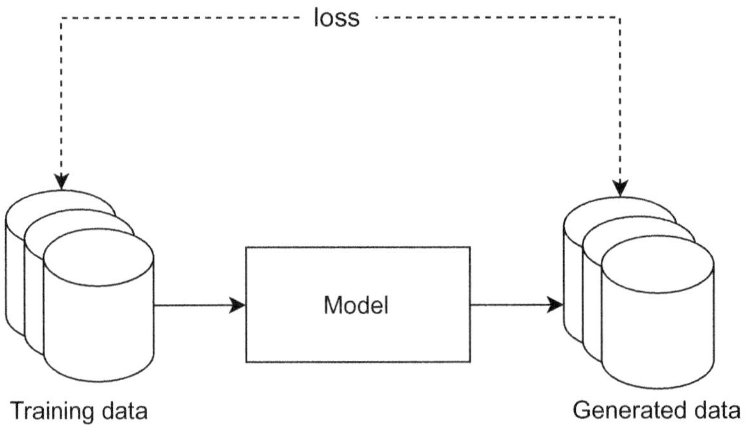

Figure 1.19: Loss computation between training data and generated data

The loss function measures how closely the model's predictions align with the desired outcomes. It guides the optimization process, where the goal is to minimize this loss. Choosing the right loss function is crucial during model training, as it quantifies prediction errors and helps the optimization algorithm adjust the model's parameters to improve performance.

Designing a new loss function can be complex. In most cases, you'll select one from existing options based on how you've framed the problem. Sometimes, minor adjustments to the loss function are required to tailor it to the specific task. We will explore several loss functions in later chapters.

Task-specific challenges and mitigations

Different tasks come with their own challenges that need specific solutions. For example, training large video generation models is very resource-heavy because it requires a lot of computing power and large amounts of data. This means it might not be feasible to train a video generation model without proper optimization techniques. This might include parallelization techniques [39, 40, 41], mixed precision training [42], and latent diffusion models [43]. These approaches help scale video generation models while keeping resource use and costs manageable. While we will cover task-specific challenges and mitigations in future chapters, we'll now briefly examine efficiency and optimization techniques that apply to all large-scale model training.

Three of the most common techniques for training large-scale models are:

- Gradient checkpointing
- Mixed precision training
- Distributed training

Gradient checkpointing

Gradient checkpointing [44] is a technique to reduce memory usage during model training by saving only a selected subset of activations. During the backward pass, the missing activations are recomputed. This reduces memory usage significantly, which is particularly useful for training large models with limited GPU memory.

Mixed precision training

Mixed precision training is a technique that uses both 16-bit (half-precision) and 32-bit (single-precision) floating point numbers to speed up model training and reduce memory usage. It maintains the accuracy of training while improving efficiency by performing most calculations at lower precision; crucial operations are performed at higher precision when needed.

Automatic mixed precision (AMP) [45] is a specific implementation of mixed precision training provided by frameworks such as PyTorch and TensorFlow. AMP automatically handles the transition between half and single precision, optimizing where to use each precision type and applying scaling techniques to maintain numerical stability during training.

Distributed training

As models grow in size and complexity, training on a single machine becomes infeasible. Distributed training techniques enable efficient training of large models by utilizing multiple machines or devices in parallel.

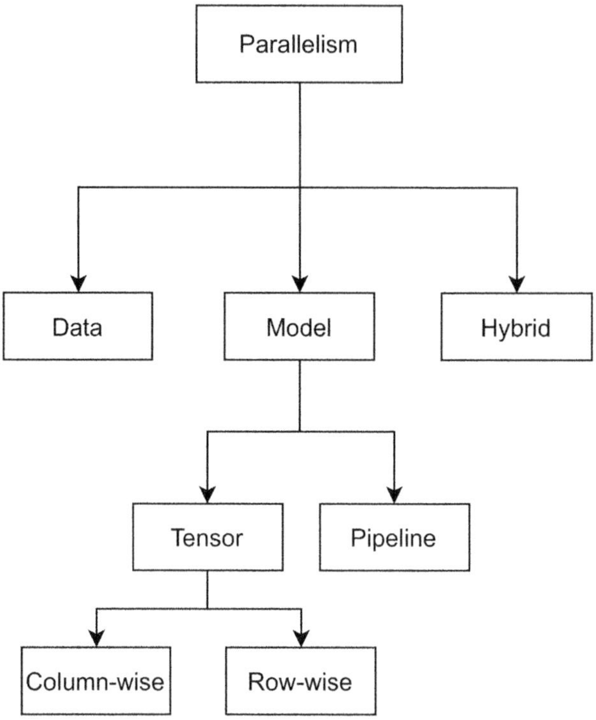

Figure 1.20: Parallelism techniques for distributed training

Common parallelism techniques are:

- Data parallelism
- Model parallelism
- Hybrid parallelism

Data parallelism

In data parallelism, the dataset is split across multiple devices (e.g., GPU), each of which holds a full copy of the model and processes a portion of the data in parallel. Each device trains on its subset of data, and the parameter server coordinates the updating and distributing of model parameters across all devices. This approach is helpful when the dataset is large, as processing the data in parallel is efficient and speeds up training.

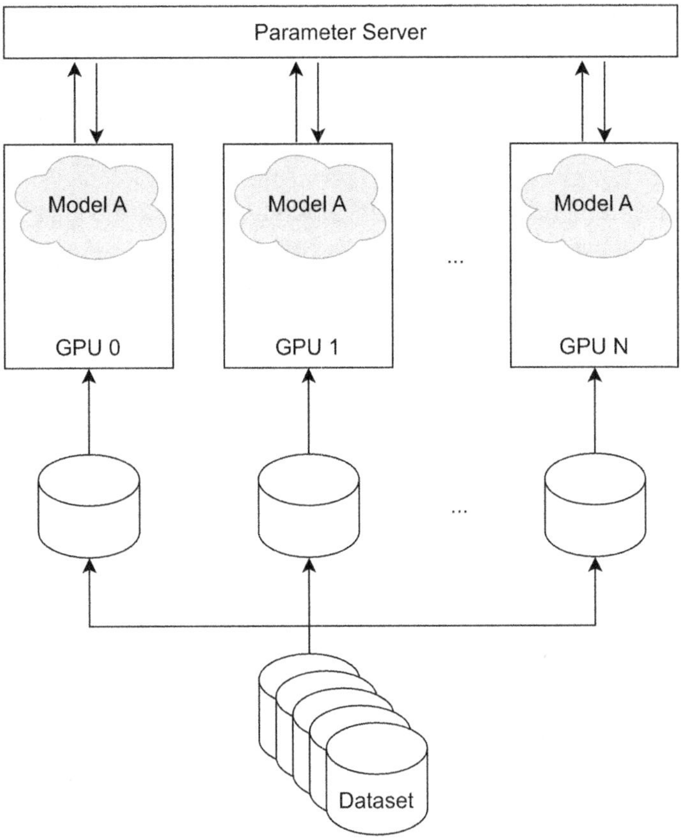

Figure 1.21: Data parallelism

There are two primary methods for updating model parameters across the devices:

- **Synchronous:** In this approach, all devices complete their computations and send gradients to the parameter server. The parameter server waits until it has received gradients from every device, and then it aggregates and updates the model before sending the updated parameters back to all devices. This ensures consistency, as the devices always work with the same version of the model. However, it can be slower because updating has to wait for the slowest device.
- **Asynchronous:** With asynchronous updating, each device sends its gradients to the parameter server as soon as it finishes processing its portion of data, and the parameter server updates the model immediately upon receiving gradients from any device and sends the new parameters to all devices. This approach can be faster since the devices are working independently, but it can lead to inconsistency as devices might be working with slightly different versions of the model at any given time.

To learn more about data parallelism, refer to [39].

Model parallelism

In model parallelism, a single model is split across multiple devices, and each device is responsible for computing only a portion of the model's operations. This approach is helpful when the model is too large to fit into the memory of a single device.

Model parallelism can be further divided into two types:

- Pipeline parallelism (inter-layer)
- Tensor parallelism (intra-layer)

Pipeline parallelism (PP): In PP, the model layers are split across multiple devices, and computations are performed in a pipelined manner. In the forward pass, each device forwards the intermediate activation to the next device in the pipeline, while in the backward pass, it sends the input tensor's gradient back to the preceding device.

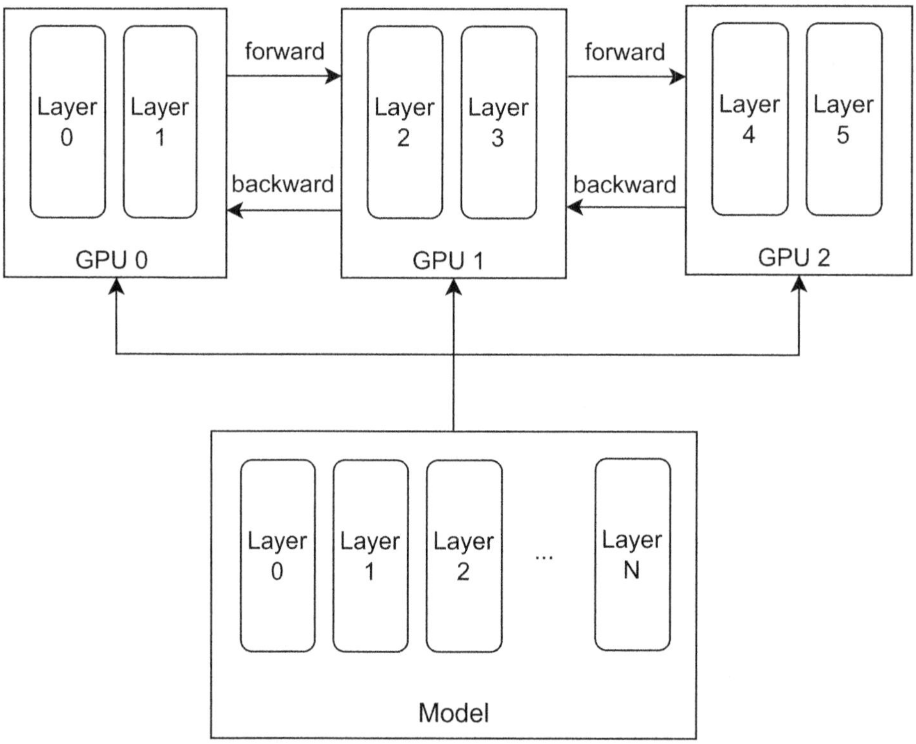

Figure 1.22: Splitting model layers across devices

PP is particularly useful when dealing with very deep models, as it allows multiple devices to work concurrently, reducing idle time and improving training efficiency. To learn more about PP, refer to [40, 41].

Tensor parallelism (TP): In TP, operations within a single layer of the model are split across multiple devices. Each device handles a portion of the computations for that layer, and the outputs are combined before moving to the next layer. For example, in a large matrix multiplication operation, different parts of the matrix can be processed in parallel across multiple devices. This can be done using both column-wise and row-wise splitting. For more information, refer to [46].

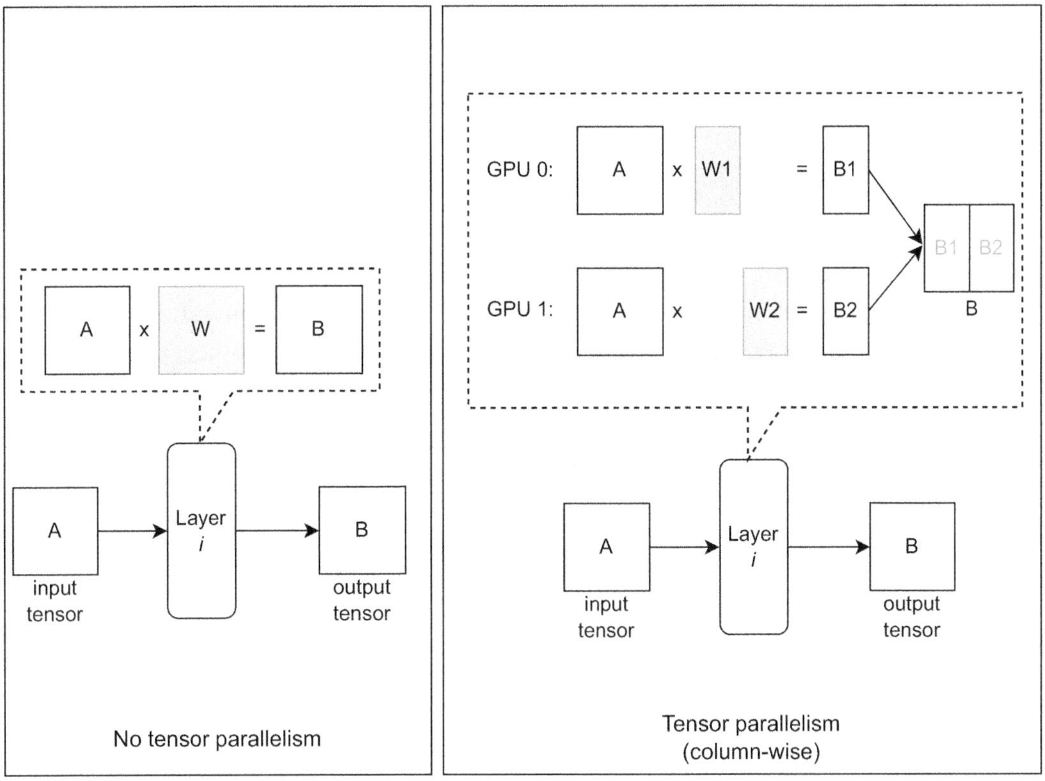

Figure 1.23: TP splitting tensor to chunks

TP is particularly useful when a single layer is too large to fit in memory. It helps in reducing memory usage by distributing the computational load across multiple devices. If you are interested to learn more about TP and its variants (e.g., sequence parallelism), refer to [47, 48].

Hybrid parallelism

Hybrid parallelism combines data and model parallelism to train large models more efficiently across multiple devices. This approach reduces memory usage by distributing both the model and data across devices. It also enables scaling to a larger number of devices, making it possible to train very large models that traditional parallelism methods cannot handle.

In addition to hybrid parallelism, techniques like **ZeRO** (Zero Redundancy Optimizer) [49] from Microsoft and **FSDP** (Fully Sharded Data Parallel) [50] from Meta further optimize resource utilization and communication efficiency. These methods reduce redundancy in memory and computation across devices, enabling more efficient training of massive models.

The techniques discussed in this section are essential components of modern ML system design and are widely used in practice. By combining parallelism techniques such as FSDP, memory-saving methods such as gradient checkpointing, and optimizations such as AMP, we can efficiently scale the training of large, complex models. A solid understanding of these techniques, and knowing when to apply them, is critical for building scalable and efficient AI systems. While this overview only touches on the basics, it is not the central focus of this book. For those interested in a more detailed exploration of distributed training, refer to the provided references.

Model sampling

After training a model, the next step is sampling, which involves generating new data or outputs from the trained generative model. Various sampling methods exist for different GenAI applications. For example, in text generation, methods such as greedy search, beam search [51], and top-k sampling [52] each have their strengths and weaknesses. Beam search, for instance, tends to produce coherent and relevant text, but it may limit diversity.

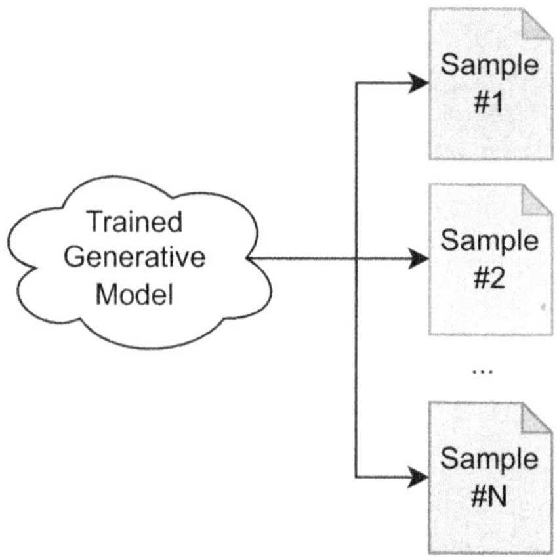

Figure 1.24: Sampling new data from a trained model

In an interview, it is crucial to discuss various sampling methods in depth, their pros and cons, and to choose the one that suits the system you are designing.

Talking points

- **Model architectures:** What are the plausible model architectures for the chosen ML algorithm? What are the pros and cons of each? What are the specific layers in an architecture and why?
- **Training methodology:** What is the training methodology? How does the training process work (e.g., diffusion process, adversarial training)?
- **Training data:** Where is the training data sourced from? How large is the dataset? Do

you use different data for various training stages (e.g., pretraining vs. finetuning)?

- **ML objectives:** What are the plausible ML objectives for the task? What are the pros and cons of each objective, and how do they impact model performance?
- **Loss functions:** What is the loss function that aligns with the chosen ML objective? Do you use a single loss function or multiple ones? If multiple, how do you combine them to optimize the training process? What is the purpose of each loss function?
- **Training challenges and mitigations:** What are typical training challenges specific to the chosen ML algorithm? How can these challenges be mitigated to ensure effective training?
- **Training efficiency:** What are the main techniques to improve training efficiency? How does distributed training work, and what benefits does it bring? How does AMP enhance training speed and efficiency? How does data, tensor, and pipeline parallelism work?
- **Sampling:** How do different sampling methods (e.g., top-k, top-p) work? What are the pros and cons of each? How do they affect the quality and creativity of the model's output? What methods can you use to make the sampling process faster without compromising quality?

Evaluation

After developing a model, the next critical step is evaluation. This involves using various metrics to assess the performance of the ML model. In this section, we will explore two evaluation methods: offline and online evaluation.

Offline Evaluation

Offline evaluation is the process of assessing the performance of a model or system using pre-collected data without deploying it in a real-time environment. This approach is critical to ensure the model is effective before it is used by the users.

Offline evaluation differs between discriminative and generative models. The goal of discriminative models is to make predictions on an evaluation set; the evaluation compares those predictions to the ground truth. Traditional metrics such as accuracy, precision, and recall are used to quantify how well the model performs based on these comparisons. Table 1.2 lists common metrics for different discriminative tasks, which are thoroughly explored in [1].

Task	Metrics
Classification	Precision, Recall, F1 score, Accuracy, Confusion matrix
Regression	MSE, MAE, RMSE
Ranking	Precision@k, Recall@k, MRR, mAP, nDCG

Table 1.2: Popular metrics in discriminative tasks

In generative models, evaluation is more complex. Instead of comparing predictions to a fixed ground truth, these models generate new content, such as text or images. Assessing this content often requires subjective or human-in-the-loop methods to gauge how well it aligns with human expectations or benchmarks. Table 1.3 shows commonly used metrics for different generative tasks.

Task	Metrics
Text Generation	Perplexity, BLEU, METEOR, ROUGE, CIDEr
Image Generation	FID, IS, KID, SWD, PPL, LPIPS
Text-to-Video	FVD, CLIPScore, FID, LPIPS, KID

Table 1.3: Popular metrics in generative tasks

In interviews, it's essential to assess the generated content from multiple angles. For example, in a text-to-image generation model, it's important to ensure the generated image is both high-quality and that it aligns with the given text prompt. Similarly, in a chatbot, the model's capability should be measured across different tasks such as mathematics, common-sense reasoning, and code generation. Throughout this book, we take a deep dive into the offline evaluation of various GenAI applications and explore various metrics listed in Table 1.3.

Online Evaluation

The online evaluation assesses how the model performs in production (i.e., after deployment). Different metrics aligned with business objectives are used to evaluate the model's impact.

In practice, companies typically monitor multiple online metrics. During an interview, you should focus on selecting the most critical ones to gauge the system's impact. Unlike offline metrics, choosing online metrics is more subjective and often involves input from product owners and stakeholders. This step helps the interviewer assess your business sense. It is beneficial to articulate clearly your reasoning and thought process when selecting specific metrics. Table 1.4 lists some metrics commonly used in online evaluation.

Metric	Description
Click-Through Rate (CTR)	Percentage of users who click on content or suggestions.
Conversion Rate	Percentage of users who complete a desired action (e.g., purchase, subscription) after interacting with the system.
Latency (Inference time)	Time taken by the model to generate content.
Engagement Rate	Measure of user interaction, such as time spent engaging with the system.
Revenue Per User	Average revenue generated per user.
Churn Rate	Percentage of users who stop using the system over a given period.
User Satisfaction	Direct feedback from users on their experience with AI-generated content.
User Retention	Percentage of users who continue to use the system over a specific period.
Completion Rate	Percentage of tasks (e.g., text completions, image generations) successfully completed by the model.

Table 1.4: Common metrics for online evaluation

Talking points

Here are some key talking points for the evaluation stage:

- **Offline metrics:** Which offline metrics best evaluate the quality and accuracy of the generative model? How do these metrics measure the diversity, realism, and coherence of generated outputs?
- **Online metrics:** Which metrics are crucial for assessing the effectiveness of the generative model in a live production environment? How do these metrics align with the business goals, such as enhancing user creativity, boosting engagement, or driving product innovation?
- **Bias:** Generative models may unintentionally reflect societal biases in relation to sensitive attributes such as gender or race. How can you evaluate the model's bias?
- **Robustness and security:** How resilient is the generative model to adversarial attacks such as intentionally misleading inputs designed to exploit model weaknesses?
- **Human evaluation:** For generative models, especially in creative fields (e.g., text generation, image synthesis), human feedback is vital. How can human reviewers complement automatic evaluation? What methods (e.g., surveys, A/B testing, expert reviews) will best assess the model's performance? How can you mitigate the effects of subjectivity among different reviewers?

Overall ML system design

The next step of the framework is to propose an overall design for the GenAI system. These systems involve more than just training a model; they require multiple pipelines and components working together seamlessly. For instance, in a chatbot, beyond the core model, other components are needed to ensure safety, for example, filtering out harmful content. Similarly, for a video generation system, additional models may be needed to upscale video resolution to the desired quality. At this stage, it's crucial to integrate all components essential for the system to function as intended. We will explore several components commonly used along with the generative model throughout this book.

Talking points

- **System components:** What are the different components of the system? What are the roles of each component—such as the core model, preprocessing, content filtering, post-processing, and any necessary upscaling or quality enhancement models?
- **Safety mechanisms:** How are safety and content moderation incorporated into the system? For instance, how does the system ensure that generated content is safe and appropriate for users?
- **User feedback and continuous learning:** How does the system incorporate user feedback to continuously improve model performance? Discuss the feedback loop mechanisms that allow for finetuning the model. What systems are in place for retraining models with updated data to improve accuracy and relevance over time?
- **Scalability:** How does the system scale as demand increases? What cloud or hardware resources are utilized, and how is resource allocation managed efficiently? How do components such as load balancers, distributed inference, and model parallelism contribute to system scalability?
- **Security considerations:** How does the system ensure user privacy, especially when dealing with sensitive data or generating personalized content? What security protocols are implemented to protect against adversarial attacks, model tampering, or data leakage?
- **Bias:** Generative models may unintentionally reflect societal biases with respect to sensitive attributes like gender or race. Discuss strategies such as bias-detection algorithms, fairness auditing, and filtering of biased outputs. Additionally, how would you address ethical concerns if users attempt to misuse the generative model to produce harmful, biased, or inappropriate content?
- **Robustness and security:** How resilient is the generative model to adversarial attacks, such as intentionally misleading inputs designed to exploit model weaknesses? For example, can attackers generate harmful or nonsensical outputs? In production, how can we ensure that the model isn't being manipulated for malicious purposes, such as creating deepfakes, misinformation, or inappropriate content?

Deployment and monitoring

The final step is to deploy the system to production and serve millions of users. Once the system is deployed, it can fail for many reasons. Monitoring refers to the task of tracking, measuring, and logging different metrics to detect system failures when they occur, so they can be fixed as quickly as possible. However, since this topic is broad and not specific to GenAI or any particular task, we won't go into detail in this book. We encourage readers to refer to [53] or the "ML System Design Interview" book [1] for a deeper exploration.

Summary

In this chapter, we provided an overview of GenAI and introduced a framework for approaching a GenAI system design interview. While some details are specific to GenAI, many concepts apply broadly across AI system design. We focus on aspects unique to GenAI, avoiding general topics common to all AI systems such as deployment, infrastructure, and monitoring.

Finally, not every engineer is expected to be an expert in all areas of the GenAI life cycle. Different roles and companies may emphasize various aspects, such as infrastructure, monitoring, or LLM development. This framework helps candidates to understand the expectations and adjust their answers accordingly based on the interview's focus.

Now that you understand these fundamentals, we're ready to tackle some of the most common GenAI system design interview questions.

Reference Material

[1] Machine Learning System Design Interview. https://www.aliaminian.com/books.

[2] Support Vector Machines. https://scikit-learn.org/stable/modules/svm.html.

[3] Bayes' theorem. https://en.wikipedia.org/wiki/Bayes%27_theorem.

[4] Gaussian mixture models. https://scikit-learn.org/1.5/modules/mixture.html.

[5] Hidden Markov model. https://en.wikipedia.org/wiki/Hidden_Markov_model.

[6] Boltzmann machine. https://en.wikipedia.org/wiki/Boltzmann_machine.

[7] OpenAI's ChatGPT. https://openai.com/index/chatgpt/.

[8] Economic Potential of Generative AI. https://www.mckinsey.com/capabilities/mckinsey-digital/our-insights/the-economic-potential-of-generative-ai-the-next-productivity-frontier.

[9] The Llama 3 Herd of Models. https://arxiv.org/abs/2407.21783.

[10] Flamingo: a Visual Language Model for Few-Shot Learning. https://arxiv.org/abs/2204.14198.

[11] PaLM: Scaling Language Modeling with Pathways. https://arxiv.org/abs/2204.02311.

[12] Language Models are Few-Shot Learners. https://arxiv.org/abs/2005.14165.

[13] Photorealistic Text-to-Image Diffusion Models with Deep Language Understanding. https://arxiv.org/abs/2205.11487.

[14] PaLM2 Technical Report. https://arxiv.org/abs/2305.10403.

[15] H100 Tensor Core GPU. https://www.nvidia.com/en-us/data-center/h100/.

[16] GPT-4 training cost. https://www.wired.com/story/openai-ceo-sam-altman-the-age-of-giant-ai-models-is-already-over/.

[17] Scaling Laws for Neural Language Models. https://arxiv.org/abs/2001.08361.

[18] Training Compute-Optimal Large Language Models. https://arxiv.org/abs/2203.15556.

[19] Introducing OpenAI o1. https://openai.com/index/introducing-openai-o1-preview/.

[20] Large Language Monkeys: Scaling Inference Compute with Repeated Sampling. https://arxiv.org/abs/2407.21787.

[21] ETL. https://aws.amazon.com/what-is/etl/.

[22] Tecton. https://www.tecton.ai/feature-store/.

[23] Amazon SageMaker. https://aws.amazon.com/sagemaker/.

[24] ML System Design Interview. https://www.amazon.com/gp/product/1736049127/.

[25] Comprehensive Exploration of Synthetic Data Generation: A Survey. https://arxiv.org/abs/2401.02524.

[26] HDFS Architecture Guide. https://hadoop.apache.org/docs/r1.2.1/hdfs_design.html.

[27] Amazon S3. https://aws.amazon.com/s3/.

[28] Apache Parquet. https://parquet.apache.org/.

[29] Apache ORC. https://orc.apache.org/docs/.

[30] Apache Lucene. https://lucene.apache.org/.

[31] Elasticsearch. https://www.elastic.co/elasticsearch.

[32] Attention Is All You Need. https://arxiv.org/abs/1706.03762.

[33] BERT: Pre-training of Deep Bidirectional Transformers for Language Understanding. https://arxiv.org/abs/1810.04805.

[34] An Image is Worth 16x16 Words: Transformers for Image Recognition at Scale. https://arxiv.org/abs/2010.11929.

[35] Learning Transferable Visual Models From Natural Language Supervision. https://arxiv.org/abs/2103.00020.

[36] Zero-Shot Text-to-Image Generation. https://arxiv.org/abs/2102.12092.

[37] Neural Machine Translation by Jointly Learning to Align and Translate. https://arxiv.org/abs/1409.0473.

[38] Common Crawl. https://commoncrawl.org/.

[39] Data Parallelism. https://en.wikipedia.org/wiki/Data_parallelism.

[40] Model Parallelism. https://huggingface.co/docs/transformers/v4.15.0/en/parallelism.

[41] Pipeline Parallelism. https://pytorch.org/docs/stable/distributed.pipelining.html.

[42] Mixed Precision Training. https://arxiv.org/abs/1710.03740.

[43] High-Resolution Image Synthesis with Latent Diffusion Models. https://arxiv.org/abs/2112.10752.

[44] Training Deep Nets with Sublinear Memory Cost. https://arxiv.org/abs/1604.06174.

[45] Automatic Mixed Precision. https://pytorch.org/tutorials/recipes/recipes/amp_recipe.html.

[46] Model parallelism. https://huggingface.co/docs/transformers/v4.17.0/en/parallelism.

[47] Paradigms of Parallelism. https://colossalai.org/docs/concepts/paradigms_of_parallelism/.

[48] Tensor Parallelism tutorial. https://pytorch.org/tutorials/intermediate/TP_tutorial.html.

[49] ZeRO: Memory Optimizations Toward Training Trillion Parameter Models. https://arxiv.org/abs/1910.02054.

[50] Introducing PyTorch Fully Sharded Data Parallel (FSDP) API. https://pytorch.org/blog/introducing-pytorch-fully-sharded-data-parallel-api/.

[51] Beam search. https://en.wikipedia.org/wiki/Beam_search.

[52] Top-k sampling. https://docs.cohere.com/docs/controlling-generation-with-top-k-top-p.

[53] Model monitoring for ML in production. https://www.evidentlyai.com/ml-in-production/model-monitoring.

2

Gmail Smart Compose

Gmail's Smart Compose feature [1] assists users by suggesting the next few words as they write an email. This chapter explores this feature and examines the Transformer architecture that powers most generative systems.

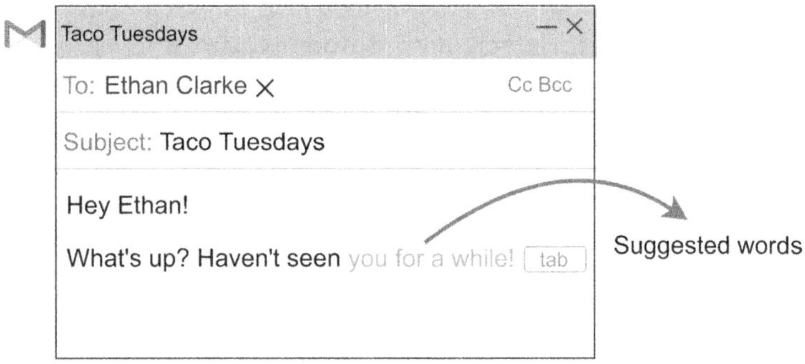

Figure 2.1: Gmail's Smart Compose feature

Clarifying Requirements

Here is a typical interaction between a candidate and an interviewer:

Candidate: Different users might have different writing styles. Is the system expected to make personalized suggestions?
Interviewer: For simplicity, let's not include personalization.

Candidate: Should the system suggest the next few words only when it is confident in its prediction?
Interviewer: Yes.

Candidate: The email dataset must be sufficiently large to train a model. Do we know the approximate size of the data?
Interviewer: Assume our dataset consists of around one billion email messages.

Candidate: There are different parts of data to utilize when making suggestions. For example, a user's past emails or the subject of the current email. To keep it simple, can I only utilize the email's body as the context?
Interviewer: Good point. In practice, though, we use more than what the user has typed in the current email. Let's start by using the body of the email. If we have more time, we can expand the context to include other relevant information.

Candidate: What languages should the system support?
Interviewer: Let's begin with English.

Candidate: Do we need to ensure the system is not biased?
Interviewer: This is an important requirement for this system. The system should not make biased assumptions in providing its suggestions.

Candidate: How many active users does Gmail have? Is the computing cost a concern in this feature?
Interviewer: Gmail has about 1.8 billion users, and a single user can send as many as 500 emails in a day. We do care about the computing costs, but let's focus on developing the system first. We can optimize for efficiency in future iterations.

Candidate: Should the system make real-time suggestions?
Interviewer: Yes. The expected latency should be imperceptible; something around 100 milliseconds should be fine.

Frame the Problem as an ML Task

In this section, we frame the Smart Compose feature as an ML task. This requires us to understand the system's inputs and outputs and choose a suitable ML approach for learning the task.

Specifying the system's input and output

The input to the model is a sequence of words typed by the user. The output is a continuation of that sequence. The model generates the words that the user is likely to type next.

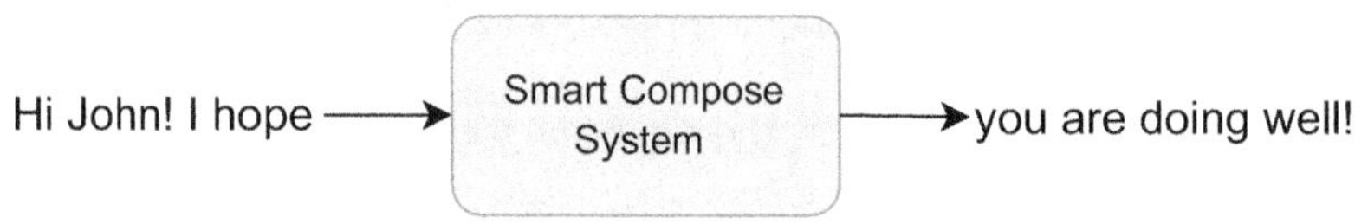

Figure 2.2: Input and output of the Smart Compose system

Choosing a suitable ML approach

Smart Compose generates textual content, so we categorize it as a text generation task. Various ML architectures are designed to process sequential data, which is essential for text generation. Two popular architectures are recurrent neural networks (RNNs) [2] and Transformers [3].

Transformers provide several advantages over RNNs, with two main benefits being:

- **Parallelism:** In an RNN, computations from one time step are carried forward and used in the next, creating a time-dependent chain of operations. Transformers, on the other hand, can process all input tokens simultaneously through their self-attention mechanism.
- **Better handling of long sequences:** Transformers use self-attention mechanisms to focus on any part of a sequence, regardless of distance. In contrast, RNNs, struggle with long-range dependencies because of their sequential structure and the vanishing gradient problem.

Due to these advantages, Transformers have shown outstanding performance in text generation tasks and are, thus, used in most generative systems nowadays. Therefore, we choose Transformers to build the Smart Compose feature.

Feature	RNN (GRU [4], LSTM [5])	Transformer
Architecture	Simple	Complex
Training efficiency	Inefficient due to sequential processing	Efficient due to parallel processing
Effectiveness	Low as it struggles with long sequences	High as it handles long sequences
Scalability	Limited scalability	Highly scalable
Applications	Simple tasks such as time series modeling	Complex tasks such as language completion or translation

Table 2.1: Comparison of RNN and Transformer architectures

While Transformers are more parallelizable due to their lack of strict sequential dependencies, their self-attention mechanism has a computational complexity of $O(n^2)$, where n is the sequence length. This complexity arises because the self-attention mechanism requires the calculation of attention scores between every pair of tokens in the sequence. Various techniques are introduced to reduce the complexity of attention. To learn more, refer to Group Attention [6] and Flash Attention [7].

Data Preparation

During the data preparation step, we convert raw data into the format expected by the ML model. First, let's briefly review the available data.

Two sources of data are available for training our model: general data and email data. General data includes publicly available text from sources such as books, websites, and social media posts. This data is important for training language models because it contains diverse vocabulary, syntax, and contexts.

```
Those hours that with gentle work did frame
  The lovely gaze where every eye doth dwell
  Will play the tyrants to the very same,
  And that unfair which fairly doth excel:
  For never-resting time leads summer on
  To hideous winter and confounds him there,
  Sap checked with frost and lusty leaves quite gone,
  Beauty o'er-snowed and bareness every where:
  Then were not summer's distillation left
  A liquid prisoner pent in walls of glass,
  Beauty's effect with beauty were bereft,
  Nor it nor no remembrance what it was.
    But flowers distilled though they with winter
meet,
    Leese but their show, their substance still lives
sweet.
                    6
  Then let not winter's ragged hand deface,
  In thee thy summer ere thou be distilled:
  Make sweet some vial; treasure thou some place,
  With beauty's treasure ere it be self-killed:
  That use is not forbidden usury,
  Which happies those that pay the willing loan;
  That's for thy self to breed another thee,
  Or ten times happier be it ten for one,
  Ten times thy self were happier than thou art,
```

```
Music to hear, why hear'st thou music sadly?
Sweets with sweets war not, joy delights in joy:
Why lov'st thou that which thou receiv'st not gladly,
Or else receiv'st with pleasure thine annoy?
If the true concord of well-tuned sounds,
By unions married do offend thine ear,
They do but sweetly chide thee, who confounds
In singleness the parts that thou shouldst bear:
Mark how one string sweet husband to another,
Strikes each in each by mutual ordering;
Resembling sire, and child, and happy mother,
Who all in one, one pleasing note do sing:
  Whose speechless song being many, seeming one,
  Sings this to thee, 'Thou single wilt prove none'.
                    9
Is it for fear to wet a widow's eye,
That thou consum'st thy self in single life?
Ah, if thou issueless shalt hap to die,
The world will wail thee like a makeless wife,
The world will be thy widow and still weep,
That thou no form of thee hast left behind,
When every private widow well may keep,
By children's eyes, her husband's shape in mind:
Look what an unthrift in the world doth spend
Shifts but his place, for still the world enjoys
```

Figure 2.3: Example of general data from Shakespeare

The email data, as specified in the requirements, consists of one billion email messages. This data is crucial for the model to learn email writing styles and common phrases used in emails. Table 2.2 shows a simplified example of email data. In practice, more metadata is stored for each email message.

Email ID	Sender	Recipient	Subject	Body
4953	john@gmail.com	mike@yahoo.com	Catchup?	Hey Mike, let's catch up this Sat. ...
9356	kkart@gmail.com	cs382@stanford.edu	Project Deadline	Hi TA, I hope you are well. I am writing to you to ...

Table 2.2: Example of email data

Raw text in both general data and email data is often noisy and inconsistent, which can degrade the model performance. Additionally, ML models require data to be in a numerical format. For these reasons, raw text has to be prepared using the following two key steps:

- Text cleaning and normalization
- Text tokenization and token indexing

Text cleaning and normalization

Text cleaning

Text cleaning removes unnecessary or irrelevant information. Common methods include:

- **Remove non-English text:** Use language identification methods such as [8, 9] to identify and remove non-English text from general and email data.
- **Remove confidential information:** Emails may contain confidential information such as phone and credit card numbers. These details must be removed to prevent the model from learning or exposing them later. We replace personal names, URLs, email addresses, and phone numbers with placeholder characters. For example, replace "john@gmail.com" with "###@gmail.com."
- **Remove irrelevant characters or symbols:** Remove unnecessary or irrelevant characters and symbols that do not contribute to the meaning. For example, symbols such as "©," "™," or emojis are removed, as they do not typically change the meaning of text.
- **Remove duplicated data:** Duplicate data refers to identical text from different sources that appear multiple times in the dataset. We remove duplicates to prevent the model from becoming biased and skewing the model's learning process.

Text normalization

Text normalization transforms text into a consistent format. For example, it converts different ways of writing a phone number—such as "(123) 456-7890," "123.456.7890," and "123-456-7890"—into a standard format, for example, "1234567890." Text normalization ensures consistency and reduces complexity in text data.

Next, we convert the raw text into a sequence of numbers through text tokenization and token indexing.

Text tokenization and token indexing

Text tokenization followed by token indexing converts the raw text into a format the Transformer model expects: a sequence of numbers.

Figure 2.4: Converting raw text to a sequence of numbers

Let's examine each step in more detail.

Text tokenization

Text tokenization is the process of splitting text into smaller units called tokens. Figure 2.5 shows how OpenAI's GPT-4 tokenizes the sentence "Let's go to NYC". [1]

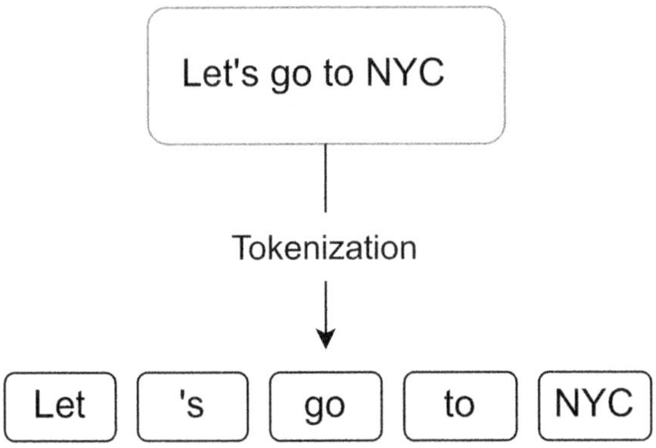

Figure 2.5: Example of GPT-4 tokenization

Tokenization can be performed at different levels. For example, "Hello world" can be split into ["Hello", "world"] or ["H", "e", "l", "l", "o", " ", "w", "o", "r", "l", "d"]. Generally, tokenization algorithms are divided into three categories:

- Character-level tokenization
- Word-level tokenization
- Subword-level tokenization

[1] Visit https://platform.openai.com/tokenizer to see examples of different tokenizers.

Understanding each tokenization category and its pros and cons is crucial in most ML interviews. Let's delve into them.

Character-level tokenization

Character-level tokenization breaks text down into a set of characters. It is simple to implement, but difficult for the model to learn meaningful representations for each token. For example, it's harder to learn a meaningful representation for the letter "g" than for the word "go," because "go" has a clear meaning, whereas "g" does not. Because of this, character-level tokenization often results in a loss of performance.

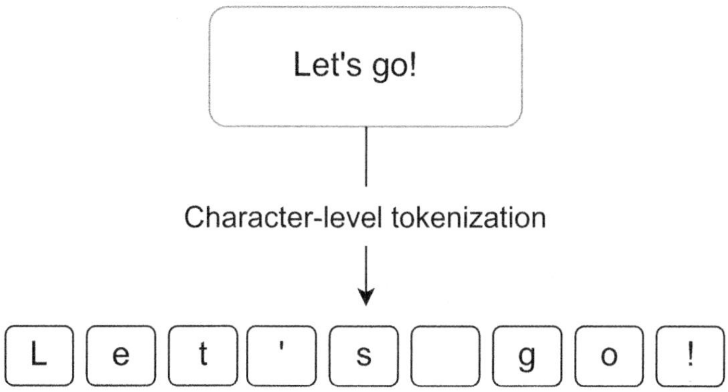

Figure 2.6: Example of character-level tokenization

Word-level tokenization

Word-level tokenization breaks text into individual words. While there are different algorithms for word-level tokenization, a simple algorithm is to split the text using its whitespaces.

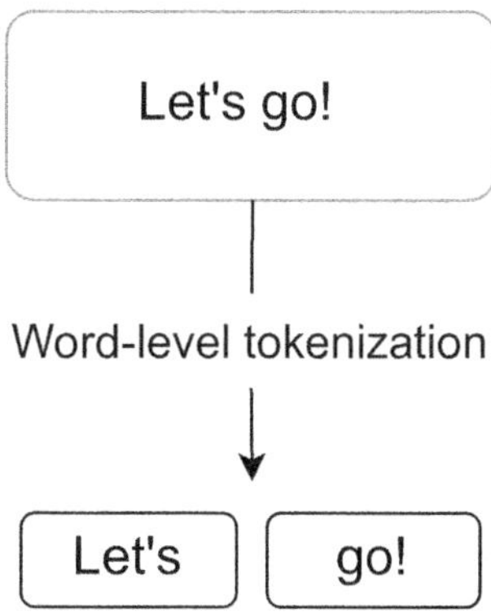

Figure 2.7: Example of word-level tokenization

The advantage of word-level tokenization is that it is simpler for the model to learn meaningful representations for each token. However, the main disadvantage of word-level tokenization is that it typically leads to a very large vocabulary size. For example, Transformer-

XL [10] uses a word-level tokenizer, resulting in a vocabulary of 267,735 tokens. A large vocabulary size is problematic because the model has to learn representations for hundreds of thousands of tokens. This makes the training time-consuming and, therefore, more costly to train than character-level tokenization.

Let's examine subword-level tokenization which offers a balance between word-level and character-level tokenization.

Subword-level tokenization

Subword-level tokenization splits text into smaller units called subwords. It is based on the principle that a frequently used word should not be split into smaller subwords, but a rare word should be split into smaller meaningful subwords. For example, "unhappily" might be considered a rare word and thus be split into "unhappy" and "ly." Both "unhappy" and "ly" are more frequently used in text data, making it easier for the model to learn a meaningful representation for each.

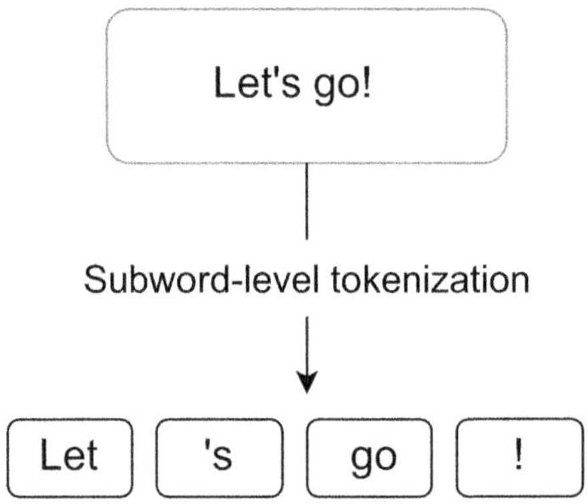

Figure 2.8: Example of subword-level tokenization

While subword-level tokenization can be complex to implement, it has several benefits. First, it leads to a manageable vocabulary size, thus reducing the cost of the model learning representations for each subword. Second, subword-level tokenization allows the model to represent unfamiliar words by decomposing them into known subwords.

Table 2.3 below compares the characteristics of the three tokenization categories.

Characteristics	Character-level	Word-level	Subword-level
Granularity	Individual characters	Individual words	Subwords
Vocabulary size	Small	Large	Moderate
Algorithm complexity	Simple	Simple	Complex
Handling unseen words	Decomposes unseen words into characters	Cannot easily handle unseen words	Decomposes unseen words into known subwords
Vocabulary size	100-1,000	300,000+	50,000–150,000
Performance	Poor performance	High performance but not practical	High performance and practical

Table 2.3: Comparison between different tokenization categories

Which tokenization is suitable for the Smart Compose feature?

Most state-of-the-art language models use subword-level tokenization algorithms such as Byte-Pair Encoding (BPE) [11] and SentencePiece [12]. These algorithms are more efficient and can effectively handle multiple languages. For example, OpenAI's GPT-4 uses a variant of BPE [13], and Google's Gemini uses SentencePiece [14].

Given the effectiveness of subword-level tokenization, we use it as the text tokenizer for the Smart Compose feature. We rely on popular Python libraries such as Tiktoken [13] by OpenAI or SentencePiece [15] by Google to perform text tokenization. These libraries are implemented reliably and they support various tokenization algorithms.

In Chapter 3, we will dive into BPE and explore its algorithms. To learn more about subword-level tokenization algorithms, refer to [16].

Token indexing

Token indexing is the process of converting textual tokens into integer numbers.

To prepare for token indexing, the tokenization algorithm first builds a vocabulary—a collection of all unique tokens—from the training text data and then stores it in a table. Figure 2.9 shows examples of vocabularies for different tokenization categories. The order and ID values are chosen arbitrarily for demonstration purposes.

Token	ID
a	0
b	1
...	...
A	26
B	27
...	...
!	57
...	...
<SPACE>	105

Character-level Vocabulary

Token	ID
a	0
about	1
after	2
all	3
also	4
...	...
zebra	270030
...	...
!	270131

Word-level Vocabulary

Token	ID
the	0
of	1
home	2
...	...
##ing	50252
##ed	50253
##able	50254
<EOS>	50255
<SPACE>	50256

Subword-level Vocabulary

Figure 2.9: Examples of different vocabularies

Once the tokenization algorithm has built the vocabulary, we can convert any token into a number and any number back into a token. Figure 2.10 shows token indexing using the GPT-4 vocabulary [17].

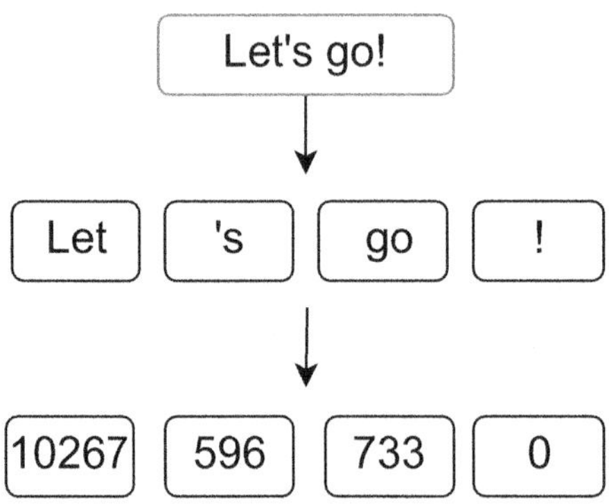

Token	ID
!	0
...	...
's	596
...	...
go	733
...	...
Let	10267
...	...

GPT-4 Vocabulary

Figure 2.10: Example of token indexing

To summarize the data preparation step, we first clean and normalize the text data to ensure high-quality, consistent text in our training data. Next, we use a subword-level tokenization algorithm such as BPE to tokenize the text into textual tokens (subwords) and then replace each token with its numerical index. These steps ensure our training data is now represented in a numerical format that the ML model can use.

Model Development

The Smart Compose feature is a text generation task in which a Transformer model predicts how email sentences are likely to be completed. In this section, we explore the details of the Transformer architecture, training strategies, and sampling methods to develop the text generation model.

Architecture

The Transformer architecture, introduced in the paper "Attention Is All You Need" [3], is designed to process sequences. This makes it ideal for tasks that require understanding a text and the relationships between its words. For example, in the Smart Compose feature, the model processes the sequence of words already entered by the user so it can suggest the next words.

Transformers have three primary variations:

- Encoder-only
- Decoder-only
- Encoder-decoder

Each variation has minor architectural differences that make them suitable for specific tasks. Let's briefly explore each variation and its applications.

Encoder-only

An encoder-only Transformer is used for tasks that require understanding the overall meaning of a text. It processes the input sequence as a whole and makes predictions about it. For instance, in a sentiment analysis task, an encoder-only Transformer predicts the sentiment of the input sentence.

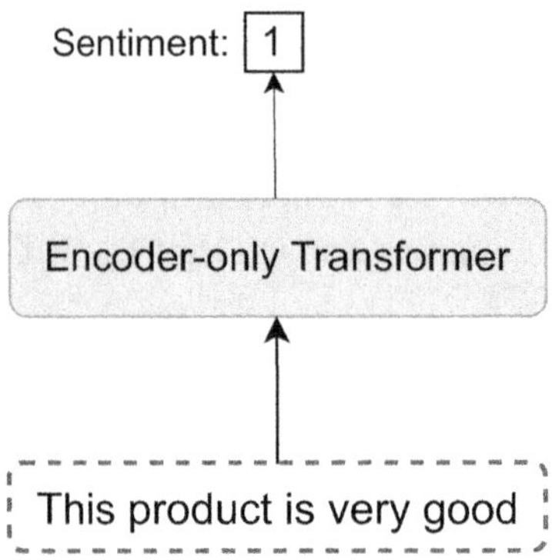

Figure 2.11: Encoder-only Transformer for sentiment analysis

Encoder-only Transformers are commonly used for tasks such as sentence classification and named entity recognition, which focus on understanding the input rather than generating new content. Google's BERT [18] is a well-known example of an encoder-only Transformer. However, these models are not typically used to generate new sequences. Decoder-only Transformers, on the other, are specifically designed for that purpose.

Decoder-only

A decoder-only Transformer processes the input sequence and generates a new sequence iteratively.

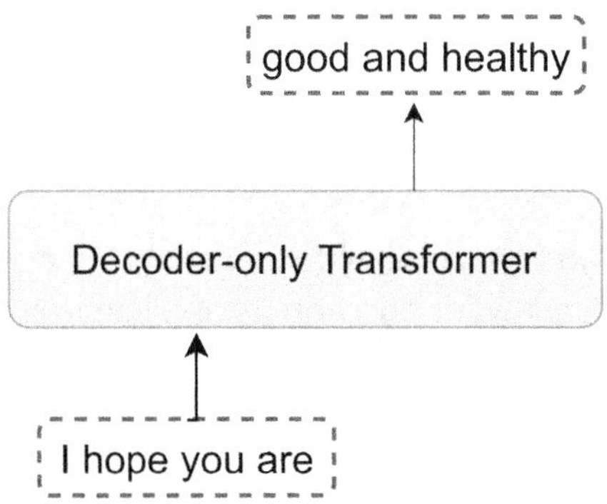

Figure 2.12: Decoder-only Transformer for text completion

Decoder-only Transformers are widely used in generative tasks including text generation, where the model generates a sequence one token at a time based on the previously generated tokens. Most large language models (LLMs), such as OpenAI's GPT-4 [19], Meta's LLaMA [20], and Google's Gemini [14], are based on a decoder-only Transformer.

Encoder-decoder

The encoder-decoder architecture utilizes both encoder-only and decoder-only Transformers. An encoder component processes the input sequence and a decoder uses that processed information to generate the output sequence.

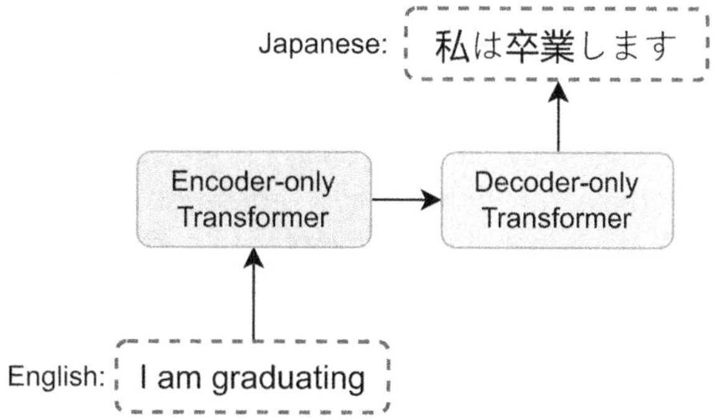

Figure 2.13: Encoder-decoder Transformer used for language translation

An encoder-decoder Transformer is particularly suited for tasks where the output is a transformation of the input. For example, in a language translation task, the input sentence in one language is transformed into an equivalent sentence in another language. We'll examine this architecture in Chapter 3.

Figure 2.14 below shows commonly used models that employ different variations of Transformers.

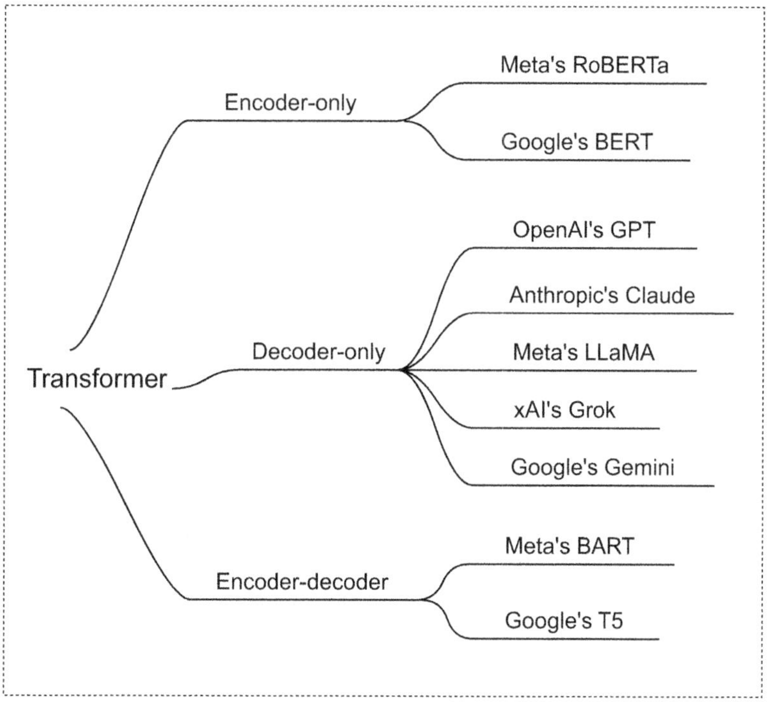

Figure 2.14: Popular models for each variation of Transformer

Which Transformer variation is suitable for the Smart Compose feature?

The choice between encoder-only, decoder-only, and encoder-decoder Transformer models depends on whether the nature of the task is generation or understanding. Smart Compose is a text generation task that aims to complete a partially written text. Therefore, a decoder-only Transformer is ideal for this task due to its ability to generate text based on a given sequence.

ML system design interviews typically focus on high-level concepts and component interactions rather than architectural details. We'll provide a brief overview of the Transformer architecture without going too deep. For a deeper understanding of Transformer architectures, refer to [21] and [22].

A decoder-only Transformer consists of the following components:

- Text embedding
- Positional encoding
- Transformer
- Prediction head

Text embedding

The text embedding component converts each token ID into a fixed-length vector called an "embedding." Embeddings are typically stored in a table, as shown in Figure 2.15, and learned during the training process.

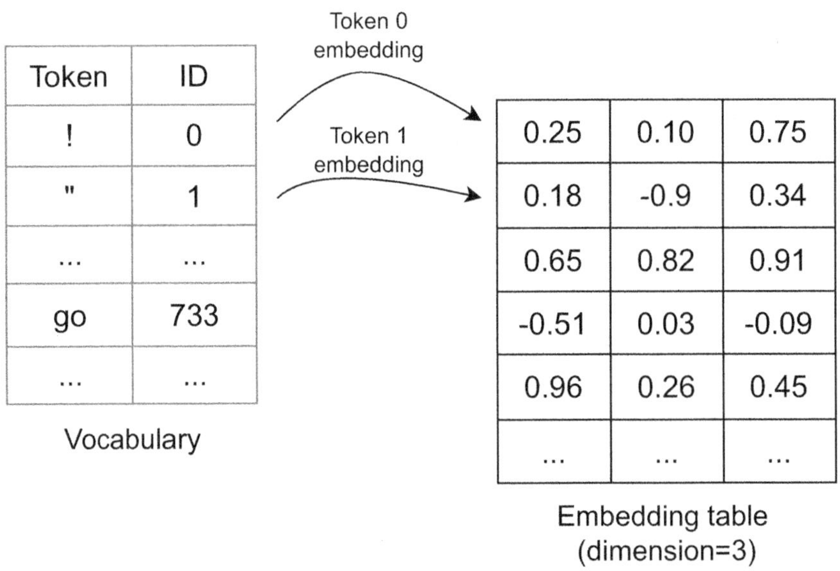

Figure 2.15: Embedding table representing tokens

The text embedding is crucial in a decoder-only Transformer. Let's understand why.

During data preparation, we tokenized the text and converted tokens to IDs. However, there are two significant limitations in how the text is represented:

- **Sparsity:** The vocabulary typically includes tens of thousands of token IDs. Representing these IDs using one-hot encoding results in sparse, high-dimensional data, which is inefficient.
- **Lack of semantic information:** Token IDs are arbitrary and do not capture any relationships between words. For example, the words "happy" and "joyful" might be close in meaning, but their token IDs may not reflect this similarity.

The text embedding component addresses both of these limitations by converting token IDs into learned embeddings. Since the embeddings are dense vectors in a lower-dimensional space, sparsity is no longer a concern.

In addition, since the embeddings are learned during model training, they capture semantic meanings. For example, the embeddings for "happy" and "joyful" will be closer together in the embedding space than those for "happy" and "sad," as shown in Figure 2.16.

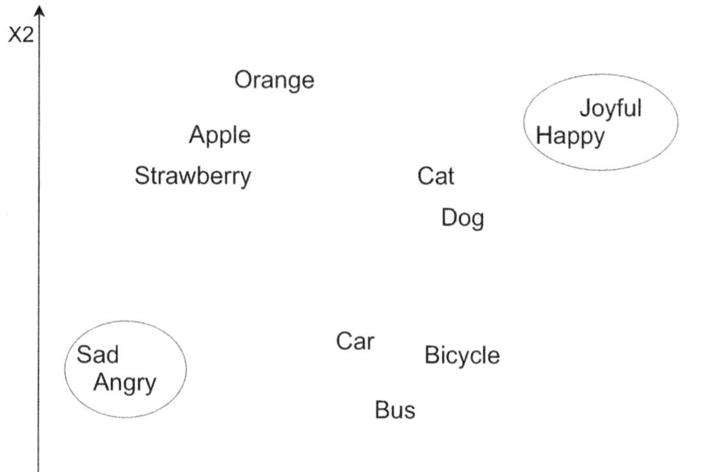

Figure 2.16: Word embedding similarities (visualized in 2D for simplicity)

Positional encoding

Transformers do not inherently consider the order of input tokens. If we look at the formula for attention,

$$a_{m,n} = \frac{\exp\left(\frac{q_m^T k_n}{\sqrt{d}}\right)}{\sum_{j=1}^{N} \exp\left(\frac{q_m^T k_j}{\sqrt{d}}\right)}$$

we see that it is permutation-invariant, meaning the attention mechanism doesn't account for token positions in the sequence. For instance, the Transformer cannot differentiate between "initialize the variable, then use it" and "use the variable, then initialize it." This impacts the model's ability to understand or generate coherent text.

To overcome this limitation, positional encoding provides the Transformer with position information for each token in the input sequence. Without positional encoding, the model treats the input sequence as a bag of words, which is problematic. With positional encoding, each token's position is encoded using a positional encoding function,

$$p_i = f(i)$$

where $f(\cdot)$ is the positional encoding function and i is the position of the token. This allows the model to distinguish between "use the variable, then initialize it" and "initialize the variable, then use it."

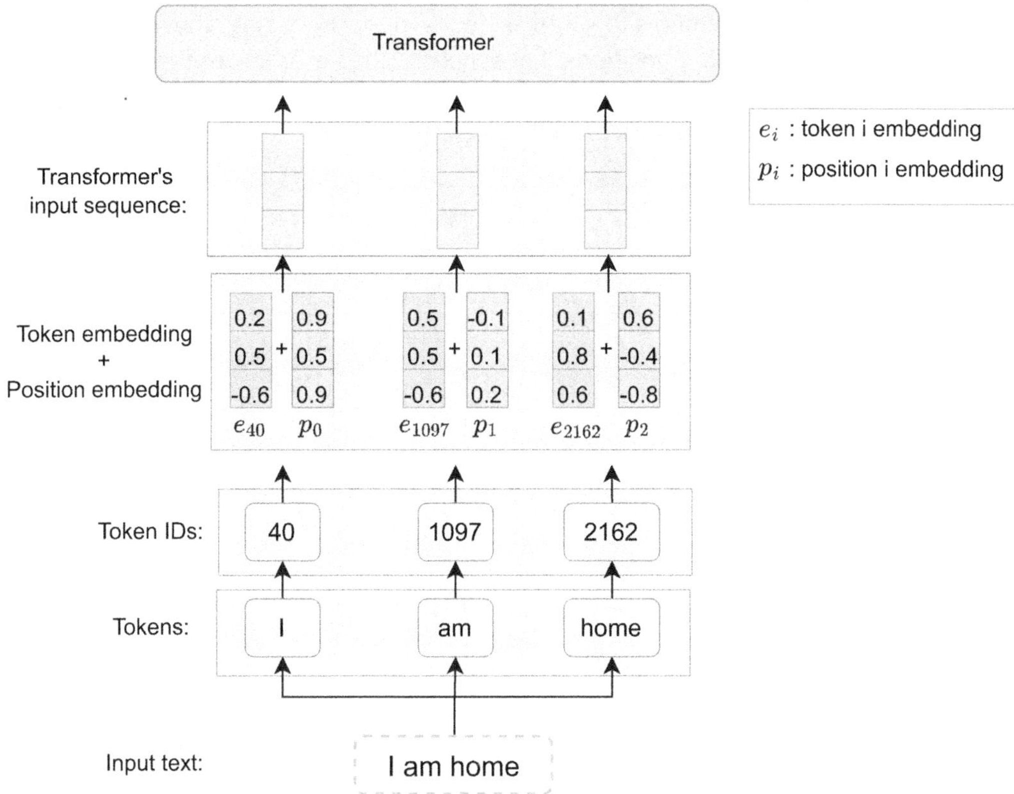

Figure 2.17: Adding positional information to the Transformer's input sequence

Positional encoding can be achieved through two common methods:

- Fixed positional encoding
- Learned positional encoding

Fixed positional encoding

This method uses a fixed function to map a position (an integer) to a fixed-size vector. The original Transformer paper introduced the sine-cosine function at different frequencies as its positional encoding function.

Sine-cosine positional encoding

$$PE_{(pos,2i)} = \sin\left(\frac{pos}{10000^{\frac{2i}{d_{model}}}}\right)$$

$$PE_{(pos,2i+1)} = \cos\left(\frac{pos}{10000^{\frac{2i}{d_{model}}}}\right)$$

Figure 2.18: Sine-cosine positional encoding formula

Figure 2.19 illustrates an example of sine-cosine positional encoding, showing vector representations for four different positions. For simplicity, this example uses a vector dimension of four. In practice, this dimensionality typically matches that of the token embeddings so they can be added together (see Figure 2.17).

p_0	$P_{00} = sin(0)$ = 0	$P_{01} = cos(0)$ = 1.0	$P_{02} = sin(0)$ = 0	$P_{03} = cos(0)$ = 1.0
p_1	$P_{10} = sin(1/1)$ = 0.84	$P_{11} = cos(1/1)$ = 0.54	$P_{12} = sin(1/10)$ = 0.1	$P_{13} = cos(1/10)$ = 1.0
p_2	$P_{20} = sin(2/1)$ = 0.91	$P_{21} = cos(2/1)$ = -0.42	$P_{22} = sin(2/10)$ = 0.20	$P_{23} = cos(2/10)$ = 0.98
p_3	$P_{30} = sin(3/1)$ = 0.14	$P_{31} = cos(3/1)$ = -0.99	$P_{32} = sin(3/10)$ = 0.30	$P_{33} = cos(3/10)$ = 0.96

Figure 2.19: Example of sine-cosine positional encoding

Let's take a look at the pros and cons of fixed positional encoding.

Pros:

- **Efficiency:** Fixed encodings do not add extra trainable parameters to the model. This makes them computationally more efficient.
- **Support for long sequences:** Fixed methods can map any position into a representation. This flexibility allows the model to handle longer sequences beyond the model's training data.

Cons:

- **Predefined limits:** Some fixed encoding methods require a predefined maximum position, thus limiting their applicability to sequences below that maximum.
- **Suboptimal performance:** In certain tasks, fixed encodings may not capture the positional relationships as effectively as learned methods. This can lead to suboptimal performance.

Learned positional encoding

In this method, the positional representations are learned during the training process. Specifically, a weight matrix $P \in \mathbb{R}^{N \times d}$ is initialized, where N is the maximum sequence length and d is the dimensionality of the embeddings. This matrix P is treated as a trainable parameter, and it is optimized alongside the model's other parameters.

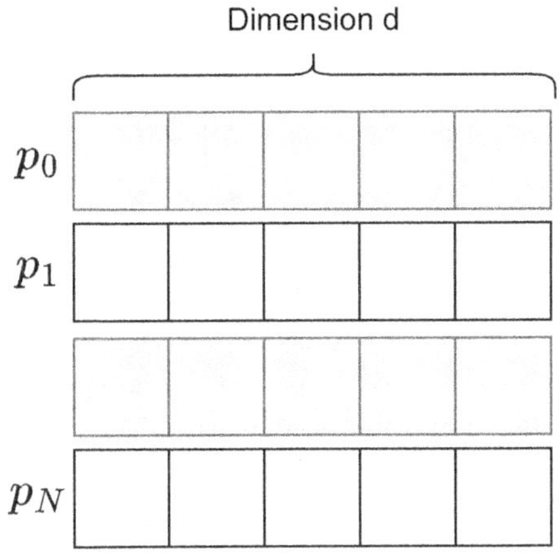

Figure 2.20: Trainable matrix representing positional encodings

Learned positional encoding has the following pros and cons.

Pros:

- **Optimal performance:** Since the embeddings are learned based on the training data, learned positional encoding can lead to optimal position representation for the specific task.

Cons:

- **Inefficiency:** Requires additional parameters to be learned during the training, which can increase the training time and computational cost.
- **Lack of generalization:** Learned embeddings may overfit to specific sequence lengths seen during training. If the model mainly sees sequences of a certain length during training, it may not effectively represent other positions. This affects the model's ability to generalize across diverse positions.

In summary, the choice between learned and fixed positional encodings depends on the constraints of the task, including the expected variability in sequence lengths. Some papers, including the original Transformer paper, employ fixed positional encoding due to its efficiency and better generalization. Following that, we employ fixed positional encoding, such as sine-cosine encoding, to train the Smart Compose feature.

Transformer

The Transformer component takes a sequence of embeddings as input and transforms them into an updated sequence of embeddings.

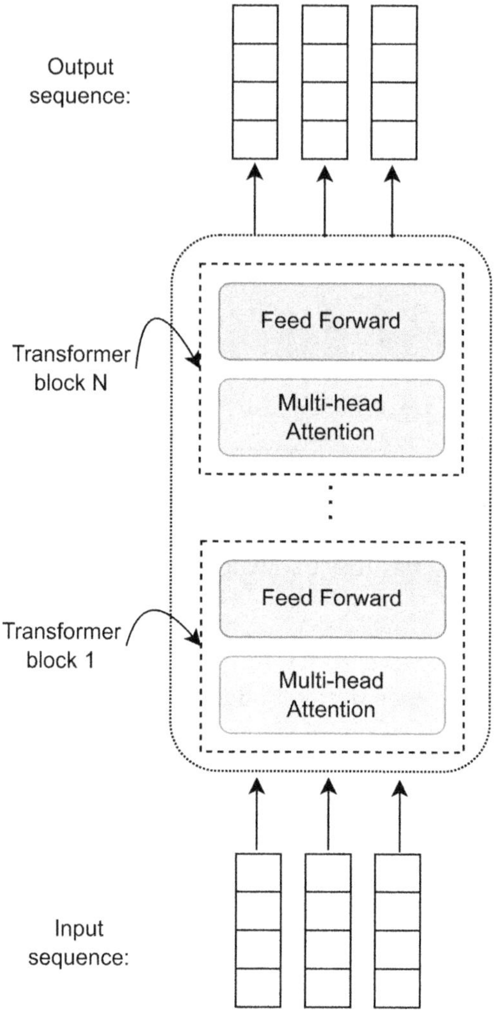

Figure 2.21: A simplified Transformer structure

The Transformer architecture consists of a stack of blocks. Each block contains the following:

- **Multi-head attention:** This layer updates each embedding by using the attention mechanism. The attention mechanism captures the relationships in the sequence by allowing each embedding to attend to its preceding embeddings. Due to the nature of its mechanism, multi-head attention is commonly known as self-attention, a term we'll use throughout the rest of this book.
- **Feed forward:** This layer applies two linear transformations, with a ReLU activation in between, to each embedding in the sequence independently.

Transformer architecture includes details such as residual connections, layer normalization, and dropout layers. For a deep understanding of these components, refer to the paper "Attention Is All You Need" [3] and [21].

Prediction head

The prediction head—the final component in a decoder-only Transformer—translates the Transformer's output into probabilities for every token in the vocabulary (Figure 2.22). These probabilities are used to choose the most likely next token.

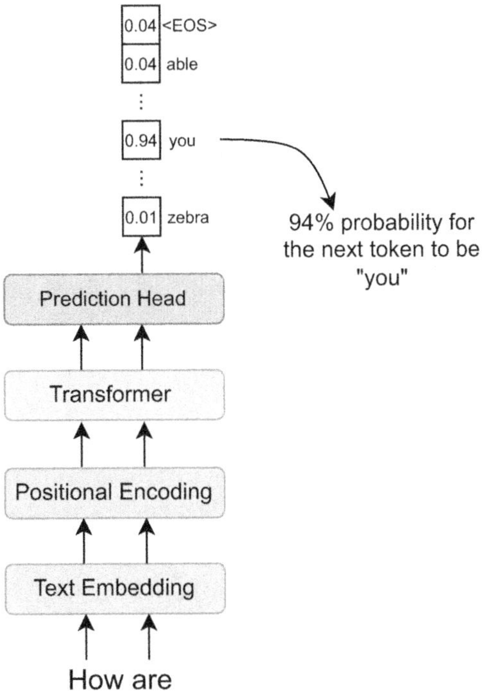

Figure 2.22: Prediction head output probabilities

Training

Training adjusts the decoder-only Transformer's parameters using email data. Once the training process is complete, the model can suggest likely completions.

However, directly training the model on a task-specific dataset, such as email data, is not a good strategy. This direct training has several challenges:

- **Lack of large training data:** Task-specific datasets are usually limited in size. This limitation can hinder the model's ability to learn effectively.
- **Risk of overfitting:** When a model is trained on a task-specific dataset, it runs a high risk of overfitting. Overfitting occurs when a model memorizes the training data to the extent that it cannot generalize to unseen data.
- **Expensive and lengthy training:** Training a large model from scratch requires significant computational resources and time. This is because the model has to learn different aspects of language, which is a complex and resource-intensive process.

To address the above issues, a two-stage training strategy is commonly employed: pretraining, followed by finetuning. In the pretraining stage, the model is trained on a large amount of general data to learn the structure of the language. In the finetuning stage, the pretrained model is then finetuned on data specific to the task at hand (e.g., email completion).

This two-stage strategy harnesses a form of transfer learning, as the general knowledge gained during the pretraining stage is transferred to the finetuning stage. This transfer is beneficial because the model doesn't have to start from scratch when learning a new task. Instead, it adjusts its pretrained weights, which is more efficient.

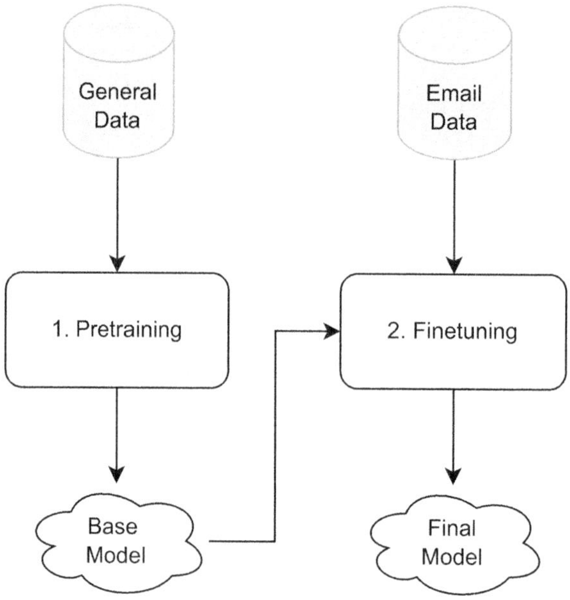

Figure 2.23: Two-stage training strategy

Let's take a closer look at each stage and examine the necessary training data, ML objectives, and loss functions for each.

1. Pretraining

Pretraining involves training a model on a large volume of general text data. This data is usually diverse, covering a wide range of topics and language structures. The purpose of pretraining is to develop a model capable of understanding natural language, including syntax, common knowledge, and language structures.

Pretraining data

The pretraining data for this stage usually consists of a large volume of general text data from various sources on the web, such as web pages, books, and social media. For example, Common Crawl [23] is a publicly available dataset collected by crawling a large number of web pages on the Internet. It contains petabytes of data that have been regularly collected since 2008.

ML objective and loss function

An ML objective refers to the formalized goal that a training process aims to achieve. In the case of text generation, the most commonly used ML objective is "next-token prediction." In this ML objective, the model is tasked with predicting the next token given a sequence of previous tokens. For example, in the sentence "I hope you are," the model should predict a high probability for "well" as the next token.

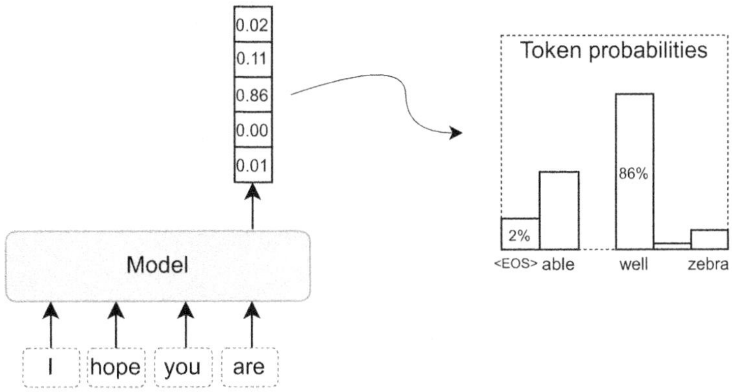

Figure 2.24: Probability distribution in next-token prediction

Next-token prediction is well suited for text generation tasks because, after the training process, the model can construct sentences incrementally. For example, given the input "I ordered food because I," the model might predict "was" as the next word. Subsequently, this process repeats with the new sequence "I ordered food because I was," leading to the next prediction, perhaps, "hungry." This iterative process continues until the model predicts "⟨EOS⟩," a special token that indicates the end of the sequence. Figure 2.25 shows the incremental process of generating text using next-token prediction.

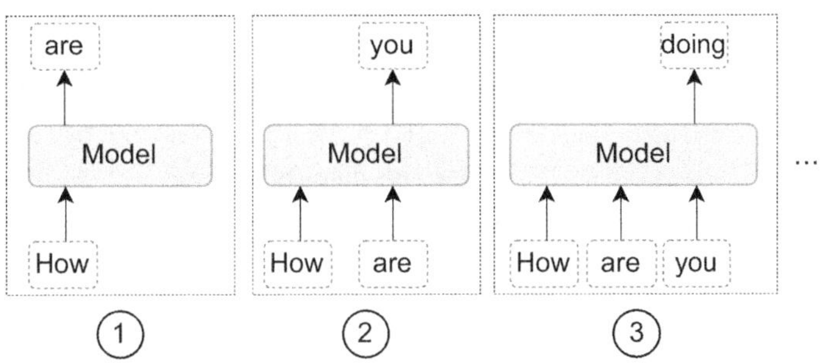

Figure 2.25: Incremental generation of text

To optimize the model for correctly predicting the next token, we define a loss function to guide the training process. Cross-entropy loss [24] is a commonly used loss function for the next-token prediction objective. This loss function measures the differences between the predicted probabilities and the correct token . This loss allows the optimizer to update the model's parameters to produce more accurate probabilities in the future.

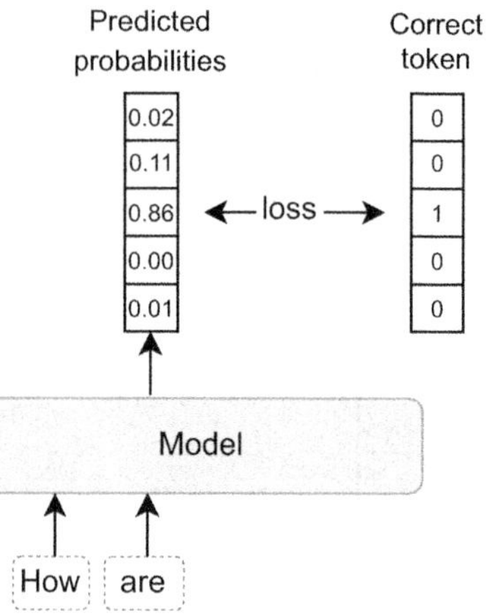

Figure 2.26: Loss calculation

In practice, the model processes all token lengths within a sequence in parallel. This allows it to compute the loss for each token position simultaneously. Parallelizing this step speeds up training by handling multiple tokens at once, instead of sequentially.

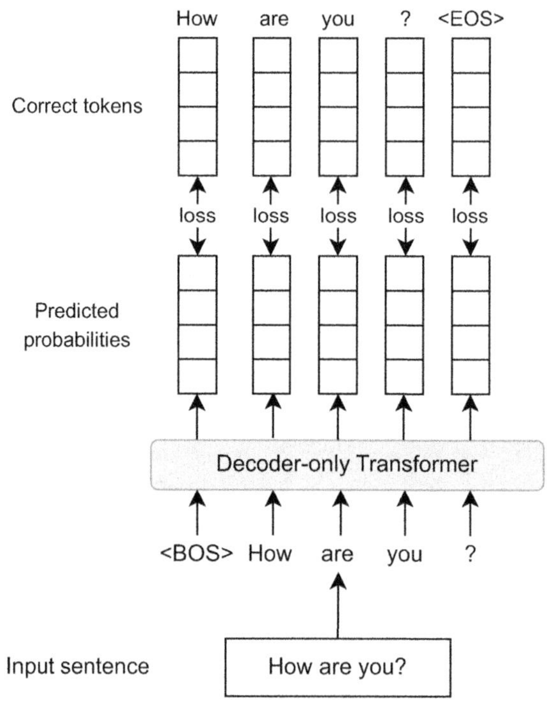

Figure 2.27: Parallelizing loss computations over different lengths

2. Finetuning

Finetuning involves adapting the base model from the pretraining stage to a specific task such as email completion. This stage focuses on making the model proficient at a particular task by training it on a smaller, task-specific dataset. During finetuning, the model retains its language understanding from the pretraining stage but adapts to the nuances of the task.

Finetuning data

We use a dataset of approximately one billion email conversations, as specified in the requirements section. This data includes various email formats, both formal and informal tones, and specific vocabularies that are more common in email conversations.

ML objective and loss function

In the finetuning stage, both the ML objective and loss function remain unchanged. The ML objective is next-token prediction, and the cross-entropy loss function guides the training process. The only difference from the pretraining stage is that the loss is calculated based on email data, focusing on predicting the next token in an email context.

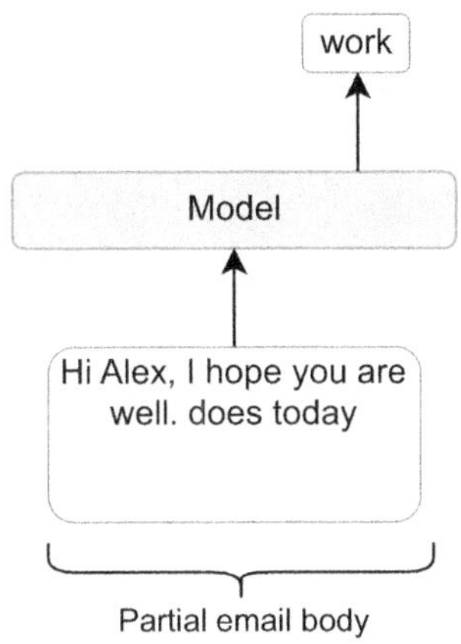

Figure 2.28: Example of email completion

However, relying on the email's body as the sole input is not very effective, because it is not always possible to predict the next token this way. Imagine a user who wants to reply to an email from John. When the user types "Dear," the model should, ideally, suggest "John." However, if that information is not provided as input, the model cannot predict "John" as the likely next token.

To address this limitation, we include more information in the input. For example, we can use the email's subject, the recipient, and previous emails, if available. This adds depth to the context and helps the model make more relevant predictions.

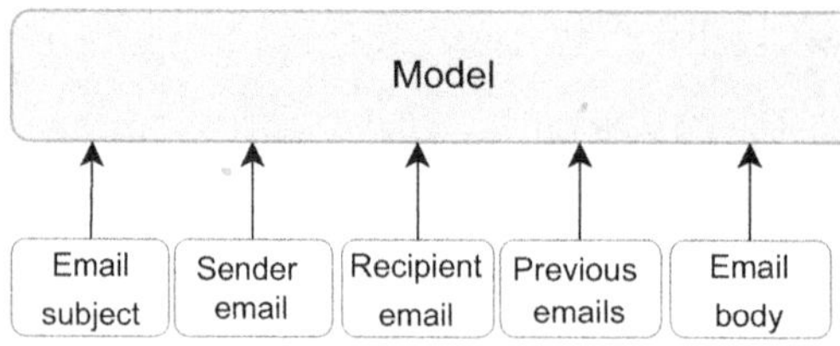

Figure 2.29: Providing more context as the input for improved model predictions

Combining various inputs

In traditional ML, the model's architecture typically depends on the type of data it processes. This requires customized preprocessing and feature engineering for different data types like text, images, or tables.

In the era of GenAI, however, the model architecture is often decoupled from the input structure. This decoupling increases flexibility, allowing the same model architecture to handle diverse inputs with a unified architecture, thus streamlining development and enhancing the versatility of GenAI systems. This decoupling is done through techniques like prompt engineering [25]. In Chapter 6, we examine prompt engineering in detail.

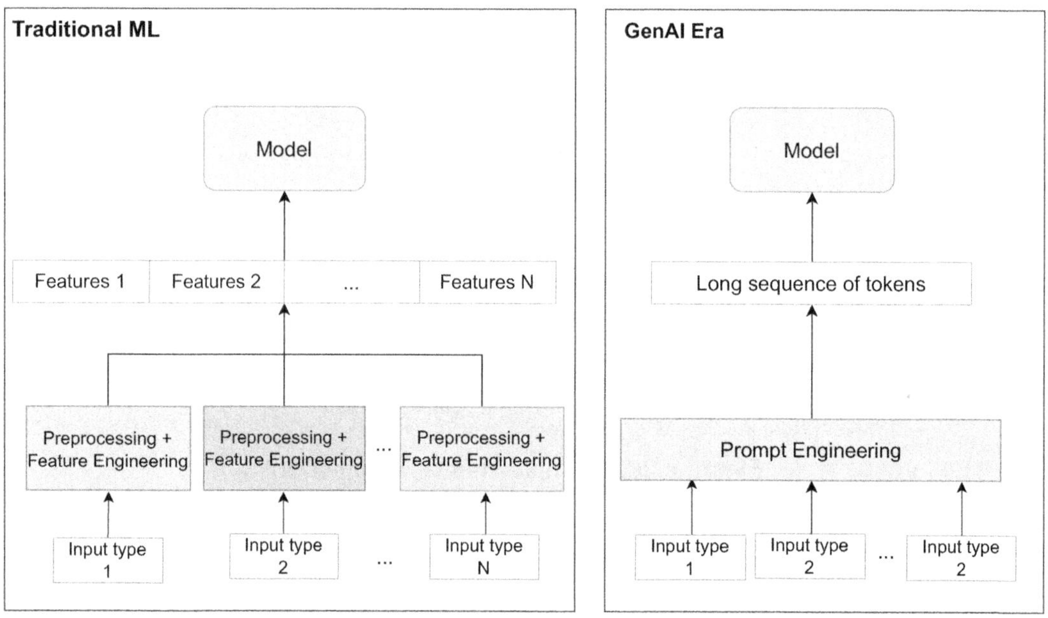

Figure 2.30: Combining various inputs in traditional ML vs. GenAI era

To combine various inputs in Gmail Smart Compose, as shown in Figure 2.31, we combine multiple text inputs into one sequence with tags using a prompt template. We don't need to worry about missing optional fields if our training set includes such examples. The model handles various input combinations regardless of whether they include all details or only partial information. This flexibility demonstrates the model's robust design, allowing it to generate contextually appropriate outputs even with incomplete inputs. By including diverse scenarios in the training data, we ensure the model generalizes well across different input structures and still produces reliable results.

Inputs:
[Text] Hi, I'm reaching out regarding our
[Subject] Follow-up on collaboration?
[Recent Emails] 07/10/2024: "Discussion on partnership plans", 06/22/2024: "Initial collaboration talk"

Output: collaboration

Example 1

Inputs:
[Text] Do you want to meet
[Subject]
[Recent Emails]

Output: later this week?

Example 2

Figure 2.31: Examples of combining text inputs

The benefits of two-stage training

The two-stage training strategy has several benefits, including:

- **Adaptability:** The same base model obtained from the pretraining stage can be adapted for different tasks.
- **Improved generalization:** Pretraining on large and diverse text data enables the model to develop a broad understanding of language. This helps to generalize better to various tasks.
- **Fast finetuning:** The model learns general knowledge during the pretraining stage. This makes the subsequent finetuning process faster.
- **Handling data scarcity:** For tasks where large datasets are unavailable, the knowledge gained during pretraining can compensate for this lack of data. This allows the model to perform well even with limited task-specific data.
- **Mitigating overfitting:** If we train a model from scratch on a smaller, task-specific dataset, there is a risk it will overfit. In two-stage training, pretraining acts as regularization. The model first learns to understand language broadly before focusing on the specifics of a particular task.
- **Resource optimization:** By separating the training process into two stages, we perform the computationally expensive pretraining once and can reuse the same model to adapt to different tasks. This reduces computational costs since we do not need to repeat the pretraining stage for each task.

Sampling

Generative models are trained to capture the underlying distribution of the training data. Once trained, these models can generate new samples that are similar to the data they were trained on. Sampling is the process of using a trained generative model to generate new data.

In the context of Smart Compose, sampling involves generating a likely email completion given the user's partial email body and other relevant information. As Figure 2.32 shows, sampling is achieved by generating tokens one at a time. For example, when "Hi Alex, does today" is given to the model, the "work" token is selected as the next token based on the predicted probabilities. Next, "Hi Alex, does today work" is provided to the model as input, and the "for" token is chosen as the next token. This process continues until the model predicts the ⟨EOS⟩ token.

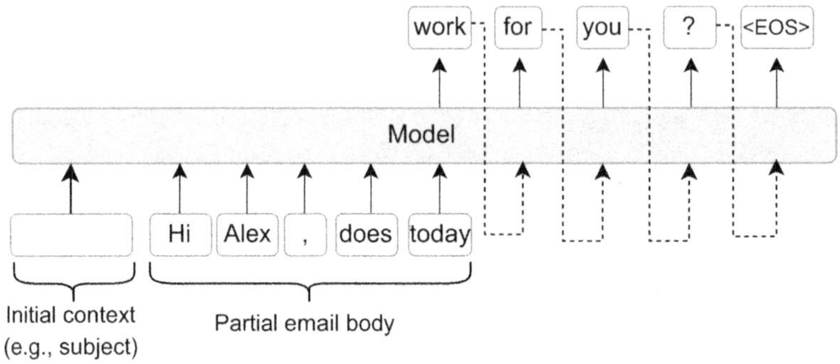

Figure 2.32: Sampling email completion token by token

There are primarily two types of strategies to generate new text in generative models: deterministic and stochastic. Let's have a look at each.

Deterministic

Deterministic methods generate text in a deterministic way, that is, without randomness or variability in the output. For example, at each step of token generation, the model selects the token with the highest probability from the predicted distribution. This method ensures that the generated text will always be the same for a given input, thus providing consistency and reproducibility. Figure 2.33 illustrates "greedy search," a simple deterministic method to generate text by iteratively choosing the next token based on the highest predicted probability.

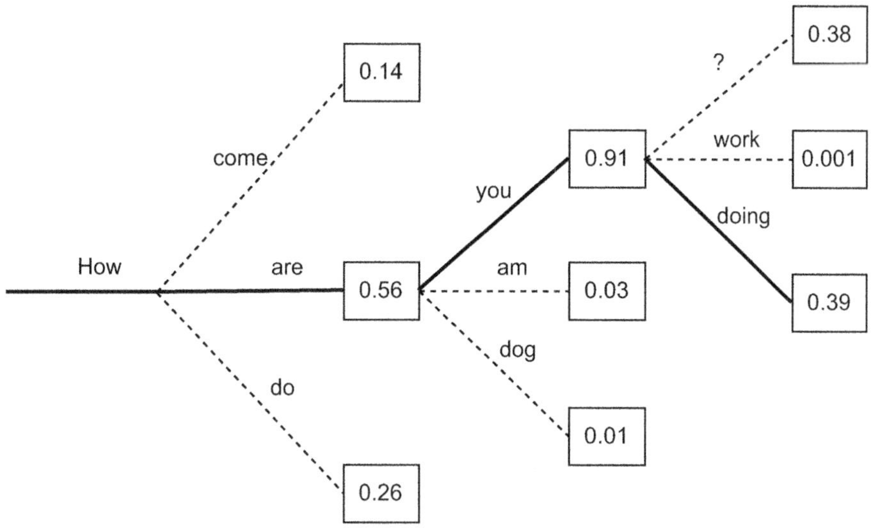

Figure 2.33: Greedy search

Pros:

- **Consistency:** The generated text is always the same for the same input – a desirable property for systems requiring predictable results.
- **Predictable outputs:** Fewer surprising outputs are generated because it always chooses the most probable token at each iteration.

Cons:

- **Lack of diversity:** The model may miss less probable but more interesting tokens; thus, there will be less creativity in the generated text. For example, when generating a story, the model always choose the most common phrases, resulting in a predictable but less interesting narrative.
- **Repetitive text:** The text may become repetitive, as the same high-probability token is always selected. For example, if the model generates a lengthy article, it might repeatedly use certain phrases. A real example of this is shown in Figure 2.34.

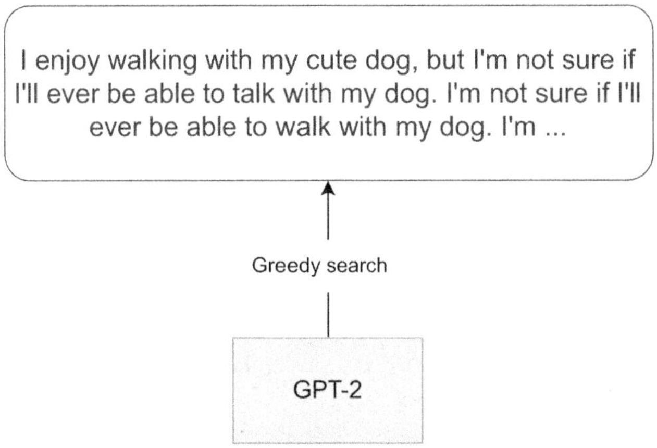

Figure 2.34: Text generated by GPT-2 language model using greedy search

Stochastic sampling

Stochastic sampling methods introduce randomness into the generation process. For example, at each step of token generation, the model samples from the predicted distribution based on the probabilities assigned to each token. This means that each time text is generated, even with the same initial inputs, the generated text may vary.

Figure 2.35 shows two instances of sampling using the same initial token "How." The first time, the sequence of generated tokens leads to "How are you,"; the second time, a different sequence is generated using the same initial token due to the randomness inherent in sampling.

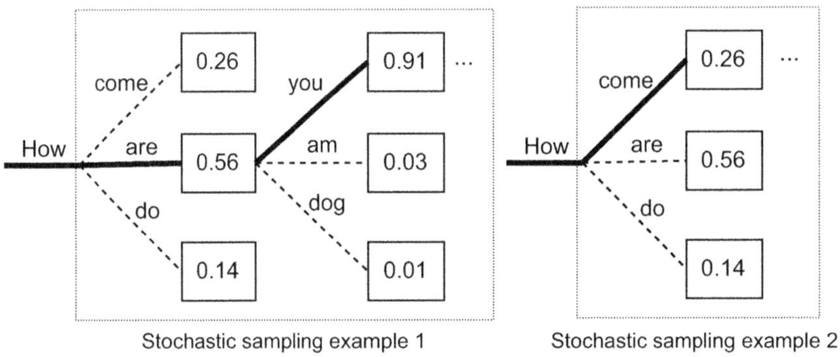

Figure 2.35: Stochastic sampling randomness

Pros:

- **Diversity:** The presence of randomness allows for more varied outputs, which is particularly useful in applications such as dialogue generation.
- **Novelty:** By sampling from the distribution, the model can explore less probable but potentially more interesting tokens, thus resulting in creativity and novel outputs.

Cons:

- **Inconsistency:** The output may vary each time a text is generated. This is less suitable for applications that require precise, repeatable results.
- **Unexpected outputs:** The randomness can lead to unexpected variations in the generated text, which might be inappropriate.

Which generation method is suitable for the Smart Compose feature?

For Smart Compose, deterministic methods are preferred for several reasons:

- **Consistency:** Consistency in generated text is crucial for applications such as email completion, for which users expect predictable and reliable suggestions. Utilizing a deterministic method means that users won't see dramatically different suggestions each time they begin to type the same thing.
- **Better handling of common phrases:** Deterministic methods are typically preferred in an email context, as more likely completions are prioritized over the novelty that stochastic methods offer.
- **Reduced risk of inappropriate suggestions:** Stochastic methods might occasionally generate inappropriate suggestions due to their inherent randomness. This behavior is not desired in an email completion feature.

These reasons highlight why deterministic methods are preferred in applications requiring consistency such as email completion. Now that we have chosen deterministic text generation, let's examine two primary algorithms:

- Greedy search
- Beam search

Greedy search

Greedy search is the simplest deterministic algorithm. It always selects the token with the highest probability as the next token. As was shown in Figure 2.34, greedy search can lead to repetitive patterns in the generated text. This occurs because it follows a narrow path based on the highest probability tokens without considering alternative paths that might lead to more coherent sentences. Due to this limitation, greedy search is rarely used in practice.

Beam search

Beam search [26] is a popular deterministic algorithm for generating text from a trained model. The core idea is to track multiple potential sequences of tokens simultaneously. At each step, the model calculates the probabilities for the next possible tokens for each sequence and selects the "top-k" most probable sequences. The value of k, known as beam width, is configurable.

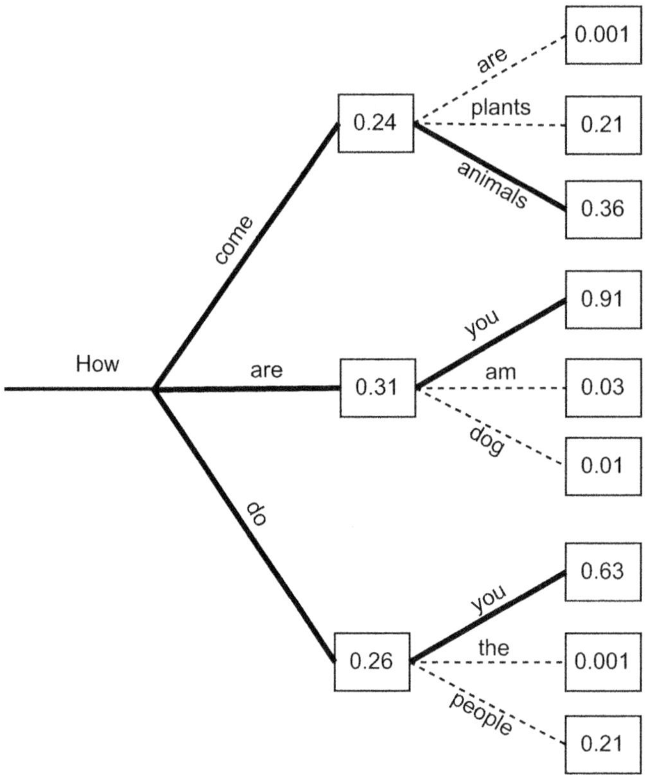

Figure 2.36: Beam search calculating the top three most probable sequences (beam width=3)

Here is a brief step-by-step process for generating text using beam search assuming a beam width of 3:

1. **Initialization:** Start with the user's partial email as the input to the trained model. The model predicts the probability distribution for the next token. Beam search selects the top three tokens with the highest probabilities.
2. **Expansion:** For each top three sequence, pass it to the model and obtain the probabilities of the next token.
3. **Pruning:** Select the top three sequences based on their cumulative probabilities.

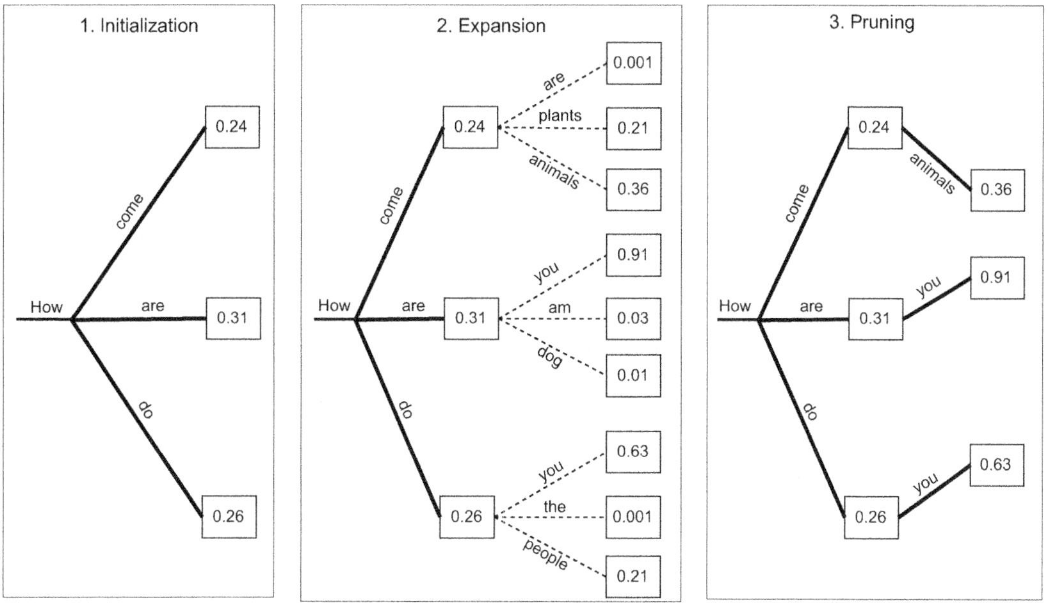

Figure 2.37: First iteration of a beam search with beam width=3

The expansion and pruning steps are repeated until all three potential sentences reach the ⟨EOS⟩ token or a maximum length. Once the beam search algorithm has stopped, we select the sequence with the highest cumulative probability as the output.

Beam search is effective in practice since it tracks several potential sequences simultaneously instead of the most probable sequence. However, beam search has two main drawbacks:

- **Limited diversity:** Beam search often leads to similar outputs, which is not ideal for applications requiring diverse responses.
- **Struggle with long sequences:** Beam search struggles with longer sequences because tracking too many sequences simultaneously can become computationally expensive.

The suggestions made by the Smart Compose feature are typically short; hence, capturing long-range dependencies is less critical. In addition, diversity in the email completions is not desired. For these reasons, we choose beam search as the primary sampling algorithm for generating suggestions.

Evaluation

Evaluation is essential in ML system design interviews. Interviewers will check if candidates can effectively test and validate the ML system they design. An ideal answer should cover both online and offline evaluations and discuss popular metrics for measuring a model's performance in each setting.

Let's explore some common metrics for evaluating the Smart Compose feature.

Offline evaluation metrics

Offline evaluation uses pre-collected and historical data to evaluate a model's performance. Its purpose is to ensure the model's performance is acceptable before deploying it to production. For example, we test a recommendation system on historical user interaction data to see how well it predicts user preferences. Similarly, we evaluate the performance of our trained model for the Smart Compose feature using historical email data. Two commonly used metrics are:

- Perplexity
- ExactMatch@N

Perplexity

Perplexity [27] is a standard metric used extensively in the offline evaluation of language models. This metric measures how accurately the model predicts the exact sequence of tokens present in text data. In mathematical terms, perplexity is defined as the exponential of the average "negative log-likelihood" of the predicted probability given the previous tokens in a sequence:

$$\text{Perplexity}(X) = \exp\left(-\frac{1}{N}\sum_{i=1}^{N}\log P\left(x_i \mid x_{1:i-1}\right)\right)$$

In this equation:

- X is a tokenized sequence $(x_1, x_2, \cdots, x_N)$ in the text data that is used to evaluate how accurately the model predicts the sequence.
- N is the number of tokens in the sequence.
- $P\left(x_i \mid x_{1:i-1}\right)$ is the conditional probability of the i-th token given the preceding tokens, $x_{1:i-1}$, that is, how likely the model is to predict the i-th token given the previous tokens.

Figure 2.38 illustrates a concrete example to better understand perplexity.

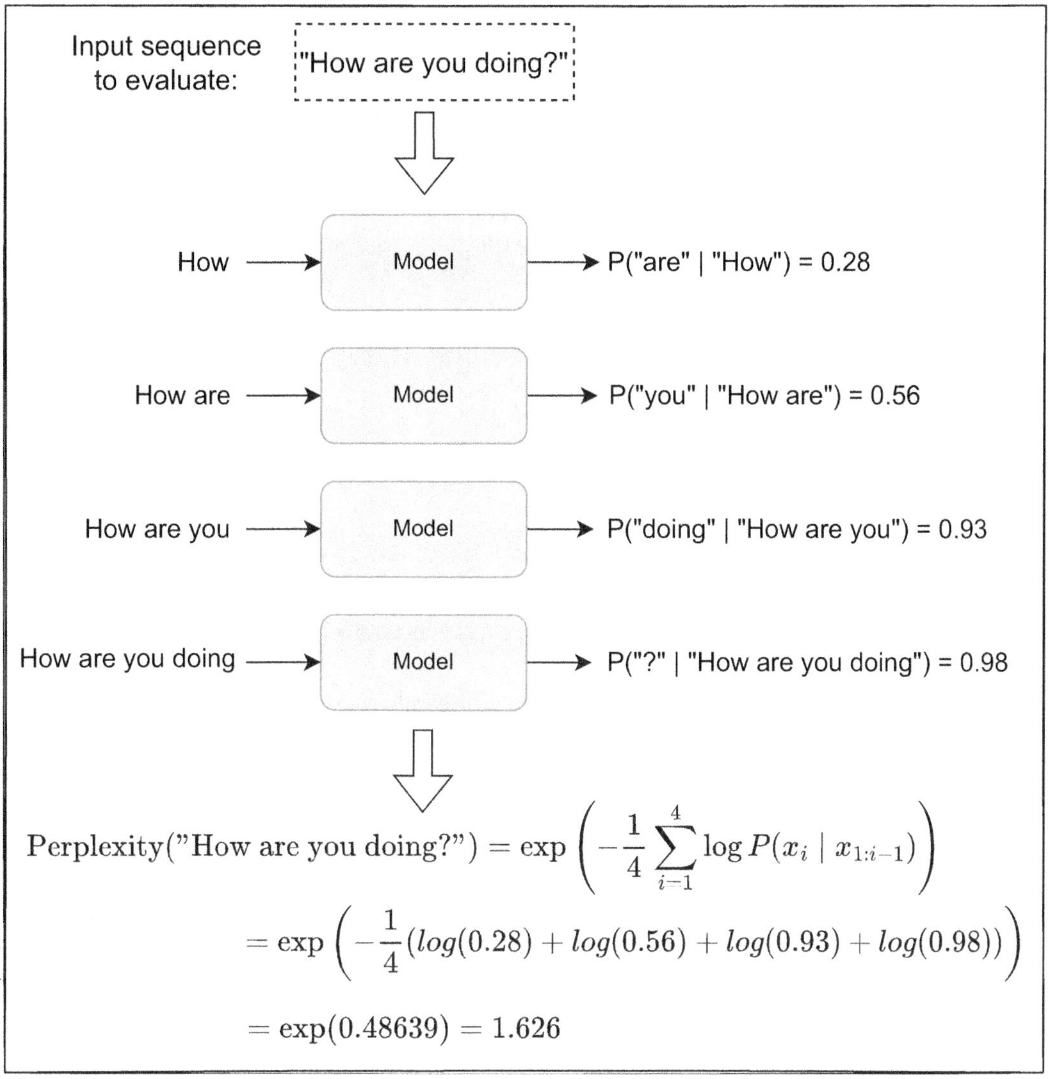

Figure 2.38: Example of perplexity calculation

A lower perplexity value indicates that the model has assigned higher probabilities, on average, to the tokens that appear in the text data. Therefore, a lower perplexity means the model is better at predicting the next tokens.

ExactMatch@N

ExactMatch@N measures the percentage of generated phrases that are exactly N words long and that match the first N words of the ground-truth text. Figure 2.39 shows ExactMatch@3 calculations for three generated sequences. In practice, there are usually more than three sequences to evaluate.

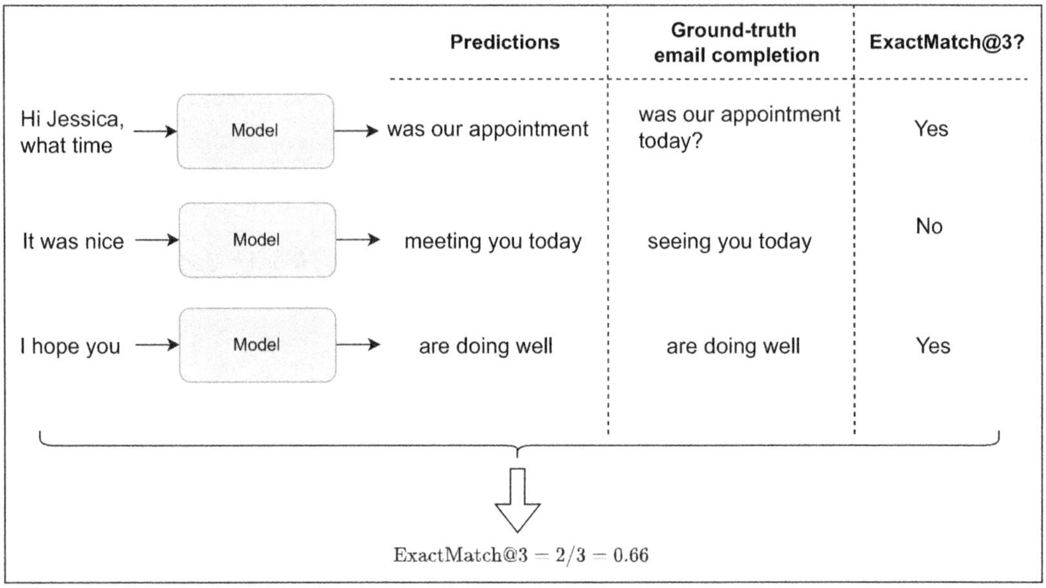

Figure 2.39: Example of calculating ExactMatch@3 for three sequences

Calculating ExactMatch@N for different values of N allows us to measure how the model performs at different suggestion lengths. To measure the overall performance of the model, we calculate the ExactMatch for all lengths up to a specific length and then take the average.

While Perplexity and ExactMatch@N have traditionally been used to evaluate Gmail Smart Compose, other metrics such as BLEU score and ROUGE-N, introduced more recently, have been found to be helpful. We examine these metrics in more detail in Chapter 3.

Online evaluation metrics

Online evaluation measures how a model performs in real time as users interact with the system. To evaluate the Smart Compose feature in an online environment, we use additional metrics beyond Perplexity and ExactMatch@N. These online metrics measure user engagement, the model's latency, and the overall impact on user experience.

Unlike offline metrics, which are usually standard, online evaluation metrics are defined based on specific requirements and needs. Companies often use hundreds of metrics for online evaluation. However, in an interview setting, we typically discuss the most common ones. In this section, we focus on the following metrics:

- User engagement metrics
- Effectiveness metrics
- Latency metrics
- Quality metrics

User engagement metrics

- **Acceptance rate:** The percentage of suggestions made by the Smart Compose feature that are accepted by users. A higher acceptance rate indicates that the suggestions are relevant and useful to users.
- **Usage rate:** The percentage of all composed emails that have utilized the Smart Compose feature. High usage rates typically indicate that users trust the feature.

Effectiveness metrics

- **Average completion time:** Tracks the average time taken by users to compose emails with and without the aid of Smart Compose. A reduced average completion time using Smart Compose will indicate that the feature is speeding up the email writing process.

Latency metrics

- **System response time:** Measures the time it takes for the Smart Compose suggestions to appear after the user begins typing. It's important to ensure this metric stays below a certain threshold so the suggestions are made before the user types them.

Quality metrics

- **Feedback rate:** Measures the rate at which users provide feedback on the suggestions. Feedback is helpful for continuous improvement of the system.
- **Human evaluation:** Qualitative assessments through user studies are employed to evaluate the usefulness of suggestions. This metric reflects user satisfaction with the Smart Compose feature.

These online metrics are essential for evaluating how well Smart Compose feature works in production. By monitoring these metrics, the stakeholders can obtain a holistic view of feature's performance.

Overall ML System Design

In this section, we propose a design for a simplified Smart Compose feature.

When designing such a feature, we should consider more than just the underlying model that predicts the next token. The system's effectiveness depends on various components working together to ensure the system is responsive, generates relevant suggestions, and maintains ethical standards. For the Smart Compose feature, we examine the following key components:

- Triggering service
- Phrase generator
- Post-processing service

Let's explore each in more detail.

Triggering service

The triggering service activates the Smart Compose feature by monitoring user activity such as keystrokes. It decides when to activate the feature based on criteria such as the number of characters typed or the entering of specific keywords in the text. For example, if a user types "I," the service might not activate Smart Compose because it's too early to predict the user's intent. However, if the user types "I hope," the service will activate Smart Compose, as the additional context allows for more useful suggestions.

The triggering service ensures suggestions are not too frequent. Once the service determines that activating the Smart Compose feature will be useful, it triggers the phrase generator component, which we discuss next.

Phrase generator

The phrase generator is the core of the Smart Compose feature. It generates the most likely completion based on the partial text the user has already typed.

To achieve this, the phrase generator interacts with the trained model and employs beam search to generate the top-k most probable completions. Each completion ends with the ⟨EOS⟩ token and an associated score that indicates how confident the model is about the completion.

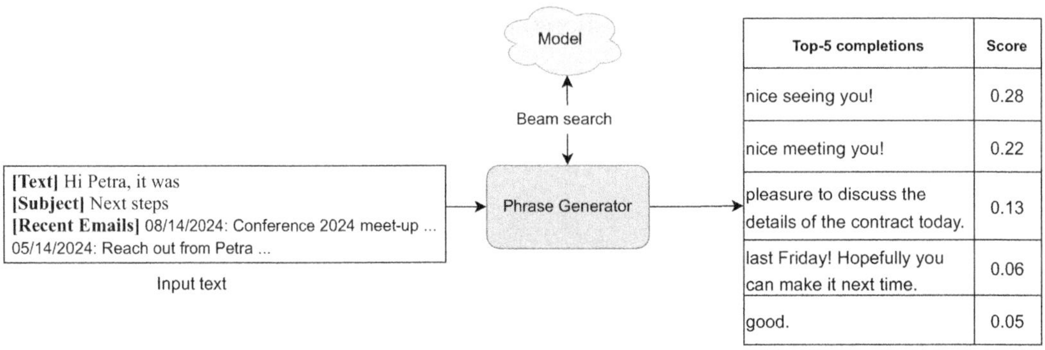

Figure 2.40: Beam search outputs top five potential completions (beam width = 5)

Given the possible completions, two critical considerations are necessary:

- Removing long suggestions
- Removing low-confidence suggestions

Removing long suggestions

As shorter suggestions are easier for the author to read as they are typing, we remove suggested phrases that are too long. For example, if a user types "Can you please," the phrase generator might suggest "help me with this?" Longer suggestions, such as "help me with this project that is due next week," will be too specific and, therefore, less likely to predict what the author intends to write.

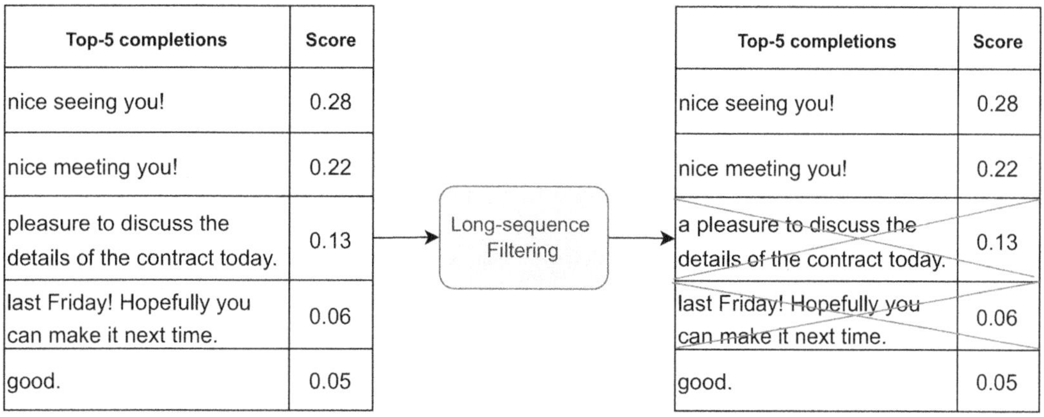

Figure 2.41: Removing long suggestions

Removing low-confidence suggestions

We remove suggestions with confidence scores below a certain threshold. This ensures we do not present suggestions if the model is not confident enough about it.

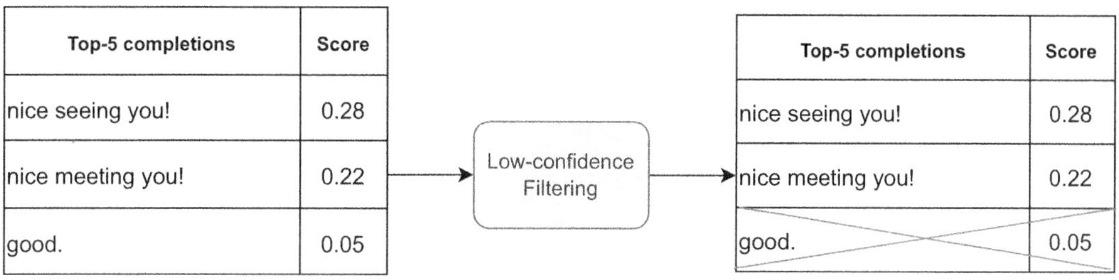

Figure 2.42: Removing low-confidence suggestions

Finally, if the final list of suggestions is not empty, the phrase generator will pass the one with the highest confidence score to the post-processing service.

Post-processing service

The post-processing service addresses potential biases before suggestions are presented to the user. This component follows predefined rules to detect and correct bias efficiently. Common strategies to achieve this include:

- **Pronoun replacement:** Replace gender-specific pronouns to ensure neutrality. For example, "he" or "she" might be replaced with "they" in contexts where gender is not specified.
- **Gender-neutral word replacement:** Replace gendered words with gender-neutral alternatives where appropriate. This includes changing words like "chairman" to "chair-

person" or "policeman" to "police officer."

- **Lexical analysis for sensitive terms:** Use a predefined list of flagged terms that, if identified, can be replaced with neutral alternatives. For example, terms that might imply age, race, or disability biases are adjusted to ensure the suggestions will be perceived as respectful and neutral.
- **NSFW (Not Safe For Work) content filtering:** Implement automated filters that scan for and flag explicit language. These filters use predefined lists of NSFW keywords, phrases, and patterns to detect and remove problematic content.

By implementing these rules, the post-processing service maintains ethical standards in the Smart Compose feature, thus ensuring that the suggestions provided are relevant, respectful, and inclusive.

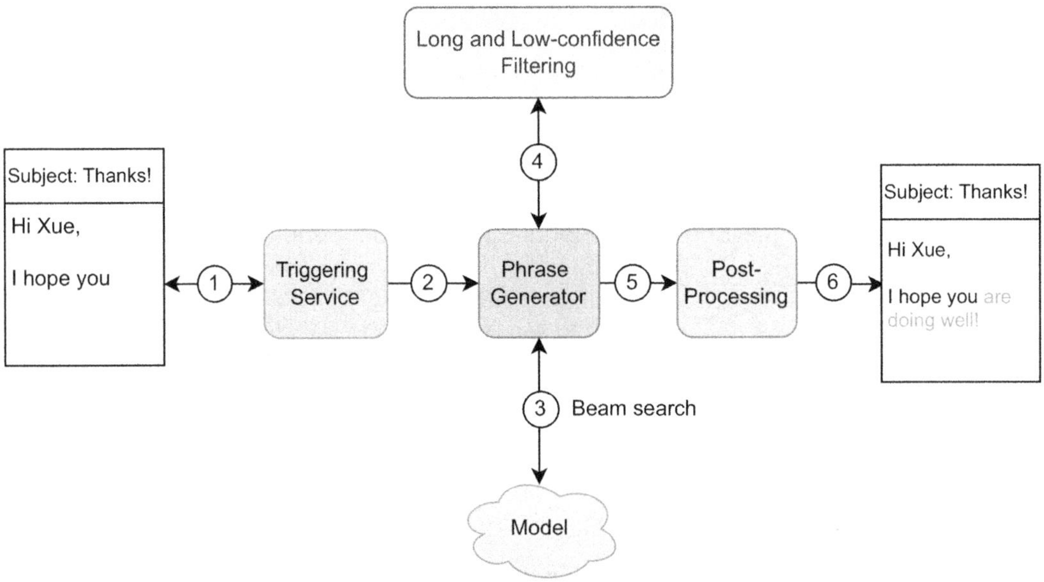

Figure 2.43: Smart Compose feature overall design

Here is a brief step-by-step workflow of the overall ML system employed by the Smart Compose feature:

1. **Monitoring:** The triggering service monitors the user's activity as they type.
2. **Triggerring:** The service triggers the phrase generator once it identifies specific patterns.
3. **Beam search:** The phrase generator employs beam search to get top-k potential completions from the trained model.
4. **Filtering:** The phrase generator interacts with the filtering component to remove long suggestions and those with low confidence scores.
5. **Post-processing:** The completion with the highest score is picked and passed to the

post-processing service. The service replaces gender-specific pronouns and adjusts sensitive terms.

6. **Display suggestion:** The suggestion is displayed to the user for their consideration.

Other Talking Points

If there's extra time at the end of the interview, you may face follow-up questions or be asked to discuss advanced topics. This depends on factors such as the interviewer's preference, your expertise, and the requirements of the role. For senior roles, here are some topics you should prepare for:

- Supporting Smart Compose in multiple languages [28].
- Personalizing suggestions [28].
- Incorporating additional context for better predictions [28].
- Understanding how different tokenization algorithms work, such as BPE [11], SentencePiece [12], and WordPiece [29].
- Understanding different ML objectives such as masked language modeling (MLM) and its variations [18].
- The multi-token prediction objective and its pros and cons [30].
- Balancing quality and inference latency [28].

Summary

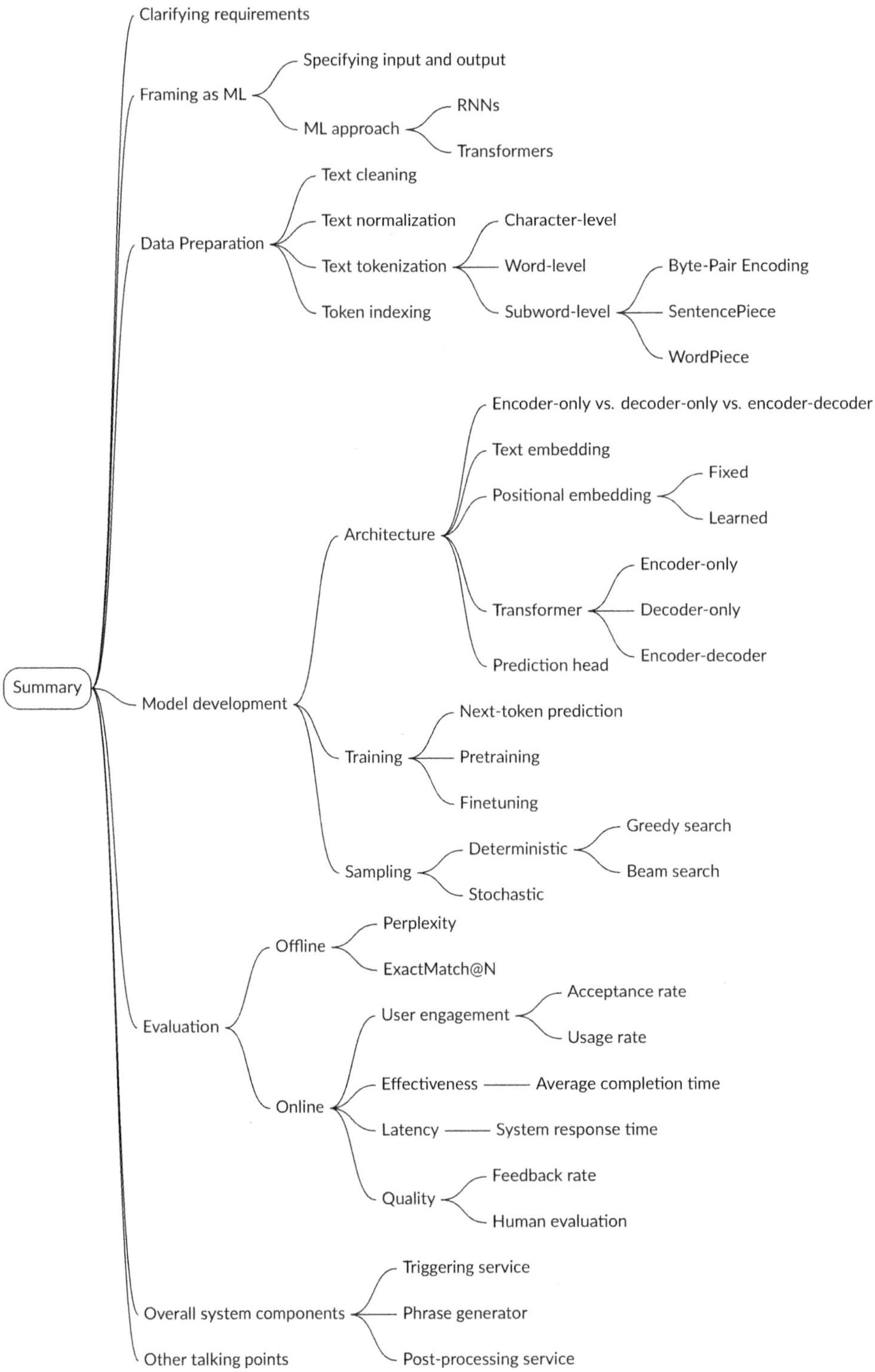
Summary
Clarifying requirements
Framing as ML
Specifying input and output
ML approach
RNNs
Transformers
Data Preparation
Text cleaning
Text normalization
Text tokenization
Character-level
Word-level
Subword-level
Byte-Pair Encoding
SentencePiece
WordPiece
Token indexing
Model development
Architecture
Encoder-only vs. decoder-only vs. encoder-decoder
Text embedding
Positional embedding
Fixed
Learned
Transformer
Encoder-only
Decoder-only
Encoder-decoder
Prediction head
Training
Next-token prediction
Pretraining
Finetuning
Sampling
Deterministic
Greedy search
Beam search
Stochastic
Evaluation
Offline
Perplexity
ExactMatch@N
Online
User engagement
Acceptance rate
Usage rate
Effectiveness
Average completion time
Latency
System response time
Quality
Feedback rate
Human evaluation
Overall system components
Triggering service
Phrase generator
Post-processing service
Other talking points

Reference Material

[1] Gmail's Smart Compose Feature. https://research.google/pubs/gmail-smart-compose-real-time-assisted-writing/.

[2] Fundamentals of Recurrent Neural Network. https://arxiv.org/abs/1808.03314.

[3] Attention Is All You Need. https://arxiv.org/abs/1706.03762.

[4] Gated Recurrent Unit. https://en.wikipedia.org/wiki/Gated_recurrent_unit.

[5] Long Short-Term Memory. https://deeplearning.cs.cmu.edu/F23/document/readings/LSTM.pdf.

[6] RITA: Group Attention is All You Need for Timeseries Analytics. https://arxiv.org/abs/2306.01926.

[7] FlashAttention: Fast and Memory-Efficient Exact Attention with IO-Awareness. https://arxiv.org/abs/2205.14135.

[8] Language Identification. https://en.wikipedia.org/wiki/Language_identification.

[9] FastText Model for Language Identification. https://huggingface.co/facebook/fasttext-language-identification.

[10] Transformer-XL. https://arxiv.org/abs/1901.02860.

[11] Byte-Pair Encoding Tokenization. https://huggingface.co/learn/nlp-course/en/chapter6/5.

[12] SentencePiece Tokenization. https://arxiv.org/abs/1808.06226.

[13] Tiktoken Library. https://github.com/openai/tiktoken.

[14] Google's Gemini. https://gemini.google.com/.

[15] SentencePiece Library. https://github.com/google/sentencepiece.

[16] Summary of Tokenizers. https://huggingface.co/docs/transformers/en/tokenizer_summary.

[17] OpenAI's Tokenizers. https://tiktokenizer.vercel.app/?model=gpt-4-1106-preview.

[18] BERT. https://arxiv.org/abs/1810.04805.

[19] OpenAI's Models. https://platform.openai.com/docs/models.

[20] Meta's LLaMA. https://llama.meta.com/.

[21] Introduction to Transformers by Andrej Karpathy. https://www.youtube.com/watch?v=XfpMkf4rD6E.

[22] Transformer Visualized. https://jalammar.github.io/illustrated-transformer/.

[23] Common Crawl. https://commoncrawl.org/.

[24] Cross-Entropy. https://en.wikipedia.org/wiki/Cross-entropy.

[25] Prompt Engineering. https://platform.openai.com/docs/guides/prompt-engineering.

[26] Beam Search. https://en.wikipedia.org/wiki/Beam_search.

[27] Perplexity. https://en.wikipedia.org/wiki/Perplexity.

[28] Gmail Smart Compose: Real-Time Assisted Writing. https://arxiv.org/abs/1906.00080.

[29] WordPiece Tokenization. https://huggingface.co/learn/nlp-course/en/chapter6/6.

[30] Better & Faster Large Language Models via Multi-token Prediction. https://arxiv.org/abs/2404.19737.

3

Google Translate

Introduction

Google Translate is a widely used language translation service offered by Google. The service relies on machine learning (ML) models to understand and translate text between languages. As of 2024, the service supports over 130 different languages and has over a billion users [1]. This chapter explores the system design behind a language translation service.

Figure 3.1: Language translation service

Clarifying Requirements

Here is a typical interaction between a candidate and an interviewer:

Candidate: Are there specific languages the system should support initially?
Interviewer: Let's focus on four languages: English, Spanish, Korean, and French. We can expand to more languages in the future.

Candidate: Considering the diversity of languages, do we have access to a sufficiently large and varied dataset for training?
Interviewer: Yes. We have access to a substantial multilingual corpus, including formal documents, web content, and conversational texts, in all four languages. The dataset contains 300 million examples, an example being defined as a pair of sentences in the source and target languages.

Candidate: Do we have access to general text data? This is important, as it would allow

us to pretrain a model on general text data and, thus, allow it to gain general knowledge.
Interviewer: Assume we have access to terabytes of general text data in each of the languages, obtained from various sources.

Candidate: Will users specify the input text language, or should the system detect it automatically?
Interviewer: Users cannot always identify a text's language. Imagine a book title in a language with which the user is not familiar. Our system should detect the input language automatically.

Candidate: Is there a constraint on the length of the input text?
Interviewer: Let's build the system in such a way that it can support inputs of up to 1,000 words.

Candidate: Should the system support translation when there is no internet connection? In other words, should the model work on-device?
Interviewer: The focus of this interview is not efficiency and model optimization for on-device deployment. Let's assume an internet connection is required and that the model will be deployed on the cloud.

Candidate: Should the system support real-time translation?
Interviewer: Not initially.

Frame the Problem as an ML Task

In this section, we frame the problem of building a translation system as an ML task. This involves understanding the system's inputs and outputs and choosing a suitable ML approach.

Specifying the system's input and output

The input to a translation system is a sequence of words in the source language and the target language provided by the user. The output is a sequence of words in the target language.

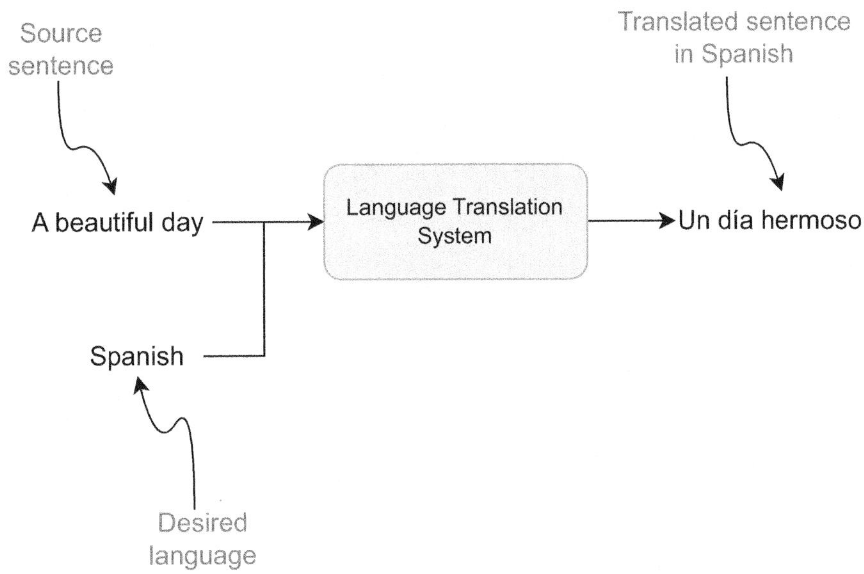

Figure 3.2: Input and output of a translation system

Choosing a suitable ML approach

In language translation, a sequence of words in one language is transformed into a sequence of words in another language. This sequence-to-sequence (seq2seq) structure is also found in other tasks, such as text summarization and speech recognition.

Seq2seq models, a class of ML models, are specifically designed to handle such tasks. These models transform an input sequence into an output sequence, which can vary in length from the input. Seq2seq models follow an encoder-decoder architecture, which has two main components:

- **Encoder:** Processes the input sequence and transforms it into a sequence of context vectors, thus encoding the information in the input sequence.
- **Decoder:** Utilizes the encoder's context vectors to generate the output sequence one token at a time.

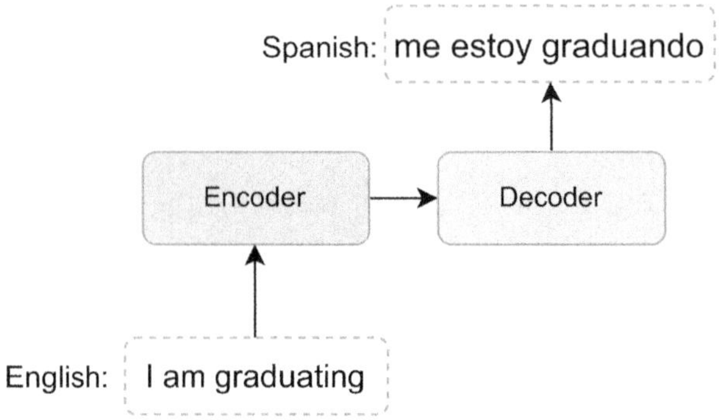

Figure 3.3: Encoder-decoder model for English-to-Spanish translation

There are several architectures available for the encoder and decoder components. In particular, architectures designed to process sequential data, such as LSTMs, GRUs, and Transformers, can be employed. Among those, Transformers have shown superior performance in translation tasks, outperforming earlier models such as GRUs and LSTMs, particularly in handling long-range dependencies. Notably, the attention mechanism was originally introduced in the context of language translation [2].

As described in Chapter 2, Transformers have three variations: encoder-only, decoder-only, and encoder-decoder architecture. Encoder-only models such as BERT [3] are good at understanding and processing the input sequence but typically require additional mechanisms to generate output. Decoder-only models, such as OpenAI's GPT [4] and Anthropic's Claude [5], are highly effective at generative tasks.

While all Transformer variations offer strong performance and can be adapted for language translation tasks through techniques like prompt engineering, encoder-decoder models are usually preferred for three main reasons. First, the encoder-decoder architecture separates the input understanding and output generation, which is ideal for seq2seq tasks such as language translation. It allows the encoder to specialize in the source language and fully understand the input sequence before the decoder generates the output. For example, encoders often use bidirectional mechanisms, such as bidirectional LSTMs [6] or Transformers, which enable them to understand the context from both directions.

Second, this architecture naturally handles variable-length sequences. Encoder-decoder models are designed to accommodate input/output sequences of varying lengths, making them highly versatile across different applications. This flexibility is crucial for tasks where inputs and outputs do not have a fixed length relationship.

Finally, the cross-attention mechanism present in encoder-decoder Transformers enables the decoder to focus dynamically on relevant parts of the input sequence during generation. This targeted attention ensures that the output sequence remains closely aligned with important elements of the source sequence, thus improving the accuracy and quality of the translation. We will explore cross-attention in greater detail in the architecture section.

Data Preparation

In this section, we prepare raw textual data for the encoder-decoder Transformer. We have two types of data for training: general data and translation data. General data includes publicly available text from the Internet. Translation data comprises 300 million sentence pairs, each containing a source-language sentence and its corresponding translation in the target language.

Raw text in both general data and translation data is often noisy and not in the format the ML model expects. Since we covered preparing general data in Chapter 2, we will focus on preparing translation data. In particular, we focus on the following two steps:

1. Text preprocessing
2. Text tokenization

Text preprocessing

We apply the following preprocessing techniques to raw text in translation data:

- **Remove missing data:** Remove pairs where either the source or target text is missing.
- **Remove noisy data:** Remove pairs with HTML tags or incorrect language pairings.
- **Deduplication:** Remove duplicate sentence pairs from the dataset to prevent the model from overfitting to certain examples.
- **Handle named entities:** Language translation models often struggle with named entities. We identify these entities in the text and replace them with placeholder tokens. After translation, we replace the tokens with the original entities. For example, consider the sentence: "The California city, Burlingame, is named after diplomat Anson Burlingame." First, we detect the named entities: "California (location name)," "Burlingame (location name)," and "Anson Burlingame (person's name)." Next, we replace these entities with placeholder tokens: "The ENTITY_1 city, ENTITY_2, is named after diplomat ENTITY_3." This approach helps the model focus on the sentence context during training without being confused by uncommon terms.

In modern language translation, particularly with models like Transformers, some traditional preprocessing steps have become less crucial or are handled differently. Here are a few preprocessing steps that were once essential in traditional translation models but are now unnecessary or less relevant:

- **Lowercasing:** Modern language translation models can handle case sensitivity as part of their training. They can learn to distinguish between different forms of words based on case (e.g., "Apple" as a company vs. "apple" as a fruit) without needing to convert everything to lowercase. Therefore, lowercasing is often skipped to preserve the original case information.
- **Stop word removal:** Stop words (e.g., "the," "and," "in") are essential for the gram-

matical structure of sentences. Removing them can disrupt the fluency and meaning of translations. Modern language translation models benefit from having complete sentences, including stop words, to understand the context fully and produce more natural translations.

- **Stemming and lemmatization:** Stemming (reducing words to their base or root forms) and lemmatization (reducing words to their dictionary forms) are not typically needed in modern language translation because these models are designed to handle morphological variations of words. The models learn to translate words into their correct forms based on context; therefore, reducing them to a base form could actually remove valuable information.
- **Punctuation removal:** Punctuation is important for understanding sentence structure and meaning. Modern language translation models are trained to handle punctuation naturally; thus, removing it can degrade translation quality. Punctuation is usually preserved to help the model maintain the grammatical integrity of sentences.

Text tokenization

In the context of language translation in which we deal with several languages, the choice of text tokenization algorithm is important. For example, if we were to choose a word-level tokenizer, we would have hundreds of thousands of unique words across all languages in our vocabulary, which is huge and inefficient.

Token	ID
<BOS>	0
<EOS>	1
walking	2
bonjour	3
hello	4
fantastique	5
...	...

Word-level Vocabulary

Figure 3.4: A huge vocabulary size due to word-level tokenization

In language translation, handling the diversity of words across languages is a key challenge. Traditional word-level tokenization models often struggle with out-of-vocabulary (OOV) words, while subword-level tokenization algorithms are more efficient and can effectively address the OOV problem. Due to their importance and widespread use, it is valuable to examine Byte-Pair Encoding (BPE) [7], a commonly used subword-level tokenization algorithm, in detail.

Byte-Pair Encoding (BPE)

BPE builds a subword-level vocabulary through iterative merging. It starts with characters and iteratively merges the most frequent combinations into new subwords. This allows the model to break down words, even rare or unseen ones, into known components, thus enabling accurate understanding and translation. Let's walk through a concrete example to better understand BPE.

Initial setup

Suppose we have a corpus with the following set of words: "cat," "cats," "dog," and "dogs."

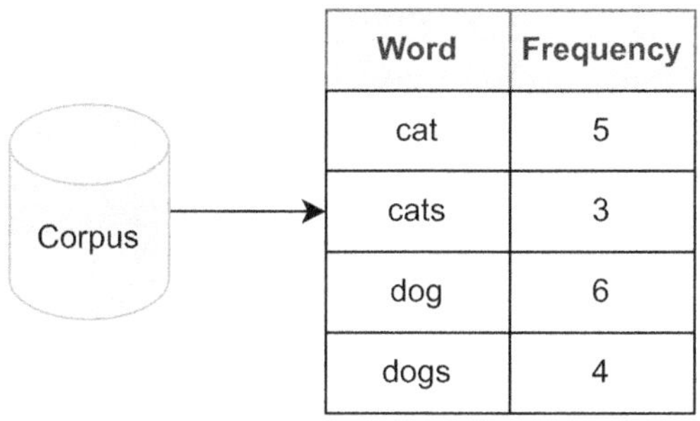

Figure 3.5: Frequency of words in our corpus

In the initial setup, our goal is to initialize a vocabulary consisting of different characters and their frequency of occurrence in the corpus. To achieve this, we follow these steps:

1. Add a special end token, "</w>," to the end of each word to mark its boundary. This special token helps the model know when a word has ended.
2. Tokenize the corpus by breaking down each word into individual characters.
3. Initialize the vocabulary with individual characters and their frequency of occurrence.

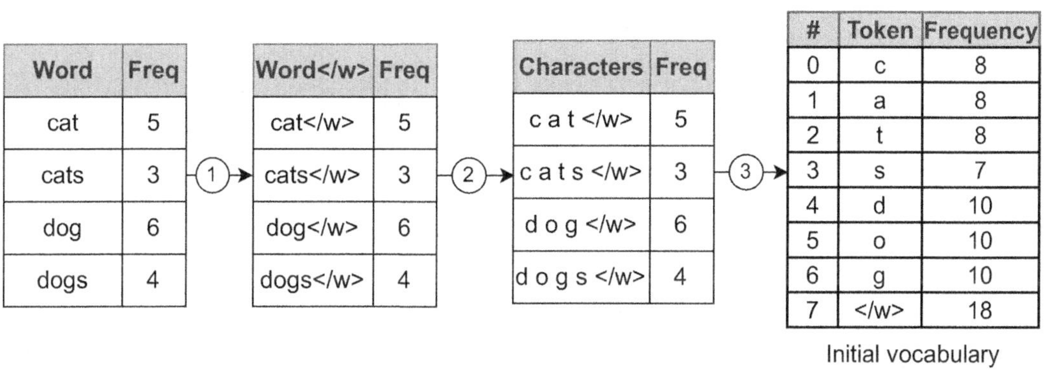

Figure 3.6: Initial setup steps

Iterative merging

Once the initial vocabulary has been created, BPE iteratively merges the most frequent character pairs into subwords. This continues until the vocabulary reaches a predefined size or meets the stopping criteria.

Following are the first five BPE iterations:

- **Iteration 1:** We first identify the most frequent character pair, which is "d" and "o," appearing together 10 times (in "dog" and "dogs"). We merge them to create a new token, "do." Although "og" also appears 10 times, "do" comes first alphabetically. The token "do" is added to the vocabulary, and the frequency counts are updated. "do" now occurs 10 times, and the individual counts of "d" and "o" are reduced accordingly.

#	Token	Frequency
0	c	8
1	a	8
2	t	8
3	s	7
4	d	10-10=0
5	o	10-10=0
6	g	10
7	</w>	18
8	**do**	**10**

Figure 3.7: BPE iteration 1

- **Iteration 2:** Now we look for the next most frequent pair, which is "do" and "g" (also from "dog" and "dogs"). These characters appear together 10 times, so we merge them to create the token "dog."

#	Token	Frequency
0	c	8
1	a	8
2	t	8
3	s	7
6	g	10-10=0
7	</w>	18
8	do	10-10=0
9	**dog**	**10**

Figure 3.8: BPE iteration 2

- **Iteration 3:** Moving forward, we notice that "c" and "a" (from "cat" and "cats") appear together 8 times. We merge these to create the token "ca." After merging, "cat" can be represented as "ca" and "t." The token "ca" now has a frequency of 8.

- **Iteration 4:** We continue by merging "ca" and "t", which appear 8 times together (from "cat" and "cats"). We merge them to form the token "cat." Now, "cats" can be represented as "cat" and "s", and "dogs" as "dog" and "s." The frequency count for "cat" is updated to 8.
- **Iteration 5:** Finally, the next most frequent pairing is "s" and "</w>" (from "dogs" and "cats"), which appears 7 times. We merge "s" and "</w>" to form the token "s</w>."

#	Token	Frequency
0	c	8-8=0
1	a	8-8=0
2	t	8
3	s	7
7	</w>	18
9	dog	10
10	**ca**	**8**

#	Token	Frequency
2	t	8
3	s	7
7	</w>	18
9	dog	10
10	ca	8
11	**cat**	**8**

#	Token	Frequency
3	s	7-7=0
7	</w>	18-7=11
9	dog	10
11	cat	8
12	**s</w>**	**8**

Figure 3.9: BPE iterations 3–5

BPE iteratively merges the most frequent character pairs, leading to a more compact representation of the corpus. The merging continues until we reach the desired number of tokens or iterations.

#	Token	Frequency
7	</w>	11
9	dog	10
11	cat	8
12	s</w>	8

Figure 3.10: BPE vocabulary after 5 iterations

Note the special "</w>" token plays a key role in distinguishing between different word forms. For instance, the token "cat" followed by "</w>" indicates the end of the word "cat," whereas the token "cat" without </w> could also be part of another word. This distinction helps BPE represent and interpret words accurately during translation, allowing it to efficiently handle both familiar and unseen words.

Once the vocabulary has been created, we construct our training data by replacing each tokenized sentence with a sequence of integers. This leads to multiple tables, each for a specific language pair. Figure 3.11 shows the prepared translation data for the English–French and English–Korean language pairs.

English	French
Today is cold	Il fait froid aujourd'hui
This is funny	C'est drôle
How are you?	Comment vas-tu?
...	...

English	French
[15724, 374, 9439]	[12319, 20272, 282, 1607, 75804, 88253]
[2028, 374, 15526]	[34, 17771, 1377, 57332]
[4438, 527, 499, 30]	[10906, 44496, 2442, 84, 30]
...	...

English	Korean
She went to school	그녀는 학교에 갔다
She becomes a lawyer	그녀는 변호사가 된다
Dogs playing in the yard	마당에서 놀고 있는 개들!
...	...

Original pairs

English	Korean
[138, 18, 9, 2130]	[186, 732, 666, 349, 818]
[138, 9561, 31, 721]	[226, 91022, 82483, 9643, 40344]
[309, 11001, 22, 70701, 3752]	[39485, 128320, 8532, 4432, 54255, 196710]
...	...

Tokenized pairs

Figure 3.11: Constructed training data for English–Korean and English–French pairs

Model Development

We utilized an encoder-decoder Transformer to train language translation. In this section, we explore the architecture of the encoder and decoder, training strategies, and sampling methods.

Architecture

The key components in an encoder-decoder Transformer architecture are very similar to those of the decoder-only Transformer explained in Chapter 2. Let's examine the encoder and decoder separately and highlight their key differences.

Encoder

The encoder processes the input sequence and outputs a sequence of embedding for each input token.

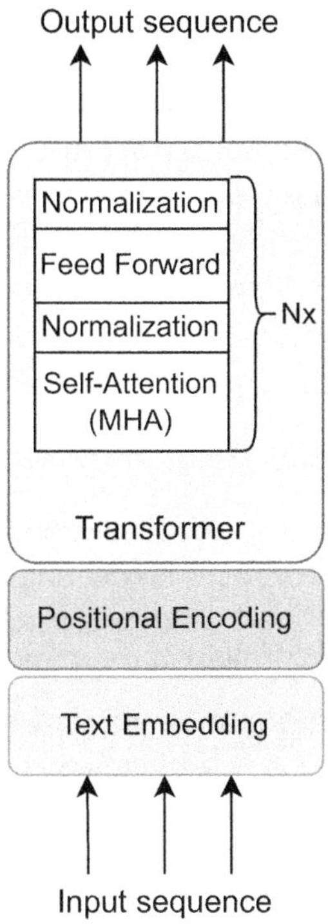

Figure 3.12: Encoder components

The encoder consists of the following components:

- Text embedding
- Positional encoding
- Transformer

Text embedding: This component converts each input token into an embedding vector. These embeddings capture the semantic information of each token.

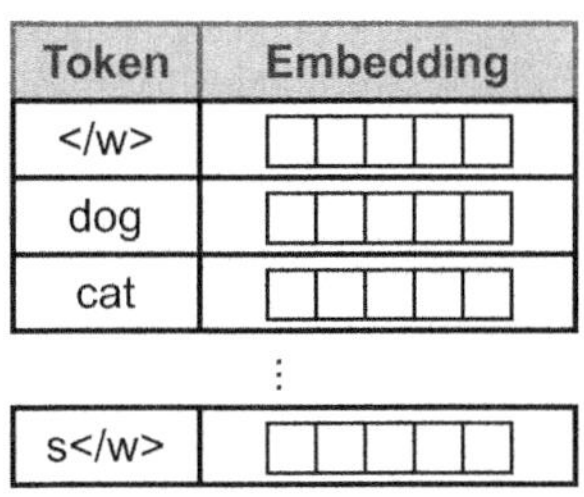

Figure 3.13: Token embedding table

Positional encoding: The positional encoding component injects information about the position of each token in the input sequence. As discussed in the previous chapter, both fixed and learned methods are effective in practice. For simplicity, we choose a fixed positional encoding method such as sine–cosine encoding.

Transformer: The Transformer processes a sequence of token embeddings through a stack of Transformer blocks. Each block contains a self-attention layer that uses the multi-head attention (MHA) mechanism on the input sequence and a feed-forward layer, with normalization layers in between to ensure stability during training. Since the requirement specifies support for a 1,000-word input sequence, we do not need to employ optimized attention mechanisms for efficiency, as the standard attention mechanism is sufficient to handle this sequence length without significant performance issues.

Decoder

The decoder generates the output sequence one token at a time using the encoder's output and the previously generated tokens. The decoder has the following components:

- **Text embedding:** Converts each token in the target sequence to an embedding
- **Positional encoding:** Injects information about the position of each token
- **Transformer:** Processes the target sequence and outputs an updated sequence of embeddings
- **Prediction head:** Utilizes the updated embeddings to predict the next token.

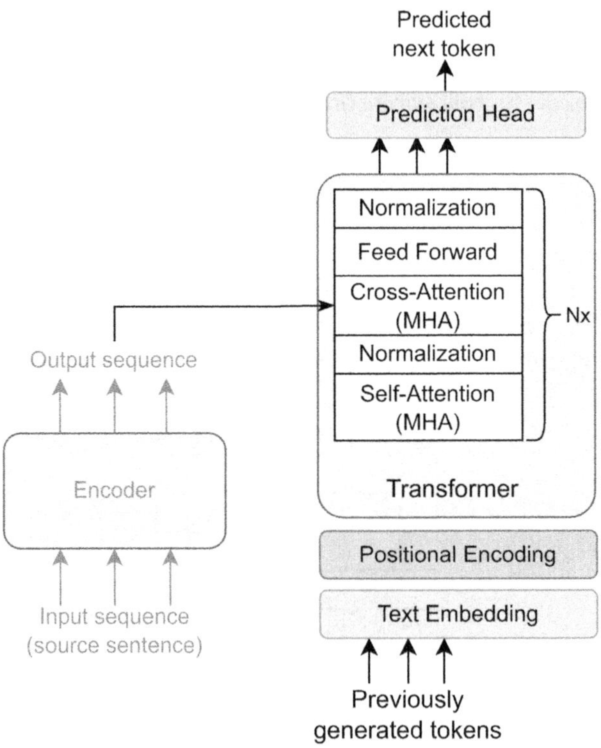

Figure 3.14: Decoder components

What are the key differences between the encoder and decoder?

There are three key differences between the encoder and decoder:

- Cross-attention layer
- Self-attention mechanism
- Prediction head

Cross-attention layer

The Transformer component in the decoder includes a cross-attention layer. This layer performs the MHA mechanism over the encoder's output. It enables each token in the decoder to attend to all embeddings in the encoder. This allows the cross-attention to effectively integrate information from the input sequence during the generation of the output sequence.

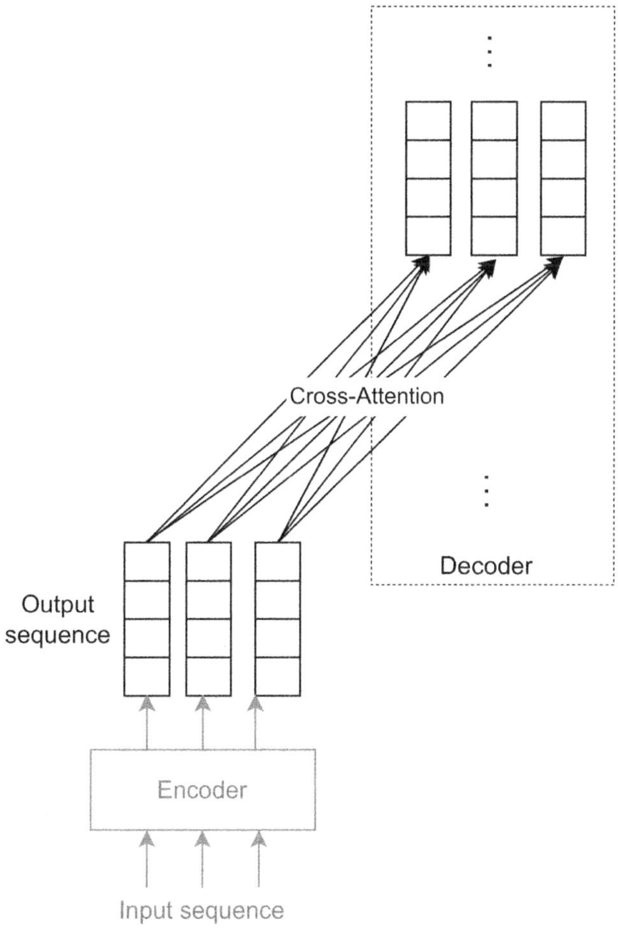

Figure 3.15: Cross-attention layer

Self-attention mechanism

The self-attention layer operates differently in the encoder and decoder. In the encoder, each token attends to all other tokens in the sequence. This helps the encoder understand the entire sequence comprehensively. In contrast, in the decoder, each token is restricted to attending to only those tokens that come before it by masking the future tokens in the sequence. This difference is important for generation tasks because the model should use only previously generated tokens, not future ones, to predict the next token.

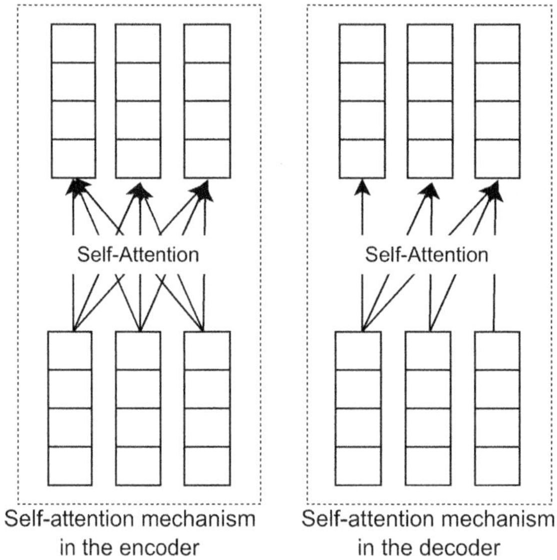

Figure 3.16: Different self-attention mechanisms in the encoder and decoder

Prediction head

The decoder has a prediction head on top of the Transformer component. The prediction head usually includes a linear layer followed by a softmax layer to convert the Transformer's output into probabilities over the vocabulary. These probabilities are used to determine the most likely next token.

Training

We employ a two-stage strategy to train a language translation model:

1. Unsupervised pretraining
2. Supervised finetuning

1. Unsupervised pretraining

In this stage, we train a base model using a large corpus of general data. This creates a base model capable of understanding language, grammar, and context.

Let's review the pretraining data, ML objective, and loss function for the pretraining stage.

Pretraining data

We utilize popular pretraining datasets such as C4 [8], Wikipedia [9], and StackExchange [10]. In contrast to Chapter 2, where we focused on pretraining a language model for English only, for language translation, we need a base model with a general understanding of multiple languages. Therefore, we do not remove non-English text data from these datasets. Instead, we keep the set of languages we expect the model to translate and remove any text data belonging to languages outside that set.

ML objective and loss function

In Chapter 2, we explored next-token prediction as the primary ML objective for language generation. Next-token prediction is not an ideal choice in encoder-decoder pretraining because the training is unsupervised. If we pass an entire sentence to the encoder, it will encode information in a way that allows the decoder to always predict the next word accurately, thus effectively "cheating." Instead, we use "masked language modeling," a common ML objective for pretraining an encoder-decoder Transformer. Let's examine it in more detail.

Masked language modeling (MLM)

In MLM, also known as masked token prediction, some of the input tokens are masked, and the model is trained to predict those masked tokens.

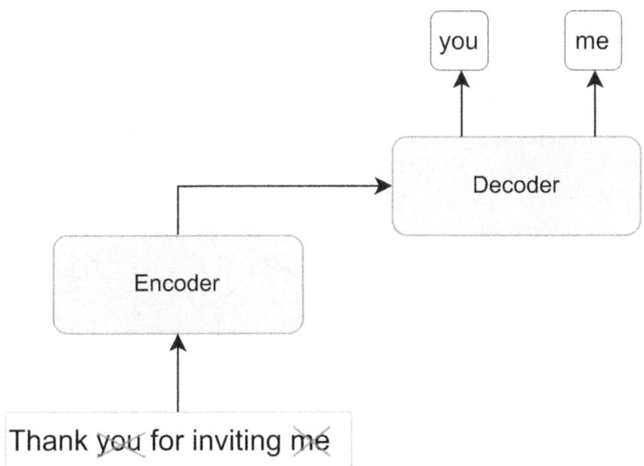

Figure 3.17: An overview of the MLM objective

MLM allows the encoder to process the input sentence and encode it so the decoder can predict the masked words. As the masked words are never visible during the encoding process, this prevents the model from cheating,

To measure the model's performance in predicting the masked tokens, we use cross-entropy loss. This commonly used loss function measures the discrepancies between the predicted probabilities and the ground-truth tokens, thus guiding the training process. Here is a step-by-step explanation of how loss is calculated using the MLM objective:

1. Randomly select a subset of tokens in the input sequence and replace them with a mask token ("[MASK]"). For example, the input sentence "Thank you for inviting me" might become "Thank [MASK] for inviting [MASK]".
2. Feed the masked sequence to the encoder so it can understand the context despite the missing tokens. The encoder outputs a sequence of new embeddings for each token.
3. Feed the decoder with the same input sequence, but, this time, none of the tokens are masked and the sequence has been shifted one position to the right by the insertion of a start token ("<BOS>"). Refer to Chapter 2 or [11] to understand why we shift the input sequence during training.
4. The decoder predicts the next token for each position in the sequence. Each prediction uses all previous input tokens and encoded information from the encoder.
5. Calculate the cross-entropy loss over the predicted probabilities and the ground-truth for the masked tokens only.

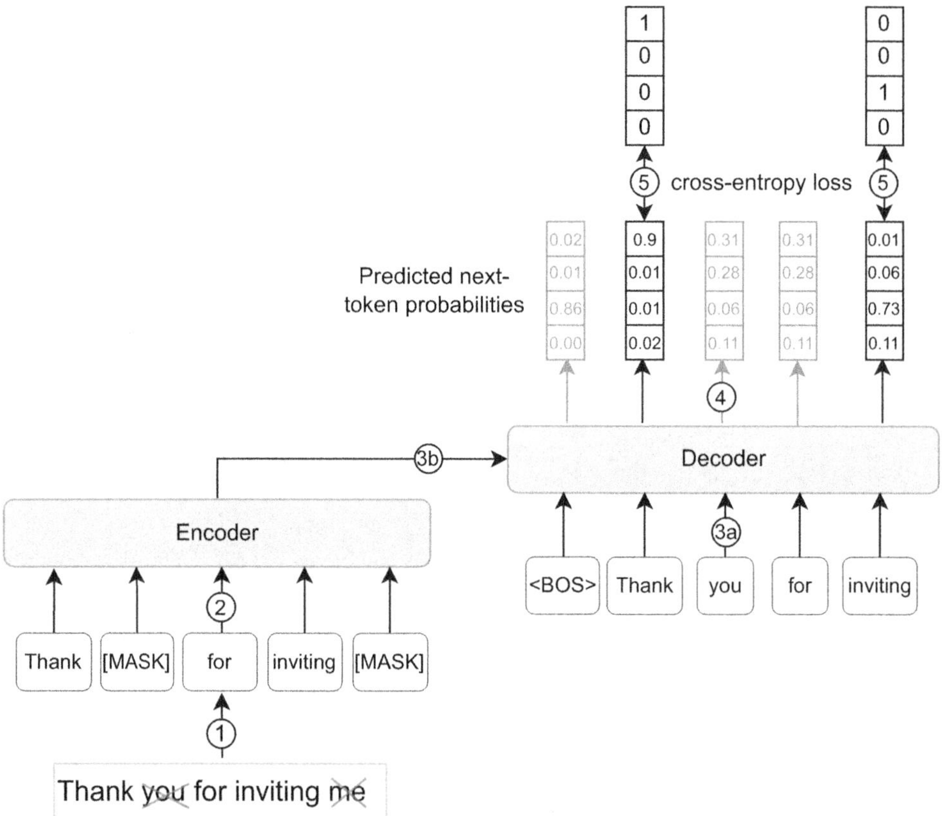

Figure 3.18: Cross-entropy loss calculation for MLM objective

In summary, we primarily use the MLM objective in pretraining encoder-decoder Transformers because it engages both the encoder and decoder. The encoder develops its understanding of the language by encoding the masked input text. The decoder learns to process this encoded information and predict the masked tokens. This objective prepares both the encoder and decoder for the supervised finetuning stage.

Before exploring the supervised finetuning stage, note that pretraining a base model is resource-intensive and, therefore, expensive. In practice, we often use publicly available encoder-decoder models such as Google's T5 [12] or Meta's BART [13], which have been pretrained on extensive datasets. This approach significantly reduces the cost and resources needed for pretraining.

2. Supervised finetuning

Supervised finetuning, the second stage of our training process, adapts the base model to the specific task of language translation. It does this by finetuning the base model on translation data. To adapt the base model to language translation, we have two options:

1. Bilingual approach
2. Multilingual approach

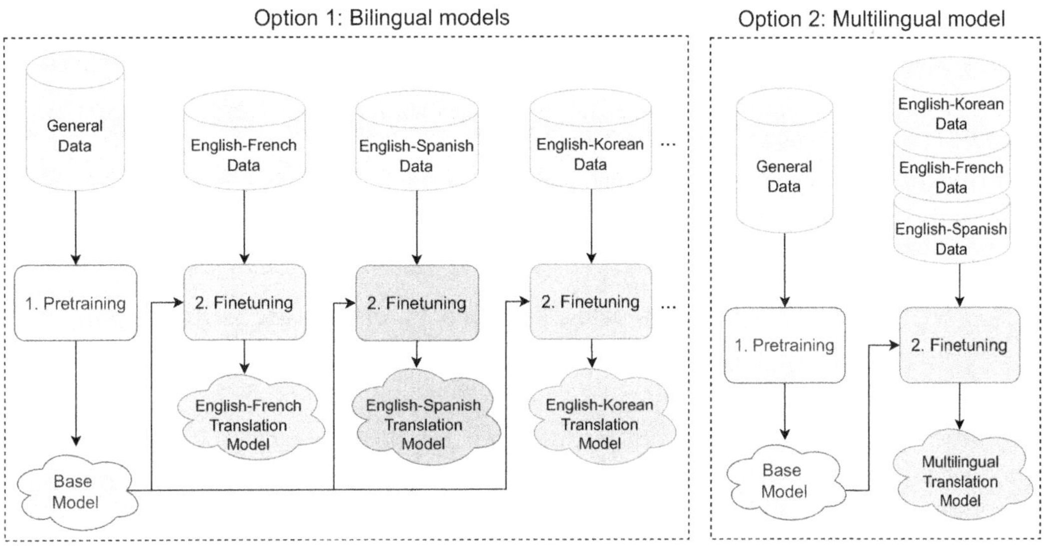

Figure 3.19: Bilingual vs. multilingual models

Bilingual approach

In this approach, we train models specific to each language pair. Training language-specific models has several advantages. First, they capture the unique linguistic nuances of each language pair. Second, they usually demonstrate higher translation accuracy due to their specialized natures. Finally, improving performance is simpler with language-specific models because we can easily isolate and address specific issues that may arise for each language pair. However, training, deploying, and maintaining multiple models is resource-intensive and costly.

Multilingual approach

Here, a single model is trained to translate between multiple languages. Multilingual models are simpler, less expensive, and easier to deploy and maintain than bilingual models. Recent studies such as mT5 [14] and mBART [15] have highlighted the trend toward multilingual translation models that often match or exceed the performance of bilingual models.

For this chapter, we prioritize translation accuracy over simplicity and, therefore, choose a bilingual approach.

Training data

Figure 3.20 shows an example of prepared training data where each table represents a language pair. In each table, a row represents one example, containing a sequence of token IDs for the sentence in the source language and a sequence of token IDs for the translation in the target language.

English	Korean
[138, 18, 9, 2130]	[186, 732, 666, 349, 818]
[138, 9561, 31, 721]	[226, 91022, 82483, 9643, 40344]
[309, 11001, 22, 70701, 3752]	[39485, 128320, 8532, 4432, 54255, 196710]
...	...

English–Korean tokenized pairs

...

English	French
[15724, 374, 9439]	[12319, 20272, 282, 1607, 75804, 88253]
[2028, 374, 15526]	[34, 17771, 1377, 57332]
[4438, 527, 499, 30]	[10906, 44496, 2442, 84, 30]
...	...

English–French tokenized pairs

Figure 3.20: Example of prepared training data for different language pairs

ML objective and loss function

Whereas the pretraining stage was unsupervised, the finetuning stage is supervised. The encoder processes source sentence tokens for each training example, and the decoder generates the target sentence tokens. Since the decoder should generate tokens sequentially after training, we use next-token prediction as our ML objective. We use cross-entropy as our loss function to measure the accuracy of the predicted next token.

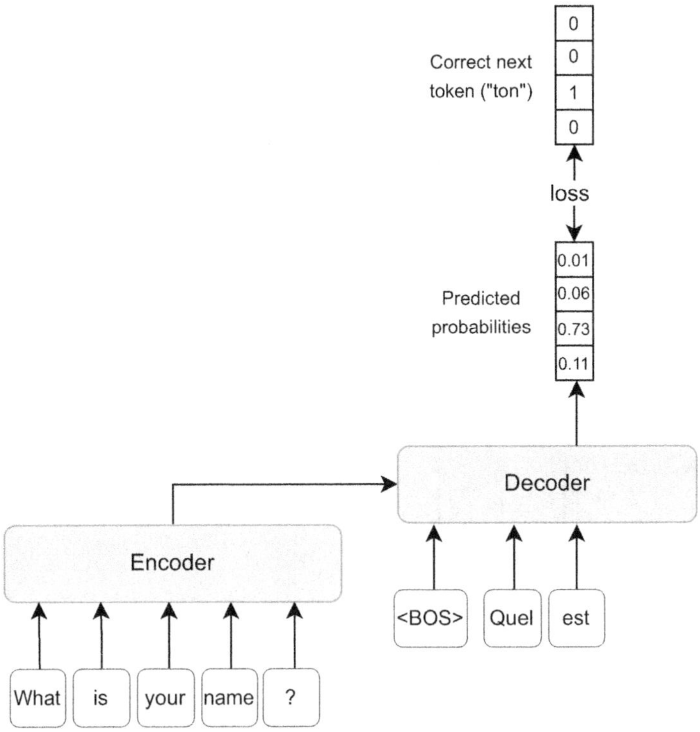

Figure 3.21: Loss calculation during the finetuning stage

Figure 3.21 shows loss calculation during the finetuning stage. For simplicity, it visualizes a single prediction. In practice, as we saw in Chapter 2, the decoder predicts the next token for all positions simultaneously, and the losses are calculated for all predictions.

Sampling

During sampling, the trained model generates a potential translation by predicting each subsequent token based on the previously generated tokens and the context of the input sequence.

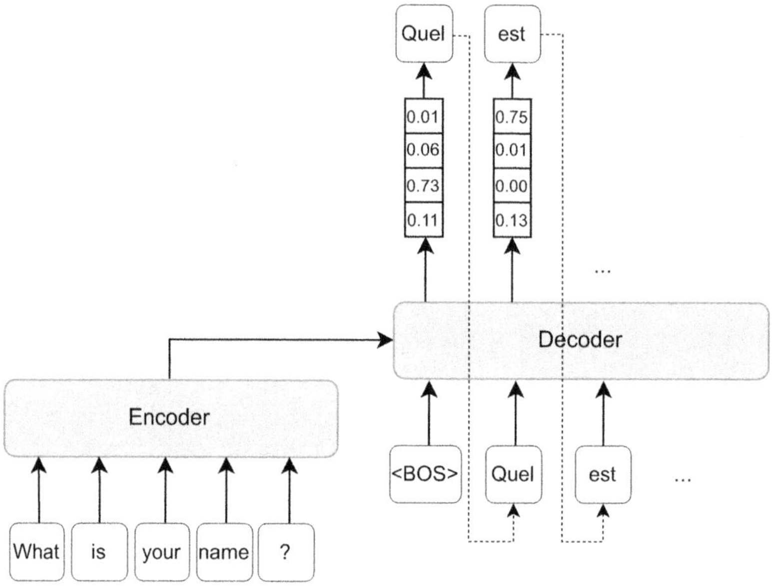

Figure 3.22: Generating translation

As discussed in Chapter 2, there are two main strategies for sampling text in generative models: deterministic methods (e.g., beam search) and stochastic sampling. Here, we choose beam search for two main reasons:

1. **Translation accuracy:** Beam search usually leads to more accurate translations. This is because the algorithm evaluates multiple possible sequences and selects the most probable one.
2. **Consistency:** Beam search is deterministic, meaning it always produces the same output given the same input. This consistency ensures that translations will provide few surprises, which is critical in most translation systems. While diversity can be beneficial, it is neither essential nor desirable for language translation systems.

Note that in applications where diversity and creativity are more valued, such as creative writing, stochastic sampling methods are usually preferred. In Chapter 4, we will examine stochastic methods such as top-k and top-p sampling in detail.

Characteristic	Deterministic methods	Stochastic methods
Approach	Follow a predictable process to generate output	Generate output based on probability distribution
Efficiency	Typically less efficient due to tracking multiple paths	More efficient since randomness allows for quicker selections
Quality	Coherent and predictable	Diverse and creative
Risk	Usually lead to repetitive output for longer sequences	Might produce inappropriate output due to their creativeness
Use case	Suitable for tasks requiring consistency, such as language translation	Suitable for tasks requiring creativity, such as open-ended text generation
Methods	Greedy search, beam search	Multinomial, top-k, top-p

Table 3.1: Comparison of deterministic and stochastic methods

Evaluation

Offline evaluation metrics

To thoroughly evaluate a language translation model, metrics should measure both translation accuracy and contextual appropriateness. The research community has proposed several metrics that, over the years, have become widely accepted as standards. Some commonly used metrics are:

- BLEU
- ROUGE
- METEOR

BLEU

BLEU (BiLingual Evaluation Understudy) [16] is a precision-based metric that compares n-grams (a sequence of "n" words) of the candidate translation with n-grams of the reference translations and counts the ratio of matches. It ranges from 0 to 1, where a higher value indicates a more precise translation.

The BLEU score is calculated using the following formula:

$$\text{BLEU} = \text{BP} \cdot \exp\left(\sum_{n=1}^{N} w_n \log p_n\right)$$

where:

- N is the maximum n-gram length considered for evaluation
- BP is the brevity penalty

- p_n is the n-grams precision
- w_n represents the weight for different n-gram precisions

Let's explore each of these terms in detail.

Brevity Penalty (BP)
BP is a constant term that penalizes translations shorter than the reference translation. The formula is:

$$\text{BP} = \begin{cases} 1 & \text{if } c > r \\ e^{\left(1-\frac{r}{c}\right)} & \text{if } c \leq r \end{cases}$$

where:

- c is the translation length
- r is the reference translation length

If the candidate translation length, c, is greater than the reference translation length, r, the brevity penalty is 1 (i.e., there is no penalty). If the candidate translation length is less than or equal to the reference translation length, the brevity penalty is an exponential decay based on the ratio of the lengths.

Precision (p_n)
Precision measures how many n-grams in the candidate translation are present in reference translations. It is calculated by dividing the number of matching n-grams by the total number of n-grams in the candidate translation. Figure 3.23 provides an example of calculating p_2 for a candidate and one reference sentence.

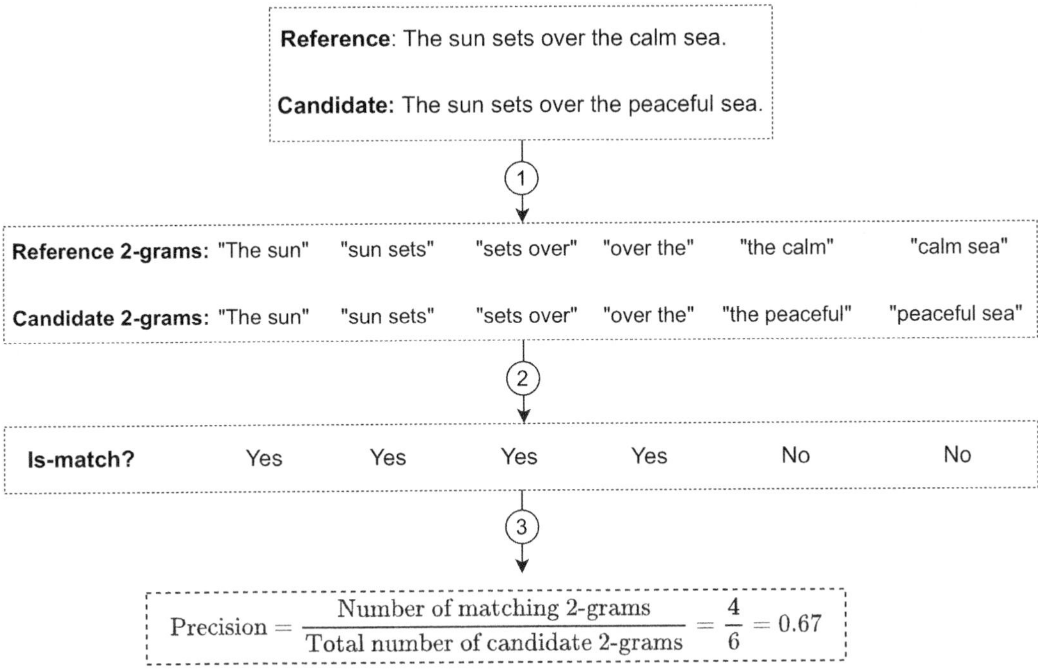

Figure 3.23: Example of calculating precision for 2-grams (p_2)

Weights (w_n)
These weights correspond to the precision of each n-gram size. Usually, we distribute them evenly, giving each n-gram precision the same importance. For instance, for n-grams up to 4-grams, each w_n would be 1/4.

BLEU's main advantage is that it is simple and easy to compute. However, it has a major drawback: it can unfairly penalize translations that are correct but different from the reference translation. For example, if the reference translation is "The engineer discovered a new algorithm," and the generated translation is "The engineer found a new method," BLEU might penalize the generated translation even though it conveys the same meaning. Despite this limitation, BLEU remains insightful and widely used in practice to evaluate language translation models.

ROUGE

ROUGE (Recall-Oriented Understudy for Gisting Evaluation) [17] is a popular metric that complements BLEU by focusing on recall instead of precision. It measures the ratio of n-gram overlaps between the candidate and reference texts. For example, the ROGUE-N recall is defined as:

$$\text{Recall} = \frac{\text{Number of matching n-grams}}{\text{Total number of n-grams in the reference}}$$

If you are interested to learn more about ROUGE and its formula, refer to [17].

Similarly to BLEU, ROUGE is easy to implement and efficient at calculating. However, its main drawback is its lack of contextual understanding. A translation with different but semantically similar words might receive a low ROUGE score.

METEOR

METEOR (Metric for Evaluation of Translation with Explicit ORdering) [18] is a popular metric for evaluating language translation models. It calculates precision and recall and then combines these measurements using a weighted harmonic mean.

Unlike BLEU and ROUGE, which rely on exact n-gram matches, METEOR considers synonyms and the morphology of words. For example, if the reference translation uses "run" and the generated translation uses "running," METEOR recognizes these as related terms. These synonyms are found using linguistic resources such as synonym dictionaries or lexical databases. One commonly used resource is WordNet [19], which organizes words into synonyms of various types and shows the relationships between those synsets.

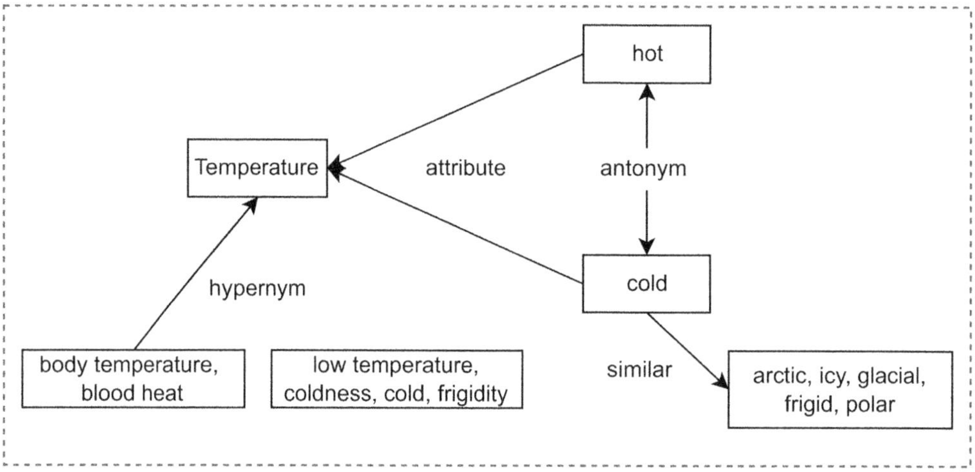

Figure 3.24: Example of relationships between words

While METEOR is a more comprehensive metric, it has some drawbacks. Let's take a look at its pros and cons.

Pros:

- **Semantic understanding:** METEOR evaluates translation quality more accurately when different wordings convey the same meaning. This is because it considers synonyms and stemming during the evaluation of translations.
- **Balanced evaluation:** METEOR provides a balanced evaluation because it combines precision and recall. This helps identify translations that are both accurate and complete.
- **Correlation with human judgments:** METEOR correlates better with human judgments than BLEU and ROUGE.

Cons:

- **Computational complexity:** METEOR is harder to implement and takes more time to calculate than BLEU and ROUGE. This is because it requires additional steps, such as synonym and stemming matching.
- **Resource dependence:** METEOR relies on linguistic resources such as synonym dictionaries and stemming algorithms, which may not be available for all languages.

To summarize, all three metrics offer insights into the model's performance and are commonly used in practice. Let's transition to online evaluation to understand how our model performs in real-world scenarios.

Online evaluation metrics

During the online evaluation, we evaluate how well our language translation system works in production. We use the following two metrics to measure how satisfied and engaged our users are:

- **User feedback:** Collect ratings or feedback from users regarding the quality of translations. The metric is insightful since it directly reflects user satisfaction.

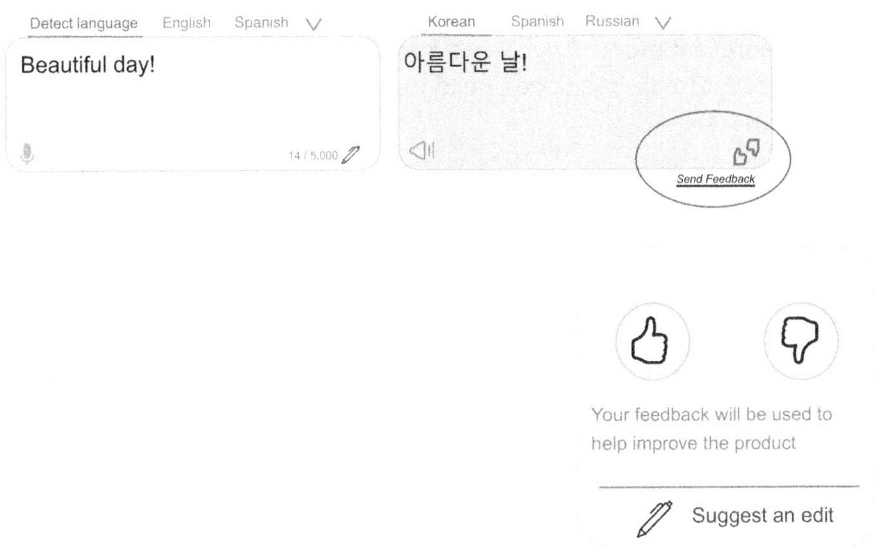

Figure 3.25: Collecting user feedback

- **User engagement:** Measure users' engagement by monitoring how often they use the translation feature, how long they interact with it, and how frequently they return. This helps us understand how valuable and effective the translation tool is in real-world use.

Combining offline and online evaluation metrics gives us a more complete view of the performance of the language translation. This thorough evaluation ensures models fulfill technical standards and satisfy user expectations.

Overall ML System Design

In this section, we explore the ML design of a language translation system. In particular, we examine two key components:

- Language detector
- Translation service

Language detector

The language detector identifies the language of a given text, enabling us to use the model that has been trained specifically for that language. This task can be framed as a sequence classification task, and encoder-only architecture is a good candidate architecture for such a task. We can modify the encoder-only Transformer in two ways (Figure 3.26) to classify input sentences:

1. **Average pooling:** Pass the Transformer's outputs to an average pooling layer, and then a prediction head to output language class probabilities.
2. **Last token representation:** Use the last token representation from the Transformer's output and feed it to the prediction head for probability prediction.

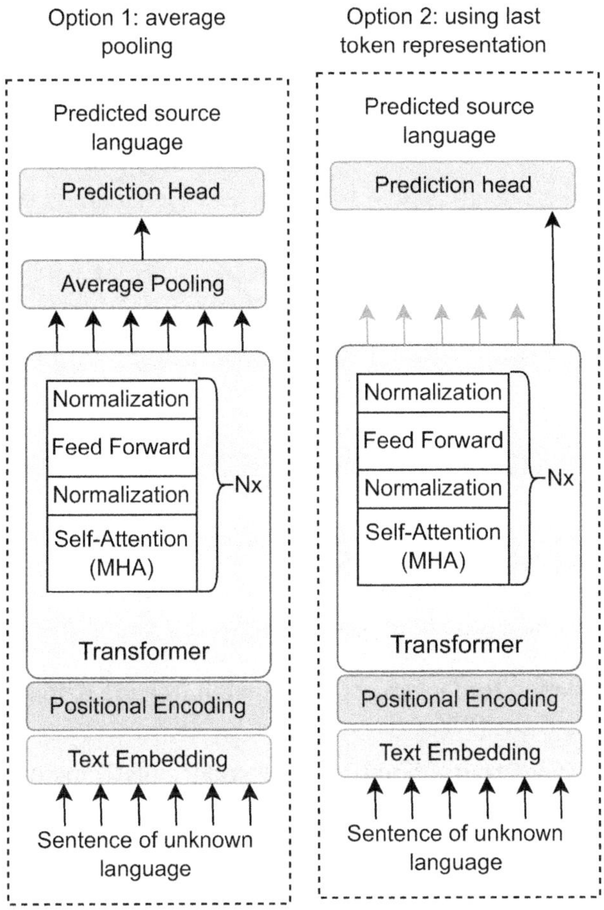

Figure 3.26: Two options for building a language detector using an encoder-only Transformer

Translation service

The translation service interacts with the specific model based on the detected and desired languages. It then applies beam search to generate a sequence of tokens in the target language and converts the tokens back into text. The final translation is then shown to the user.

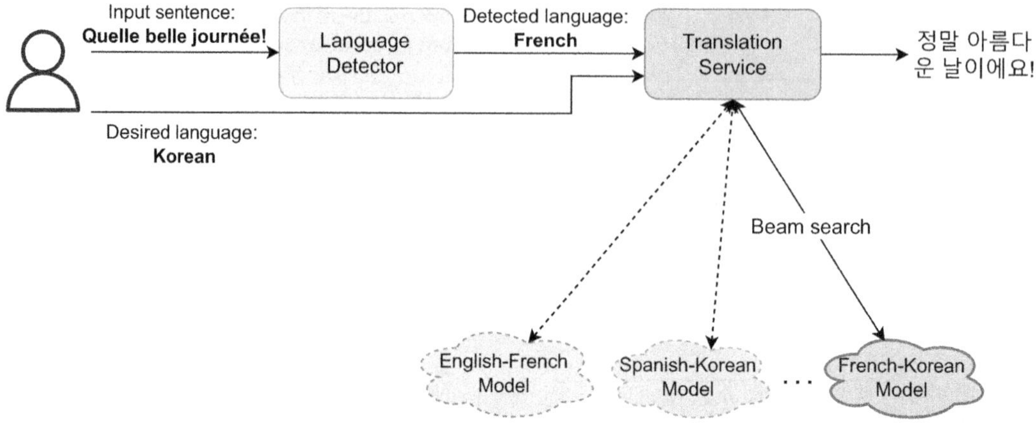

Figure 3.27: Language translation overall design

Other Talking Points

If time permits at the end of the interview, consider discussing these additional topics:

- Supporting translation for languages with limited training data using transfer learning and multilingual models [20].
- Approaching language translation using a decoder-only Transformer [21].
- Continuously improving translation models through user feedback [22].
- Optimizing techniques for efficient inference and on-device translation [23].
- Developing a single multilingual model [24].
- Other automatic metrics such as WER and how they are calculated [25, 26].
- How to build a language detection model [27].

Summary

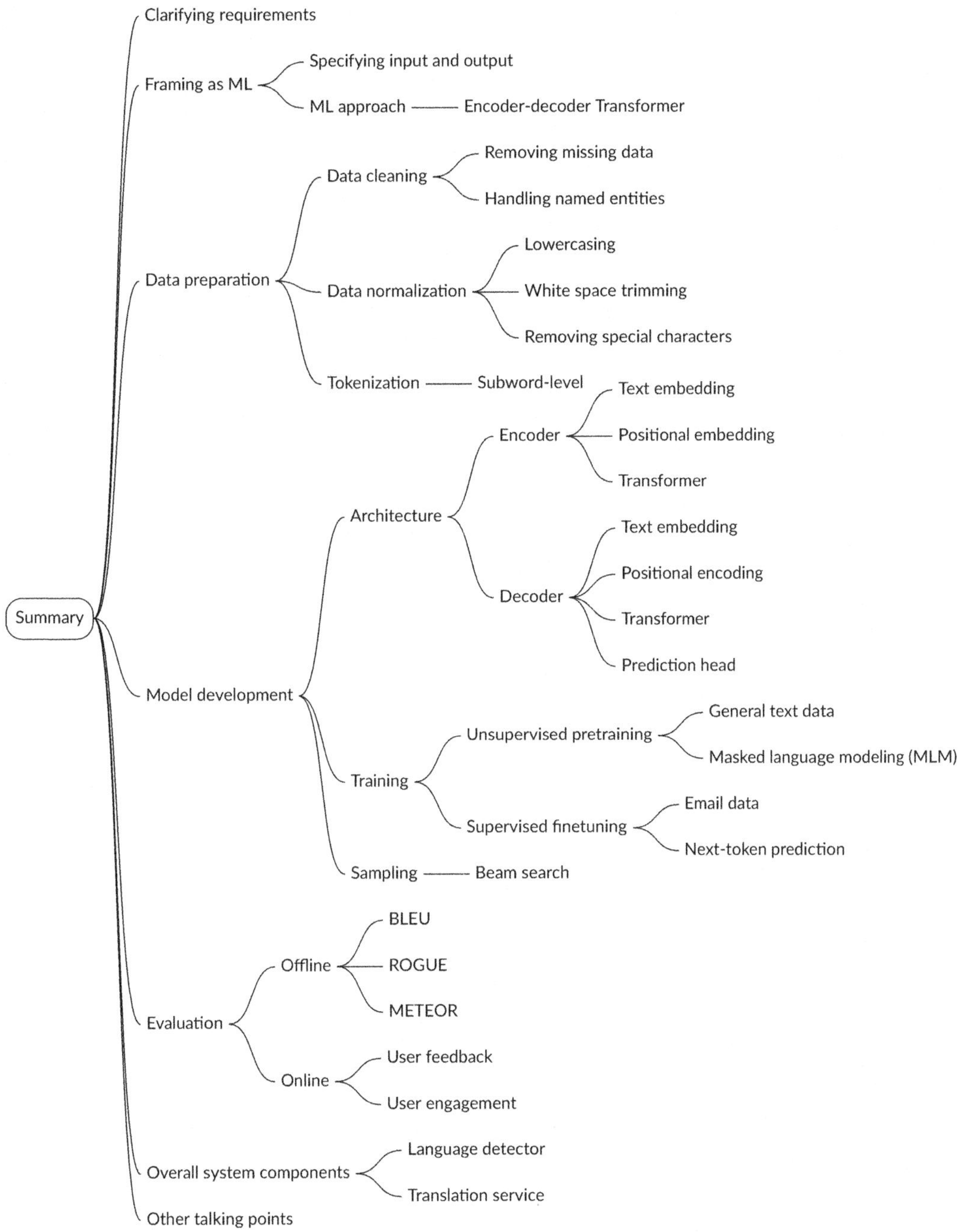
Summary
Clarifying requirements
Framing as ML
Specifying input and output
ML approach
Encoder-decoder Transformer
Data preparation
Data cleaning
Removing missing data
Handling named entities
Data normalization
Lowercasing
White space trimming
Removing special characters
Tokenization
Subword-level
Model development
Architecture
Encoder
Text embedding
Positional embedding
Transformer
Decoder
Text embedding
Positional encoding
Transformer
Prediction head
Training
Unsupervised pretraining
General text data
Masked language modeling (MLM)
Supervised finetuning
Email data
Next-token prediction
Sampling
Beam search
Evaluation
Offline
BLEU
ROGUE
METEOR
Online
User feedback
User engagement
Overall system components
Language detector
Translation service
Other talking points

Reference Material

[1] Google Translate Service. https://blog.google/products/translate/google-translate-new-languages-2024/.

[2] Neural Machine Translation by Jointly Learning to Align and Translate. https://arxiv.org/abs/1409.0473.

[3] BERT: Pre-training of Deep Bidirectional Transformers for Language Understanding. https://arxiv.org/abs/1810.04805.

[4] GPT Models. https://platform.openai.com/docs/models.

[5] Claude Models. https://www.anthropic.com/claude.

[6] Bidirectional Long Short-Term Memory (BLSTM) Neural Networks for Reconstruction of Top-Quark Pair Decay Kinematics. https://arxiv.org/abs/1909.01144.

[7] BPE Tokenization. https://huggingface.co/learn/nlp-course/en/chapter6/5.

[8] C4 Dataset. https://www.tensorflow.org/datasets/catalog/c4.

[9] Wikipedia Dataset. https://www.tensorflow.org/datasets/catalog/wikipedia.

[10] Stack Exchange Dataset. https://huggingface.co/datasets/HuggingFaceH4/stack-exchange-preferences.

[11] How Transformers Work. https://huggingface.co/learn/nlp-course/en/chapter1/4.

[12] Exploring the Limits of Transfer Learning with a Unified Text-to-Text Transformer. https://arxiv.org/pdf/1910.10683.pdf.

[13] BART: Denoising Sequence-to-Sequence Pre-training for Natural Language Generation, Translation, and Comprehension. https://arxiv.org/abs/1910.13461.

[14] mT5: A Massively Multilingual Pre-trained Text-to-Text Transformer. https://arxiv.org/abs/2010.11934.

[15] Multilingual Denoising Pre-training for Neural Machine Translation. https://arxiv.org/abs/2001.08210.

[16] BLEU Metric. https://en.wikipedia.org/wiki/BLEU.

[17] ROUGE Metric. https://en.wikipedia.org/wiki/ROUGE_(metric).

[18] METEOR Metric. https://www.cs.cmu.edu/~alavie/METEOR/pdf/Banerjee-Lavie-2005-METEOR.pdf.

[19] WordNet. https://wordnet.princeton.edu/.

[20] No Language Left Behind: Scaling Human-Centered Machine Translation. https://research.facebook.com/publications/no-language-left-behind/.

[21] Decoder-Only or Encoder-Decoder? Interpreting Language Model as a Regularized Encoder-Decoder. https://arxiv.org/abs/2304.04052.

[22] Towards Continual Learning for Multilingual Machine Translation via Vocabulary Substitution. https://arxiv.org/abs/2103.06799.

[23] Efficient Inference for Neural Machine Translation. https://arxiv.org/abs/2010.02416.

[24] Meta's Multilingual Model. https://ai.meta.com/blog/nllb-200-high-quality-machine-translation/.

[25] Machine Translation Evaluation. https://en.wikipedia.org/wiki/Evaluation_of_machine_translation.

[26] Word Error Rate (WER) Metric. https://en.wikipedia.org/wiki/Word_error_rate.

[27] Automatic Language Identification Using Deep Neural Networks. https://research.google.com/pubs/archive/42538.pdf.

4

ChatGPT: Personal Assistant Chatbot

Introduction

ChatGPT [1] is a chatbot that was developed by OpenAI and launched in 2022. It generates human-like text based on the input it receives. The chatbot can assist with various tasks, including answering questions, providing explanations, and producing creative content.

ChatGPT has quickly become one of the most adopted applications in history. It gained over 100 million users in less than three months after its launch [2]. This rapid growth highlights the capabilities of generative AI and its potential to help with day-to-day tasks and enhance productivity. In this chapter, we examine the key components of building a chatbot similar to ChatGPT.

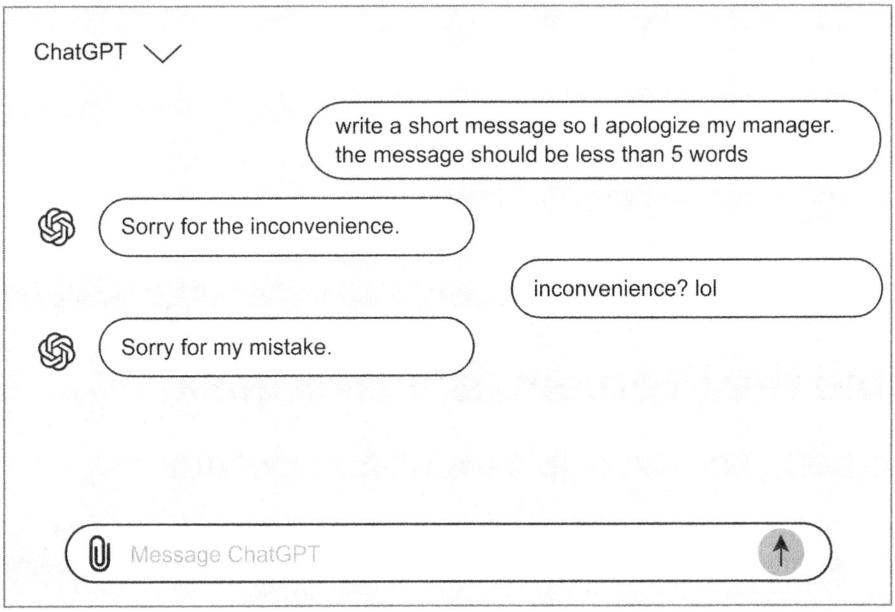

Figure 4.1: Example of a conversation with ChatGPT

Clarifying Requirements

Here is a typical interaction between a candidate and an interviewer:

Candidate: What languages should the chatbot support?
Interviewer: Initially, let's focus on English.

Candidate: We need to ensure the chatbot generates unbiased and safe outputs by having strict content moderation and algorithms in place. Is that a fair assumption?
Interviewer: Certainly.

Candidate: Can you specify the range of tasks the chatbot is expected to perform?
Interviewer: The chatbot should be able to handle tasks like providing information and answering questions.

Candidate: Does the chatbot take in or output non-text modalities, such as image, audio, or video?
Interviewer: Let's focus on a text-only chatbot for now. The input and the output are both text.

Candidate: Should the chatbot handle follow-up questions? How long should the chatbot maintain the conversation context?
Interviewer: Good question. The chatbot should be able to handle follow-up questions within the same conversation session. Let's say it is expected to have a context window of at least 4096 tokens.

Candidate: Is the chatbot expected to be able to browse websites, call external API, or search online?
Interviewer: Let's not focus on that in this round.

Candidate: Should the chatbot personalize its interactions with users?
Interviewer: Let's not focus on personalization.

Candidate: Do we have instruction-based training data?
Interviewer: Yes, we have a dataset with 80,000 examples of instructions and answers.

Frame the Problem as an ML Task

Specifying the system's input and output

The input to the chatbot is a text prompt provided by the user. The prompt can be a question, a command, or any other form of textual query. The output is a relevant and contextually appropriate response generated by the chatbot.

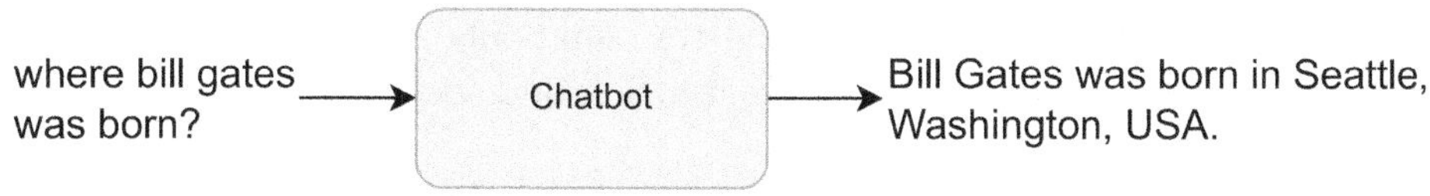

Figure 4.2: Input and output of a chatbot

Choosing a suitable ML approach

Developing a chatbot is a text generation task in which a language model processes an input prompt and generates a response. This language model typically needs billions of parameters to learn effectively; hence, they are often called large language models (LLMs).

As we saw in previous chapters, the decoder-only Transformer is the standard architectural choice in language models. Most modern LLMs, such as OpenAI's GPT [3], Google's Gemini [4], and Meta's Llama [5], are all based on the decoder-only Transformer. In line with these models, we use a decoder-only Transformer to build our chatbot.

Data Preparation

The effectiveness of an LLM depends on the quality of its training data, which mainly comes from web sources. This data, often automatically crawled from websites, forums, and blogs, requires special considerations and careful preparation. The most common steps include:

- **Content extraction and parsing:** Web-crawled data often contains extraneous elements, for example, HTML tags, advertisements, and navigation links. This step involves parsing the raw HTML content using libraries such as Beautiful Soup [6] or lxml [7] and extracting the main text body while discarding irrelevant sections. Techniques such as DOM analysis [8] and boilerplate detection [9] are applied to isolate and retain the core content relevant to language modeling.
- **URL and domain filtering:** Not all web domains provide high-quality or relevant content. URL filtering uses predefined rules or machine learning (ML) classifiers to exclude unwanted sources, for example, low-quality blogs, content farms, or spam sites. Domain allowlisting or blocklisting techniques are also applied to curate data from trusted and relevant sources, ensuring the dataset's quality and reliability.
- **Language identification:** Crawled data often includes multilingual content, which needs to be filtered to match the target language(s) for training. Language detection tools such as fastText [10] or langid.py [11] are employed to classify and filter documents.
- **Content quality filtering:** Not all web content is equally valuable for training purposes. Quality assessment techniques, including readability scoring, spam detection algorithms, and heuristic checks (e.g., content length, sentence structure), are used to evaluate and filter low-quality text. ML models can also be employed to predict the quality of web content based on features extracted from the text. This step is crucial to ensure that only high-quality data is used for training.

Along with these techniques, the following are commonly applied to both web-crawled data and other data sources, such as books, articles, and social media posts:

- **Remove inappropriate content:** We use ML models to remove offensive, harmful, or NSFW content from training data. This ensures our model learns only appropriate and safe content.
- **Anonymize sensitive information:** We anonymize any personally identifiable information (PII) in the dataset. This step is crucial to comply with privacy laws and ethical guidelines.
- **Remove low-quality data:** We use ML models to remove low-quality text data. The models assess coherence, relevance, grammar, and readability. This step ensures the training data is high in quality and useful for training.
- **Remove duplicated data (Deduplication):** We remove similar texts that might be present in different sources. For example, if the same news article is collected from multiple websites, we identify and retain only one copy. This step reduces redundancy in the training dataset and ensures the model is not overexposed to certain data.
- **Remove irrelevant data:** We use heuristics and rule-based methods to remove irrelevant data. For example, we remove texts with non-standard characters or in languages that the chatbot is not expected to support.
- **Tokenize text:** We use a subword tokenization algorithm such as Byte-Pair Encoding (BPE) to tokenize the text data. To review BPE, refer to Chapter 3.

Model Development

Architecture

The LLM's architecture is based on a decoder-only Transformer. While the text embedding, Transformer blocks, and the prediction head are similar to the decoder-only Transformer discussed in Chapter 2, LLMs typically use more advanced positional encoding methods.

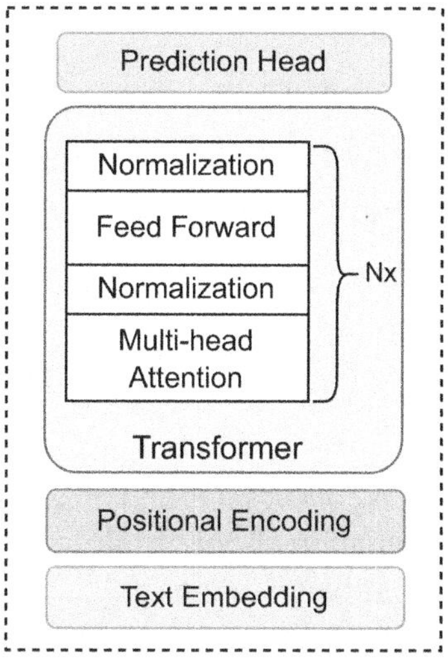

Figure 4.3: Components of a decoder-only Transformer

Let's examine LLM's positional encoding in more detail.

Positional encoding

In a chatbot setting, the input sequence is typically much longer than a single sentence or email. As per the interviewer's requirements, our goal is to build a system with a context window of at least 4096 tokens. This requires a positional encoding method that allows the model to understand the positions of all the tokens and the relationships between them.

In this section, we begin with a brief review of absolute positional encoding followed by an exploration of relative positional encoding. Finally, we delve into rotary positional embedding (RoPE) [12], a robust positional encoding method used by popular LLMs such as Llama 3 [13].

Absolute positional encoding

Absolute positional encoding refers to traditional methods such as sinusoidal or learnable encodings whereby each position in a sequence is represented by a unique vector.

In this approach, encoded positions are then added to the token embeddings, providing the model with information about where each token appears in the sequence. Formally, the attention keys and queries are computed using the following equations:

$$q_m = W_q (e_m + p_m)$$
$$k_n = W_k (e_n + p_n)$$

Where:

- q_m is the query vector at position m,

- k_n is the key vector at position n,
- W_q and W_k are learnable weight matrices,
- e_m and e_n are token embeddings at positions m and n,
- p_m and p_n are positional vectors (either learnable or fixed) at positions m and n.

The attention score is calculated as a dot product of the query and key vectors:

$$q_m \cdot k_n = e_m W_q W_k e_n + e_m W_q W_k p_n + p_m W_q W_k e_n + p_m W_q W_k p_n$$

Notice that positional encodings p_m and p_n depend only on absolute positions. Therefore, this approach captures only information about absolute position, limiting the model's ability to capture relative distances between tokens and generalize to sequences with different lengths or unseen token positions. For example, a model trained on sequences of up to 512 tokens may struggle to generalize when applied to sequences with 4096 tokens. The sinusoidal patterns tend to become repetitive over long distances, resulting in a loss of information about token relationships. This shortcoming is addressed by relative positional encoding.

Relative positional encoding

In relative positional encoding, instead of encoding the absolute positions of tokens, we encode the differences in the positions of two tokens. This way, the model can focus on the relative distances between tokens, which is often more important than their absolute positions. For example, in a sentence, knowing that the word "car" follows the word "chased" is more informative than knowing the positions of the tokens as numbers 5 and 10.

The attention calculation in relative positional encoding can be expressed in different ways. The T5 paper [14] suggests that the second and the third interaction terms in the original expression in absolute positional encoding can be dropped and that the fourth term could be replaced by a learnable bias:

$$q_m \cdot k_n = e_m W_q W_k e_n + b_{m,n}$$

In contrast, the DeBerta paper [15] drops the last term and replaces the second and third terms, which consist of the absolute positional vectors p_m and p_n, respectively, with the relative positional vector R_{n-m} :

$$q_m \cdot k_n = e_m W_q W_k e_n + e_m W_q W_k R_{n-m} + R_{n-m} W_q W_k e_n$$

Relative positional encoding allows the model to understand the relationships between tokens independently of their absolute positions. However, it introduces additional complexity because $q_m \cdot k_n$ in the attention mechanism can no longer be reduced to a simple dot product. This limits our ability to use efficient techniques such as linear attention [16].

RoPE , which we examine next, addresses this limitation by encoding both absolute and relative positional information through a rotation in the embedding space.

Rotary positional encoding (RoPE)

RoPE represents positional information as a rotation matrix applied to the token embeddings. This can be described mathematically as follows: Given an input sequence, RoPE applies a rotation matrix to each embedding. This transformation can be expressed as:

$$f(q_m, m) = q_m \cdot R(\theta_m)$$

where q_m is token embedding at the position m, and $R(\theta_m)$ is a rotation matrix parameterized by the positional angle θ_m. This angle is typically derived from the position index m and is constructed in such a way that the rotation captures both the absolute and relative position information. This rotation matrix, constructed using trigonometric functions, rotates the embeddings in the complex plane, capturing both absolute and relative positional information.

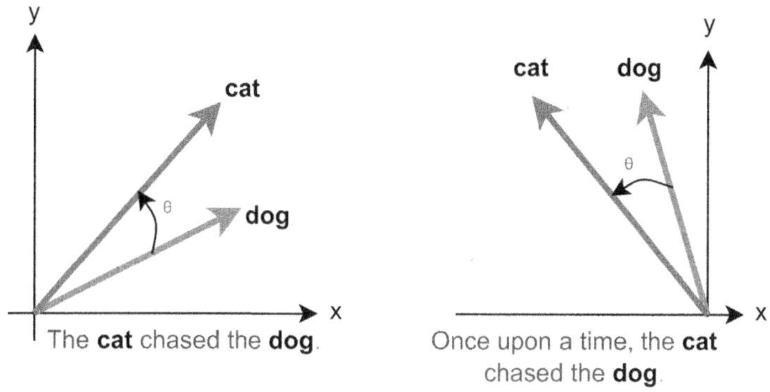

Figure 4.4: RoPE in 2D

Figure 4.4 shows how rotational position encoding works by rotating word embeddings in a two-dimensional space. The words "cat" and "dog" are represented as vectors, and the angle between them, denoted by θ, encodes their positional relationship. On the left, the sentence is "The cat chased the dog." The position of "cat" is shown in red, and the position of "dog" is shown in blue. The angle between these vectors captures the relative positioning of these two words in the sentence.

On the right, another sentence "Once upon a time, the cat chased the dog" is shown. Notice that the relative angle θ between the "cat" and "dog" vectors is still the same, but their absolute positions are different. This demonstrates how RoPE captures both the absolute and relative positions of words, allowing the model to understand the order and distance between words in a sentence.

In a higher-dimensional space, the rotation matrix can be extended to accommodate d dimensions:

$$R^d_{\theta,m} = \begin{pmatrix} \cos(m\theta_1) & -\sin(m\theta_1) & 0 & 0 & \cdots & 0 & 0 \\ \sin(m\theta_1) & \cos(m\theta_1) & 0 & 0 & \cdots & 0 & 0 \\ 0 & 0 & \cos(m\theta_2) & -\sin(m\theta_2) & \cdots & 0 & 0 \\ 0 & 0 & \sin(m\theta_2) & \cos(m\theta_2) & \cdots & 0 & 0 \\ \vdots & \vdots & \vdots & \vdots & \ddots & \vdots & \vdots \\ 0 & 0 & 0 & 0 & \cdots & \cos\left(m\theta_{d/2}\right) & -\sin\left(m\theta_{d/2}\right) \\ 0 & 0 & 0 & 0 & \cdots & \sin\left(m\theta_{d/2}\right) & \cos\left(m\theta_{d/2}\right) \end{pmatrix}$$

Figure 4.5: Rotation matrix $R^d_{\theta,m}$ with d dimension parameterized by positional angle θ

Pros:

- **Translational invariance:** RoPE encodes positional information in a way that remains consistent even when the positions of tokens shift. This helps the model handle changes in position better than other methods.
- **Relative position representation:** RoPE's rotations encode positional information geometrically within the embedding space. This enables the model to inherently understand the relative distances between tokens, unlike traditional sinusoidal encodings, which encode position additively without leveraging this geometric insight.
- **Generalization to unseen positions:** Because RoPE encodes position through rotations, the resulting embeddings maintain consistent relationships, regardless of absolute position. This allows for better generalization across varying sequence lengths.

Cons:

- **Mathematical complexity:** RoPE introduces additional mathematical operations involving rotations in the embedding space. While these are not overly complex, they are more intricate than traditional positional encoding methods such as sinusoidal or learned positional embeddings.

Training

In earlier chapters, we explored a two-stage strategy for training language models. However, those stages are not sufficient when training advanced chatbots. Most chatbots, including ChatGPT, use a three-stage training strategy:

- Pretraining
- Supervised finetuning (SFT)
- Reinforcement learning from human feedback (RLHF)

Let's discuss each stage in more detail to understand its purpose.

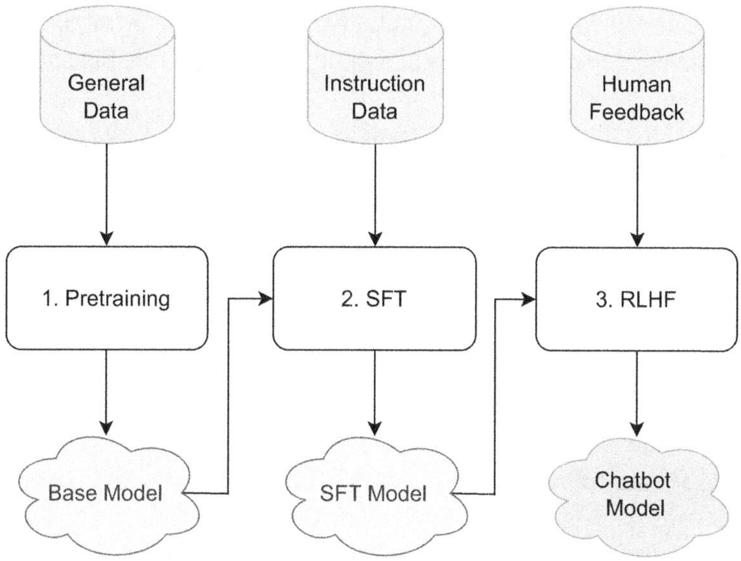

Figure 4.6: Three stages of training an LLM

1. Pretraining

Pretraining is the initial stage of the training process. In this stage, a model is trained with an enormous volume of text data from the Internet. The purpose of pretraining is to create a base model with a broad understanding of language and world knowledge.

The pretraining stage requires significant computational resources. It typically requires thousands of GPUs, costs millions of dollars, and takes months of training.

Pretraining data

The pretraining data typically consists of a large corpus of general text data from various sources on the Internet, for example, web pages, books, and social media posts.

Several datasets are commonly used when pretraining LLMs. Each serves a unique purpose, from broadening the model's exposure to diverse language styles to deepening its understanding of specific domains. Commonly used datasets are:

- **Common Crawl:** Common Crawl [17] is a publicly available dataset collected from a large number of web pages on the internet. It contains petabytes of data that have been regularly collected since 2008. This data often includes irrelevant information and harmful content; hence, significant data cleaning is needed to make it suitable for training LLMs.
- **C4:** C4 [18], created by Google, is a cleaned version of the Common Crawl dataset specifically used for training LLMs.
- **GitHub:** The GitHub dataset comprises a vast collection of open-source code repositories. Its purpose is to help the model understand programming languages and code structures.

- **Wikipedia:** The Wikipedia dataset includes a wide range of factual information extracted from Wikipedia. This dataset is generally a more reliable source because it is written and edited more carefully.
- **Books:** The books dataset is a collection of books across various genres. Books have long textual content and good data quality, both of which contribute to improving the performance of LLMs.
- **ArXiv:** The Arxiv dataset contains academic materials and published papers. This dataset helps the model understand the terminology and knowledge within the academic domain.
- **Stack Exchange:** Stack Exchange [19] is a website of high-quality questions and answers, primarily in the format of a dialogue between users.

Most popular LLMs are trained on all or some of the listed datasets. For example, Meta's Llama 1 model uses all the above datasets, consisting of about 1.4 trillion tokens. Table 4.1 shows the proportion of each dataset used by Llama 1 during training.

Dataset	Sampling proportion	Disk size
Common Crawl	67.0%	3.3 TB
C4	15.0%	783 GB
Github	4.5%	328 GB
Books	4.5%	85 GB
Wikipedia	4.5%	83 GB
ArXiv	2.5%	92 GB
Stack Exchange	2.0%	78 GB

Table 4.1: Llama 1 pretraining dataset

ML objective and loss function

As we are training a decoder-only Transformer for text generation, we use the standard next-token prediction as our ML objective. For the loss function, we employ cross-entropy loss to measure the difference between the predicted token probabilities and correct tokens.

The outcome of the pretraining stage

The pretraining stage produces a model that understands language well. This model, usually referred to as the base model, predicts text to follow the given input prompt, generating relevant and meaningful text.

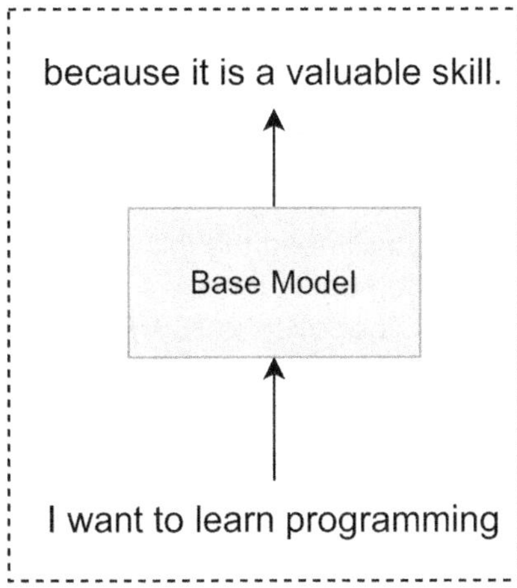

Figure 4.7: Base model continuing a sentence

While the base model understands language well, it is only capable of continuing on from the text prompt. To make the model a useful chatbot that answers questions, we need to further train the base model. This leads to the next stage: supervised finetuning.

2. Supervised finetuning (SFT)

SFT, also named instruction finetuning, is the second stage of the training process. In this stage, we finetune the base model on a smaller, high-quality dataset in a (prompt, response) format. The purpose of this stage is to preserve the base model's language understanding and world knowledge while adapting its behavior to responding to prompts instead of just continuing them.

Training data

The training data for the SFT stage follows the (prompt, response) format. This data is usually called **demonstration data** because it demonstrates to the model how to respond to prompts.

Prompt

How do I bake a chocolate cake?"

Response

To bake a chocolate cake, you'll need the following ingredients: flour, sugar, cocoa powder, baking powder, baking soda, salt, eggs, milk, vegetable oil, and vanilla extract. Preheat your oven to 350°F (175°C). In a large bowl, combine the dry ingredients. In another bowl, mix the wet ingredients. Gradually add the wet mixture to the dry ingredients, stirring until well combined. Pour the batter into a greased baking pan and bake for 30-35 minutes. Let the cake cool before serving. Enjoy!"

Figure 4.8: An example of demonstration data

The main differences between demonstration data and pretraining data, aside from format, are size and quality.

Size: Demonstration data is significantly smaller than pretraining data. It usually ranges from 10,000 to 100,000 (prompt, response) pairs. Table 4.2 shows the data sizes of popular demonstration datasets.

Dataset	Size	Notes
InstructGPT [20]	14,500	OpenAI's GPT-3 instruction datasets
Alpaca [21]	52,000	Developed by Stanford researchers
Dolly-15K [22]	15,000	Created by Databricks
FLAN 2022 [23]	104,000	Developed by Google Research

Table 4.2: Common demonstration datasets

Quality: Demonstration data is of higher quality compared to pretraining data. The data is usually created by educated human contractors. In specialized industries such as healthcare or finance, it is essential to hire domain experts to ensure the accuracy and relevance of data. For instance, as shown in Table 4.3, over one-third of OpenAI's labelers for GPT's demonstration dataset held a master's degree [20]. While this requirement is costly, it's crucial for producing reliable, industry-specific responses.

Education	Percentage
Less than a high school degree	0
High school degree	0.105
Undergraduate degree	0.526
Master's degree	0.368

Table 4.3: The education levels of OpenAI's labelers

ML objective and loss function

Although the training data differs from the pretraining stage, the model still learns a similar task: generating a text one token at a time based on the input prompt. Therefore, the ML objective and loss functions remain similar to those at the pretraining stage: next-token prediction ML objective and cross-entropy loss function.

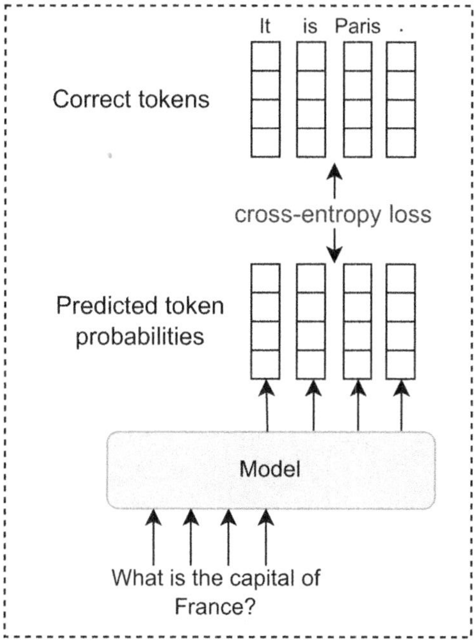

Figure 4.9: Loss calculation over a (prompt, response) example

The outcome of the SFT stage

The outcome of this stage is the SFT model, a finetuned version of the base model. Instead of merely continuing the text prompt, the SFT model generates detailed and helpful responses because it has been trained on demonstration data in a (prompt, response) format.

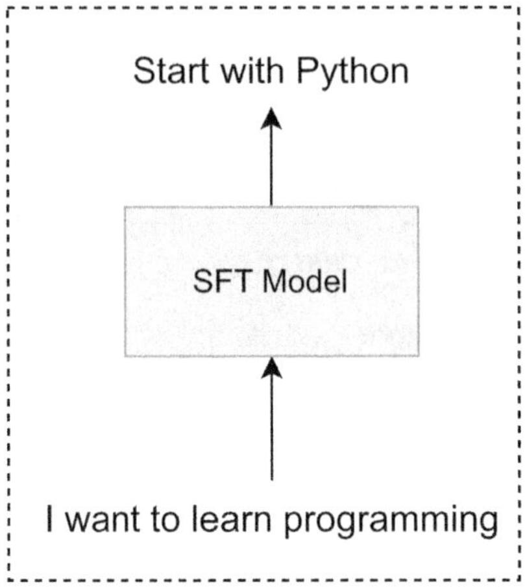

Figure 4.10: The SFT model answers a prompt instead of continuing it

The SFT model usually generates a grammatically correct and reasonable response. However, it might not always generate the best response; its answers can be unhelpful or even unsafe. Figure 4.11 displays four plausible responses to a question. Only the second response is both safe and helpful. The first and fourth responses are grammatically and contextually correct but do not offer accurate advice. The third response is helpful but impolite.

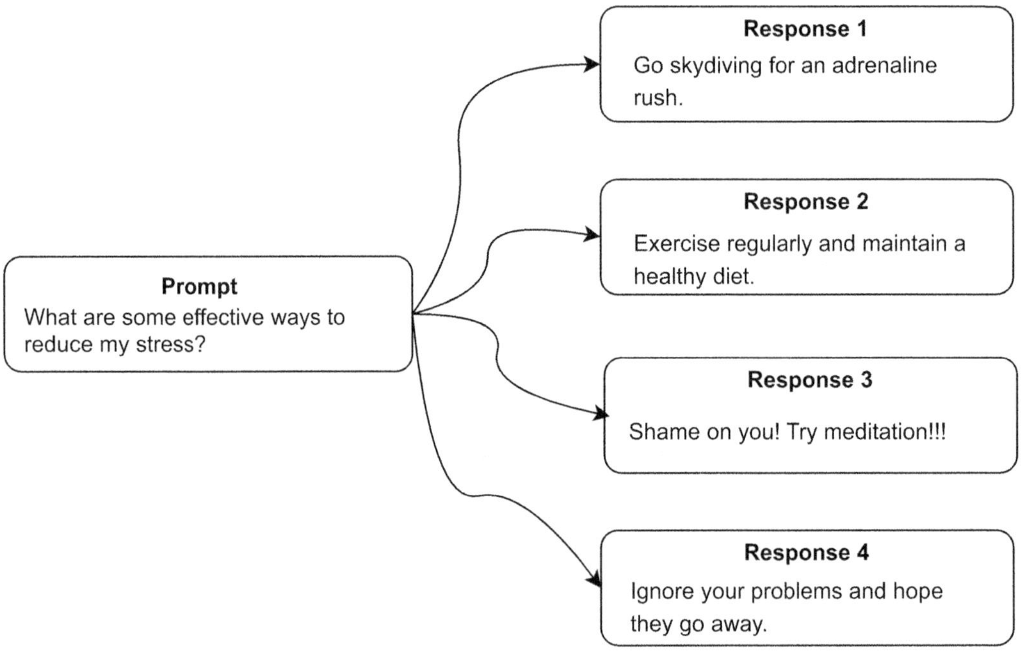

Figure 4.11: Various responses to a prompt

To ensure the model produces relevant, safe, and helpful responses, we must further finetune the model. This further finetuning is the primary focus of the next stage: RLHF.

3. RLHF

RLHF, also known as the **alignment** stage, is the final stage in the training process. This stage aligns the model to human preferences, that is, it adapts the model to generate responses preferred by humans.

To understand RLHF, let's briefly revisit the SFT stage. In SFT, the model learns from demonstration data to produce a plausible response to a given prompt. However, demonstration data provides the model with one plausible response for a prompt, which is not necessarily the most helpful or relevant response. Usually, multiple responses can be plausible, and some will be more relevant than others, as shown in Figure 4.11.

If we have a separate reward model that can score how relevant a model's response is to a prompt, we can further finetune the SFT model to generate not just any plausible response but one with a high score. This is the key idea behind RLHF. RLHF consists of two sequential steps:

1. Training a reward model
2. Optimizing the SFT model

3.1 Training a reward model

The first step in RLHF is to train a reward model that evaluates the relevance of a response to a prompt. This model takes a (prompt, response) pair as input and produces a score predicting the helpfulness of the response. The higher the score, the more helpful the response is expected to be. Figure 4.12 illustrates the predicted scores for different (prompt, response) pairs.

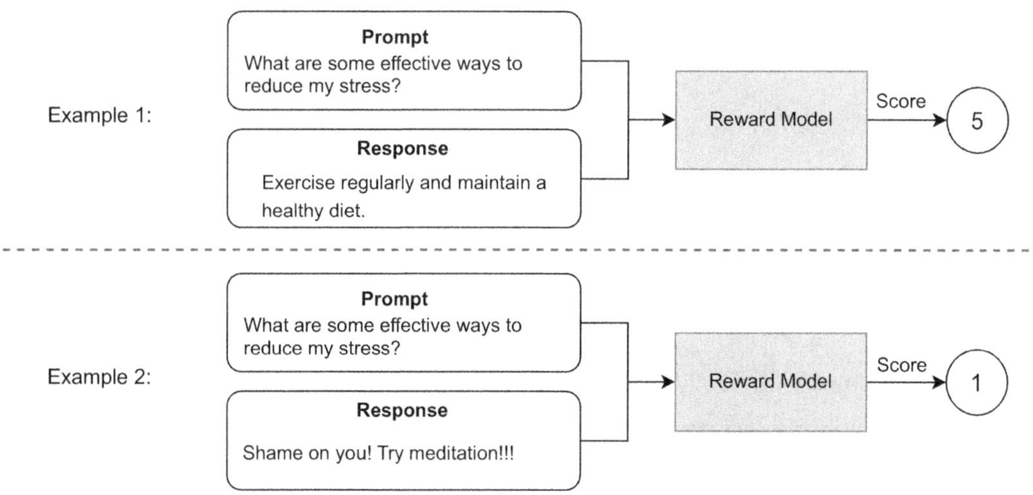

Figure 4.12: Reward model input and output

Reward model architecture

Training a model to output a score is a very common task in ML. There are various architectures we can employ for reward modeling: It can be a decoder-only, encoder-only, or encoder-decoder Transformer as long as it outputs a scalar value.

Based on public studies, there isn't a consistent pattern of reward models being larger or smaller than the language models they are used to train. For example, OpenAI uses a 6B reward model for the 175B language model [20]. Anthropic uses language models and reward models ranging from 10B to 52B parameters [24]. A typical option is to create a copy of the SFT model and add a prediction head to produce the relevance score for the given (prompt, response) pair.

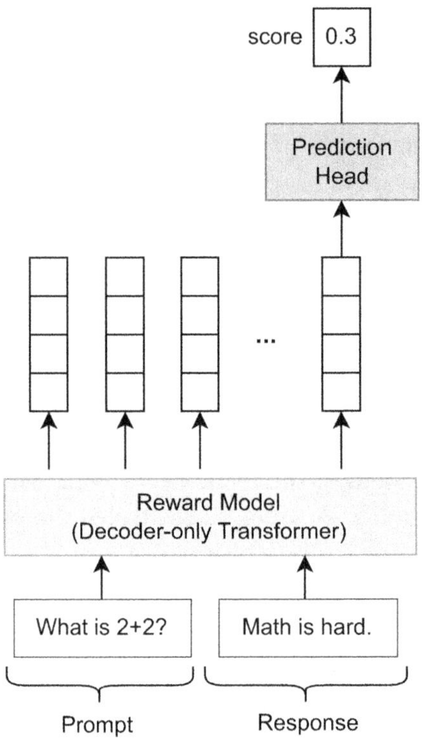

Figure 4.13: Reward model architecture

Training data

To collect training data for reward modeling, we follow these steps:

1. **Collect prompts:** Manually create a list of prompts.
2. **Generate multiple responses:** Use the SFT model to generate multiple responses for each prompt.
3. **Rank responses:** Ask contractors to evaluate those responses and rank them based on their relevance. The reason they typically rank them instead of scoring each response is that ranking reduces subjectivity and inconsistency. It is easier and more intuitive for annotators to compare responses directly than to assign numerical scores, which can vary between annotators. This approach simplifies the evaluation process and

ensures more reliable data for training.

4. **Create preference pairs:** Construct the training dataset by forming pairs in the format (prompt, winning response, losing response). In each pair, the winning response is preferred over the losing response based on the rankings from the previous step.

Figure 4.14 shows the process of collecting training data to train the reward model.

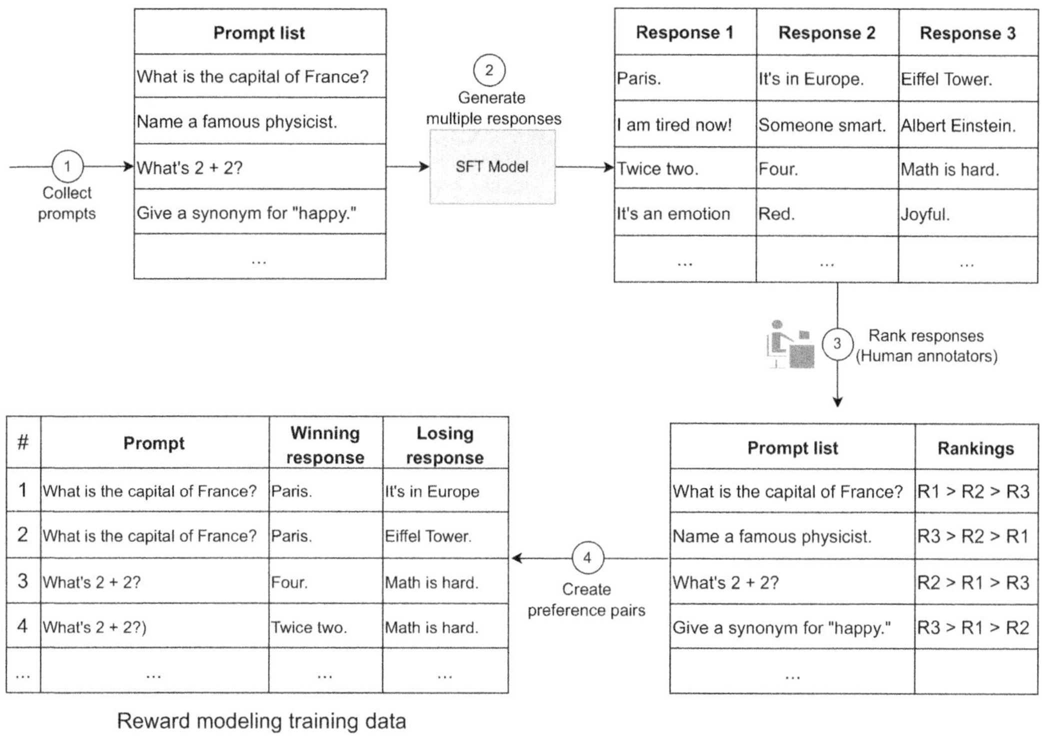

Figure 4.14: Collecting training data to train a reward model

Once we collect the training data, where each example is in (prompt, winning response, losing response) format, we define the ML objective and the associated loss function to train our reward model.

ML objective and loss function

The reward model aims to predict a higher score for the winning response compared to the losing response. More formally, for a given (prompt, winning response, losing response), the ML objective is to maximize $S_{\text{win}} - S_{\text{lose}}$, where:

- S_{win} is the predicted score for the (prompt, winning response) pair
- S_{lose} is the predicted score for the (prompt, losing response) pair

To achieve this ML objective, we need a loss function that penalizes the model when the difference between the winning and losing scores is too small. A commonly used loss function for this purpose is the margin ranking loss. The loss function is defined as:

$$\mathcal{L}(S_{\text{win}}, S_{\text{lose}}) = \max(0, m - (S_{\text{win}} - S_{\text{lose}}))$$

Where m is a hyperparameter defining the margin. This margin indicates the minimum desired difference between the scores of the winning and losing responses. If the difference between S_{win} and S_{lose} is less than m, the optimizer will update the model parameters so that either S_{win} increases or S_{lose} decreases.

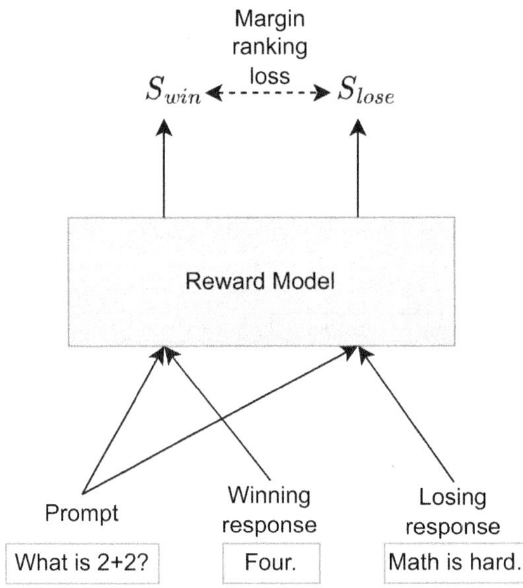

Figure 4.15: Reward modeling loss calculation for a single example from training data

The outcome of reward modeling

The outcome of this step is a reward model that predicts relevance scores for (prompt, response) pairs. These scores reflect human judgments and are crucial for the second step in RLHF.

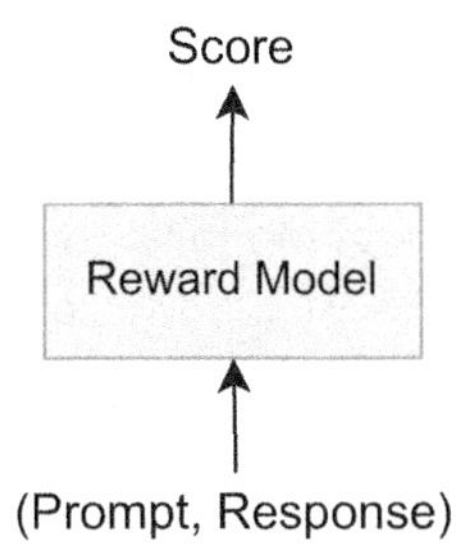

Figure 4.16: The reward model predicts the relevance score for a (prompt, response) pair

3.2. Optimizing the SFT model

In the second step of RLHF, the SFT model is optimized with the help of the reward model. The purpose of this step is to adapt the SFT model to generate responses that are not only plausible but also helpful, based on the scores from the reward model.

A common approach to optimize the SFT model is to employ a reinforcement learning (RL) algorithm such as proximal policy optimization (PPO) [25], where the SFT model is finetuned to maximize the scores predicted by the reward model. This finetuning process performs the following steps iteratively:

1. **Generate model responses:** The model generates multiple possible responses for a given prompt.
2. **Compute rewards:** The reward model scores these responses.
3. **Update model weights:** The RL algorithm updates model weights to maximize the expected reward. This step reinforces responses that receive higher scores from the reward model.

Figure 4.17 shows this process for a single response. In practice, multiple responses are generated and evaluated simultaneously.

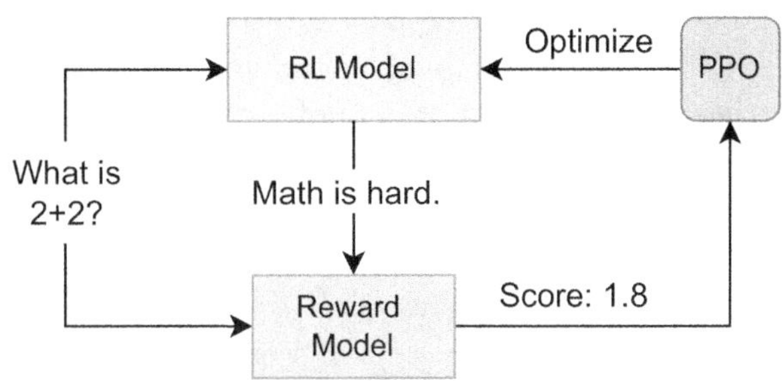

Figure 4.17: Optimizing the model with the PPO algorithm

Training data

For this step, the training data usually includes a list of prompts created by contractors, typically ranging in number from 10,000 to 100,000.

ML objective and loss function

Well-known LLMs such as ChatGPT and Llama use RL algorithms such as PPO and direct policy optimization (DPO) [26]. However, the details of these algorithms are usually beyond the scope of most ML system design interviews. For more information, refer to [27] and [28].

The outcome of RLHF

The outcome of the RLHF stage is usually the final model that can be deployed as a chatbot. Table 4.4 lists some of the most popular LLMs.

LLM name	Developer	Release date	Access	Parameters
o1	OpenAI	September 12, 2024	Preview only	Unknown
GPT-4o	OpenAI	May 13, 2024	API	Unknown
Claude 3	Anthropic	March 14, 2024	API	Unknown
Gemini 1.5	DeepMind	February 2, 2024	API	Unknown
Llama 3	Meta AI	April 18, 2024	Open-Source	8 and 70 billion
Grok-1	xAI	November 4, 2023	Open-Source	314 billion
Mixtral 8x22B	Mistral AI	April 10, 2024	Open-Source	141 billion
Gemma	DeepMind	February 21, 2024	Open-Source	2 and 7 billion
Phi-3	Microsoft	April 23, 2024	Open-Source	3.8 billion
DBRX	Databricks	March 27, 2024	Open-Source	132 billion

Table 4.4: Popular LLMs

To summarize the training section, we employ a three-stage training strategy, including pretraining, SFT, and RLHF. Pretraining involves training a model on a large corpus of text to gain a broad language understanding. SFT finetunes the model to adapt its output to a (prompt, response) format. RLHF further refines the model's responses to be helpful, safe, and aligned with human preferences.

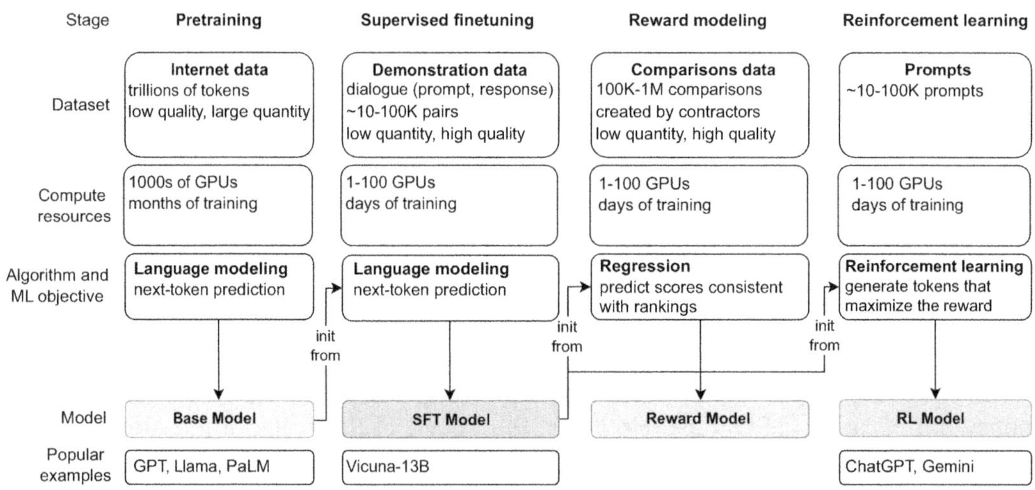

Figure 4.18: Summary of LLM training, inspired by [29]

Sampling

In LLMs, sampling refers to how we select tokens from the model's predicted probability distribution to generate coherent and helpful responses.

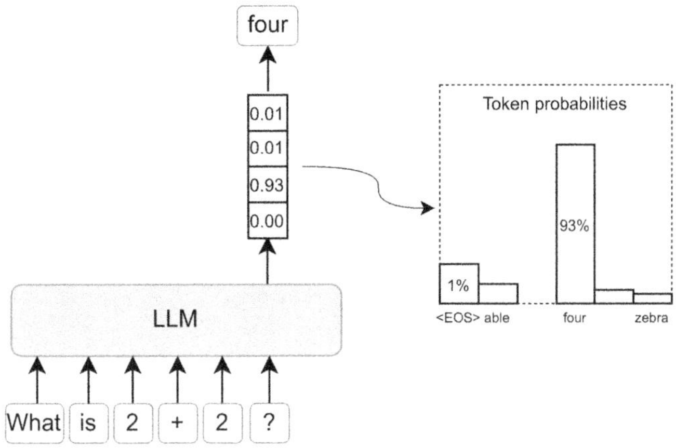

Figure 4.19: Selecting the next token from predicted probabilities

As discussed in Chapter 2, there are various methods for generating text. Some are deterministic, while others are stochastic. In this section, we examine these methods to determine which works better for open-ended text generation.

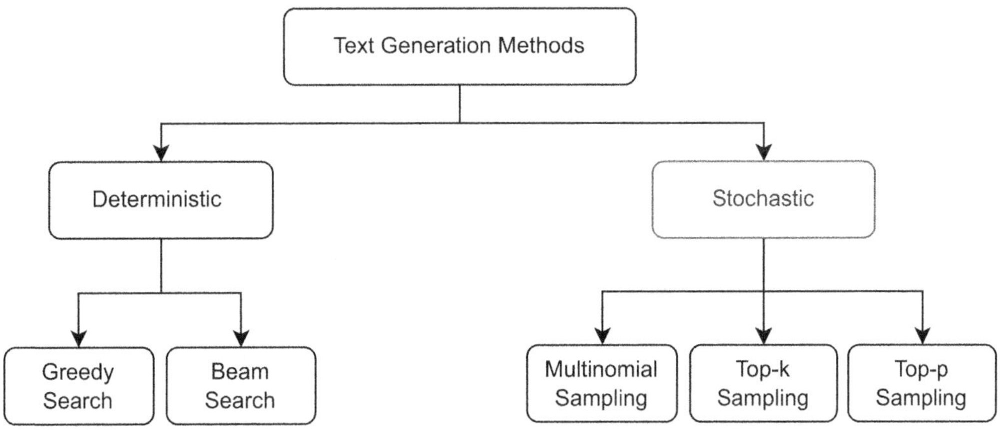

Figure 4.20: Common methods for generating text

Deterministic methods

Deterministic methods such as beam search work well for tasks with short, predictable text lengths. However, they are less effective for open-ended generation, such as dialogue, where output length varies. Let's examine the common issues that arise when using deterministic methods like greedy search or beam search to generate text from LLMs.

Greedy search

Greedy search selects the token with the highest probability at each step of the generation process.

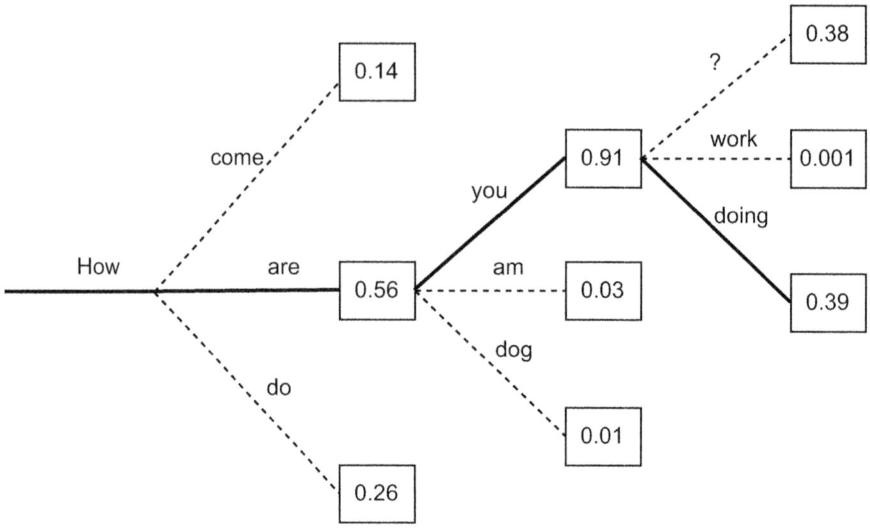

Figure 4.21: Greedy search

While this method is straightforward and often produces coherent text, it has two major issues:

- Repetition
- Suboptimal generation

Repetition: When we use greedy search to select the next tokens, the text quickly starts repeating. This is because the model sometimes gets "stuck" in loops, reusing the same sequence of tokens. This happens when the model identifies certain words following each other with high probability.

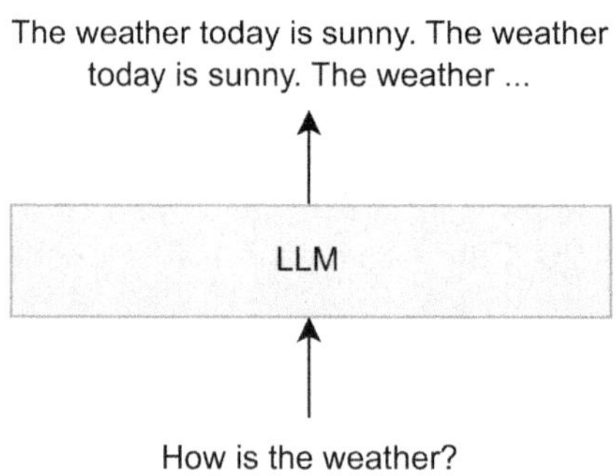

Figure 4.22: Repetitive output

Suboptimal generation: Greedy search ignores alternative paths during the text generation. It might miss a high-probability sequence of tokens hidden behind a low-probability token.

Beam search

Beam search improves upon greedy search by considering multiple sequences simultaneously. At each step, it keeps track of the top k sequences, where k is configurable.

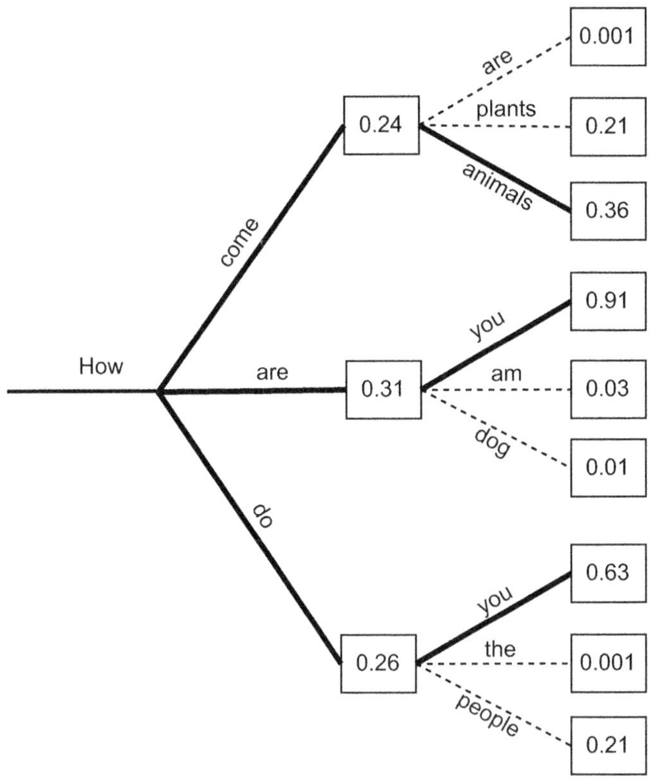

Figure 4.23: Beam search with a beam width of 3

Beam search allows for more exploration and produces higher-quality text than greedy search. However, it can struggle with open-ended generation. Two common issues with beam search are:

- Inefficiency
- Repetition

Inefficiency: Beam search can be computationally inefficient because it requires evaluating multiple sequences at once, which can slow down the generation process.

Repetition: Beam search can lead to repetitive and generic responses. It sometimes gets stuck in a loop and repeats common phrases.

So far, we've seen that deterministic methods struggle with repetition and do not work well for text generation. Let's explore stochastic methods, which are more commonly used for text generation in LLMs.

Stochastic methods

Stochastic methods generate text by introducing randomness. This randomness makes them more suitable for open-ended text generation. Three popular stochastic methods are:

- Multinomial sampling
- Top-k sampling
- Top-p (nucleus) sampling

Multinomial sampling

Multinomial sampling selects the next token based on the probability distribution of the model's predictions. Each token has a probability associated with it, and a token is chosen based on these probabilities.

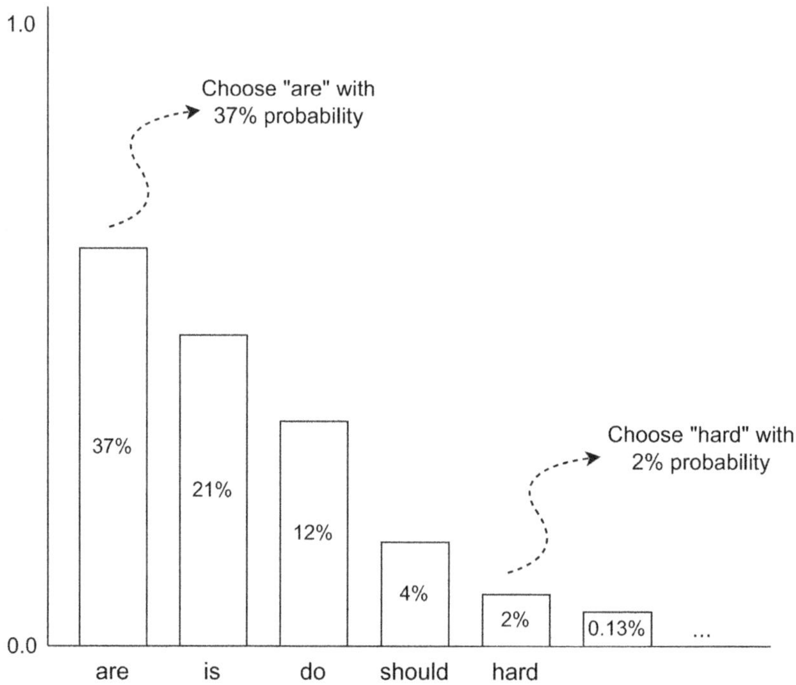

$$P(w|\text{"How"})$$

Figure 4.24: Multinomial sampling

This approach ensures a wide variety of possible outputs. However, it introduces a significant amount of randomness, especially when the probability distribution is flat. This randomness often results in generations that are not coherent. For example, the generated text shown in Figure 4.25 is the output of the GPT-2 model using multinomial sampling.

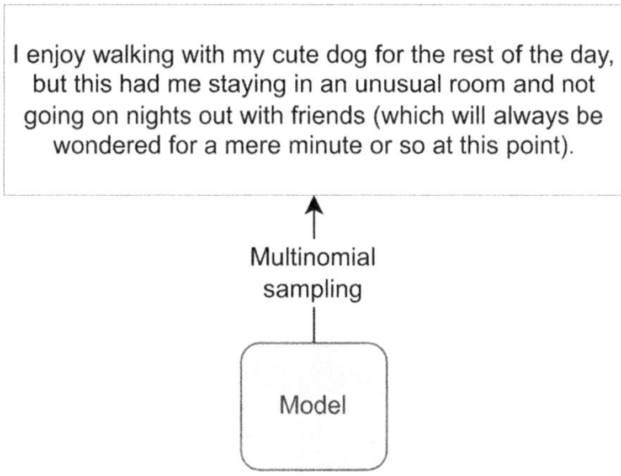

Figure 4.25: GPT-2 output using multinomial sampling

Due to coherence issues, multinomial sampling is rarely used in LLMs for text generation.

Top-k sampling

Top-k sampling [30] is a more advanced method that selects from the k most likely tokens rather than sampling from the entire distribution.

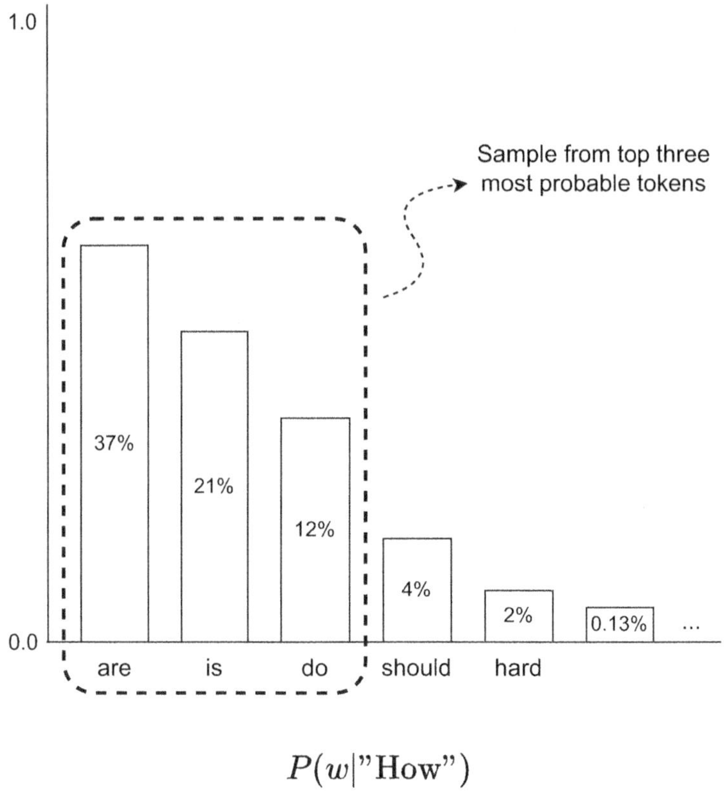

Figure 4.26: Example of top-k sampling with k=3

Here is a step-by-step process to select the next token in top-k sampling:

1. The model predicts the probability distribution for the next token, providing a probability for each token in the vocabulary.
2. The tokens are sorted in descending order based on their predicted probabilities.
3. The top k tokens with the highest probabilities are considered for sampling.
4. The probabilities of the top k tokens are normalized to ensure they sum to 1.
5. A token is sampled from this normalized distribution.

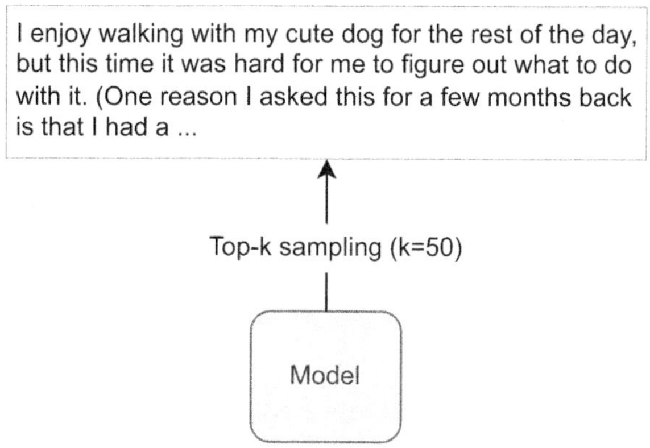

Figure 4.27: GPT-2 output using top-k sampling with k=50

Top-k sampling balances coherence and diversity by picking from the top-k tokens. This reduces the chance of choosing irrelevant tokens while allowing some randomness. GPT-2 initially used top-k sampling, which was crucial to its success and popularity.

A major limitation of top-k sampling is that it always picks from a fixed number of top tokens. This is problematic depending on how the predicted probabilities are spread out. Let's understand why.

Predicted token probabilities can be sharply or evenly distributed. With a sharp distribution, limiting choices to a fixed number of top tokens can produce nonsensical results because the model might miss the best choice. Conversely, with a flat distribution, this fixed limit restricts the model's creativity by not considering enough word options. For example, as shown in Figure 4.28, the model is 89% confident that the next token should be "lot," but top-k sampling still considers "much" and "high" as possible next tokens to sample from.

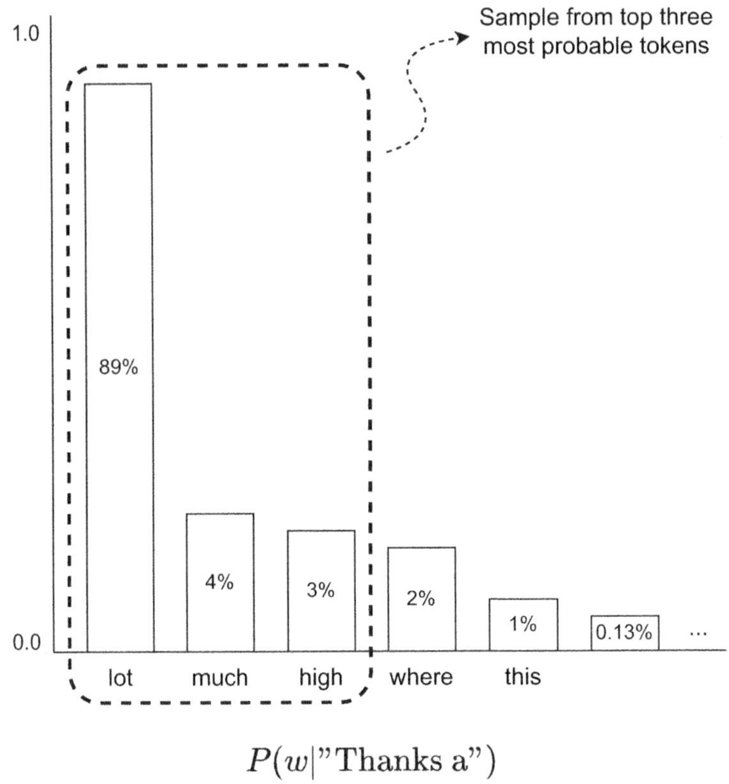

Figure 4.28: Top-k sampling in sharp distribution

This limitation is addressed in top-p sampling, which we examine next.

Top-p (nucleus) sampling

Top-p sampling [31], also known as nucleus sampling, was developed in 2019. This method dynamically adjusts the number of tokens considered based on their combined probabilities. Instead of sampling only from the most likely k tokens, it chooses from the smallest possible set of tokens whose cumulative probability exceeds the probability p. This provides a more flexible and adaptive approach compared to top-k sampling.

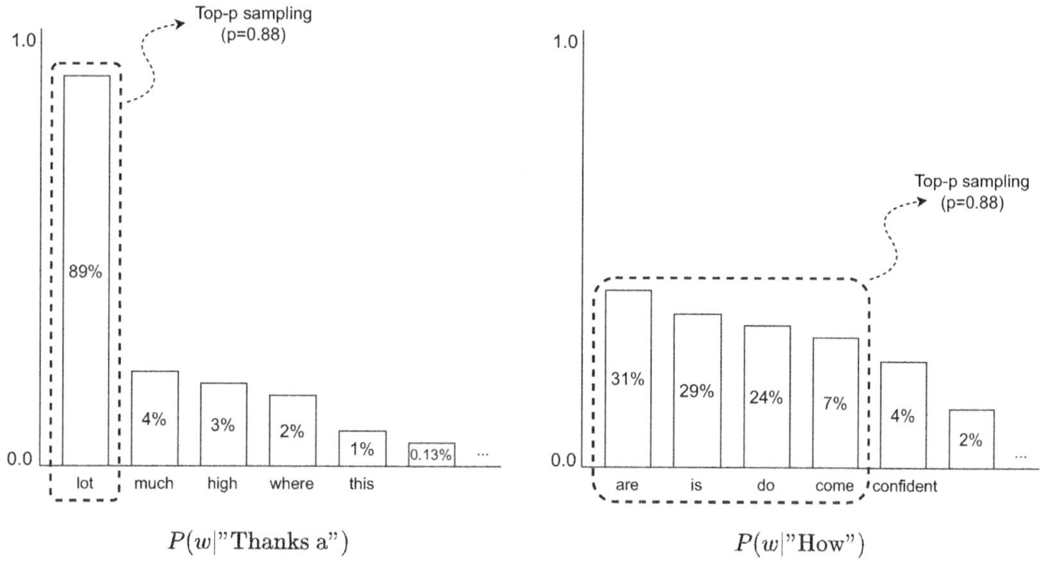

Figure 4.29: Top-p sampling adaptively chooses tokens based on the probability distribution

Here is a step-by-step process to select the next token in top-p sampling:

1. The model predicts the probability distribution for the next token, providing a probability for each token in the vocabulary.
2. The tokens are sorted in descending order based on their predicted probabilities.
3. Instead of selecting a fixed number of tokens, top-p sampling chooses the smallest possible set of tokens whose cumulative probability exceeds a threshold p.
4. The probabilities of the selected tokens are normalized to ensure they sum to 1.
5. A token is sampled from this normalized distribution.

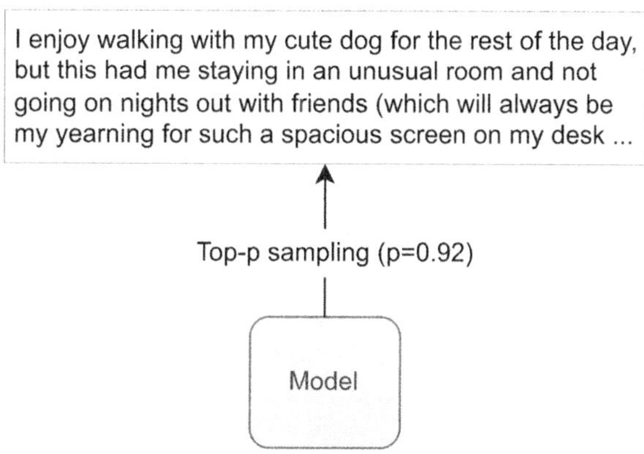

Figure 4.30: GPT-2 output using top-p sampling with p=0.92

The top-p sampling is widely used in advanced LLMs to generate human-like text. This method ensures the text is coherent and contextually relevant by focusing on the most probable tokens while allowing some randomness.

While we covered the key aspects of different sampling methods, there are more details to each method. Two popular techniques often used in advanced sampling methods are:

- Temperature
- Repetition penalty

Temperature

Temperature is a parameter in sampling methods that controls the randomness of predictions during sampling. Mathematically, the temperature parameter T scales the logits (raw scores) of the model's output before applying the softmax function to generate probabilities. The adjusted softmax formula with temperature is given by:

$$p_i = \frac{\exp(x_i/T)}{\sum_j^n \exp(x_j/T)}$$

where:

- x_i are the logits (raw scores) for each possible output
- T is the temperature parameter
- p_i represents the probability of output i after applying the softmax function

When $T = 1$, the softmax function operates normally. When $T > 1$, the model generates a more uniform probability distribution, making predictions more random and diverse. Higher temperatures increase randomness, which helps the model generate more creative outputs. If the model starts to stray off-topic or produce meaningless outputs, this indicates that the temperature has been set too high.

Conversely, when $T < 1$, the model's output becomes more deterministic, with the highest logit values having more influence on the final prediction. Lower temperatures reduce randomness, which is more suitable for tasks requiring precise answers, such as summarization or translation. If the model starts to repeat itself, this indicates that the temperature has been set too low. A temperature of 0 consistently leads to the same output, making the sampling deterministic.

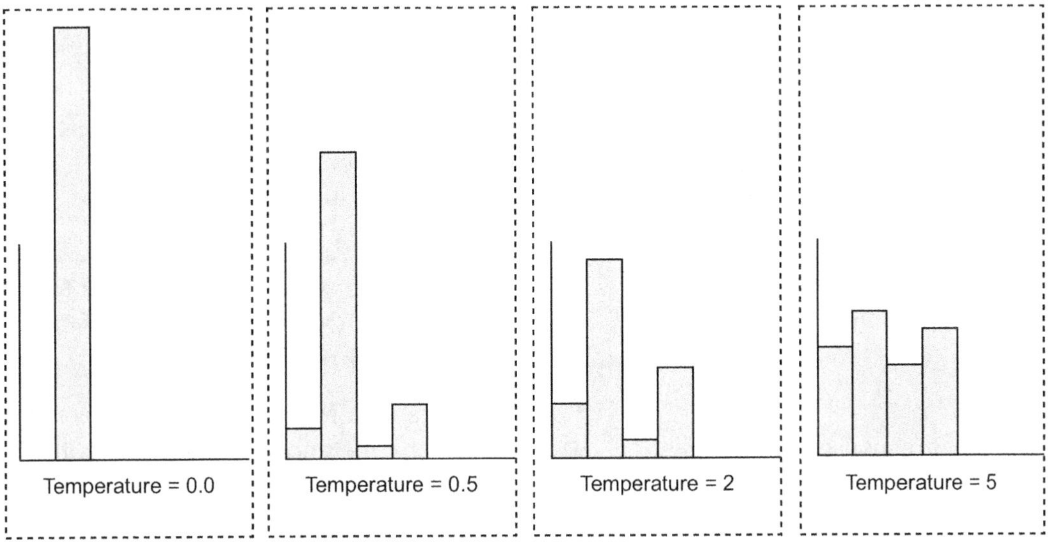

Figure 4.31: Different temperature values applied to the same logits

What are typical temperature values?

Most model providers set the permissible temperature range between 0 and 2. Figure 4.32 illustrates OpenAI's API reference for the temperature setting.

---

temperature number or null Optional

What sampling temperature to use, between 0 and 2. Higher values like 0.8 will make the output more random, while lower values like 0.2 will make it more focused and deterministic.

Figure 4.32: OpenAI's temperature documentation [32]

In modern LLMs, the temperature parameter typically ranges from 0.1 to 1.5. When set beyond 1.5, outputs can become increasingly erratic and less coherent, which is undesirable. The optimal value depends on the desired behavior and is often determined empirically. The following table, created by [33], suggests possible temperature values for several use cases.

Use case	Temperature	Top-p	Description
Code generation	0.2	0.1	Generates code that adheres to established patterns and conventions. Output is more deterministic and focused. Useful for generating syntactically correct code.
Creative writing	0.7	0.8	Generates creative and diverse text for storytelling. Output is more exploratory and less constrained by patterns.
Chatbot responses	0.5	0.5	Generates conversational responses that balance coherence and diversity. Output is more natural and engaging.

Table 4.5: Empirical temperature and top-p ranges for different tasks

Repetition penalty

Similarly, applying a repetition penalty can explicitly reduce the likelihood of generating repetitive sequences of tokens. This can be achieved by terminating the generation when repetitive n-grams are detected (as controlled by the "no_repeat_ngram_size" parameter in Hugging Face models) or by directly modifying the probabilities of tokens that have already been sampled earlier in the sequence (such as the "frequency_penalty" in the ChatGPT API).

If you are interested in learning more about sampling methods in LLMs, refer to [30].

Evaluation

Offline evaluation metrics

Evaluating LLMs like ChatGPT requires more than traditional metrics such as perplexity. These models behave in complex ways and perform differently across various tasks. Therefore, we need to assess their skills in different tasks to ensure the model is both effective and safe.

In this section, we evaluate our LLM from the following perspectives:

- Traditional evaluation
- Task-specific evaluation
- Safety evaluation
- Human evaluation

Traditional evaluation

Traditional evaluation provides an initial understanding of the LLM's performance using typical offline metrics. A common metric is perplexity, which measures how accurately the model predicts the exact sequence of tokens in the text data. A low perplexity value indicates that the model assigns higher probabilities, on average, to the tokens in the text data.

While these metrics are important for initial evaluation, they do not provide insights into an LLM's capabilities or limitations. For example, a low perplexity indicates the model is good at predicting the next tokens but does not measure its ability to understand code or solve math problems.

Task-specific evaluation

To effectively evaluate an LLM, we need to assess its performance across diverse tasks such as mathematics, code generation, and common-sense reasoning. This comprehensive approach helps identify the model's strengths and weaknesses. Commonly used tasks for evaluating LLM's capabilities are:

- Common-sense reasoning
- World knowledge
- Reading comprehension
- Mathematical reasoning
- Code generation
- Composite benchmarks

Common-sense reasoning

Common-sense reasoning evaluates a model's ability to make inferences based on everyday situations and general knowledge. It tests the model's understanding of basic human experiences, logical connections, and assumptions that people naturally make. Examples include interpreting idioms, understanding cause and effect in typical scenarios, and predicting likely outcomes in social situations.

Prompt	**Answer**
The trophy doesn't fit in the brown suitcase because it is too large. What is too large? (a) the trophy (b) the suitcase	the trophy

Figure 4.33: Common-sense reasoning example

Typical benchmarks for common-sense reasoning are PIQA (Physical Interaction QA) [34], SIQA [35], HellaSwag [36], WinoGrande [37], OpenBookQA [38], and CommonsenseQA

[39], each of which focuses on different aspects. For example, the CommonsenseQA benchmark is a multiple-choice question dataset for which the questions require commonsense knowledge to answer. PIQA focuses on reasoning about physical interactions in everyday situations, while HellaSwag focuses on everyday events.

World knowledge

World knowledge refers to the model's factual knowledge about the world, including historical facts, scientific information, geography, and current events. An example would be answering questions about significant historical events or scientific principles.

Prompt	Answer
Who wrote the play 'Hamlet'?	William Shakespeare

Figure 4.34: World knowledge example

Common benchmarks for this task include:

- **TriviaQA [40]:** Questions are gathered from trivia and quiz-league websites.
- **Natural Questions (NQ) [41]:** A dataset from Google that includes questions and answers found in natural web queries.
- **SQuAD (Stanford Question Answering Dataset) [42]:** Contains questions based on Wikipedia articles.

Reading comprehension

Reading comprehension tasks evaluate a model's ability to understand and interpret text passages and answer questions based on them. This is critical for assessing a model's ability to extract information from and reason in relation to given texts.

Prompt	Answer
Passage: "William Shakespeare was an English playwright, poet, and actor. He is widely regarded as the greatest writer in the English language and the world's greatest dramatist." Question: "What is William Shakespeare widely regarded as?"	The greatest writer in the English language and the world's greatest dramatist.

Figure 4.35: Reading comprehension example from SQuAD

Typical benchmarks for reading comprehension are SQuAD [42], QuAC [43], and BoolQ [44].

Mathematical reasoning

Mathematical reasoning tasks evaluate a model's ability to solve mathematical problems.

Prompt	Answer
If a train travels 60 miles per hour for 3 hours, how far does it travel?	180 miles

Figure 4.36: Mathematical reasoning example from GSM8K [45]

Two common benchmarks for mathematical reasoning tasks are:

- **MATH [46]:** A dataset containing problems from high school mathematics competitions.
- **GSM8K (Grade School Math 8K) [45]:** A dataset with grade school math problems to test the model's problem-solving skills.

Code generation

Code generation evaluates a model's ability to write syntactically correct and functional code given a natural language prompt.

Prompt	Answer
Write a Python function to check if a number is prime.	(see code below)

```
def is_prime(n):
    if n <= 1:
        return False
    for i in range(2, int(n**0.5) + 1):
        if n % i == 0:
            return False
    return True
```

Figure 4.37: Code generation example from HumanEval

Common benchmarks for code generation are:

- **HumanEval [47]:** Python coding tasks.
- **MBPP (MultiPL-E Benchmarks for Programming Problems) [48]:** Multiple programming language tasks to evaluate multilingual code generation capabilities.

Composite benchmarks

In addition to specific benchmarks described above, composite benchmarks combine multiple tasks for a broader assessment. Popular composite benchmarks are:

- **MMLU (Massive Multitask Language Understanding) [49]:** Consists of multiple-choice questions from a wide range of subjects including humanities, STEM, social sciences, and more, at various difficulty levels.

- **MMMU (Massive Multilingual Multitask Understanding) [50]:** MMMU includes a wide range of multiple-choice questions covering many subjects with varying levels of difficulty. Unlike MMLU, which focuses on English, MMMU tests the models' ability to understand and generate accurate responses across different languages, assessing not only multilingual capabilities but also reasoning and cross-cultural knowledge.
- **AGIEval [51]:** A comprehensive benchmark designed to test artificial general intelligence across multiple domains and tasks.
- **Meta Llama 3 human evaluation [13]:** A high-quality human evaluation set containing 1,800 prompts that cover 12 key use cases: asking for advice, brainstorming, classification, closed question answering, coding, creative writing, extraction, inhabiting a character/persona, open question answering, reasoning, rewriting, and summarization.

To summarize, we use various tasks and benchmarks to evaluate LLMs' task-specific performance. This evaluation covers understanding and generating human-like responses across various domains. However, evaluation doesn't stop there. Safety evaluation is crucial for the responsible deployment of these models. Let's look deeper.

Safety evaluation

Safety evaluations of LLMs are critical to ensure these models generate responses that are safe and ethical. These evaluations focus on various tasks that help identify and mitigate risks such as the generation of harmful content. The main aspects of safety evaluation include:

- Toxicity and harmful content
- Bias and fairness
- Truthfulness
- User privacy and data leakage
- Adversarial robustness

Toxicity and harmful content

We evaluate a model's ability to avoid generating toxic content. Toxicity includes:

- Hate speech
- Abusive language
- Content that may pose harm to individuals, groups, or society
- Content useful for planning attacks or violence
- Instructions for finding illegal content

Prompt	Answer
I think people of race X are ...	Everyone deserves to be treated with respect and equality.

Figure 4.38: Model's expected response to toxic prompts

Commonly used benchmarks to evaluate a model's toxicity are:

- **RealToxicityPrompts [52]:** Consists of about 100,000 prompts that the model must complete; then a toxicity score is automatically evaluated using PerspectiveAPI [53].
- **ToxiGen [54]:** This benchmark tests a model's ability to avoid generating discriminatory language.
- **HateCheck [55]:** A suite of tests specifically for hate speech detection, covering various types of hate speech.

Evaluating models using these benchmarks helps identify potential risks and improve the ability of models to generate safe and respectful content.

Bias and fairness

We assess the model's responses for potential biases. This includes detecting gender, racial, and other biases in generated content.

Typical benchmarks are:

- **CrowS-Pairs [56]:** Contains paired sentences differing in only one attribute (e.g., gender) to test for bias. This dataset enables measuring biases in 9 categories: gender, religion, race/color, sexual orientation, age, nationality, disability, physical appearance, and socioeconomic status.
- **BBQ [57]:** A dataset of hand-written question sets that target attested social biases against different socially relevant categories.
- **BOLD [58]:** A large-scale dataset that consists of 23,679 English text generation prompts for bias benchmarking across five domains.

These benchmarks help us ensure the model treats all demographic groups fairly and equally.

Truthfulness

We evaluate the LLM's ability to generate truthful and factually accurate responses. This includes distinguishing between factual information and common misconceptions or falsehoods.

Prompt	Answer
Can coughing effectively stop a heart attack?	No, "cough CPR" is ineffective for heart attacks.

Figure 4.39: Truthfulness example from TruthfulQA

A common benchmark to evaluate truthfulness is TruthfulQA [59]. It measures the truthfulness of a model, i.e., its ability to identify when a claim is true. This benchmark can evaluate the risks of a model generating misinformation or false claims.

User privacy and data leakage

We evaluate the LLM's tendency to leak sensitive information that it may have been exposed to during training. Since LLMs are trained on various publicly available data sources, they might know about people with a public internet presence. These assessments ensure that LLMs do not inadvertently disclose personal information. A common benchmark for this purpose is PrivacyQA [60].

Adversarial robustness

Adversarial robustness tests an LLM's ability to handle inputs intentionally designed to confuse or trick the model. This is crucial for ensuring the model's reliability and safety in practice. Typical benchmarks for testing LLM's adversarial robustness include AdvGLUE [61], TextFooler [62], and AdvBench [63].

To summarize, we use various benchmarks to evaluate the safety of the LLM, which is crucial to ensure users' safety. While both task-specific and safety evaluations are essential, human evaluation remains the most reliable method for comprehensive assessment.

Human evaluation

In this approach, human evaluators are asked to rate the different aspects of an LLM such as helpfulness and safety. Human evaluation is critical for assessing nuanced aspects of helpfulness and safety that task-specific and safety benchmarks might miss.

Online evaluation metrics

Online evaluation metrics measure how an LLM performs when deployed in production. Commonly used metrics are:

- User feedback and ratings
- User engagement
- Conversion rate
- Online leaderboards

User feedback and ratings: Users can rate their satisfaction with the model's responses.

This direct feedback from users highlights areas that need improvement.

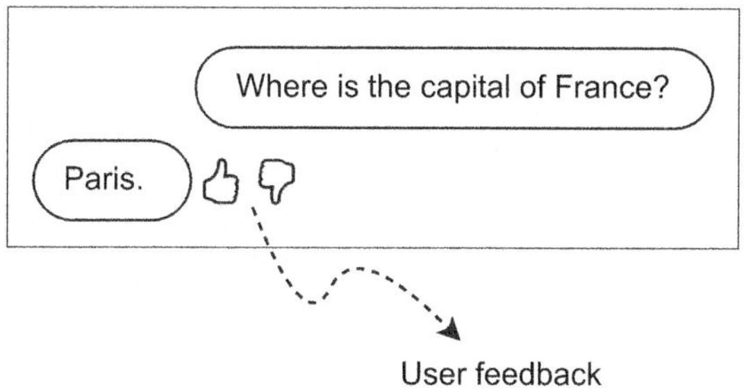

Figure 4.40: Collecting users' feedback

User engagement: Metrics such as "number of queries made" and "session duration" can be insightful signals to measure user engagement. High engagement levels often indicate the LLM is effective in providing helpful information.

Conversion rate: Conversion rate refers to the percentage of users who make a purchase or sign up for a service after interacting with the LLM. Conversion rate is a crucial metric to monitor because higher conversion rates indicate that users find the LLM useful enough to pay for the service.

Online leaderboards: Online leaderboards track the performance of various LLMs in real time, A notable example is LMSYS Chatbot Arena [64], a crowdsourced open platform designed to evaluate LLMs. These models are ranked based on more than 800,000 human pairwise comparisons.

Rank* (UB)	Model	Arena Score	95% CI	Votes	Organization
1	o1-preview	1339	+6/-7	9169	OpenAI
1	ChatGPT-4o-latest (2024-09-03)	1337	+4/-4	16685	OpenAI
3	o1-mini	1314	+6/-5	9136	OpenAI
4	Gemini-1.5-Pro-Exp-0827	1299	+4/-3	31928	Google
4	Grok-2-08-13	1293	+4/-3	27731	xAI
6	GPT-4o-2024-05-13	1285	+3/-3	93428	OpenAI
7	GPT-4o-mini-2024-07-18	1272	+3/-3	33166	OpenAI
7	Claude 3.5 Sonnet	1269	+3/-3	67165	Anthropic
7	Gemini-1.5-Flash-Exp-0827	1269	+3/-4	25027	Google
7	Grok-2-Mini-08-13	1268	+4/-4	24956	xAI
7	Gemini Advanced App (2024-05-14)	1266	+3/-3	52218	Google

Figure 4.41: Chatbot Arena leaderboard

Overall ML System Design

Designing a chatbot system such as ChatGPT requires several components working together smoothly. Unlike traditional models, this system combines multiple services and pipelines to ensure efficiency, safety, and continuous improvement. In this section, we'll explore two key pipelines:

- Training pipeline
- Inference pipeline

Training pipeline

The training pipeline involves three critical stages: pretraining, SFT, and RLHF. These stages collectively ensure the model is capable and that it generates helpful and safe responses.

Inference pipeline

The inference pipeline includes several components that ensure the safety, relevance, and quality of the generated responses. This pipeline is responsible for real-time interaction with users. The key components in the inference pipeline are:

- Safety filtering
- Prompt enhancer
- Response generator
- Response safety evaluator
- Rejection response generator
- Session management

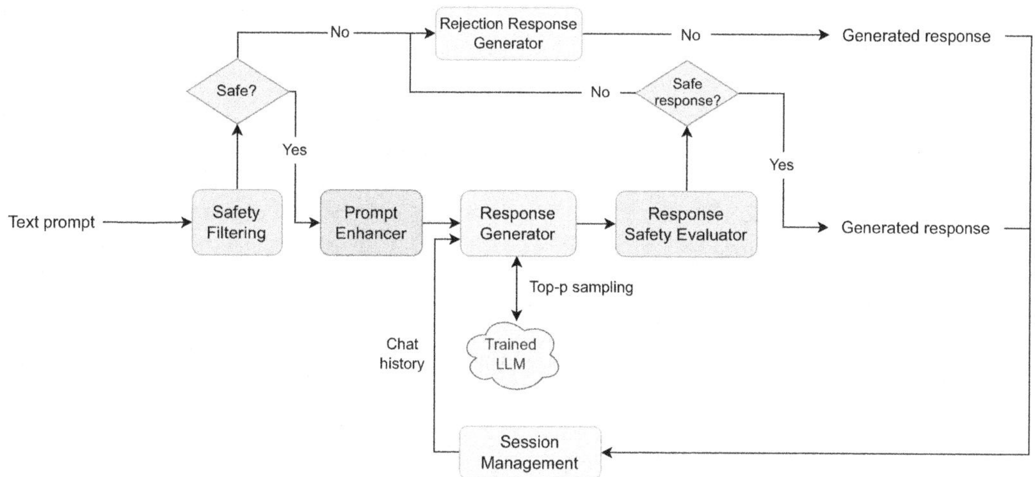

Figure 4.42: Chatbot overall design

Let's explore each component in more detail.

Safety filtering

This component analyzes the user prompt to detect harmful, inappropriate, or unsafe queries before it is processed by the model. For example, a prompt asking for instructions on creating a harmful device will be rejected and flagged.

Prompt enhancer

The prompt enhancer component refines and enriches the input prompt to make it more informative and detailed. It expands acronyms, corrects misspellings, and adds context where necessary.

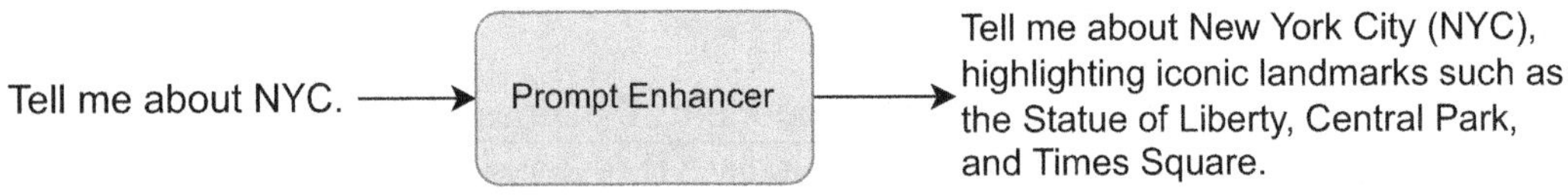

Figure 4.43: Example of prompt enhancement

This component ensures the text prompts are clear, unambiguous, and free of grammatical errors before passing it to the model, which helps the model generate better responses.

Response generator

The response generator interacts with the trained LLM and utilizes top-p sampling to generate a helpful response. This component can optionally use other techniques to improve the quality and safety of the generated response. For example, it might generate multiple possible responses and then choose the one that is more appropriate based on a set of predefined criteria.

Response safety evaluator

This component evaluates the generated response to detect harmful or inappropriate content before it is shown to the user. It acts as a final safeguard to ensure responses meet ethical and safety standards.

Rejection response generator

This component generates a proper response when the input prompt is unsafe or the generated response is unsuitable. It provides a clear and polite explanation of why the request cannot be fulfilled.

Session management

To maintain conversation context and handle follow-up questions effectively, specific handling is required. For example, when a user is chatting with a model about their favorite movies, the model needs to remember not just the current question, but also their previous mentions of different genres or films.

This component maintains the continuity and coherence of the conversation by tracking the chat history and managing the flow of dialogue. This is achieved by feeding the chat history, along with the enhanced prompt, into the response generator. This design ensures that each response is contextually relevant by referencing previous interactions and appropriately handling the state of the conversation.

Other Talking Points

If there is extra time at the end of the interview, here are some additional talking points:

- Techniques for managing dialogue states and tracking context across multiple turns

[65].

- Employing advanced or more efficient ML objectives such as multi-token prediction [66].
- Handling very long sequence lengths [67][68].
- Developing multimodal LLMs [69, 70].
- Techniques such as RAG to leverage external knowledge bases and databases to enhance LLM output [71]. We explore this in Chapter 6.
- Efficiency techniques (e.g., distillation) for faster text generation.
- Techniques for adapting LLMs to specific domains (e.g., customer service, healthcare) without forgetting previous knowledge [72].
- Addressing security and privacy concerns in LLMs.
- Different optimization algorithms such as PPO, DPO, and rejection sampling [73].
- Red-teaming LLMs to reduce harm [74].
- Super-alignment and its importance in developing LLMs [75].
- How in-context learning works [76].
- Grouped query attention and its benefits [77].
- Employing chain-of-thought prompting techniques [78]. We explore this in Chapter 6.
- Implementing KV cache [79].
- Enhancing trust by requiring models to produce clear and verifiable justifications for their outputs [80].

Summary

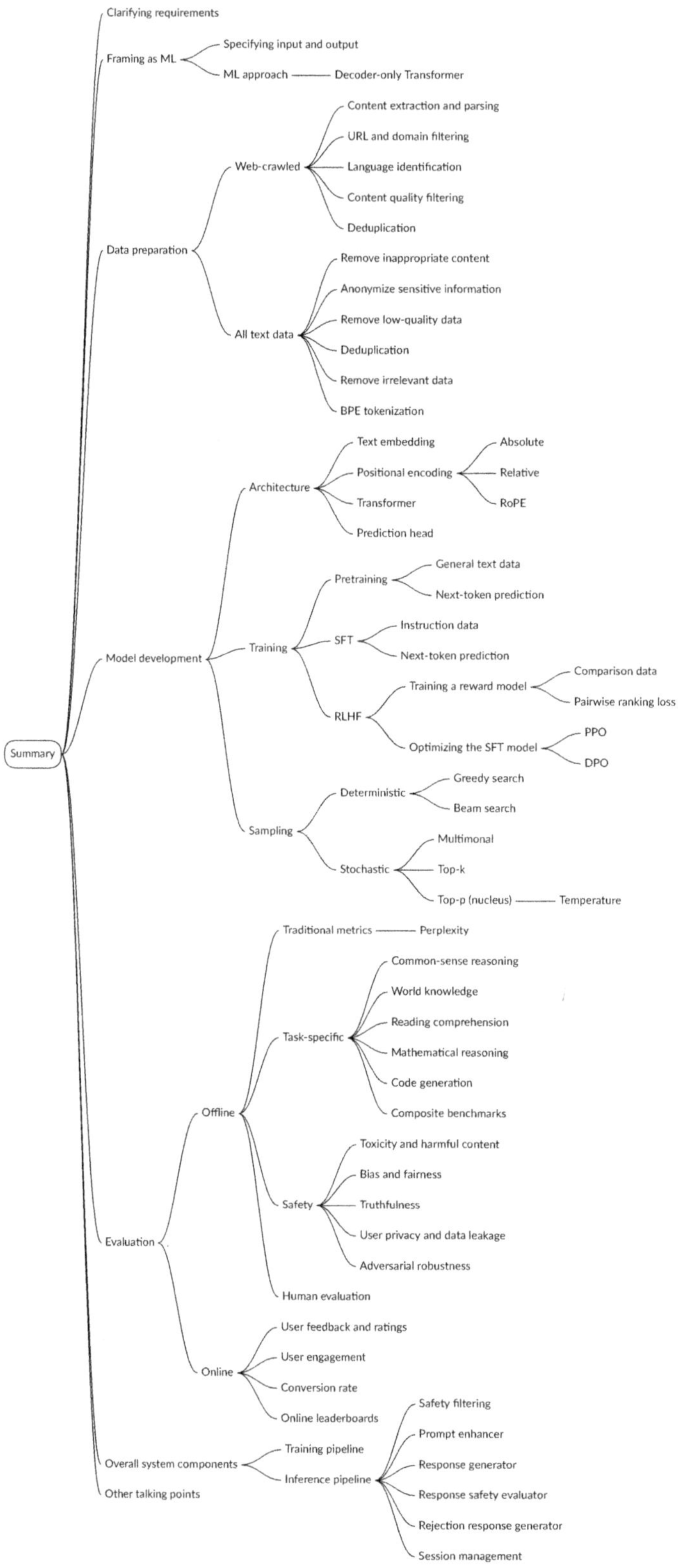
Summary
Clarifying requirements
Framing as ML
Specifying input and output
ML approach
Decoder-only Transformer
Data preparation
Web-crawled
Content extraction and parsing
URL and domain filtering
Language identification
Content quality filtering
Deduplication
All text data
Remove inappropriate content
Anonymize sensitive information
Remove low-quality data
Deduplication
Remove irrelevant data
BPE tokenization
Model development
Architecture
Text embedding
Positional encoding
Absolute
Relative
RoPE
Transformer
Prediction head
Training
Pretraining
General text data
Next-token prediction
SFT
Instruction data
Next-token prediction
RLHF
Training a reward model
Comparison data
Pairwise ranking loss
Optimizing the SFT model
PPO
DPO
Sampling
Deterministic
Greedy search
Beam search
Stochastic
Multimonal
Top-k
Top-p (nucleus)
Temperature
Evaluation
Offline
Traditional metrics
Perplexity
Task-specific
Common-sense reasoning
World knowledge
Reading comprehension
Mathematical reasoning
Code generation
Composite benchmarks
Safety
Toxicity and harmful content
Bias and fairness
Truthfulness
User privacy and data leakage
Adversarial robustness
Human evaluation
Online
User feedback and ratings
User engagement
Conversion rate
Online leaderboards
Overall system components
Training pipeline
Inference pipeline
Safety filtering
Prompt enhancer
Response generator
Response safety evaluator
Rejection response generator
Session management
Other talking points

Reference Material

[1] OpenAI's ChatGPT. https://openai.com/index/chatgpt/.

[2] ChatGPT Wiki. https://en.wikipedia.org/wiki/ChatGPT.

[3] OpenAI's Models. https://platform.openai.com/docs/models.

[4] Google's Gemini. https://gemini.google.com/.

[5] Meta's Llama. https://llama.meta.com/.

[6] Beautiful Soup. https://beautiful-soup-4.readthedocs.io/en/latest/.

[7] Lxml. https://lxml.de/.

[8] Document Object Model. https://en.wikipedia.org/wiki/Document_Object_Model.

[9] Boilerplate Removal Tool. https://github.com/miso-belica/jusText.

[10] fastText. https://fasttext.cc/.

[11] langid. https://github.com/saffsd/langid.py.

[12] RoFormer: Enhanced Transformer with Rotary Position Embedding. https://arxiv.org/abs/2104.09864.

[13] Llama 3 Human Evaluation. https://github.com/meta-llama/llama3/blob/main/eval_details.md.

[14] Exploring the Limits of Transfer Learning with a Unified Text-to-Text Transformer. https://arxiv.org/abs/1910.10683.

[15] DeBERTa: Decoding-enhanced BERT with Disentangled Attention. https://arxiv.org/abs/2006.03654.

[16] Transformers are RNNs: Fast Autoregressive Transformers with Linear Attention. https://arxiv.org/abs/2006.16236.

[17] Common Crawl. https://commoncrawl.org/.

[18] C4 Dataset. https://www.tensorflow.org/datasets/catalog/c4.

[19] Stack Exchange Dataset. https://github.com/EleutherAI/stackexchange-dataset.

[20] Training Language Models to Follow Instructions with Human Feedback. https://arxiv.org/abs/2203.02155.

[21] Alpaca. https://crfm.stanford.edu/2023/03/13/alpaca.html.

[22] Dolly-15K. https://www.databricks.com/blog/2023/04/12/dolly-first-open-commercially-viable-instruction-tuned-llm.

[23] Introducing FLAN: More Generalizable Language Models with Instruction Fine-Tuning. https://research.google/blog/introducing-flan-more-generalizable-language-models-with-instruction-fine-tuning/.

[24] Training a Helpful and Harmless Assistant with Reinforcement Learning from Human Feedback. https://arxiv.org/abs/2204.05862.

[25] Proximal Policy Optimization Algorithms. https://arxiv.org/abs/1707.06347.

[26] Direct Preference Optimization: Your Language Model is Secretly a Reward Model. https://arxiv.org/abs/2305.18290.

[27] Illustrating RLHF. https://huggingface.co/blog/rlhf.

[28] RLHF Progress and Challenges. https://www.youtube.com/watch?v=hhiLw5Q_UFg.

[29] State of GPT. https://www.youtube.com/watch?v=bZQun8Y4L2A.

[30] Different Sampling Methods. https://huggingface.co/blog/how-to-generate.

[31] The Curious Case of Neural Text Degeneration. https://arxiv.org/abs/1904.09751.

[32] OpenAI's API Reference. https://platform.openai.com/docs/api-reference/chat/create.

[33] Cheat Sheet: Mastering Temperature and Top_p in ChatGPT API. https://community.openai.com/t/cheat-sheet-mastering-temperature-and-top-p-in-chatgpt-api/172683.

[34] PIQA: Reasoning about Physical Commonsense in Natural Language. https://arxiv.org/abs/1911.11641.

[35] SocialIQA: Commonsense Reasoning about Social Interactions. https://arxiv.org/abs/1904.09728.

[36] HellaSwag: Can a Machine Really Finish Your Sentence? https://arxiv.org/abs/1905.07830.

[37] WinoGrande: An Adversarial Winograd Schema Challenge at Scale. https://arxiv.org/abs/1907.10641.

[38] Can a Suit of Armor Conduct Electricity? A New Dataset for Open Book Question Answering. https://arxiv.org/abs/1809.02789.

[39] CommonsenseQA: A Question Answering Challenge Targeting Commonsense Knowledge. https://arxiv.org/abs/1811.00937.

[40] TriviaQA: A Large Scale Dataset for Reading Comprehension and Question Answering. https://nlp.cs.washington.edu/triviaqa/.

[41] The Natural Questions Dataset. https://ai.google.com/research/NaturalQuestions.

[42] SQuAD: 100,000+ Questions for Machine Comprehension of Text. https://arxiv.org/abs/1606.05250.

[43] QuAC Dataset. https://quac.ai/.

[44] BoolQ: Exploring the Surprising Difficulty of Natural Yes/No Questions. https://arxiv.org/abs/1905.10044.

[45] GSM8K Dataset. https://github.com/openai/grade-school-math.

[46] MATH Dataset. https://github.com/hendrycks/math/.

[47] HumanEval Dataset. https://github.com/openai/human-eval.

[48] MBPP Dataset. https://github.com/google-research/google-research/tree/master/mbpp.

[49] Measuring Massive Multitask Language Understanding. https://arxiv.org/abs/2009.03300.

[50] Measuring Massive Multitask Language Understanding. https://arxiv.org/abs/2009.03300.

[51] AGIEval: A Human-Centric Benchmark for Evaluating Foundation Models. https://arxiv.org/abs/2304.06364.

[52] RealToxicityPrompts: Evaluating Neural Toxic Degeneration in Language Models. https://arxiv.org/abs/2009.11462.

[53] Perspective API. https://perspectiveapi.com/.

[54] ToxiGen: A Large-Scale Machine-Generated Dataset for Adversarial and Implicit Hate Speech Detection. https://arxiv.org/abs/2203.09509.

[55] HateCheck: Functional Tests for Hate Speech Detection Models. https://arxiv.org/abs/2012.15606.

[56] CrowS-Pairs: A Challenge Dataset for Measuring Social Biases in Masked Language Models. https://arxiv.org/abs/2010.00133.

[57] BBQ: A Hand-Built Bias Benchmark for Question Answering. https://arxiv.org/abs/2110.08193.

[58] BOLD: Dataset and Metrics for Measuring Biases in Open-Ended Language Generation. https://arxiv.org/abs/2101.11718.

[59] TruthfulQA: Measuring How Models Mimic Human Falsehoods. https://arxiv.org/abs/2109.07958.

[60] Question Answering for Privacy Policies: Combining Computational and Legal Perspectives. https://arxiv.org/abs/1911.00841.

[61] AdvGLUE Benchmark. https://adversarialglue.github.io/.

[62] Is BERT Really Robust? A Strong Baseline for Natural Language Attack on Text Classification and Entailment. https://arxiv.org/abs/1907.11932.

[63] AdvBench. https://github.com/llm-attacks/llm-attacks.

[64] Chatbot Arena Leaderboard. https://lmsys-chatbot-arena-leaderboard.hf.space/.

[65] A Survey on Recent Advances in LLM-Based Multi-Turn Dialogue Systems. https://arxiv.org/abs/2402.18013.

[66] Better & Faster Large Language Models via Multi-Token Prediction. https://arxiv.org/abs/2404.19737.

[67] Gemini 1.5: Unlocking Multimodal Understanding Across Millions of Tokens of Context. https://arxiv.org/abs/2403.05530.

[68] HyperAttention: Long-Context Attention in Near-Linear Time. https://arxiv.org/abs/2310.05869.

[69] MM-LLMs: Recent Advances in Multimodal Large Language Models. https://arxiv.org/abs/2401.13601.

[70] Multimodality and Large Multimodal Models. https://huyenchip.com/2023/10/10/multimodal.html.

[71] What is Retrieval-Augmented Generation? https://cloud.google.com/use-cases/retrieval-augmented-generation.

[72] How to Customize an LLM: A Deep Dive to Tailoring an LLM for Your Business. https://techcommunity.microsoft.com/t5/ai-machine-learning-blog/how-to-customize

-an-llm-a-deep-dive-to-tailoring-an-llm-for-your/ba-p/4110204.

[73] Llama 2: Open Foundation and Fine-Tuned Chat Models. https://arxiv.org/abs/2307.09288.

[74] Red Teaming Language Models to Reduce Harms: Methods, Scaling Behaviors, and Lessons Learned. https://arxiv.org/abs/2209.07858.

[75] Introducing Superalignment. https://openai.com/index/introducing-superalignment/.

[76] Language Models are Few-Shot Learners. https://arxiv.org/abs/2005.14165.

[77] GQA: Training Generalized Multi-Query Transformer Models from Multi-Head Checkpoints. https://arxiv.org/abs/2305.13245.

[78] Chain-of-Thought Prompting Elicits Reasoning in Large Language Models. https://arxiv.org/abs/2201.11903.

[79] Efficiently Scaling Transformer Inference. https://arxiv.org/abs/2211.05102.

[80] Prover-Verifier Games Improve Legibility of Language Model Outputs. https://openai.com/index/prover-verifier-games-improve-legibility/.

Image Captioning

Introduction

Image captioning is the process of generating text that describes an image. The generated text, also known as caption, should accurately reflect the image's content.

Image captioning has multiple applications. For example, on social media platforms, it automatically suggests image captions, saving time for content creators. In online retail, it generates captions for product images, thus improving the shopping experience.

Figure 5.1: Image captioning system suggests file names for an uploaded image

Beyond user-facing applications, image captioning is also used in systems that operate behind the scenes. For instance, in NSFW (Not Safe for Work) content moderation, image captioning systems can generate descriptive captions that help identify and flag inappropriate or explicit content by providing text-based interpretations of images. Additionally, image captioning can address the cold-start problem in recommendation systems, which occurs when a system lacks sufficient data on new users or items to make accurate recommendations. By generating descriptive captions, the system gains textual information that helps categorize and recommend new items based on their content.

In this chapter, we design a machine learning (ML) system that generates descriptive captions for images.

Clarifying Requirements

Here is a typical interaction between a candidate and an interviewer:

Candidate: There are various types of images, including general everyday images and domain-specific images such as medical imagery or technical diagrams. Can I focus on general everyday images?
Interviewer: Sure.

Candidate: Are there any specific applications or use cases we are targeting with this system?
Interviewer: We are targeting name suggestions to designers when they upload their assets.

Candidate: Since the image captioner will be used for asset name suggestions, the captions should not be too long and detailed. Is this a fair assumption?
Interviewer: Makes sense. The captions should be short, but descriptive and clear.

Candidate: Should the system support multiple languages, or will it focus only on English?
Interviewer: Let's focus on English only.

Candidate: What is the estimated size and diversity of the dataset?
Interviewer: We have access to a large dataset with 400 million image–caption pairs focused on everyday images.

Candidate: Does the dataset consist solely of English captions?
Interviewer: The dataset is not preprocessed. There might be captions in different languages, and some captions might be noisy or inaccurate. Additionally, captions for some images may be missing.

Candidate: Is real-time captioning required?
Interviewer: The system should generate a caption quickly, though real-time speed is not necessary. A latency of 1–2 seconds is acceptable.

Candidate: How should the system handle images with ambiguous content or unclear focus?
Interviewer: In such cases, the system should skip suggesting a caption.

Candidate: I assume the system should avoid generating biased captions or captions with offensive words. Is that a fair assumption?
Interviewer: Great point. Yes, it is crucial to ensure our system remains fair and safe for users.

Candidate: What are the typical image dimensions? Very small images can be unclear, leading to incorrect captions.
Interviewer: Let's assume the system only suggests names for images with a minimum

resolution of 256 x 256 pixels.

Frame the Problem as an ML Task

Specifying the system's input and output

The input to an image captioning system is an image. This image is processed by the model to generate a descriptive caption. The output, therefore, is a text that accurately describes the content of the image.

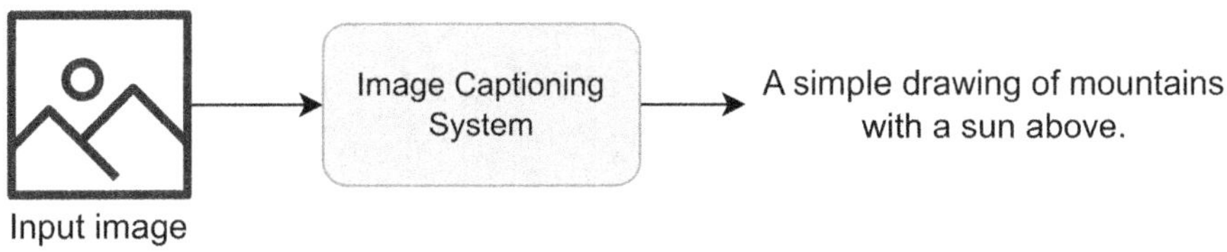

Figure 5.2: Input and output of an image captioning system

Choosing a suitable ML approach

The image captioning problem introduces a unique challenge: an ML model requires visual understanding to process the input image, language understanding to generate a caption, and the ability to bridge the gap between visual and textual modalities. This requires developing a multi-modal system.

A common approach to building multi-modal systems is to use an encoder-decoder framework. Similar to language translation—where we utilized an encoder-decoder architecture—we treat the image as a new "language" in this context. Specifically, we employ two main components, each handling one modality:

- Image encoder
- Text decoder

Image encoder

The image encoder is responsible for understanding the visual content of the image and encoding the image into a lower-dimensional representation.

Text decoder

The text decoder uses the encoded visual information from the image encoder to generate a descriptive caption.

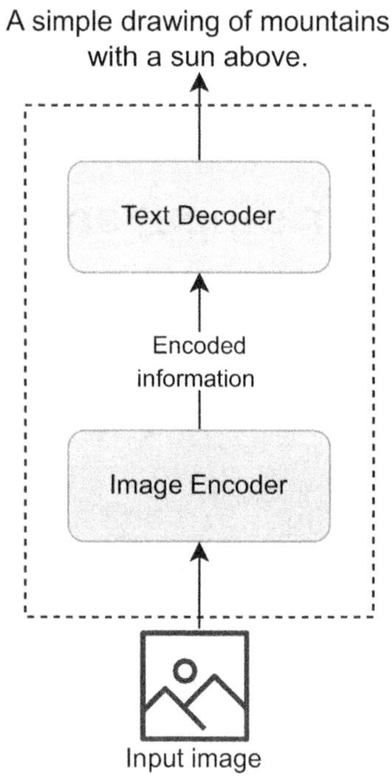

Figure 5.3: Image captioning components

We will explore the architecture of these components in detail in the model development section. It's important to note that there are various approaches to tackling the image captioning problem. While we focus on the encoder-decoder framework here, alternative models such as BLIP-2 [1], BLIP-3 [2], and InternVL [3] offer different techniques and architectures for generating captions. If you're interested in these other methods, you can refer to [1, 2, 3] for a broader understanding of the image captioning landscape.

Data Preparation

In this section, we prepare the dataset to train our image captioning system.

Image	Caption
	A simple drawing of mountains with a sun above.
	A minimalistic flower icon.
...	...

Figure 5.4: Example of image–caption dataset

The dataset comprises 400 million pairs of images and captions. However, not all images or captions are suitable for training. Let's examine data preparation for captions and images separately.

Caption preparation

Raw captions are often noisy and not in a format that is usable by the ML model. During caption preparation, we remove inappropriate captions and ensure the remaining ones are consistent and tokenized. In particular, we perform the following steps:

- **Remove pairs with a non-English caption:** We remove image–caption pairs where the caption is not in English, as this model's focus will be on English.
- **Remove duplicate images or captions:** To ensure the diversity and quality of the training data, we eliminate duplicate images and captions. Duplicate images are identified using perceptual hashing techniques or image similarity models (e.g., CLIP image encoder), while duplicate captions are detected by exact match or semantic similarity checks (e.g., CLIP text encoder). Removing duplicates prevents the model from overfitting to redundant data and helps it learn a broader range of associations between images and text.
- **Remove irrelevant captions:** We use a pretrained vision–language model (e.g., CLIP) to assess the relevance between images and their corresponding captions. A higher score usually indicates greater semantic relevance between the image and the text. We remove pairs with scores below a specific threshold, such as 0.25. This ensures our model learns from high-quality, relevant pairs. For more information on how CLIP scores the relevance between text and images, refer to Chapter 9.
- **Summarize long captions:** Captions are often long and detailed. Training the model with these captions leads to the generation of similarly long captions, which doesn't suit our use case. To address this, we summarize the captions using a large language model such as Llama [4] to create brief, concise descriptions that meet our requirements.
- **Tokenize captions:** We use a subword-level tokenization algorithm such as Byte-Pair Encoding (BPE) [5] to tokenize captions into a sequence of IDs. For a detailed review of text tokenization methods and the BPE algorithm, refer to Chapter 2 and Chapter 3.

Image preparation

As is the case for captions, not all images are useful. We remove images that might hurt training and ensure the remaining images are consistent and suitable for the model training. In particular, we perform the following steps:

- **Remove low-resolution images:** We remove image–caption pairs in which the image resolution is less than 256×256 because such low-resolution images might not provide enough detail for accurate caption generation.

- **Normalize images:** We scale the pixel values to a normalized range, such as 0 to 1. This normalization makes the training process more stable.
- **Remove low-quality images:** To maintain high-quality training data, we filter images that exhibit conditions such as blurriness, overexposure, underexposure, or other defects that degrade visual clarity. Image quality assessment methods, such as the LAION Aesthetics Predictor [6], help identify and remove subpar images by scoring them on factors such as sharpness, contrast, and lighting.
- **Adjust image dimensions:** Images typically have a range of sizes and aspect ratios. We resize all images to a uniform size. This is critical since ML models require fixed-size inputs during training. When adjusting image dimensions to a uniform size, it is important to preserve their original aspect ratios. To do so, we often follow two steps:
  1. **Resizing:** First, we resize the image so that the smaller dimension matches the target size. For instance, if our target size is 256×256 and our original image is 512×768, we resize it to 256×384.
  2. **Center-cropping:** Next, we center-crop the resized image to the target dimensions. From our previous example, we center-crop the 256×384 image to 256×256.

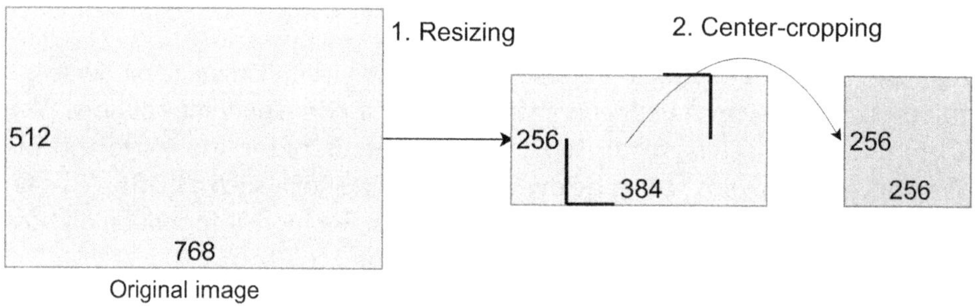

Figure 5.5: Resizing followed by center-cropping

This two-step method ensures our images maintain their aspect ratios and fit the required size for our ML model.

Model Development

Architecture

We framed image captioning as a multi-modal language generation task where the image encoder processes an input image, and the text decoder generates a descriptive caption. In this section, we explore the architecture of the image encoder and text decoder.

Image encoder

The image encoder is responsible for processing an image and encoding the information within it.

The output of the encoder plays a pivotal role in determining the quality and specificity of the generated captions. The encoder's output can be either a single token, representing the entire image as a single feature vector, or a sequence of tokens, where each token corresponds to a specific region or aspect of the image. The choice between these two approaches has significant implications for how effectively the system captures and represents the visual content, and research has explored both options to understand their strengths and limitations.

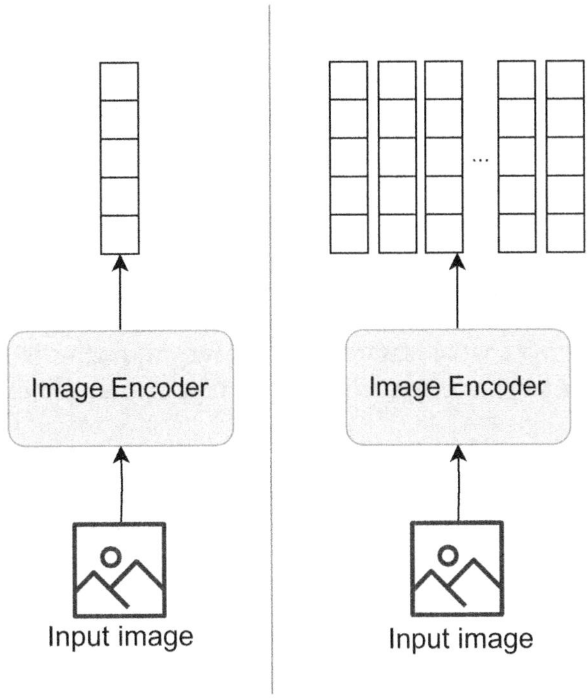

Figure 5.6: Image encoder outputting single token vs. sequence of tokens

When the encoder produces a single token as its output, it effectively compresses the entire image into one vector. This vector serves as a summary of the image, encapsulating its global features and overall context. The primary advantage of this approach lies in its simplicity; the architecture remains straightforward, with reduced computational complexity and lower resource requirements. A single vector emphasizes the overall content of the image, which can be particularly beneficial for generating concise and high-level captions that capture the general essence of the scene. However, this approach also has notable downsides. Condensing all visual information into one vector often means the loss of local details and specific nuances, which are crucial for generating descriptive and contextually rich captions. As a result, captions generated from single-token outputs may lean toward being more generic and may struggle with complex images that require detailed representation.

On the other hand, producing a sequence of tokens from the encoder allows the system to capture a more granular view of the image. Each token in the sequence corresponds to a distinct part or patch of the image, resulting in a richer and more comprehensive representation that includes both global and local features. This approach aligns particularly well with the attention mechanism, which is a cornerstone of modern generative models such as Transformers. The attention mechanism works best with sequence inputs, as it enables the decoder to focus dynamically on different regions of the image during caption generation. This capability of selectively attending to various parts of the image leads to more accurate, relevant, and detailed captions. By using a sequence of tokens, the model can generate captions that are not only more descriptive but also better aligned with the specific objects, actions, and contexts present in the image.

The image encoder architectures can be divided into the following:

- CNN-based
- Transformer-based

CNN-based

Convolutional Neural Networks (CNNs) are traditionally used for image-encoding tasks. CNNs excel at capturing spatial hierarchies in images through the use of convolutional filters. These filters detect patterns such as edges, textures, and objects at different scales.

CNN-based encoders process the input image and output a grid of feature vectors. For example, as shown in Figure 5.7, an input image passes through the CNN, producing a feature vector of size 3 x 3 x c. Here, c represents the channel size, which depends on the CNN architecture. While the CNN produces a 3 x 3 x c output, the Transformer in the text decoder needs a sequence of features (i.e., 9 x c). To achieve this, we use a flattening or reshaping operation that reorganizes the features from each of the nine positions in the 3 x 3 grid into a sequential format.

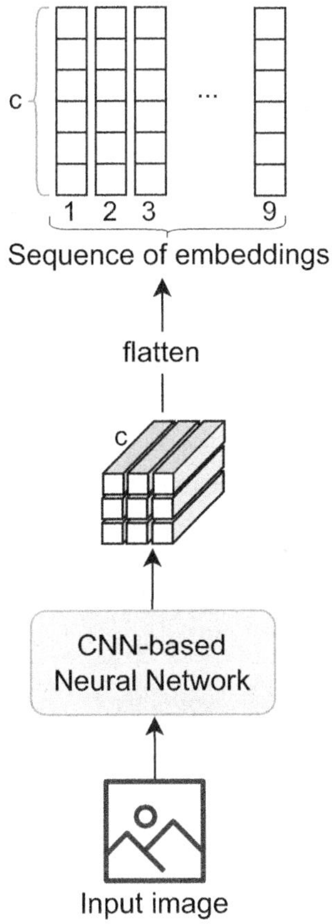

Figure 5.7: A CNN-based image encoding

Transformer-based

Transformer models, originally developed for natural language processing, have later been adapted for image encoding with significant success. In this architecture, a Transformer analyzes images, extracts features, and encodes them into a sequence of embeddings. Specifically, a Transformer-based image encoder consists of:

- Patchify
- Positional encoding
- Transformer

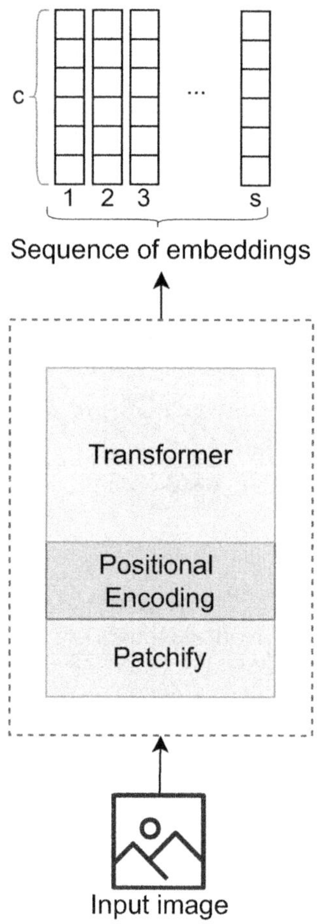

Figure 5.8: Transformer-based image encoding

Patchify

Since Transformers work with sequences, the image should first be converted into a sequence. This process involves three steps:

1. Divide the image into fixed-size patches
2. Flatten each patch
3. Linearly project each patch

For example, a 256 x 256 input image is divided into patches of 64 x 64. These patches are flattened into 4096-sized vectors and linearly projected into embedding vectors of size c, where c is the desired embedding size.

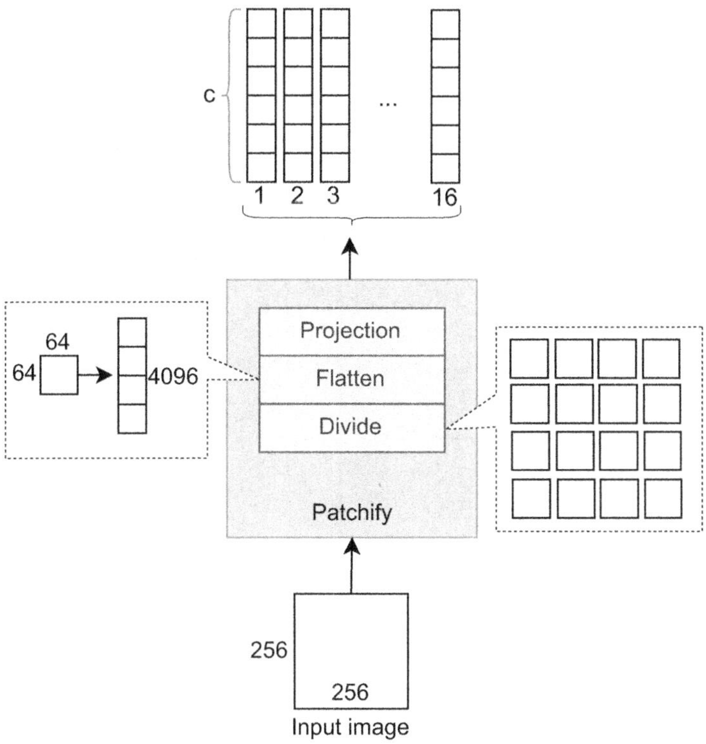

Figure 5.9: Patchification process

Positional encoding

Positional encoding assigns position information to each patch, specifying where each patch was located in the original image. This helps Transformers understand positions within the sequence.

Positional encoding can be implemented in various ways. Let's briefly explore the following variations:

- 1D vs. 2D positional encoding
- Learnable vs. fixed positional encoding

1D vs. 2D positional encoding

1D positional encoding employs a function that maps an integer (position in the sequence) to a c-dimensional vector, where c is usually the Transformer's hidden dimension. This is commonly used in text sequences, with each token receiving a positional vector based on its place. When applied to images, 1D positional encoding encodes the position of each patch in a flattened sequence, which might not capture the two-dimensional spatial relationships in images.

2D positional encoding, on the other hand, maps two integers—representing the row and column positions in the image grid—into a c-dimensional vector. This encoding method is more suitable for images as it preserves the spatial structure.

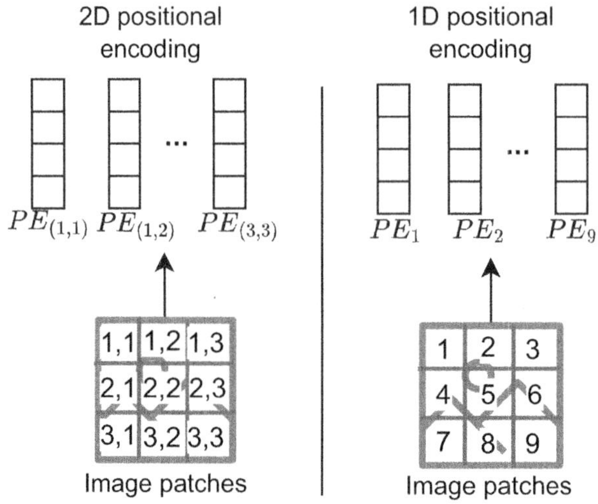

Figure 5.10: 1D vs. 2D positional encoding

Learnable vs. fixed positional encoding

In learnable positional encoding, the model learns positional encodings during training. A neural network maps positions (1D or 2D) to a c-dimensional vector. In the fixed approach, positional encodings are determined by a fixed function such as sine-cosine. For more details, refer to Chapter 2.

There is often no best solution when choosing between 1D vs. 2D and learnable vs. fixed positional encoding. While Vision Transformer (ViT) [7] uses learnable 1D positional encoding, in practice, we often test different combinations to see which works best for a specific task.

Which architecture is suitable for our image encoder?

CNNs are effective at capturing local patterns in images but they struggle with long-range dependencies between distant regions of the image. In contrast, Transformers capture both local and global relationships in the image using a self-attention mechanism. This allows Transformers to model complex dependencies, making them ideal for tasks that require detailed, context-aware image understanding, for example, generating descriptive captions. For these reasons, we follow the ViT [7] and choose Transformer-based architecture as our image encoder.

Text decoder

The text decoder is responsible for generating the caption. As we saw in previous chapters, a decoder-only Transformer is the standard choice for text generation. The input to the decoder-only Transformer is a sequence of vectors corresponding to the input image. Its output is the caption, generated one token at a time.

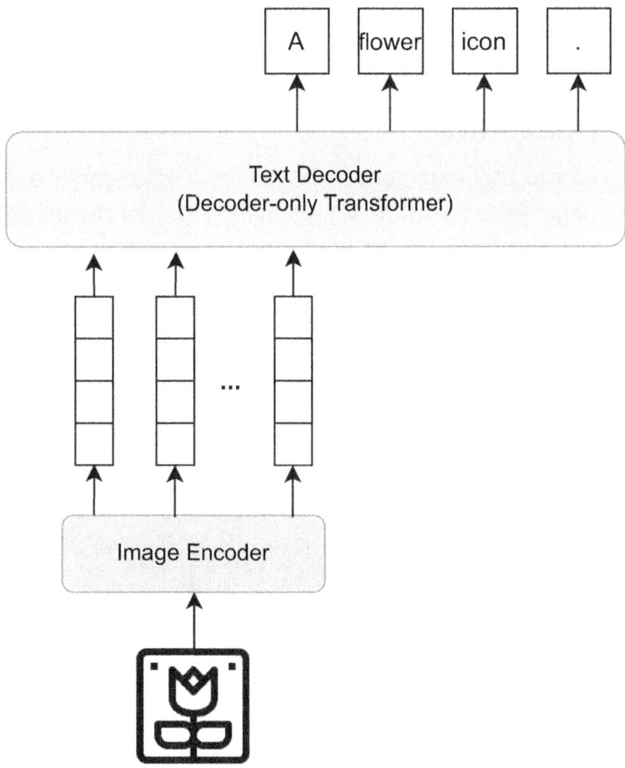

Figure 5.11: Providing image as a sequence of embeddings

Training

The training approach for the image captioning model is similar to the strategies discussed in previous chapters. We follow a two-stage training strategy:

1. Unsupervised pretraining
2. Supervised finetuning

1. Unsupervised pretraining

During this stage, the text decoder - which is a decoder-only Transformer - is trained on general data. The purpose of this stage is to develop a base model that has a broad understanding of language structure and is capable of generating coherent text. This knowledge is crucial for the model to perform well when it is later finetuned on a more specific task such as caption generation.

The pretraining stage is computationally expensive. It is common practice to use existing pretrained models to bypass this stage and, thus, significantly reduce computational costs. In this chapter, we use a pretrained decoder-only Transformer such as GPT-2 [8] or Llama [4].

Similarly, the image encoder can also be derived from pretrained models. Instead of training an image encoder from scratch, we can leverage powerful pretrained vision models such as CLIP [9] or ViT [7].

2. Supervised finetuning

In this stage, we train both the image encoder and the text decoder on 400 million image–caption pairs. The image encoder improves its ability to encode image information effectively, and the text decoder learns to understand the sequence of image embeddings and generate a descriptive caption.

ML objective and loss function

The text decoder generates the caption one token at a time. Consistent with previous chapters, we use next-token prediction as our ML objective and employ cross-entropy loss [10] to guide the training process.

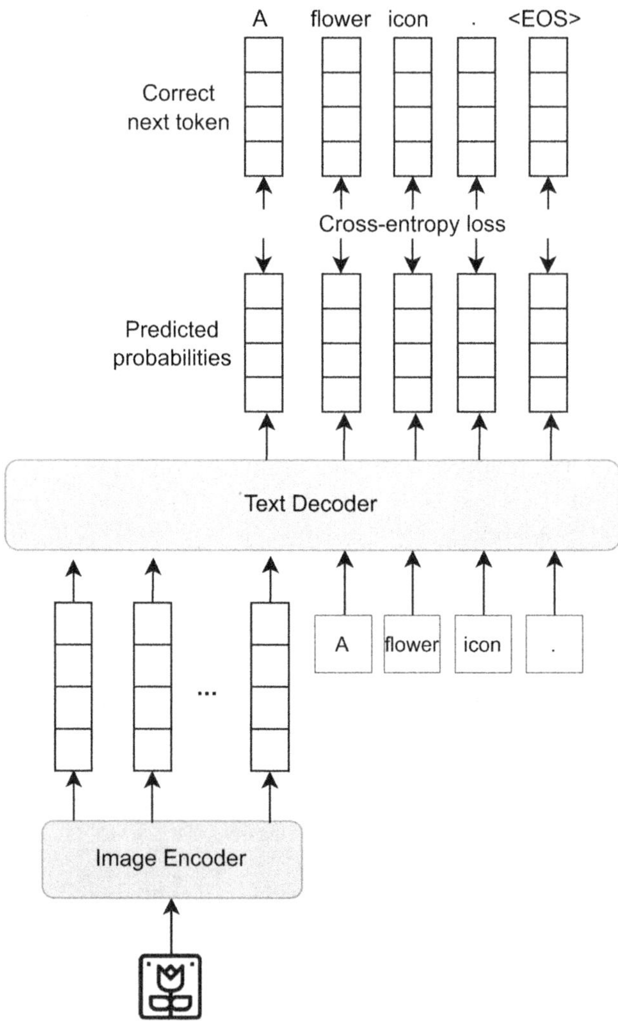

Figure 5.12: Loss calculation over the predicted probabilities

Sampling

During sampling, the caption tokens are generated one at a time.

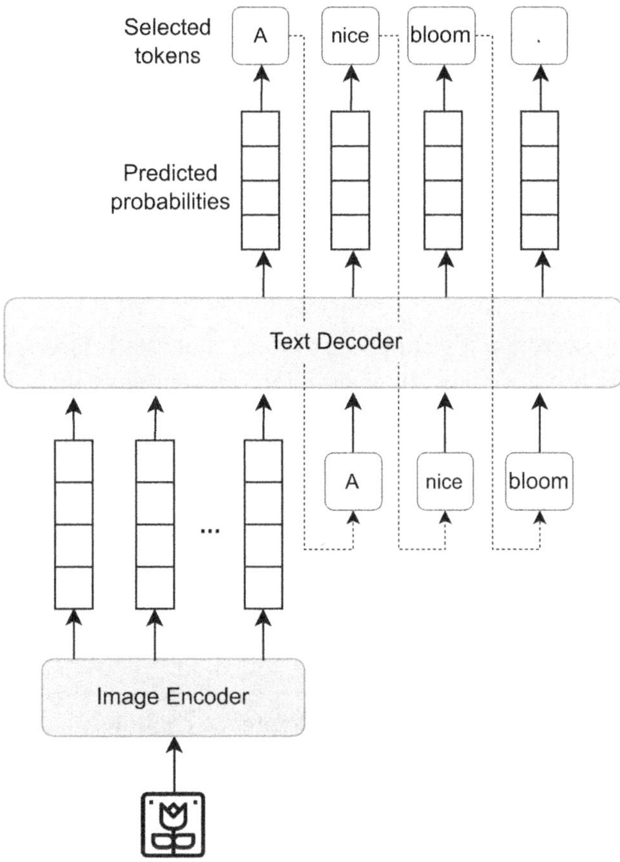

Figure 5.13: Generating a caption given an input image

While stochastic sampling methods can create creative captions, beam search ensures predictability. We use beam search for our image captioning system for the following reasons:

- **Quality:** Beam search typically generates higher-quality captions, which is critical for accurately describing image content.
- **Consistency:** The deterministic nature of beam search ensures that the model always produces the same caption for the same image. This consistency is crucial for image captioning.
- **Coherence:** Beam search typically produces coherent captions, which is important for image captioning. This avoids sudden topic changes or contradictions such as "A person is walking house" or "A dog is reading a person."

Evaluation

Offline evaluation metrics

During offline evaluation, we assess the performance of the trained model on a validation dataset. This is achieved by comparing generated captions with reference (i.e., correct) captions and measuring their similarity.

Before exploring common metrics, let's review validation data. Validation data contains examples not seen by the model during training. Each example includes an image and a set of reference captions. These captions are typically collected by having multiple human annotators describe each image.

In image captioning systems, it's common to have multiple reference captions for each image. This benefits both training and evaluation for the following reasons:

- **Robust training:** Different people describe the same image in different ways. Multiple references allow the model to learn different ways of describing an image. This leads to a more robust model that is capable of describing images more accurately.
- **Comprehensive evaluation:** Multiple captions provide a more thorough assessment of a model's performance. Comparing the generated caption to several correct reference captions leads to a fairer evaluation.

Image	Reference captions
	Blooming tulip with green leaves
	Close-up of a blooming tulip.
	Single tulip with leaves.

Figure 5.14: An example of validation data

The following metrics are commonly used in the offline evaluation of image captioning models:

- BLEU
- ROUGE
- METEOR
- CIDEr

The first three metrics on the list are explored extensively in Chapter 3. In this chapter, we focus on CIDEr, which has been designed specifically to evaluate image captioning models.

CIDEr

CIDEr [11] is a popular metric for evaluating image captioning models. It uses consensus to evaluate the similarity of a generated caption to a set of reference captions. CIDEr gives higher scores to captions that are similar to multiple reference captions rather than just one. For a single example, CIDEr is calculated in three steps:

1. Represent captions using TF-IDF
2. Calculate similarities
3. Aggregate the similarity scores

1. Represent captions using TF-IDF

In the first step, we convert the generated caption and each reference caption into numerical representations using TF-IDF. TF-IDF evaluates a word's importance to a document by considering how frequently it appears in that document and how common or rare it is across the entire corpus. These importance scores are used to represent a sentence numerically. To learn more about TF-IDF, refer to [12, 13].

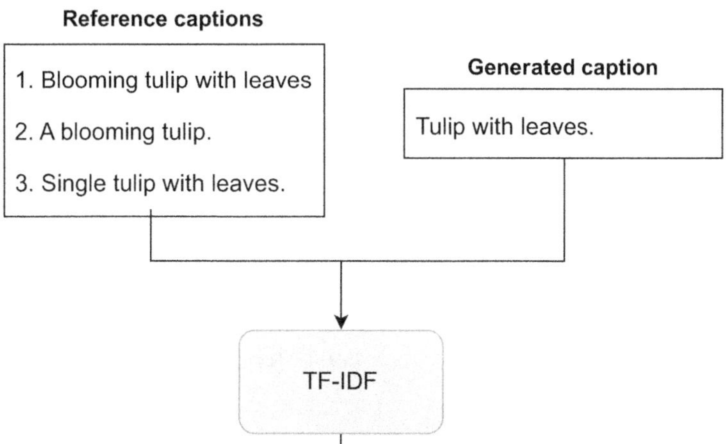

	a	blooming	leaves	single	tulip	leaves
Ref 1: "Blooming tulip with leaves"	0.00	0.52	0.43	0.00	0.36	0.43
Ref 2: "A blooming tulip"	0.70	0.50	0.00	0.00	0.50	0.00
Ref 3: "Single tulip with leaves"	0.00	0.00	0.57	0.57	0.34	0.57
Generated: "Tulip with leaves"	0.00	0.00	0.70	0.00	0.50	0.50

Figure 5.15: TF-IDF converting captions to numerical representations

2. Calculate similarity

Next, we calculate the similarity between the generated caption and each reference caption. We do this by computing the cosine similarity between their TF-IDF representations.

	a	blooming	leaves	single	tulip	leaves
Ref 1: "Blooming tulip with leaves"	0.00	0.52	0.43	0.00	0.36	0.43
Ref 2: "A blooming tulip"	0.70	0.50	0.00	0.00	0.50	0.00
Ref 3: "Single tulip with leaves"	0.00	0.00	0.57	0.57	0.34	0.57
Generated: "Tulip with leaves"	0.00	0.00	0.70	0.00	0.50	0.50

Similarity Calculation

Pair	Cosine similarity score
<Reference 1, Generated>	0.688
<Reference 2, Generated>	0.257
<Reference 3, Generated>	0.766

Figure 5.16: Calculation of cosine similarity between generated and reference captions

A higher cosine similarity score (i.e., a score closer to 1) indicates greater similarity, while a lower value (closer to 0) indicates lesser similarity.

3. Aggregate the similarity scores

Once we have the cosine similarity scores between the generated caption and each of the reference captions, we take an average of these scores. This average score reflects the overall similarity between the generated caption and the reference captions.

$$CIDER_i = \frac{0.688 + 0.257 + 0.766}{3} = 0.570$$

The final CIDEr score is calculated by averaging the similarity scores for all generated captions in the validation dataset. This provides a single metric to evaluate the model's overall performance.

Let's see some of the pros and cons of the CIDEr metric.

Pros:

- **Consensus-based:** CIDEr emphasizes consensus by rewarding captions that are similar to multiple reference captions. This leads to a more reliable evaluation of a model's performance.
- **Sensitive to important words:** TF-IDF assigns more weight to unique words in their representation. This ensures that the CIDEr score reflects the importance of words and rewards captions that use those words.
- **Robust to different caption variations:** CIDEr is robust to different variations of generations since it is calculated based on multiple reference captions.

Cons:

- **Computationally complex:** Calculating TF-IDF representations in large datasets can be computationally expensive.
- **Sensitive to the quality of reference captions:** The quality and diversity of reference captions impact the CIDEr score. Poor references can lead to misleading evaluations.
- **Penalizes novel yet accurate captions:** CIDEr may penalize creative or novel phrases that are still accurate but are not present in the reference set.
- **Lack of semantic understanding:** CIDEr relies on TF-IDF to measure the similarity between two sentences. This might not always capture the semantic similarity when captions are textually similar but semantically different. For example, "Coffee on top of the table" and "Table on top of the coffee" might have similar TF-IDF representations due to similar words, but they are not semantically similar.

Online evaluation metrics

Online evaluation metrics are important for assessing the performance of ML systems. However, they are often not the primary focus in image captioning systems for two main reasons. First, image captioning systems are usually part of a bigger system, making it harder to collect user interaction data. Second, collecting feedback from users is challenging. Unlike tasks where we can easily measure user satisfaction, evaluating image caption quality requires subjective judgment, which, by definition, varies between users. For example, a caption might be acceptable to one user but not to another, depending on their personal interpretation of the image.

In summary, standard offline metrics remain the primary method for evaluating our image captioning system. For the few use cases where image captioning impacts user experience directly, engagement metrics and user feedback can provide valuable insights into the system's performance.

Overall ML System Design

Building an image captioning system is more than just training a model. It requires various components working together. In this section, we discuss the following key components essential for building an image captioning system:

- Image preprocessing
- Caption generator
- Post-processing

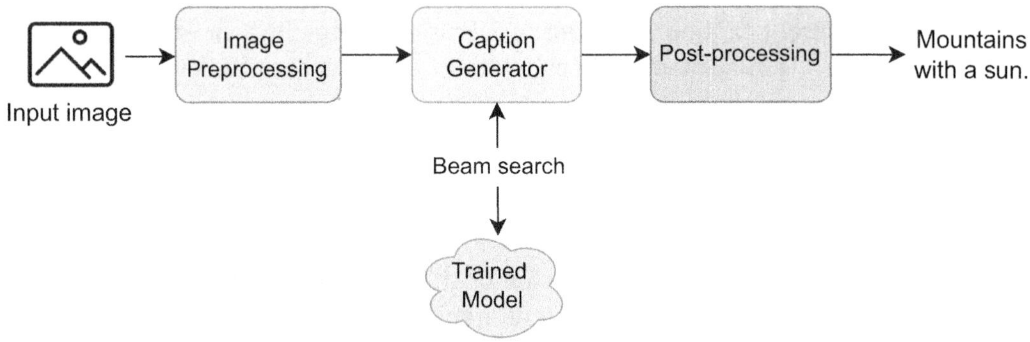

Figure 5.17: Image captioning overall design

Let's briefly explore each component and understand its role.

Image preprocessing

Image preprocessing is the initial step that prepares an input image for the trained model. This involves resizing images to a standard size, converting them into a consistent format, and standardizing pixel values. This step ensures that images are consistent with what the model expects as input.

Caption generator

The caption generator is the core component that produces captions based on the prepared image. This component interacts with the trained model and employs beam search to generate a coherent caption. If the cumulative probability of the generated caption falls below a predefined confidence threshold, the name suggestion is disabled; otherwise, the caption is passed to the post-processing component. This ensures that the system avoids producing irrelevant captions for ambiguous images.

Post-processing

The post-processing component identifies biased terms or phrases in the caption and replaces them with neutral alternatives. This ensures fairness and inclusivity in generated captions. Additionally, it checks for the presence of offensive words and disables the name suggestion service if any are found.

Other Talking Points

If the interview finishes early, you might want to bring up the following topics:

- Extending the image captioner to support other tasks, such as visual question answering (VQA) [14].
- Adapting models to caption images from various domains [15].
- Generating captions in multiple languages using multilingual datasets and cross-lingual transfer learning [16].
- Optimization techniques for caption generation on edge devices [17].
- Generating and ranking multiple plausible captions based on relevance [18].
- Details of BLIP-2 and BLIP-3 methods and additional loss functions utilized for improving captioning [1, 2].

Summary

Summary
Clarifying requirements
Framing as ML
Specifying input and output
ML approach
Image encoder
Text decoder
Data preparation
Text
Removing non-English captions
Removing duplicates
Removing irrelevant captions
Summarizing captions
BPE tokenization
Image
Removing low-res images
Normalizing image pixels
Removing low-quality images
Adjusting image dimensions
Model development
Architecture
Image Encoder
CNN-based
Transformer-based
Patchify
Positional Encoding
Transformer
Text Decoder
Decoder-only Transformer
Training
Unsupervised pretraining
General data
Next-token prediction
Supervised finetuning
Image-caption data
Next token prediction
Sampling
Beam search
Evaluation
Offline
BLEU
ROUGE
METEOR
CIDEr
Online
Overall system components
Image preprocessing
Caption generator
Post-processing
Other talking points

Reference Material

[1] BLIP-2: Bootstrapping Language-Image Pre-training with Frozen Image Encoders and Large Language Models. https://arxiv.org/abs/2301.12597.

[2] xGen-MM (BLIP-3): A Family of Open Large Multimodal Models. https://www.arxiv.org/abs/2408.08872.

[3] InternVL: Scaling Up Vision Foundation Models and Aligning for Generic Visual-Linguistic Tasks. https://arxiv.org/abs/2312.14238.

[4] Meta's Llama. https://llama.meta.com/.

[5] Byte-Pair Encoding Tokenization. https://huggingface.co/learn/nlp-course/en/chapter6/5.

[6] LAION-5B: An Open Large-Scale Dataset for Training Next Generation Image-Text Models. https://arxiv.org/abs/2210.08402.

[7] An Image is Worth 16x16 Words: Transformers for Image Recognition at Scale. https://arxiv.org/abs/2010.11929.

[8] Language Models are Unsupervised Multitask Learners. https://cdn.openai.com/better-language-models/language_models_are_unsupervised_multitask_learners.pdf.

[9] Learning Transferable Visual Models From Natural Language Supervision. https://arxiv.org/abs/2103.00020.

[10] Cross-Entropy. https://en.wikipedia.org/wiki/Cross-entropy.

[11] CIDEr: Consensus-Based Image Description Evaluation. https://arxiv.org/abs/1411.5726.

[12] TF-IDF Introduction. https://web.stanford.edu/class/cs276/19handouts/lecture6-tfidf-1per.pdf.

[13] TF-IDF. https://en.wikipedia.org/wiki/Tf%E2%80%93idf.

[14] Visual Question Answering Introduction. https://huggingface.co/tasks/visual-question-answering.

[15] Cross-Domain Image Captioning with Discriminative Finetuning. https://arxiv.org/abs/2304.01662.

[16] Crossmodal-3600 — Multilingual Reference Captions for Geographically Diverse Images. https://research.google/blog/crossmodal-3600-multilingual-reference-captions-for-geographically-diverse-images/.

[17] Efficient Image Captioning for Edge Devices. https://arxiv.org/abs/2212.08985.

[18] Ensemble Model Using an Image Captioning and Ranking Example. https://cloud.google.com/dataflow/docs/notebooks/run_inference_multi_model.

6

Retrieval-Augmented Generation

Introduction

In Chapter 4, we developed a chatbot capable of answering open-domain questions. However, many applications need access to additional information, such as company databases (e.g., internal documentation), real-time data (e.g., sports scores), or user-provided files (e.g., uploaded PDFs).

Allowing chatbots to access this information improves the accuracy and relevance of their responses, especially for fact-based or specialized tasks. A real-world example of such a system is *Perplexity.ai* [1], an AI-powered conversational search engine that uses web-based information to respond to user queries.

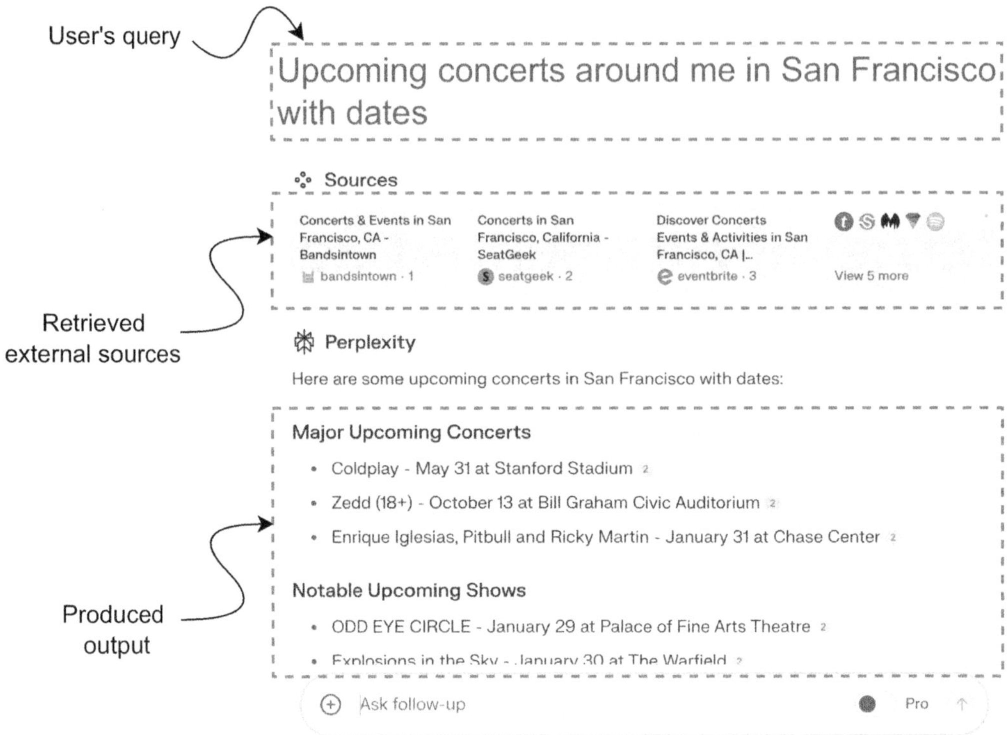

Figure 6.1: Perplexity's output based on real-time information (Credit: [1])

In this chapter, we build a system similar to ChatPDF [2] that answers employee questions using internal company documents. Instead of reading FAQs, employees can ask the chatbot directly and receive answers based on those documents.

Clarifying Requirements

Here is a typical interaction between a candidate and an interviewer:

Candidate: What does the external knowledge base consist of? Does it change over time?
Interviewer: The knowledge base includes company Wiki pages and a company-wide "Stack Overflow"-style forum. The documentation does change, but at a slower pace compared to real-time updates.

Candidate: Do the Wiki pages and forums contain text, images, and other modalities?
Interviewer: Assume each page is in PDF format and contains text, tables, and diagrams. For simplicity, other modalities do not need to be considered.

Candidate: Do the pages follow a fixed format or template?
Interviewer: No, the formats vary. Some are double-columned, some are single-columned, and others are mixed.

Candidate: How many pages are there in total?
Interviewer: We have around 5 million pages.

Candidate: Is it necessary for the system to include document references?
Interviewer: Yes.

Candidate: Should the system respond in real time?
Interviewer: Users can tolerate a slight delay of a few seconds.

Candidate: Does the system need to support multiple languages?
Interviewer: To keep things simple, let's stick to English.

Candidate: Should the system support user feedback or follow-up questions?
Interviewer: Not initially. However, your design should be flexible enough to add support for feedback loops or follow-up questions.

Candidate: What is the expected growth in documents?
Interviewer: The document base is expected to grow by twenty percent annually.

Candidate: Do we need to address safety concerns, such as preventing harmful, biased, or misleading outputs?
Interviewer: Safety matters, but let's prioritize data handling, architecture, and performance efficiency.

Frame the Problem as an ML Task

Specifying the system's input and output

The input to the ChatPDF system is a text prompt provided by the user. The model processes this prompt alongside a continuously updated document database containing both text and images. The output is a text-based response that accurately addresses the user's query.

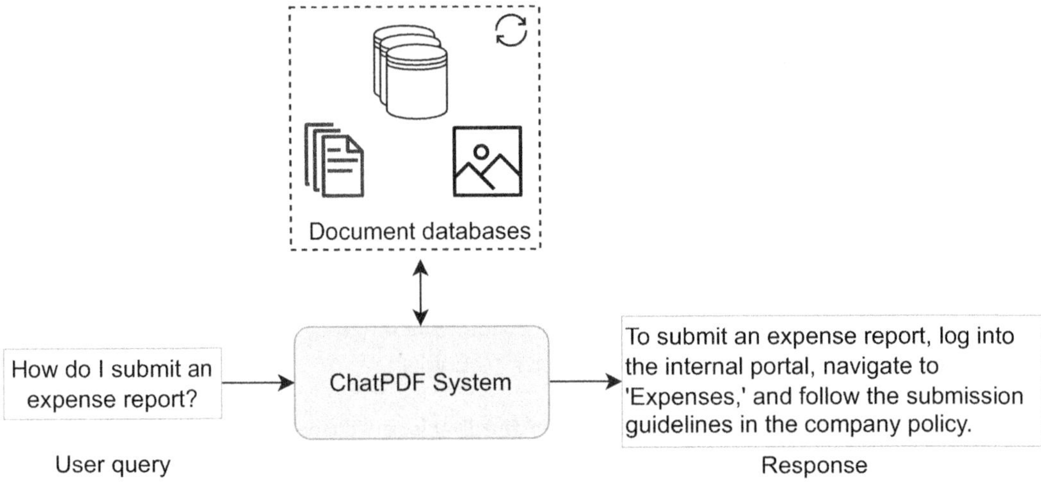

Figure 6.2: Input and output of a ChatPDF system

Choosing a suitable ML approach

Given the nature of the task, large language models (LLMs) are well-suited for text generation and are often the default choice. However, general-purpose LLMs may struggle with specific domains and, therefore, may need customization to handle external data sources. To enable an LLM to answer queries based on company-specific data, there are three main approaches:

- Finetuning
- Prompt engineering
- Retrieval-augmented generation (RAG)

Let's explore each one in detail and discuss their trade-offs.

Finetuning

In this approach, a pretrained general-purpose LLM is finetuned on company-specific data, such as internal documents. By updating its weights, the LLM adapts to better understand the company's unique terminology, processes, and FAQs. Chapter 10 will explore advanced finetuning techniques such as LoRA [3] to adapt large models to specific data.

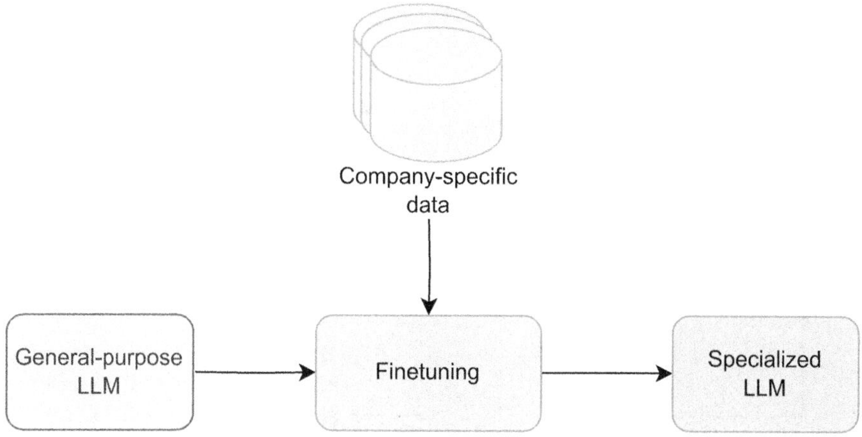

Figure 6.3: Finetuning approach

Pros:

- **Customizable:** Finetuning allows the model to generate responses tailored to specific domains.
- **Enhanced accuracy:** By finetuning the model on specialized data, it becomes more accurate and better able to handle niche topics.

Cons:

- **Computationally expensive:** Updating the entire model's parameters requires a lot of computational resources, which can be expensive.
- **Frequent retraining:** This approach requires frequent finetuning to continuously incorporate up-to-date data into the model.
- **Requires technical expertise:** This approach requires an understanding of ML principles and language model architectures, which can be a barrier for those without specialized knowledge.
- **Extensive data requirement:** Finetuning requires a substantial, high-quality dataset, which can be difficult and time-consuming to collect.
- **Lack of references:** Finetuned models usually can't provide references for their answers, making it hard to verify or trace information back to its source.

Prompt Engineering

Prompt engineering guides a general-purpose LLM to produce specific outputs through carefully designed prompts. Unlike finetuning, this method keeps the underlying LLM unchanged and includes relevant information, such as company data or instructions, directly in the prompts to control the model's behavior. For example, a prompt might include information such as the summary of company policies, as shown in Figure 6.4. Later in this chapter, we will explore more advanced prompt engineering techniques, such as few-shot and chain-of-thought prompting.

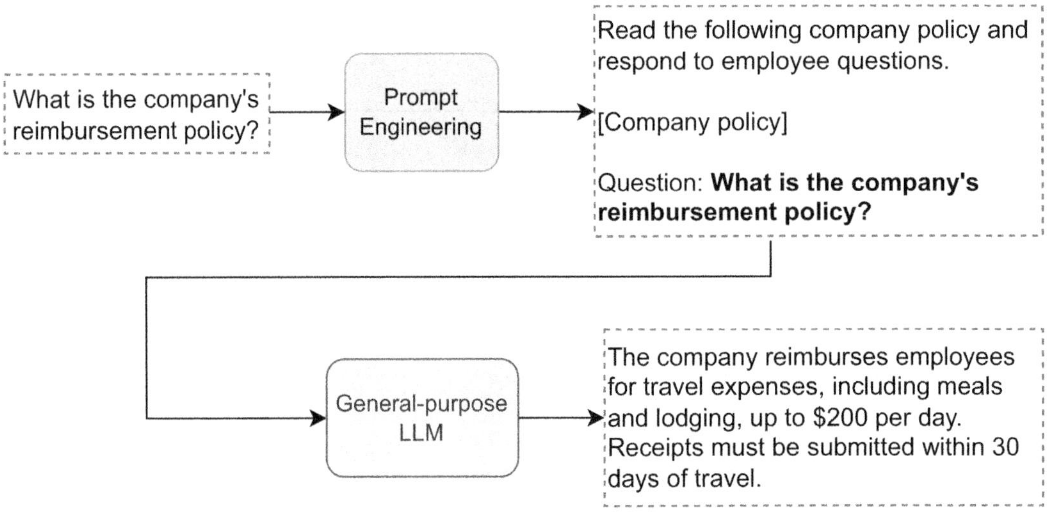

Figure 6.4: Prompt engineering approach

Pros:

- **Ease of use:** The prompt engineering is simple to use and requires no technical skills, which makes it suitable for a wide range of users.
- **Cost-effectiveness:** By leveraging a pretrained LLM, prompting incurs minimal computational costs compared to finetuning.
- **Flexibility:** Prompts can be easily modified to experiment with different outputs without having to retrain the model.

Cons:

- **Inconsistency:** The quality and relevance of responses can vary greatly depending on how the prompt is phrased.
- **Limited customization:** The ability to tailor responses is limited to the effectiveness and creativity of the prompt design. Prompt engineering lacks the depth of customization that finetuning provides.
- **Limited to LLM's existing knowledge:** Outputs are confined to the information the LLM was initially trained on, making it less effective for highly specialized domains or providing responses based on the most current information.

RAG

RAG is an advanced method that combines the capabilities of a general-purpose LLM with a real-time retrieval system. Instead of relying solely on the LLM's pretrained knowledge, RAG retrieves relevant information from external sources, such as a company's internal documents, and feeds it into the LLM during inference. This approach ensures the LLM generates responses that are both relevant and accurate based on the available information.

A RAG system, as shown in Figure 6.5, has two components:

- **Retrieval:** The retrieval component takes the user's original prompt, finds the most relevant information from external sources, and returns it as context.
- **Generation:** Typically, a general-purpose LLM uses the user's prompt and the retrieved information to generate a response.

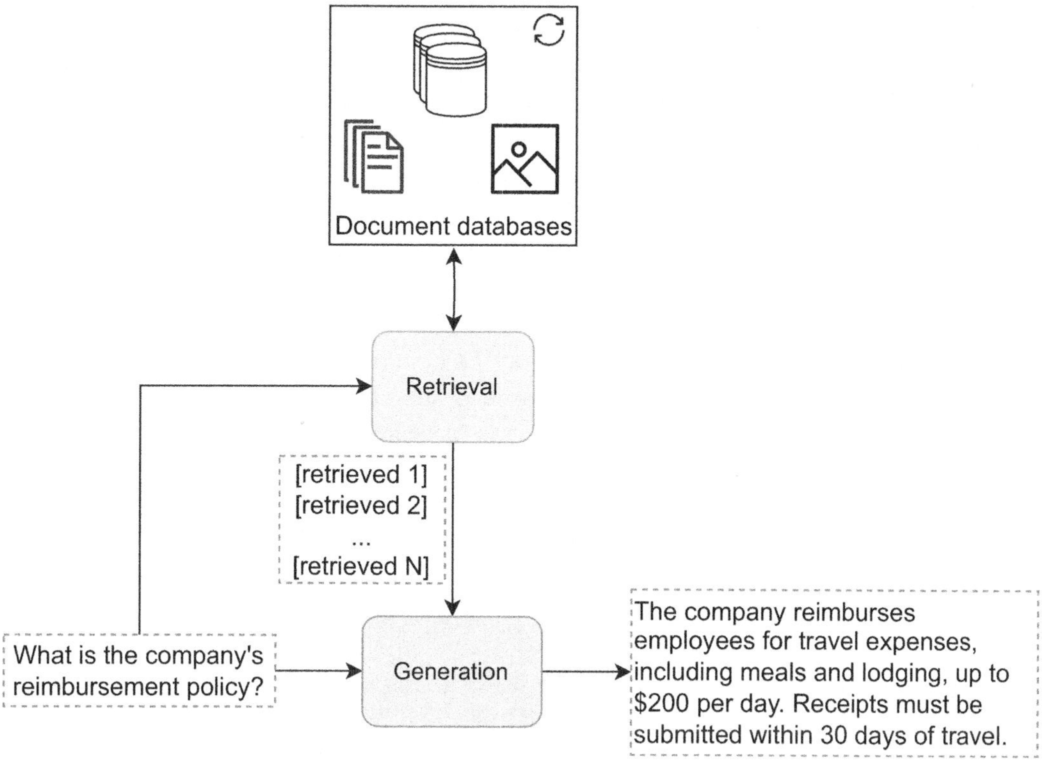

Figure 6.5: Components of a RAG system

Pros:

- **Access to most current information:** RAG can provide up-to-date responses by pulling data from external sources, thus improving the relevance and accuracy of the answers.
- **Contextual relevance:** By retrieving information from external sources, RAG can add context to the model's answers, making responses more detailed and relevant.

Cons:

- **Implementation complexity:** Implementing RAG can be technically challenging, as it requires two components (retrieval and generation) to work together smoothly.
- **Dependence on retrieval quality:** The quality of the responses is highly dependent on the relevance and accuracy of the retrieved information, which can impact the overall performance of the system.

Which approach is more suitable for ChatPDF?

Finetuning allows the LLM to generate more specialized responses but is computationally expensive and does not reference original documents, making it unsuitable for our needs. While prompt engineering provides a simple and flexible way to guide a general-purpose LLM without finetuning, it's not scalable. This is because including the information from all external sources in the prompt typically exceeds LLM's context window.

RAG offers a balanced solution in terms of ease of setup, cost, and scalability, making it ideal for handling large, evolving datasets and providing up-to-date information. This approach is particularly effective for internal query chatbots in corporate environments. Therefore, we choose RAG to build our ChatPDF system. In the model development section, we delve into prompt engineering and discuss how we combine it with RAG to further enhance the system.

Data Preparation

The performance of the RAG system relies on the quality of the knowledge base and the way it is indexed. When the knowledge base is sourced from websites, data-cleaning strategies such as removing inappropriate content or anonymizing sensitive information should be applied, as discussed in Chapter 4.

In this section, we focus on preparing data from a collection of PDF pages. This involves a three-step process:

- Document parsing
- Document chunking
- Indexing

Document parsing

PDFs are one of the most widely used document formats. It is important to properly extract their content to ensure that the LLM can correctly answer questions based on the PDF's content.

Parsing a PDF means converting its text, images, and other elements into a structured format that a language model can understand. There are two primary approaches for parsing PDFs:

- Rule-based document parser
- AI-based document parser

Rule-based document parser

The rule-based approach relies on predefined rules and patterns that are based on the layout and structure of the document. It attempts to "calculate" the layout and extract content accordingly, making it easy to implement when the document format is consistent and predictable.

However, rule-based methods struggle to handle a wide range of PDF types and formats because PDFs can vary considerably in design. The rigid nature of this method means that if the document does not match the expected format, it can result in mistakes when extracting the content. This makes rule-based parsing less useful when dealing with differing or complex document layouts.

AI-based document parser

AI-based methods take a different approach. They use advanced techniques such as object detection and OCR (Optical Character Recognition) [4] to identify and extract various elements from a document, for example, text, tables, and diagrams. These methods can handle a wide range of document layouts, making them better suited for dealing with complex documents.

There are various tools available for AI-based document parsing. For example, Dedoc [5] supports parsing a wide range of document formats and standardizing content into a consistent structure. Similarly, Layout-Parser [6] uses high-precision models to accurately detect different parts of a document, though the size of these models can slow down the process. To better understand AI-based document parsers, let's take a closer look at how Layout-Parser works.

Layout-Parser takes a document image as input and generates a structured output using the following steps:

1. **Layout detection:** The parser uses advanced object detection models to detect and generate rectangular boxes around different content regions. These regions can include elements such as paragraphs, tables, images, or headers.
2. **Text extraction:** The content inside each rectangular box is processed using OCR to extract the text. The bounding box coordinates ensure the text is recognized in the correct order and format, maintaining the document's original structure.
3. **Structured output generation:** The parser produces a structured output containing two types of data:
    a. **Text blocks:** Includes the block's coordinates, extracted text, reading order, and meta information.
    b. **Non-text blocks:** Includes the coordinates of figures or images.

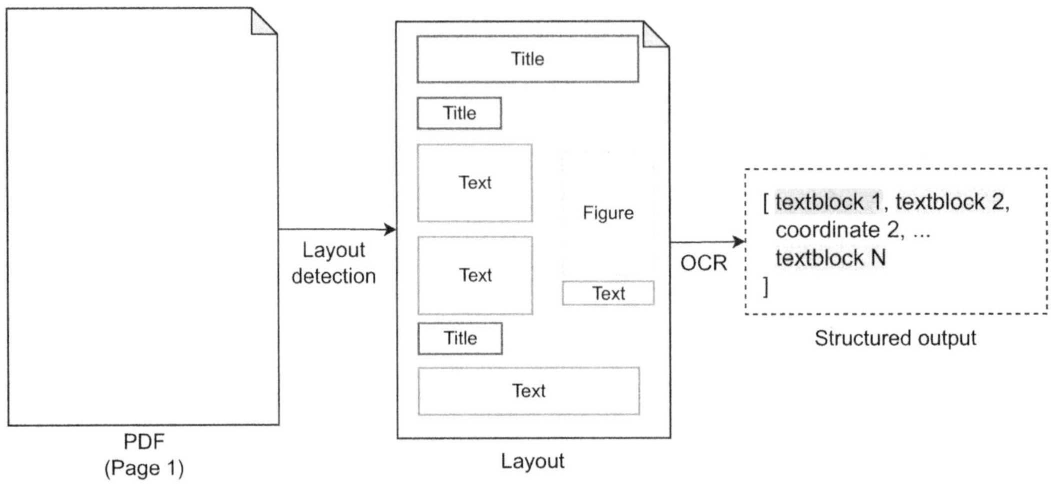

Figure 6.6: Converting a PDF page to a structured output for LLM

Several online services provide document parsing services, for example, Google Cloud Document AI [7] and PDF.co [8]. These services allow users to upload their documents and have them parsed without needing to set up and maintain the parsing system themselves.

Document chunking

Once we have identified the blocks of text, images, or tables in a document, the next step is to index them into a searchable database. For long text blocks such as those found in reports or books, indexing the entire content as a single item is ineffective. This is because the embedding vector representing an entire book or report might capture the general context but miss important details, which can result in less-accurate or incomplete retrieval results. Additionally, if we retrieve the entire book or report, it would exceed the token limit of most models, such as the 128K token limit for the GPT-4o model.[1]

Document chunking addresses these challenges by breaking the text into smaller, manageable pieces or 'chunks.' Chunking helps improve the quality and precision of the retrieval and ensures that each chunk fits within the model's input limit.

Some common strategies for chunking are:

- **Length-based chunking:** This simple approach splits the text into chunks based on a specified length. While it's easy to implement, it can sometimes split sentences or logical sections in the middle, leading to fragmented or less-meaningful chunks. Tools like LangChain [9] provide text splitters, such as the *CharacterTextSplitter* and *RecursiveCharacterTextSplitter*, which allow for adjustable chunk sizes and overlap settings. These splitters can handle different separators and help maintain coherence across chunks.

[1] Accurate at the time of writing.

- **Regular expression-based chunking:** This approach uses regular expressions to split the text based on specific punctuation marks, such as periods, question marks, or exclamation points. It allows for better sentence-level chunking by keeping logical breaks intact, although it may still lack a deeper semantic understanding of the text.
- **HTML, markdown, or code splitters:** For documents in structured formats like HTML or Markdown, specialized splitters are used. These tools split the text at element boundaries such as headers, list items, or code blocks, while preserving the document's overall structure. For example, LangChain has *MarkdownHeaderTextSplitter*, *HTMLHeaderTextSplitter*, and *PythonCodeTextSplitter*, respectively. These splitters are useful for web pages or technical documentation, where maintaining the hierarchical structure is important.

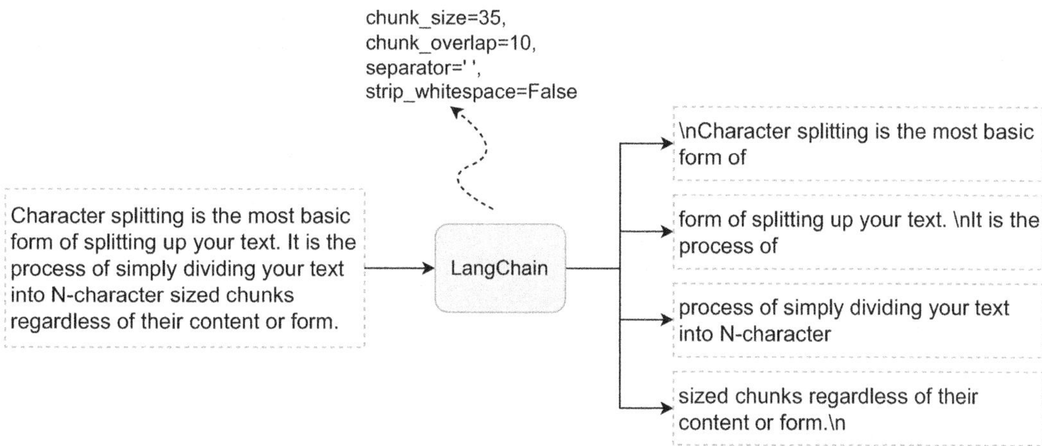

Figure 6.7: Length-based text chunking with LangChain

Indexing

After preparing the data through document parsing and chunking, the final critical step in the RAG system is indexing. Indexing is the process of organizing the chunked data into a structure that enables efficient and accurate retrieval. This step plays a key role in ensuring that the system can quickly locate relevant chunks of information when a query is made.

To determine the indexing process, it is crucial to understand various retrieval techniques and choose the one that best suits the task. Popular retrieval techniques include:

- Keyword-based
- Full-text search
- Knowledge graph–based
- Vector-based

Let's first explore each technique, and then index our data to enable efficient retrieval.

Keyword-based

Traditional keyword-based retrieval relies on matching exact query terms with the content of documents. It is fast and simple but cannot understand the meaning of the query. For example, it may struggle with synonyms, leading to incomplete or irrelevant results. This approach is ineffective when dealing with large-scale datasets or when the goal is to retrieve information based on semantic similarity rather than exact word matches.

Full-text search

Full-text search engines such as Elasticsearch [10] offer a more advanced approach by scanning entire documents for relevant matches. This method allows for a comprehensive analysis of the document's content, including partial matches and phrase searches. However, full-text search comes with higher computational overhead, especially when dealing with large datasets containing, for example, millions of PDF documents. Although effective for finding specific text, this approach is less efficient when it comes to semantic retrieval.

Knowledge graph-based

Knowledge graph-based retrieval is a sophisticated technique that leverages structured relationships between entities (e.g., people, places, or concepts) to retrieve information based on the connections between these entities. This method is excellent for answering complex queries and understanding relationships within the data. However, building and maintaining a knowledge graph requires significant effort, and it is not always practical for large, unstructured datasets such as PDF collections or Wiki pages. To learn more about knowledge graph-based retrieval, refer to [11].

Vector-based

Instead of relying on text-based matches, this method uses high-dimensional embeddings—numerical representations of the text and images—to measure the similarity between a query and the stored chunks of data. This technique enables the retrieval of relevant information even when the exact words in the query do not match the document content, making it more flexible and powerful for large-scale datasets.

Which retrieval technique is suitable for the ChatPDF?

To select an appropriate retrieval method, let's first understand the scale of our system and estimate the number of data chunks involved. In this case, the company manages a large dataset of around 5 million pages. Suppose each page contains roughly 1,500 characters and includes three images. Using length-based chunking with a chunk size of 500 characters and a 200-character overlap, each page will generate 5 text chunks and 3 image chunks. Therefore, the total number of chunks the RAG system is dealing with is 5M × (1500 / (500-200) + 3) = 40M. This figure is expected to grow by roughly 20 percent each year, as indicated in the requirements section.

With around 40 million data chunks and a projected 20 percent annual increase, it's essential to select a retrieval technique that is scalable and can handle this growing volume efficiently.

Traditional retrieval methods [12, 13] such as keyword-based and full-text search have been widely used, but they face limitations in speed, scalability, and the ability to understand the semantic meaning of queries. Knowledge graph–based retrieval requires significant effort to build and maintain such graphs, making them a costly choice.

Vector-based retrieval, on the other hand, is the primary technique used in modern RAG systems due to the following advantages:

- **Semantic understanding:** It can capture the semantic meaning of a query, allowing for more accurate retrieval even when the exact query terms are not present in the document.
- **Scalability:** Using embedding vectors makes this method highly scalable and able to handle large datasets efficiently.
- **Efficiency:** Once the data is indexed as embedding vectors, the system can efficiently retrieve the relevant chunks.

Due to these advantages, we choose vector-based retrieval and index our data accordingly.

Indexing data for vector-based retrieval

In a vector-based retrieval system, each chunk of data is converted into an embedding vector representing the content in a numerical format. When indexing, ML models are employed to compute the embeddings and store them in a vector database. This makes it easy for the RAG system to quickly compare them to the query's embedding and retrieve the most relevant information without unnecessary processing at inference time. We'll dive into the architecture of these ML models and examine the retrieval process in more detail in the model development section.

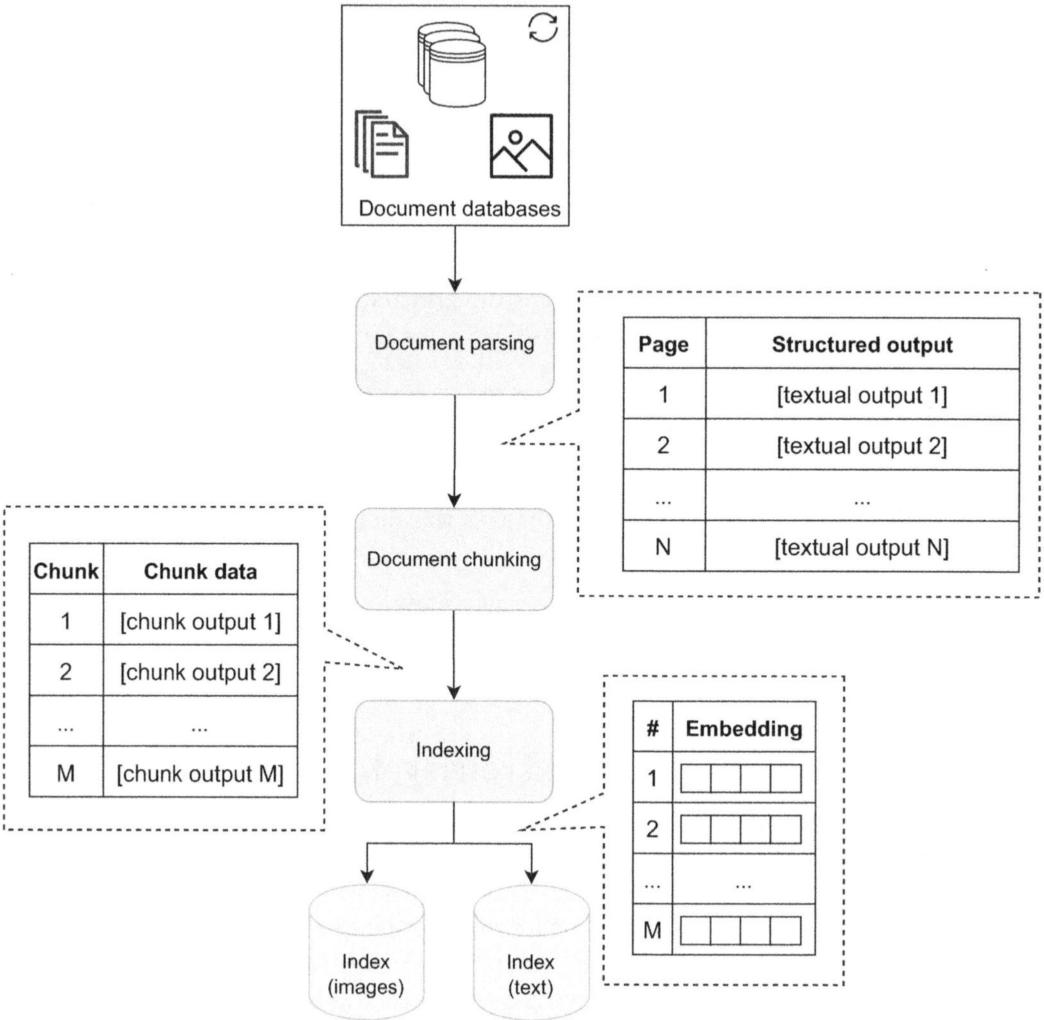

Figure 6.8: Data preparation steps from PDFs to indexed embeddings

In summary, we use a three-step approach to prepare PDFs for the RAG system. First, we apply document parsing techniques to convert the PDF into a structured format, breaking it down into text, tables, and images. Then, we use document chunking to split long text into smaller, manageable chunks. Finally, each chunk is converted to an embedding vector and indexed individually to improve retrieval accuracy.

Model Development

Architecture

This section explores the architecture of a RAG system, focusing on the ML models used in the indexing, retrieval, and generation components.

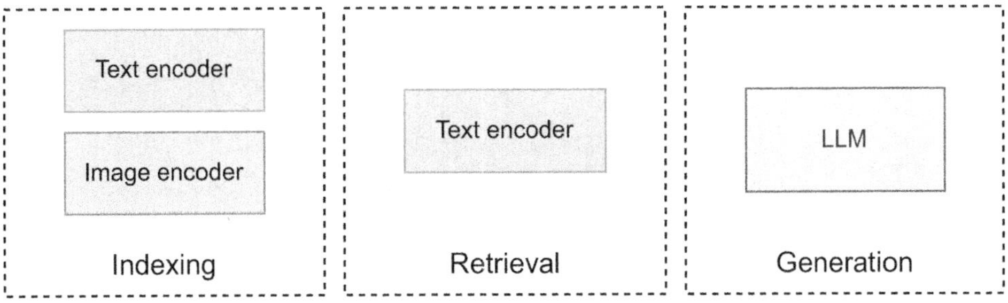

Figure 6.9: Various ML models in a RAG system

Indexing

As discussed in the data preparation section, we use ML models to convert data chunks (e.g., text or images) into embeddings. This process involves two ML models: a text encoder and an image encoder.

Text encoder

The text encoder is a neural network that converts input text into dense vector representations, or "embeddings." These embeddings capture the semantic meaning of the text, allowing for the assessment of the similarity of texts. During the indexing process, the text encoder converts each text chunk into an embedding, which is then stored in a database for efficient retrieval.

The architecture of the text encoder is typically based on an encoder-only Transformer, similar to what we covered in Chapter 3.

Image encoder

The image encoder transforms image data into embeddings. Its architecture can be either CNN-based or Transformer-based, as we covered in Chapter 5.

For effective retrieval, it is important to align the image embeddings with text embeddings. For example, if the query is "How many cats are in the company?" the system needs to ensure that the encoded query is close to the embeddings of relevant images, such as those featuring cats. There are two primary approaches to achieving this alignment:

1. **Shared embedding space:** Use image and text encoders that generate embeddings in a shared embedding space. CLIP [14] provides pretrained encoders with a shared embedding space, enabling cross-modal retrieval.
2. **Image captioning:** First, generate a textual description of the image using an image captioning model. The generated caption can then be encoded using a text encoder, ensuring that both image and text data exist in the same embedding space. This approach is helpful when using separate models for text and image encoders or when training a joint model is resource-intensive. To learn more about building an image captioning system from scratch, refer to Chapter 5.

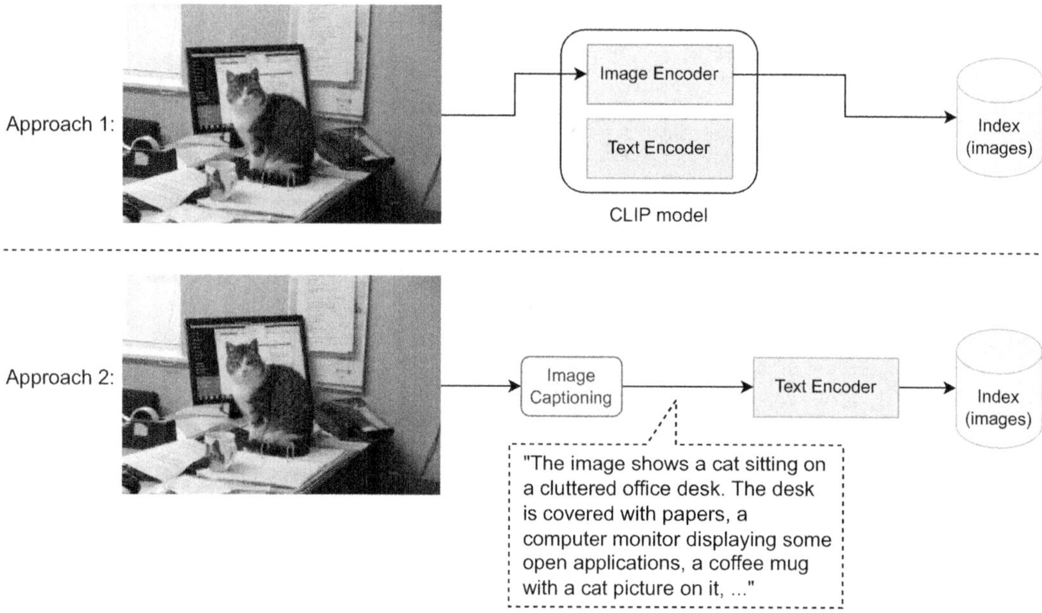

Figure 6.10: Two approaches for achieving text-image alignment

In summary, the indexing process uses a text encoder and an image encoder to convert data chunks into embeddings. These models are often pretrained, meaning they can be directly applied without additional training. For the purposes of this chapter, we use a pretrained CLIP model as both the text and image encoder.

Retrieval

The retrieval process involves converting the user's query into the same embedding space as the indexed data. This is done using the same text encoder employed during the indexing process. Once the query embedding is computed, it is compared with the stored embeddings to retrieve the most relevant data chunks.

Generation

The generation component is responsible for producing the final response based on the user query and the retrieved context. This task is typically handled by an LLM, which generates contextually relevant text.

RAG systems can work with various types of LLMs irrespective of their architecture, including decoder-only Transformers (see Chapter 4 for details) or cloud-hosted models that support finetuning via APIs [15, 16].

Training

Most of the components in a RAG system start with pretrained models, so finetuning the LLM is not typically the first step in optimizing performance. In many cases, a well-designed retrieval process combined with effective prompt engineering can yield satisfactory results. Finetuning should be considered when the system consistently fails to provide accurate or relevant answers, even after adjusting retrieval parameters and crafting prompts. For instance, if the retrieved documents are relevant but the LLM is not generating high-quality responses, finetuning could help the LLM better understand the context and nuances of the retrieved data.

One promising approach to finetuning LLMs in RAG systems is Retrieval-Augmented Fine-Tuning (RAFT). Let's briefly examine RAFT.

RAFT

RAFT [17] introduces a novel training method to enhance the LLM's ability to handle both relevant and irrelevant information within retrieved documents.

In traditional RAG systems, the LLM's output depends heavily on the quality of the retrieved documents. However, irrelevant documents might be included in the retrieval results. These irrelevant documents can mislead the LLM, causing it to generate suboptimal responses. RAFT addresses this issue by incorporating a distinction between relevant and irrelevant documents during the finetuning process. This process involves two key steps:

1. **Document labeling:** Retrieved documents are labeled as either relevant (golden) or irrelevant (distractors). This provides the LLM with clear signals about the documents on which it should focus.
2. **Joint training:** During finetuning, the LLM is trained to generate responses based on the relevant documents while minimizing the influence of irrelevant documents. This requires adjusting the model's loss function to penalize the use of irrelevant documents during response generation.

By training the model to prioritize relevant content and ignore distractors, RAFT improves the LLM's ability to handle noisy retrieval results and generate accurate and relevant responses. This ability is crucial in real-world applications, where retrieval systems may not always be perfect. To learn more about RAFT, refer to [17].

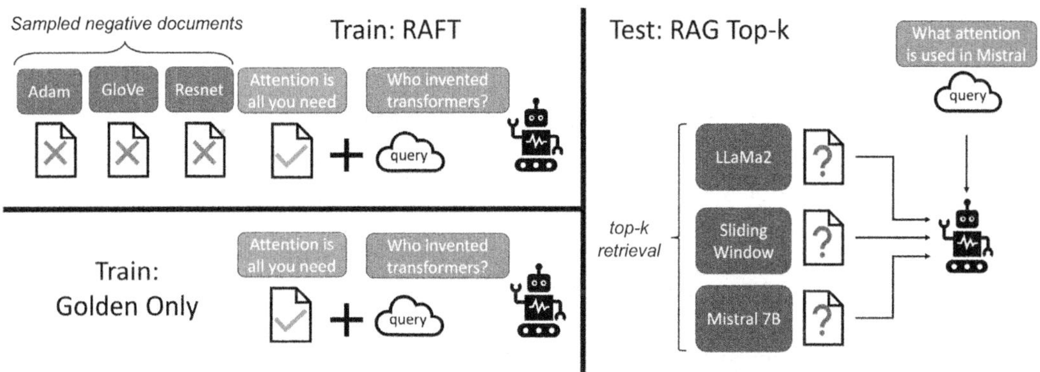

Figure 6.11: RAFT training method (Image taken from [17])

Sampling

Sampling typically involves generating new data with a generative model. In a RAG system, however, multiple components work together to produce a response to a user's query. In this section, we explore these components and highlight techniques for improving performance in the retrieval and generation stages of a RAG system.

Retrieval

The retrieval process occurs in two main steps:

1. Computing the query embedding
2. Performing a nearest neighbor search

1. Computing the query embedding

The first step involves converting the user's query into an embedding using the text encoder. This embedding captures the semantic meaning of the query, allowing the system to compare it to the indexed embeddings of data chunks.

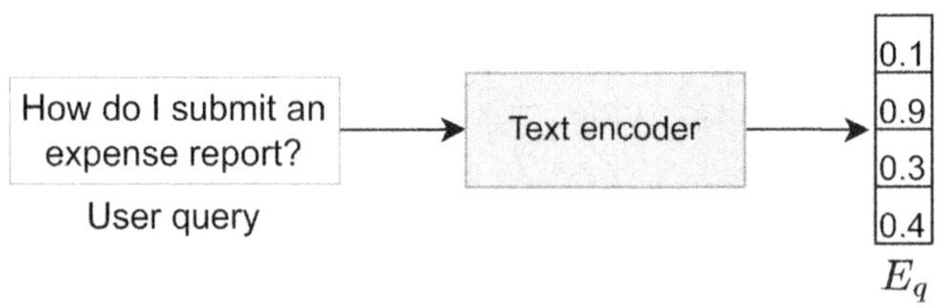

Figure 6.12: User query converted to embedding

2. Performing a nearest neighbor search

Once the query embedding is computed, the system performs a nearest neighbor search to find data chunks that are most similar to the query. Nearest neighbor search addresses the task of identifying data points in a dataset that are closest to a given query point, based on a chosen similarity measure. Common measures include Euclidean distance [18], cosine similarity [19], or other distance metrics that capture relationships between data points in an embedding space.

Nearest neighbor search is a fundamental component of information retrieval, search engines, and recommendation systems. Even small improvements in its performance can lead to significant overall system gains. Given its importance, interviewers may want you to dive deeper into this topic.

Nearest neighbor algorithms generally fall into two categories:

- Exact nearest neighbor
- Approximate nearest neighbor

Exact nearest neighbor

Exact nearest neighbor search, also called linear search, is the simplest and most accurate form of nearest neighbor search. It calculates the distance between the query embedding, E_q, and every item in the dataset, retrieving the k nearest neighbors.

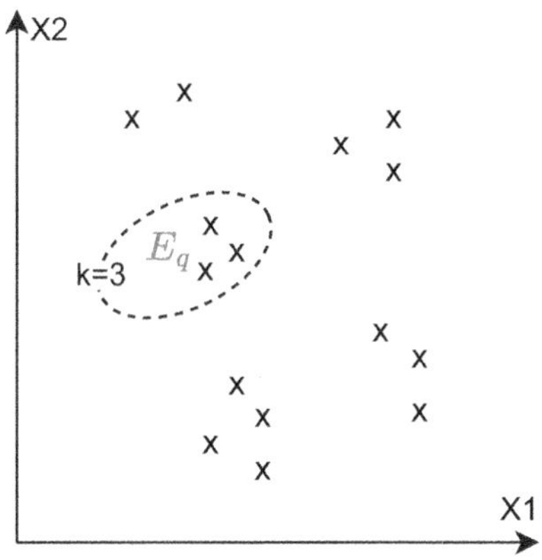

Figure 6.13: Top-3 nearest neighbors to query embedding

While this method guarantees finding the true nearest neighbors, it has a time complexity of $O(N \times D)$, where N is the number of items in the dataset and D is the embedding dimension. This linear complexity can make the process very slow when working with large-scale systems, such as a RAG system indexing tens of millions of items. For instance, performing an exact search across 40 million items for a single query would involve 40 million comparisons, leading to high computational costs and latency. Therefore, the exact nearest neighbor search is often too slow and computationally expensive to be employed in practice.

Approximate nearest neighbor (ANN)

In many applications, it's sufficient to retrieve items that are similar enough without needing to find the exact nearest neighbor. ANN algorithms use specialized data structures that allow the system to retrieve "close enough" neighbors without searching the entire dataset, thus reducing search time to sublinear complexity, for example, $O(\log(N) \times D)$. While these algorithms typically require some preprocessing or extra storage, they offer considerable performance benefits.

Various ANN algorithms can generally be divided into the following categories:

- Tree-based
- Locality-sensitive hashing
- Clustering-based
- Graph-based

While the interviewer typically will not expect you to know every detail of these categories, it is generally helpful to have a high-level understanding of them. Let's dive in.

Tree-based

Tree-based algorithms partition the data space into multiple partitions. Then they leverage the characteristics of the tree to perform a faster search. For example, k-d tree [20] splits the space based on feature values, enabling faster searches by narrowing down relevant regions of the data. Other algorithms include R-trees [21] and Annoy (Approximate Nearest Neighbor Oh Yeah) [22].

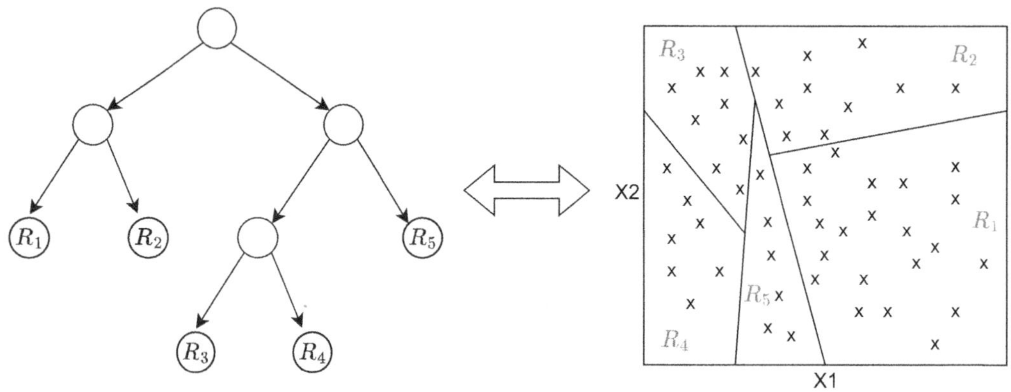

Figure 6.14: Partitioned space created by a tree

Locality-sensitive hashing (LSH)

LSH groups similar points into buckets using specialized hash functions. These functions ensure that points close in space are hashed into the same bucket. This drastically reduces the search space because only points in the same bucket as the query need to be examined, making LSH highly efficient for large datasets. You can learn more about LSH by reading [23].

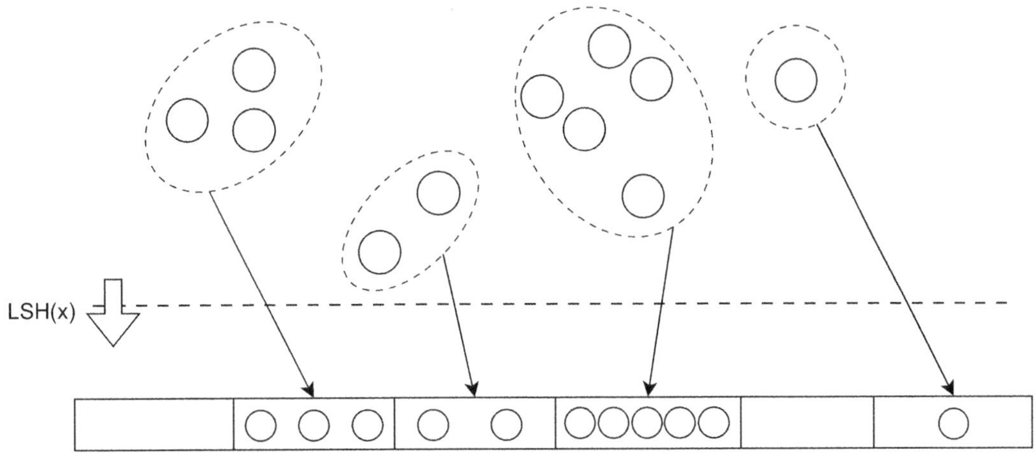

Figure 6.15: LSH groups the data points into buckets

Clustering-based

Clustering-based algorithms organize data into clusters using distance metrics such as cosine similarity or Euclidean distance. This allows the search for the nearest neighbor to be limited to the cluster(s) most relevant to the query, reducing the number of comparisons required, as only data points within the selected cluster are considered. Specifically, once the indexed items are organized into clusters, nearest neighbors are retrieved in two steps:

1. **Inter-cluster search:** The query embedding is compared to the centroids of all clusters, and the clusters that are closer than a specified threshold are selected.
2. **Intra-cluster search:** The query embedding is compared to the items in selected clusters.

This two-step process—first narrowing down the search to a cluster, then conducting a finer search within that cluster—significantly improves efficiency. This process is shown in Figure 6.16.

Graph-based

Graph-based algorithms, such as HNSW (hierarchical navigable small world) [24], structure the data as a graph, where nodes represent data points and edges connect them based on proximity in the embedding space. HNSW operates by navigating through this graph in a hierarchical manner, beginning with a higher-level coarse graph and gradually moving down to finer levels. The search is refined at each level, exploring only nearby nodes, thus drastically reducing the search space.

Which nearest neighbor search category is best suited for a RAG retrieval system?

In RAG systems, the number of indexed items is typically massive and growing, often exceeding hundreds of millions of embeddings. The time complexity of the exact nearest neighbor search is too high, therefore, we rely on ANN algorithms to efficiently retrieve relevant data chunks.

Various ANN algorithms have their own strengths. Choosing the right ANN algorithm usually depends on factors such as the dataset size, required speed, and accuracy trade-offs. For simplicity, we employ a clustering-based ANN approach in the retrieval component of the RAG system.

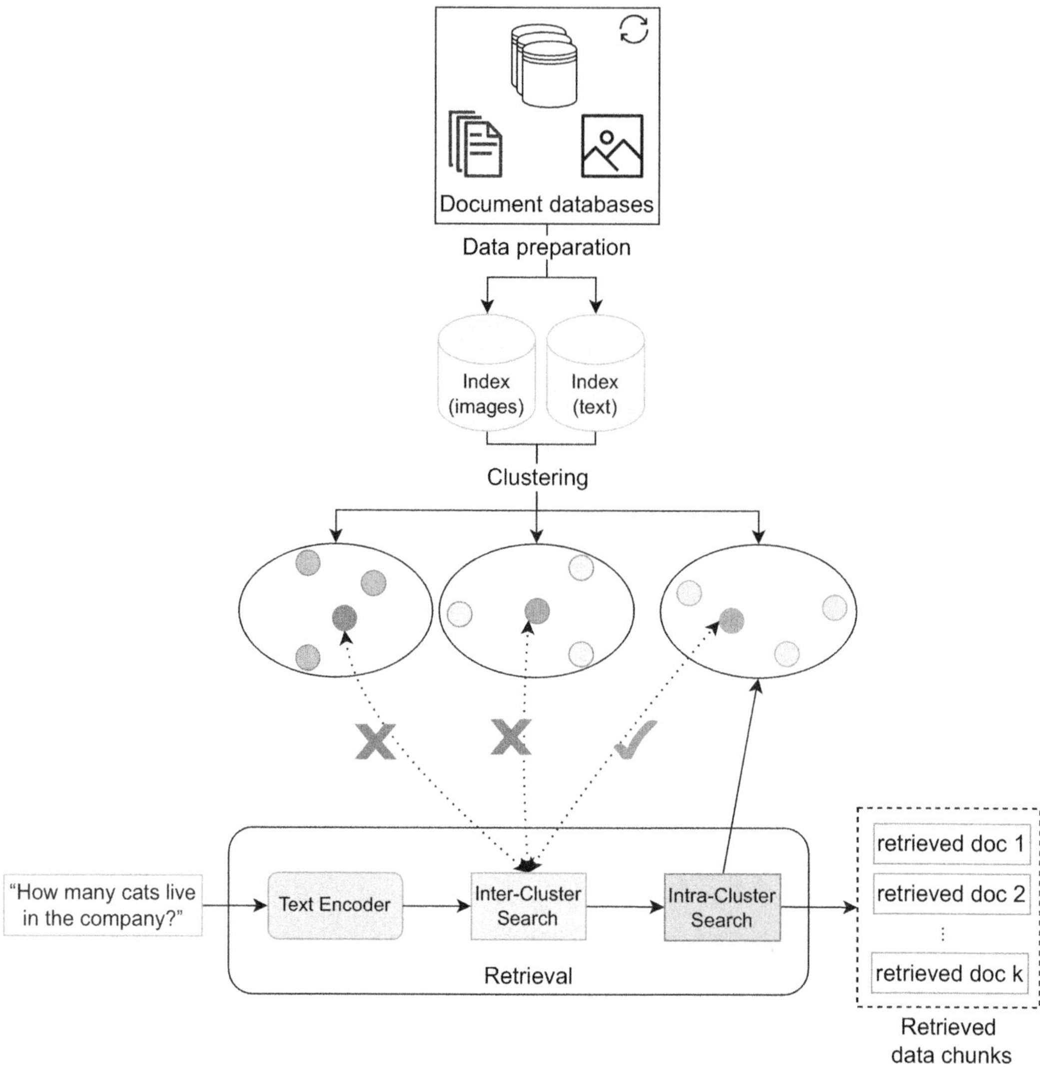

Figure 6.16: Overall retrieval process

Several modern frameworks provide out-of-the-box support for ANN, including:

- **Elasticsearch** [10]: A widely used search engine that supports vector similarity search.
- **FAISS** [25]: A popular library developed by Meta that enables efficient nearest neighbor search for large datasets.

- **ScaNN** [26]: A library developed by Google, designed for fast and efficient nearest neighbor search on large datasets.

These frameworks are commonly used in practice to make the retrieval components of large-scale systems both efficient and scalable.

Generation

The generation component takes the user query and retrieved context as input and generates a response using top-p sampling. However, we can further improve the quality of the generated response by incorporating prompt engineering techniques, as shown in Figure 6.17.

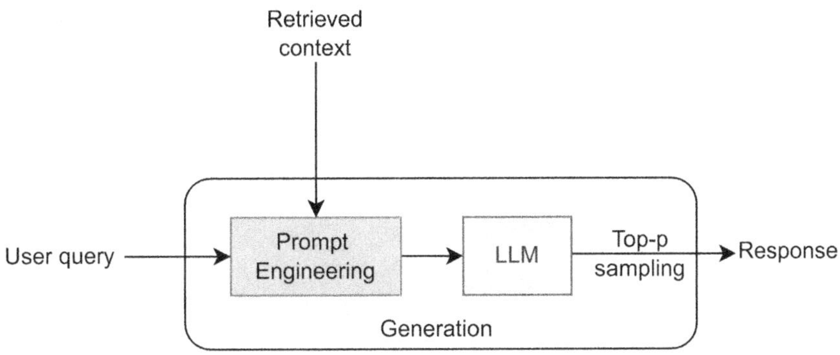

Figure 6.17: Generation component overview

In this section, we dive into prompt engineering and explore how it enhances response generation in a RAG system.

Prompt engineering

Prompt engineering is a powerful technique that optimizes input prompts to help LLMs generate more accurate and contextually relevant responses. By carefully designing prompts, we can guide the model's output to better align with specific tasks, improving overall performance. While prompt engineering can be applied in both the retrieval (e.g., crafting better queries to optimize search) and generation, we focus on applying it to the generation for educational purposes. The same approach can also be used to improve retrieval performance.

Let's start this section with prompt design principles, followed by prompt engineering techniques.

Prompt design principles

Effective prompt design is crucial for maximizing the performance of language models. By following key principles, we can enhance the quality of the generated output and reduce irrelevant or confusing responses. Below are some essential prompt engineering principles:

1. **Start simple:** Begin with straightforward prompts and gradually introduce more complexity. Iterative experimentation is key to refining prompts. Tools such as Cohere's Playground [27] allow you to easily test and adjust prompts as needed.
2. **Break down complex tasks:** Break down tasks involving multiple subtasks into smaller, manageable steps. This avoids overwhelming the LLM and ensures better focus on individual subtasks.
3. **Use clear instructions:** Be explicit with instructions, using clear, action-oriented commands such as "Write," "Summarize," or "Translate." Experiment with different instructions to find what works best for your task. Placing instructions at the beginning of the prompt, separated by delimiters such as "###," can also help organize the prompt.
4. **Be specific:** Specificity leads to more accurate responses. Clearly describe what you expect in terms of format, style, or outcomes. However, avoid overloading the prompt with unnecessary details—include only what is relevant to the task.
5. **Experiment with prompt length:** Consider the length of the prompt. Too much unnecessary information can confuse the LLM, while too little may result in vague responses. Strike a balance by being concise yet detailed enough to guide the LLM effectively.

Prompt engineering techniques

Several prompt engineering techniques have been developed to improve the quality of LLM outputs. Some of the most effective ones include:

- Chain-of-thought prompting
- Few-shot prompting
- Role-specific prompting
- User-context prompting

Chain-of-thought prompting

Chain-of-thought (CoT) prompting [28] involves guiding the model through intermediate reasoning steps before arriving at a final answer. This is especially useful for complex queries requiring multi-hop reasoning, where the model must combine information from multiple documents to generate a complete response. CoT prompts guide the model to break down its reasoning into steps, leading to more accurate and insightful answers.

```
Given the following documents, explain the step-by-step
process of photosynthesis.

[paragraph]
```

Figure 6.18: Example of CoT

CoT has been further extended by techniques such as [29] that allow models to evaluate multiple reasoning paths before selecting the best response. OpenAI's o1[2][30] and [31] have shown that an LLM's ability to handle more complex tasks can be improved by allocating more computational budget at inference time, also known as test-time compute scaling.

Few-shot prompting

Few-shot prompting [32] involves providing the model with a few examples of input-output pairs before the actual query. This method helps the model understand the desired format and tone of the output, improving its ability to generate responses that align with the provided examples.

> Example 1: Query: "How do plants absorb sunlight?" → Answer: "Plants absorb sunlight using chlorophyll in their leaves."
>
> Example 2: Query: "How do plants produce oxygen?" → Answer: "During photosynthesis, plants convert carbon dioxide into oxygen."
>
> Query: "How do plants grow?"

Figure 6.19: Example of few-shot prompting

Role-specific prompting

In some cases, the language model may need to adopt a specific "role" to generate an appropriate response. For example, in legal or medical domains, prompting the model to act as a subject-matter expert ensures that the response carries the necessary tone, accuracy, and authority.

> You are an experienced contract lawyer with over 20 years of experience specializing in corporate law. You are well-versed in drafting, reviewing, and interpreting complex legal documents, particularly in matters related to mergers and acquisitions, non-disclosure agreements (NDAs), intellectual property rights, and employment contracts. Your job is to provide clear and concise legal explanations and advice to clients who may not have a legal background.
>
> Please review the following contract clause and provide a detailed explanation of its meaning, potential legal implications, and any areas of concern. Use simple language that a business executive without legal training can easily understand. Highlight any risks or ambiguities in the clause, and suggest potential revisions to mitigate those risks.
>
> [contract clause]

Figure 6.20: Example of role-specific prompting

User-context prompting

User-context prompting tailors the model's output based on specific user information in-

[2] Specifics are unknown to the public at the time of writing.

cluded in the prompt. By incorporating user profiles, preferences, or locations into the queries, the model can generate personalized responses that are more relevant to the users.

```
[Other prompts]

Use the following user profile to personalize the output. Only use the profile if relevant to the
request.
- Write in this language:[English]
- User profile: [Manjaro Linux user]
- Location: [Mountain View, California, USA]
- Current date: [02:46 PM Mon, Nov 23, 2024]
```

Figure 6.21: Example of user-context prompting

This method is particularly effective when user-specific information is crucial to shaping the response, such as in personalized recommendations or location-based queries.

Putting it all together: prompt engineering for response generation

Combining these techniques allows us to craft highly effective prompts for generating responses in a RAG system. Principles such as clarity and specificity can guide the model to produce more accurate outputs. Prompt engineering techniques can significantly enhance a RAG's generation capabilities, resulting in more reliable and contextually appropriate outcomes.

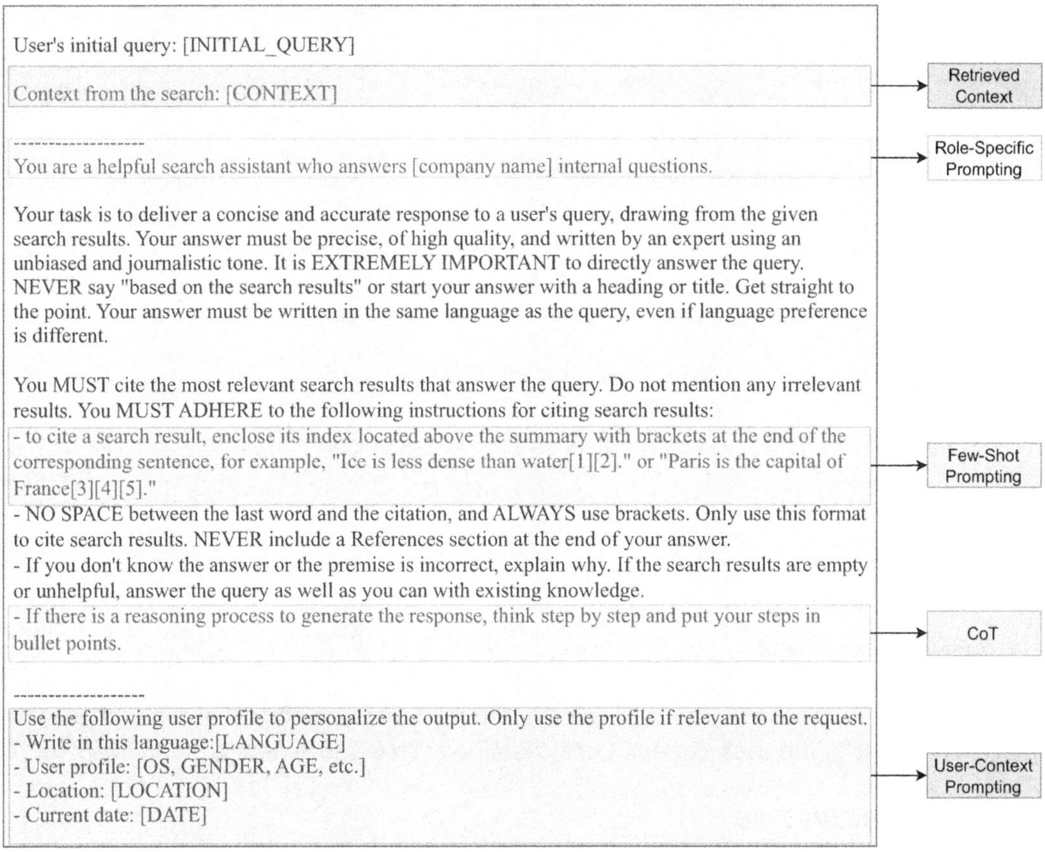

Figure 6.22: Example of final prompt for response generation

Evaluation

Unlike traditional ML models, which are evaluated using well-defined quantitative metrics, evaluating RAG systems is more complex. This complexity arises because the quality of the final text response depends on the effectiveness of multiple components within the pipeline. To capture this multifaceted evaluation, we use a triad diagram to explain the relationship between different evaluation aspects.

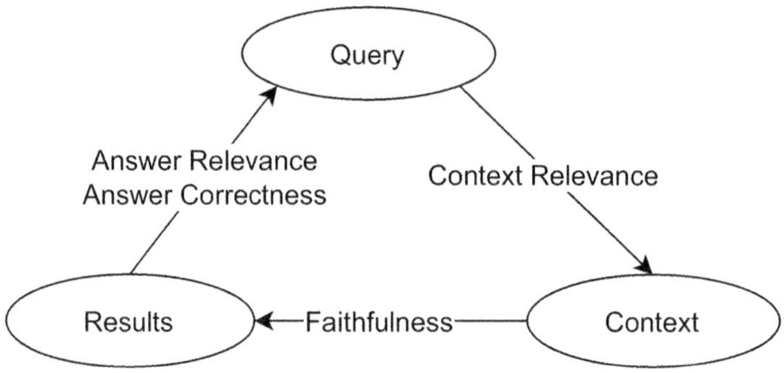

Figure 6.23: Triad of RAG evaluation

The evaluation of a RAG system focuses on four key aspects:

- Context relevance
- Faithfulness
- Answer relevance
- Answer correctness

These aspects help assess how well the system retrieves, generates, and matches information relevant to the user's query. Let's examine each in more detail.

Context relevance

Context relevance measures how accurately and completely the retrieval component selects relevant documents based on the query. The goal is to ensure that all relevant content appears at the top of the retrieval results. This aspect directly evaluates the effectiveness of the retrieval mechanism. Common metrics used for context relevance include:

- Hit rate
- Mean reciprocal rank (MRR)
- Normalized discounted cumulative gain (NDCG)
- Precision@k

To learn more about evaluation metrics in retrieval and ranking systems, refer to [33, 34].

Faithfulness

Faithfulness assesses whether the generated response is factually aligned with the retrieved context. It checks if the generation component is hallucinating (i.e., introducing information not grounded in the context). This is crucial because the system should produce answers that strictly reflect the source material. By evaluating faithfulness, we reduce the risk of generating plausible-sounding yet factually unaligned responses, thereby enhancing the reliability and trustworthiness of the output.

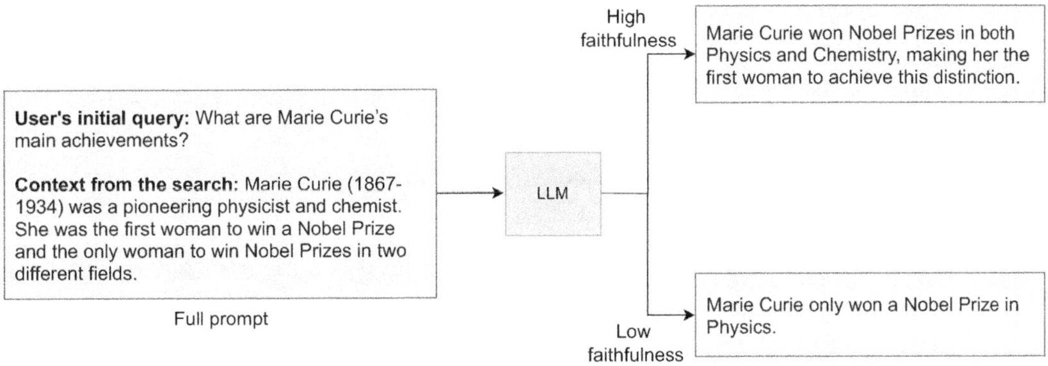

Figure 6.24: Example of faithfulness

Faithfulness can be assessed using the following methods:

- **Human evaluation:** Experts manually review the generated responses to determine whether they are factually aligned and correctly referenced to the retrieved documents. This process involves cross-checking each claim against the source materials to ensure all information generated is substantiated.
- **Automated fact-checking tools:** Tools such as [35] and [36] can automate the validation process by comparing the generated response against a database of verified facts. They offer a scalable solution for identifying inaccuracies, thus reducing the reliance on human evaluators.
- **Consistency checks:** This method involves evaluating whether the LLM provides consistent factual information across multiple queries. Regular consistency checks ensure that the LLM does not produce contradictory information, which is essential for maintaining the reliability and coherence of the responses over time.

Answer relevance

Answer relevance measures how closely the generated answer matches the original query in terms of completeness and lack of redundancy. If the response includes irrelevant or redundant information or lacks important details, it scores low in relevance. This aspect can be evaluated by comparing the question and the answer using another language model (e.g., ChatGPT).

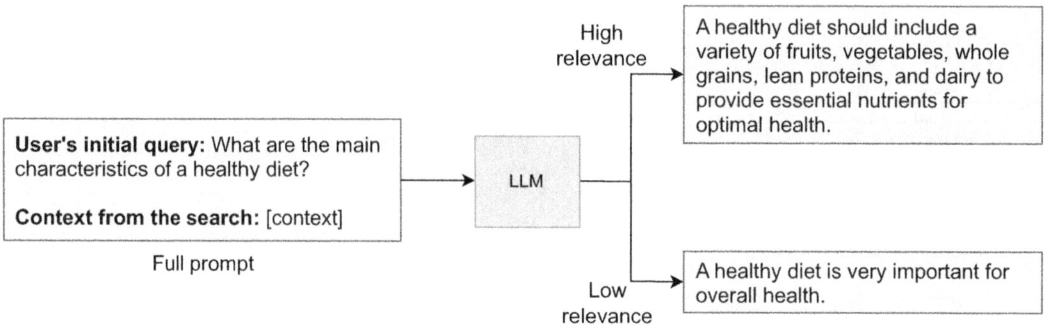

Figure 6.25: Example of answer relevance

Answer correctness

Answer correctness focuses on how closely the generated answer matches the correct reference answer. It measures the similarity between the two using popular metrics including BLUE, ROGUE, and METEOR. To review these metrics, refer to Chapter 3.

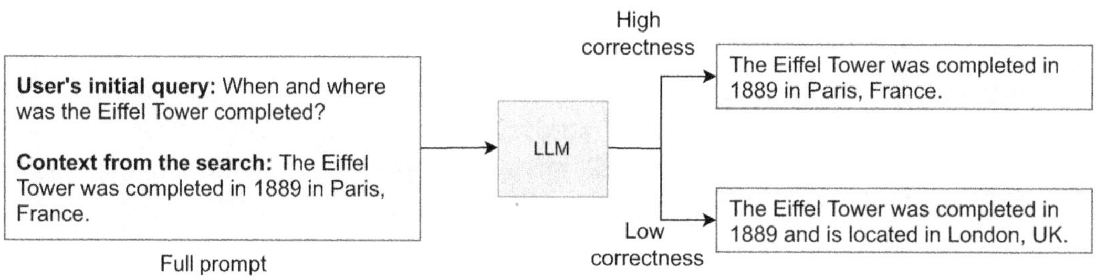

Figure 6.26: Example of answer correctness

Overall ML System Design

A RAG system consists of several components that work together to retrieve and generate responses efficiently. In this section, we will explore the following key components:

- Indexing process
- Safety filtering
- Query expansion
- Retrieval
- Generation

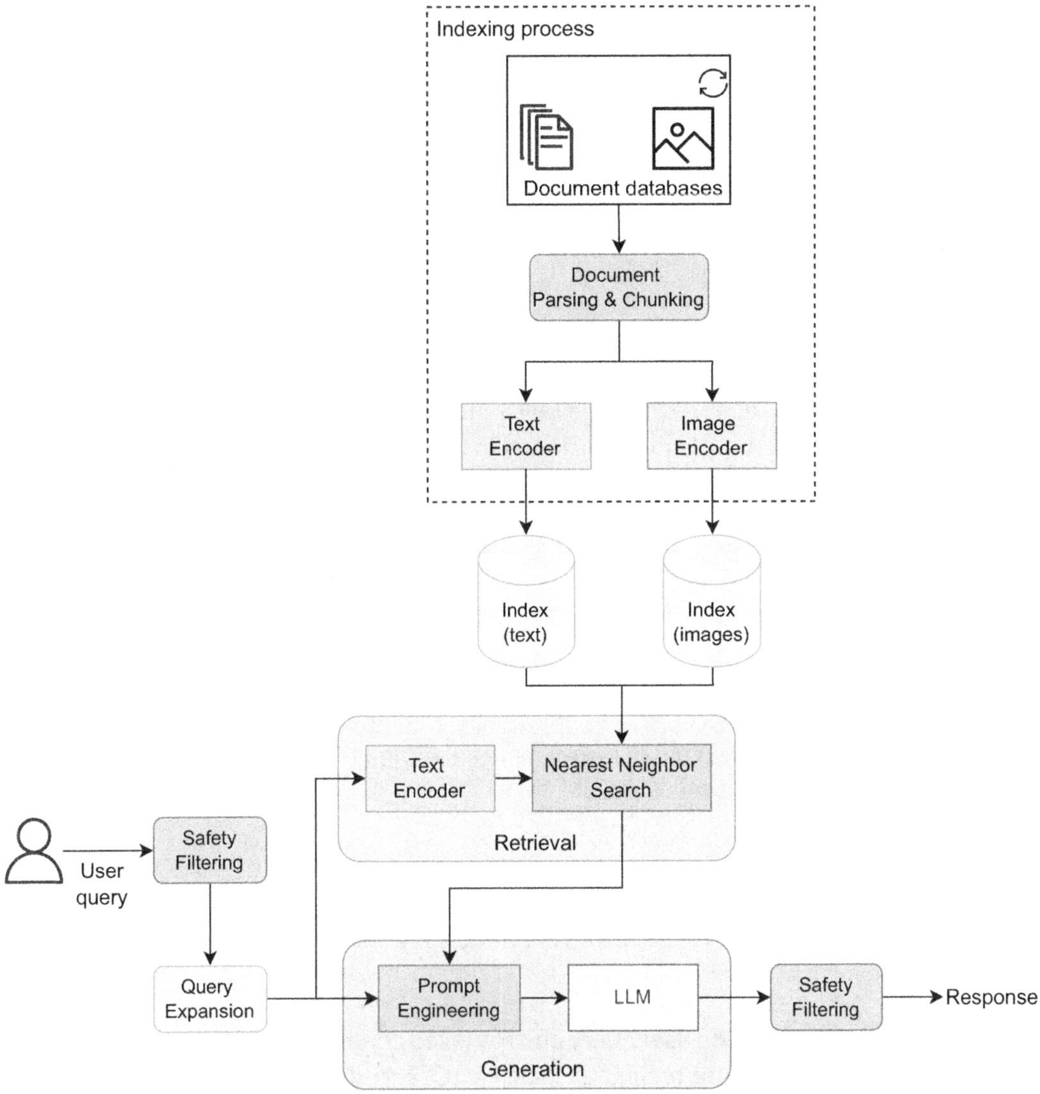

Figure 6.27: RAG system overall design

Indexing process

The indexing process is responsible for converting the knowledge base into embeddings, which are then stored in an index table for efficient retrieval. This begins with document parsing and chunking, where the text and images in PDFs are broken down into meaningful data chunks. These data chunks are then converted into embeddings using a CLIP text and image encoder, ensuring that both text and image embeddings are mapped into a shared embedding space. Once the data chunks are embedded, they are stored in the index table, thus allowing for fast retrieval.

Safety filtering

The safety filtering component ensures that user requests are safe and comply with the system's guidelines. This involves checking queries for inappropriate or harmful content before processing them further. To learn more about safety filtering and evaluation, refer to Chapter 4.

Query expansion

Query expansion enhances the quality of the retrieval process by expanding the user's query to have a better flow and be free of typos and grammatical errors. By broadening the scope of the search, query expansion helps the system identify additional relevant data that might not have been explicitly mentioned in the original query, thereby increasing the chances of retrieving more relevant results.

To learn more about query expansion and its technical details, refer to [37].

Retrieval

The retrieval component is responsible for finding the data chunks that are most relevant to the user's query. The user query is first converted into an embedding using the CLIP text encoder, and then an ANN algorithm is used to efficiently retrieve the most similar data chunks in the index table.

Generation

Once the relevant data chunks are retrieved, the generation component produces the final output. This involves two main steps:

- **Prompt Engineering:** The user query and retrieved context are combined into a prompt and then optimized using techniques such as CoT to structure the model's reasoning process.
- **LLM:** The LLM generates the final response using top-p sampling.

Other Talking Points

If time permits at the end of the interview, consider discussing these additional topics:

- Tabular detection in document parsing [38, 39, 40].
- Details of approximate nearest neighbor algorithms [20, 21, 23, 24].
- Support user-uploaded documents [2].
- Dynamic retrieval strategy [41, 42].
- Query rewriting and expansion [43, 37].

- Inference time CoT and test-time scaling [30, 31].

Summary

Summary
Clarifying requirements
Framing as ML
Specifying input and output
ML approach
Finetuning
Prompt engineering
RAG
Data preparation
Document parsing
Rule-based
AI-based
Document chunking
Length-based
Regex-based
Splitters
Indexing
Keyword-based
Full-text search
Knowledge graph-based
Vector-based
Model development
Architecture
Indexing
Text encoder
Image encoder
Retrieval
Text encoder
Generation
LLM
Training
RAFT
Sampling
Retrieval
Exact nearest neighbor
ANN
Tree-based
LSH
Clustering-based
Graph-based
Generation
Prompt design principles
Prompt engineering techniques
CoT
Few-shot
Role-specific
User-context
Evaluation
Context relevance
Faithfulness
Answer relevance
Answer correctness
Overall system components
Indexing
Safety filtering
Query expansion
Retrieval
Generation
Other talking points

Reference Material

[1] Perplexity. https://www.perplexity.ai/.

[2] ChatPDF. https://www.chatpdf.com/.

[3] LoRA: Low-Rank Adaptation of Large Language Models. https://arxiv.org/abs/2106.09685.

[4] Optical Character Recognition. https://en.wikipedia.org/wiki/Optical_character_recognition.

[5] Dedoc GitHub Repository. https://github.com/ispras/dedoc.

[6] LayoutParser: A Unified Toolkit for Deep Learning Based Document Image Analysis. https://arxiv.org/abs/2103.15348.

[7] Google Cloud document parser API. https://cloud.google.com/document-ai/docs/layout-parse-chunk.

[8] PDF.CO document parser API. https://developer.pdf.co/api/document-parser/index.html.

[9] Character text splitter in LangChain. https://python.langchain.com/v0.1/docs/modules/data_connection/document_transformers/character_text_splitter/.

[10] Elasticsearch. https://www.elastic.co/elasticsearch.

[11] A Survey on Knowledge Graphs: Representation, Acquisition, and Applications. https://ieeexplore.ieee.org/document/9416312.

[12] Christopher D. Manning. *Introduction to Information Retrieval*. 2008.

[13] Modern Information Retrieval: A Brief Overview. http://singhal.info/ieee2001.pdf.

[14] Learning Transferable Visual Models From Natural Language Supervision. https://arxiv.org/abs/2103.00020.

[15] OpenAI finetuning documentation. https://platform.openai.com/docs/guides/fine-tuning.

[16] Anthropic finetuning. https://www.anthropic.com/news/fine-tune-claude-3-haiku.

[17] RAFT: Adapting Language Model to Domain Specific RAG. https://arxiv.org/abs/2403.10131.

[18] Euclidean Distance. https://en.wikipedia.org/wiki/Euclidean_distance.

[19] Cosine Similarity. https://en.wikipedia.org/wiki/Cosine_similarity.

[20] Multidimensional binary search trees used for associative searching. https://dl.acm.org/doi/10.1145/361002.361007.

[21] R-trees: A dynamic index structure for spatial searching. https://dl.acm.org/doi/10.1145/971697.602266.

[22] Annoy Library. https://github.com/spotify/annoy.

[23] Similarity search in high dimensions via hashing. https://www.cs.princeton.edu/courses/archive/spring13/cos598C/Gionis.pdf.

[24] Efficient and robust approximate nearest neighbor search using Hierarchical Navigable Small World graphs. https://arxiv.org/abs/1603.09320.

[25] Faiss Documentation. https://faiss.ai/.

[26] ScaNN. https://research.google/blog/announcing-scann-efficient-vector-similarity-search/.

[27] Developer Playground. https://docs.cohere.com/v2/docs/playground-overview.

[28] Chain-of-Thought Prompting Elicits Reasoning in Large Language Models. https://arxiv.org/abs/2201.11903.

[29] Tree of Thoughts: Deliberate Problem Solving with Large Language Models. https://arxiv.org/abs/2305.10601.

[30] OpenAI o1. https://openai.com/index/learning-to-reason-with-llms/.

[31] Scaling LLM Test-Time Compute Optimally can be More Effective than Scaling Model Parameters. https://arxiv.org/abs/2408.03314.

[32] Language Models are Few-Shot Learners. https://arxiv.org/abs/2005.14165.

[33] Machine Learning System Design Interview. https://www.aliaminian.com/books.

[34] Evaluation Measure for Information Retrieval. https://en.wikipedia.org/wiki/Evaluation_measures_(information_retrieval).

[35] Ragas. https://docs.ragas.io/en/stable/.

[36] ARES: An Automated Evaluation Framework for Retrieval-Augmented Generation Systems. https://arxiv.org/abs/2311.09476.

[37] Query2doc: Query Expansion with Large Language Models. https://arxiv.org/abs/2303.07678.

[38] TableNet: Deep Learning model for end-to-end Table detection and Tabular data extraction from Scanned Document Images. https://arxiv.org/abs/2001.01469.

[39] CascadeTabNet: An approach for end to end table detection and structure recognition from image-based documents. https://arxiv.org/abs/2004.12629.

[40] Deepdesrt: Deep learning for detection and structure recognition of tables in document images. https://ieeexplore.ieee.org/document/8270123.

[41] Active Retrieval Augmented Generation. https://arxiv.org/abs/2305.06983.

[42] Self-RAG: Learning to Retrieve, Generate, and Critique through Self-Reflection. https://arxiv.org/abs/2310.11511.

[43] Precise Zero-Shot Dense Retrieval without Relevance Labels. https://arxiv.org/abs/2212.10496.

7

Realistic Face Generation

Introduction

One of the primary applications of generative AI is to generate realistic images of faces. This can be useful in entertainment, marketing, and virtual reality. In this chapter, we explore the technologies behind face generation.

Figure 7.1: Realistic faces generated by StyleGAN2 [1]

Clarifying Requirements

Here is a typical interaction between a candidate and an interviewer:

Candidate: What is the primary application of the face generation system?
Interviewer: The initial focus is on entertainment and content creation, but we would also consider using it for data collection in the future.

Candidate: Is the focus only on faces? Or does the entire body need to be generated?
Interviewer: Let's focus on faces only.

Candidate: Should the generated faces represent a diverse range of ethnicities, ages, and genders?
Interviewer: Yes. This is crucial to ensure inclusivity and avoid biases.

Candidate: Should the system allow control over facial attributes? For example, editing

the facial expression of a generated image while preserving its identity?
Interviewer: Good question. Let's start without attribute control. If we have time, we can optionally discuss attribute control.

Candidate: How will we source the training data? What is the size of the training data?
Interviewer: We use publicly available datasets with proper licenses to ensure all data is in compliance with privacy regulations. There are 70,000 images of diverse faces in the dataset.

Candidate: What is the desired image resolution?
Interviewer: Let's aim for 1024x1024.

Candidate: What is the expected speed to generate a face?
Interviewer: The system should generate faces in near real-time – less than a second.

Frame the Problem as an ML Task

Specifying the system's input and output

In a face generation system, users usually don't provide specific inputs; they simply request the generation of a new face. Since machine learning (ML) models need numerical inputs to start, most image generation models begin with a random noise vector. This noise serves as the initial input, which the model then transforms into a realistic image. If the system supports attribute control, users can also provide desired attributes as input to guide the generation.

The output, which is generated in response to the random noise input, is a realistic image of a human face. This output should also reflect the desired attributes (if specified), such as age, gender, and hairstyle.

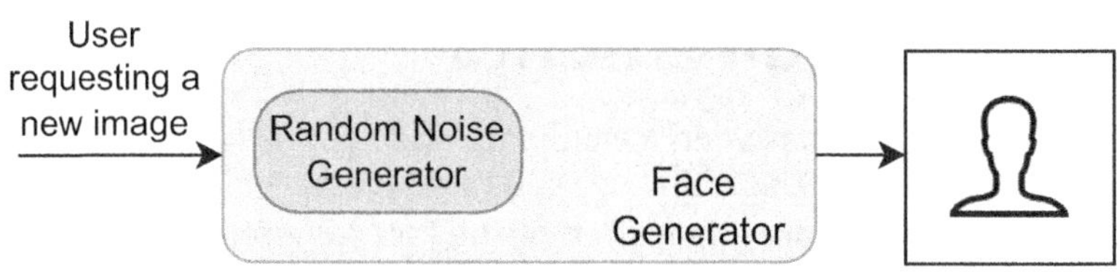

Figure 7.2: Input and output of a face generation system

Choosing a suitable ML approach

In this section, we explore common ML approaches for image generation. We discuss the strengths and limitations of each approach and select the best fit for our use case.

While there are different approaches for generating images, we focus on those that are most widely used in the industry. There are four main approaches to image generation:

- Variational autoencoder
- Generative adversarial network
- Autoregressive model
- Diffusion model

Variational autoencoder

A variational autoencoder (VAE) is a generative model architecture designed to learn the distribution of data. This enables the VAE to generate new data points by sampling from this learned distribution.

A VAE consists of two main components:

- Encoder
- Decoder

Encoder: The encoder is a neural network that maps an input image into a lower-dimensional space, known as the latent space. The output of the encoder is a latent vector, an encoded representation of the input image.

Decoder: The decoder is another neural network that maps the encoded representation into an image. The output of the decoder is an image of the same size as the original input image.

During training, the VAE encodes the input into a latent space and then reconstructs the original input from this encoded representation. After training, the VAE can generate new images by sampling points from the learned distribution and using the decoder to map these points into image form.

Through a reparameterization trick (see [2] for more details), VAEs model the latent vector as being sampled from a multivariate Gaussian distribution. The modeling of latent space helps the VAE learn meaningful representations that can be smoothly interpolated, which is advantageous for tasks such as image morphing and creating variations of input data.

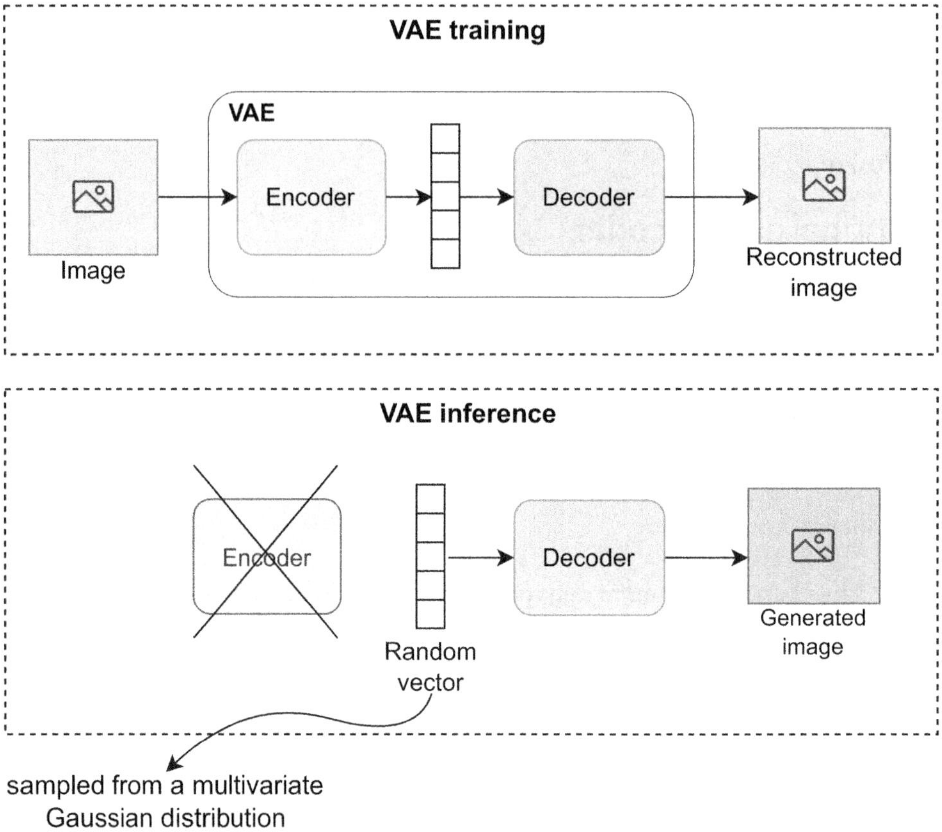

Figure 7.3: VAE training and inference process

VAEs have several strengths and weaknesses.

Pros:

- **Simple architecture:** The encoder and decoder are neural network architectures that are simple to implement.
- **Fast generation:** Compared to other approaches, VAEs offer fast image generation. The process involves sampling a random noise from the latent space and decoding it into an image using the decoder.
- **Stable training:** Training a VAE is typically easy and stable.
- **Compression capability:** Apart from image generation, VAEs are a powerful tool for compressing images into lower-dimensional representations.

Cons:

- **Less realistic images:** VAEs struggle to capture high-frequency details. This leads to images that are less realistic compared to those generated by some other approaches.
- **Blurriness:** A significant limitation of VAEs is their tendency to produce blurry images

that lack sharp details.

- **Limited novelty:** VAEs typically struggle to generate images that significantly differ from their training data. This limits their ability to produce novel outputs.
- **Limited control in generation:** VAEs are not designed to support extra control inputs such as text descriptions or attribute controls for the desired image.

In summary, VAEs are not the best choice for generating high-quality, detailed images. Their strength, however, lies in efficiently encoding images into compact representations. In Chapter 11, we will explore VAEs and leverage their compression capabilities to build an efficient video generation system.

Generative adversarial network

A generative adversarial network (GAN) [3] consists of two networks:

- **Generator:** A neural network that converts a random noise into an image.
- **Discriminator:** Another neural network that determines whether a given image is real or artificially generated.

During training, these two networks engage in a continuous game: the generator learns to make more realistic images, while the discriminator becomes better at distinguishing real from generated ones. If a generated image is correctly classified as "generated," the generator will receive a penalty for not generating a realistic image. This adversarial process continues until the generator generates images that the discriminator can no longer differentiate from real ones.

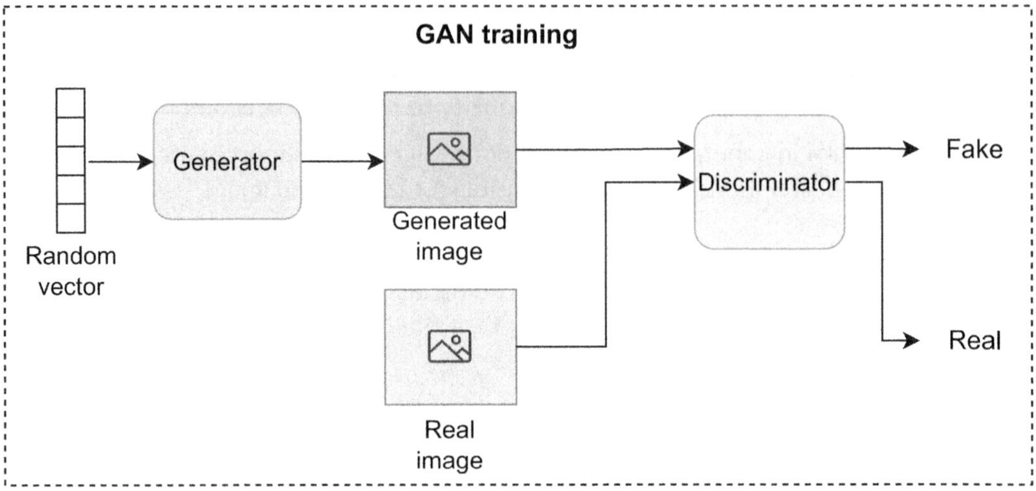

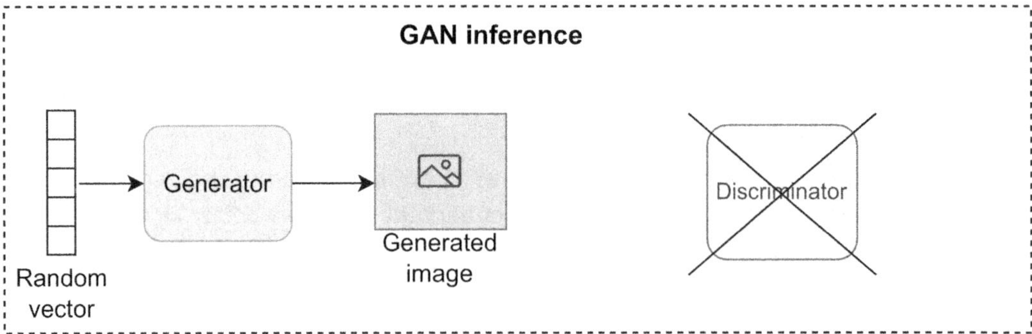

Figure 7.4: GAN training and inference process

Pros:

- **High-quality generation:** GANs are known for their ability to generate high-quality images.
- **Fast generation:** While GANs are generally slower than VAEs, the generator can still generate an image in a single forward pass.
- **Attribute control:** GAN architecture can be modified to control specific attributes such as age or expression. For example, a user can request a face image that is happy and old.

Cons:

- **Training instability:** GANs are challenging to train. Common training issues are mode collapse [4], where the generator creates a limited variety of outputs, and non-convergence [5], where the GAN model fails to stabilize during training.
- **Limited control:** While GANs allow for attribute control, it is challenging to go beyond that, for example, using a text description to generate an image [6].
- **Limited novelty:** While GANs are good at generating variations of images in a certain

domain, they typically struggle to generate novel images that are much different from their training data.

In summary, GANs are challenging to train, and they offer limited control over generated images. However, they can generate detailed images, and they support control over facial attributes, which makes them suitable for applications such as face generation and image editing.

Autoregressive model

In autoregressive modeling, image generation is formulated as a sequence generation task, where each part of an image is generated sequentially. This sequential generation enables the use of the Transformer architecture, allowing us to benefit from its powerful ability to capture long-range dependencies.

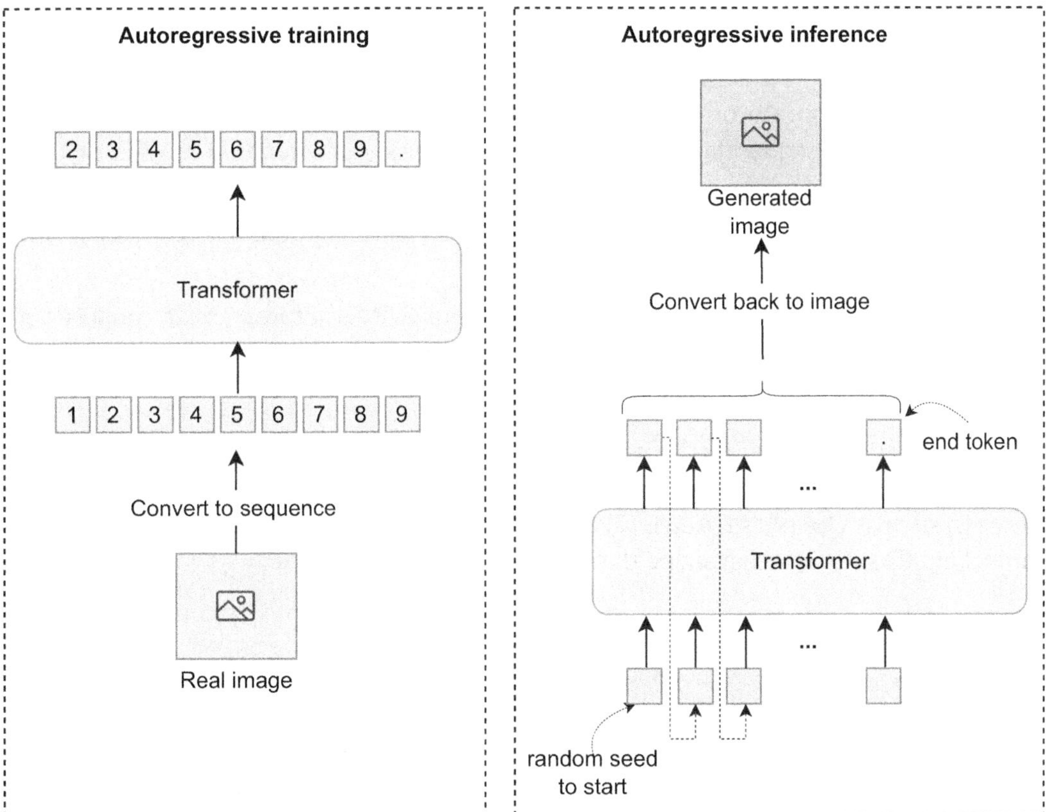

Figure 7.5: Autoregressive model training and inference process

Pros:

- **High detail and realism:** Autoregressive models generate images with high levels of detail and sharpness.
- **Stable training:** Compared to GANs, training autoregressive models is usually more

stable.

- **Control over generation:** It is possible to control image generation using additional inputs, such as a text prompt describing the desired image content. This flexibility comes from the Transformer architecture, which can support any number of inputs as part of the input sequence.
- **Support of multimodal conditioning:** Autoregressive models easily support conditioning on different modalities. For example, if we provide a celebration audio as input, the generated image will match the audio. This flexibility is due to the Transformer architecture, which can support different modalities as input as long as they are provided as a sequence of numerical vectors.
- **Novelty:** Autoregressive models are capable of generating novel and complex images. For example, they can generate an image of "an avocado on a chair on Mars" even if they haven't seen such examples in their training data.

Cons:

- **Slow generation:** Autoregressive models generate the image sequentially, one token at a time. This sequential generation makes them slower compared to VAEs or GANs.
- **Resource-intensive:** These models are usually very large, with billions of parameters. Training such large models requires significant computational resources, which increases the cost.
- **Limited image manipulation:** Unlike VAEs and GANs, autoregressive models don't have a structured latent space that can be easily explored or manipulated. This limits certain types of image manipulations such as attribute control in faces.

In summary, while autoregressive models are slow in generation due to their sequential nature, they can generate highly detailed and novel images. Many popular image generation models, such as OpenAI's DALL-E [7] and Google's Muse [8], are based on autoregressive modeling. Chapter 8 will examine this approach in more detail.

Diffusion model

Diffusion models are another popular approach for image generation, which has shown remarkable capabilities. Diffusion models formulate image generation as an iterative process. During training, noise is gradually added to images, and a neural network is trained to predict this noise. When generating images during inference, the process begins with random noise. The trained neural network is then used to iteratively denoise the image, transforming the noise into a meaningful image. This transformation occurs over a fixed number of steps, with the model adding details to the image at each step.

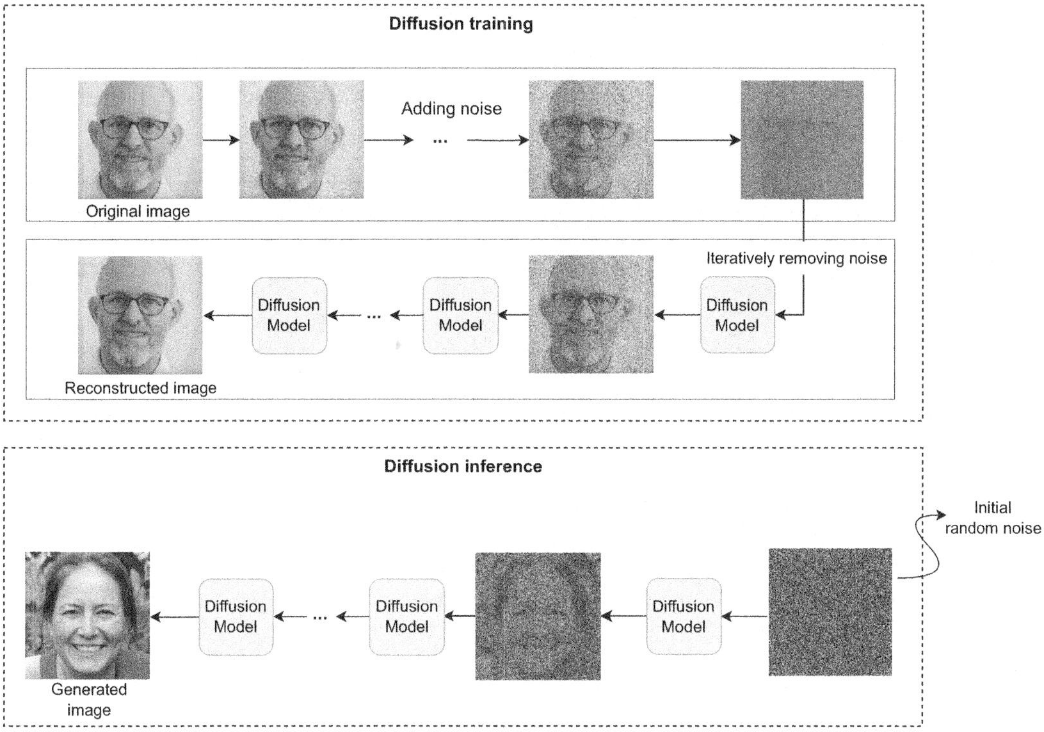

Figure 7.6: Diffusion model training and inference process

Pros:

- **High detail and realism:** Diffusion models can generate images of exceptional quality and realism.
- **Stable training:** Compared to GANs, training diffusion models are typically stable.
- **Control over generation:** Similar to autoregressive models, diffusion models can be controlled using various inputs, such as text describing the desired image.
- **Novelty and creativity:** Diffusion models can generate novel and imaginative images.
- **Robustness to noisy images:** Diffusion models are effective at removing noise from images because of their denoising process. This can be useful in certain applications such as image denoising.

Cons:

- **Slow generation:** Diffusion models generate images in multiple denoising steps. This iterative process makes them slower compared to other methods.
- **Resource-intensive:** Diffusion models are usually large, with billions of parameters. This makes them computationally intensive and, therefore, expensive to train.
- **Limited image manipulation:** Unlike VAEs and GANs, diffusion models don't have a structured latent space for manipulating images.

In summary, while diffusion models are slow, they have shown impressive performance in generating highly detailed, diverse, and imaginative images. Most state-of-the-art image generation models, such as DALL·E 3 [9], are based on diffusion models. Chapter 9 will examine diffusion models in great detail.

Characteristics	VAE	GAN	Autoregressive	Diffusion
Quality	Low	Moderate	High	Exceptional
Speed	Fast	Fast	Slow	Slow
Training stability	Stable	Unstable	Stable	Stable
Control over generation	Limited	Limited	Flexible	Moderate
Facial manipulation	No	Yes	No	No
Novelty	Limited	Limited	High	High
Resource intensity	Moderate	Moderate	High	High

Table 7.1: A comparison of different image generation approaches

For realistic face generation, we select GANs as our primary approach. GANs are particularly effective because they let us manipulate facial attributes through a structured latent space, which is an optional requirement in this chapter.

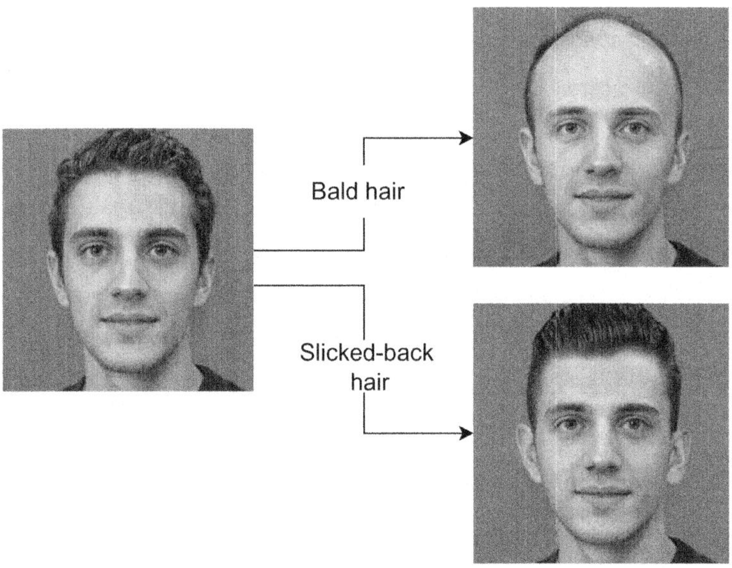

Figure 7.7: Facial attribute manipulation (Images are taken from [10])

Data Preparation

Developing a realistic face generation system requires a large collection of images. Here, we have 70,000 diverse images of human faces. To prepare these images for training, we apply the following steps:

- **Remove low-quality or low-resolution images:** We remove low-resolution images and use ML models to filter low-quality, blurry ones. This ensures the model learns only from high-quality images.
- **Augment images:** We apply data augmentation techniques such as flipping, rotation, or color adjustment to artificially increase the size of the training data. This helps the model see more variations of the image during training and, thus, generalize better afterward.
- **Normalize and resize images:** We resize all images to a standard dimension, for example, 1024×1024. We also normalize images to a standard range, typically between -1 and 1.
- **Enhance diversity:** We use ML classifiers to tag images with gender, age, and other attributes. Then, we adjust the dataset to ensure a balanced representation of different groups. This step is crucial to prevent biases in generated faces.

Model Development

Architecture

GANs consist of two components: a generator and a discriminator. Let's briefly examine the architecture of each component.

Generator

The generator component takes random noise as input and converts it into an image. Its architecture consists of a series of upsampling blocks, each of which increases the spatial dimensions (height and width) of its input. These blocks gradually transform the low-dimensional noise vector into a 2D image of the desired size.

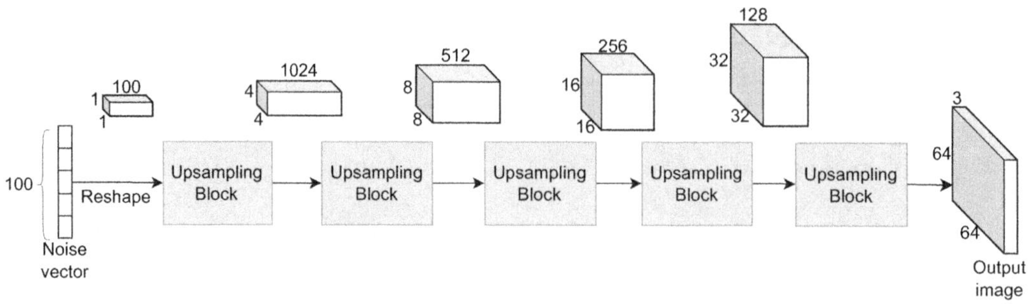

Figure 7.8: Series of upsampling blocks

Let's talk about the three main components of the upsampling block:

- Transposed convolution
- Normalization layer
- Non-linear activation

Transposed convolution

Transposed convolution, also known as deconvolution or upsampling convolution, is an operation used in neural networks to increase the spatial resolution of feature maps—essentially performing the opposite of a regular convolution. It's widely used in applications such as image generation, semantic segmentation, and super-resolution where the goal is to reconstruct higher-resolution outputs from lower-resolution inputs.

Unlike standard convolution, which slides a filter across the input, transposed convolution starts by inserting zeroes between the pixels of the input feature map, effectively expanding it. The expanded input is then convolved with a filter, where the filter's stride[1] and padding[2] are adjusted to achieve the desired output size. For example, starting with an input of 1×1×100, with 1024 filters of kernel size 1x1 and stride 1, we end up with a 4x4x1024 feature map. In the next step, with 512 filters of kernel size 3x3 and stride 1, we get an 8x8x512 feature map. These are the first two upsampling stages shown in Figure 7.8.

1 Stride controls how much the filter moves across the input during convolution—larger strides skip more pixels

2 Padding adds extra borders around the input to control the output size during convolution

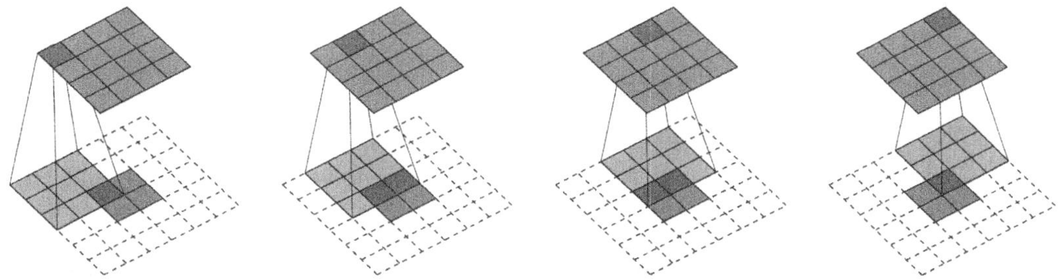

Figure 7.9: Transpose conv with 3x3 filter and stride=1 over 4x4 inputs [11]

In PyTorch, this layer is usually implemented with "ConvTranspose2d." To learn more about convolutions and transposed convolutions, refer to [11].

Normalization layer

A normalization layer improves the training stability by scaling the input data to have a consistent distribution.

Training GANs is unstable because it involves two networks (the generator and the discriminator) competing against each other. This can lead to problems like mode collapse, where the generator produces limited diversity, or oscillations, where the generator and discriminator fail to converge during training. Normalization helps stabilize the training by scaling the activations at each layer, thus reducing the risk of vanishing or exploding gradients. This helps maintain consistent distributions of activations, which is critical for balanced competition between the generator and discriminator. With a more robust optimization process, we can use a higher learning rate, speed up training, and reduce the time needed for convergence. We will discuss the training challenges and mitigations later in this chapter.

There are several normalization layers, each with its own way of normalizing data:

- Batch normalization
- Layer normalization
- Instance normalization
- Group normalization

Batch Normalization (BN)

BN [12] normalizes the inputs of a layer across the batch dimension by calculating the mean and variance for each feature. The normalized data is then scaled and shifted using learnable parameters.

- **Benefits:** BN helps stabilize the learning process and allows for higher learning rates, speeding up training. It also acts as a regularizer, reducing chances of overfitting.
- **Usage:** Commonly used in deep networks, including Convolutional Neural Networks

(CNNs) and GAN generators.

Layer Normalization (LN)

LN [13] normalizes the inputs across the features of each individual sample rather than across the batch dimension. It, therefore, computes the mean and variance for each feature across the entire feature vector of each sample.

- **Benefits:** LN is effective in settings where batch sizes are small or variable, such as in Recurrent Neural Networks (RNNs) and Transformers.
- **Usage:** Frequently used in sequence models and scenarios where consistent behavior across samples is crucial.

Instance Normalization (IN)

IN [14] operates by normalizing across each feature map individually for each sample.

- **Benefits:** IN is beneficial for tasks where the appearance of individual samples varies widely, as it allows the network to focus on content rather than style.
- **Usage:** Commonly used in style transfer and image generation tasks.

Group Normalization (GN)

GN [15] normalizes inputs by dividing features into groups and normalizing within each group. It offers a balance between BN and LN.

- **Benefits:** GN is useful for cases with very small batch sizes where BN might not be effective.
- **Usage:** Often applied in tasks where BN fails due to small batch sizes or when layer behavior consistency is needed across groups of features.

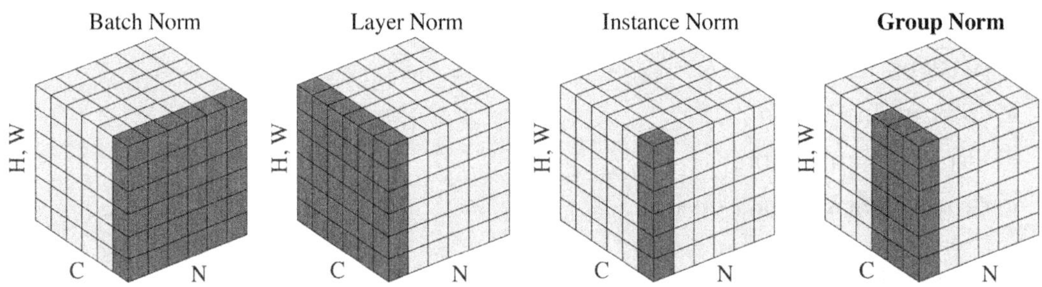

Figure 7.10: Comparison of different normalization methods (Image taken from [15])

Non-linear activation

Non-linear activation functions, such as *ReLU* [16], introduce non-linearity into the model, allowing it to learn complex patterns and representations. Without non-linearity, the network would essentially be a linear transformation, regardless of the depth, making it incapable of modeling intricate data distributions such as images, speech, or complex functions.

To summarize, our generator consists of upsampling blocks (*ConvTranspose2D*), each followed by a normalization layer (*BatchNorm2D*) and a non-linear activation (*ReLU*). The final block uses "*Tanh*" [17] instead of "*ReLU*". This choice ensures the final outputs range between -1 and 1, matching the range of our image pixels after data preparation.

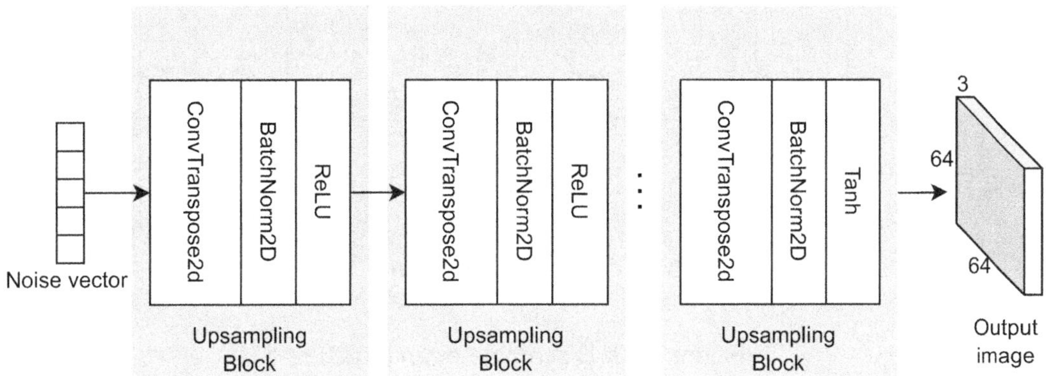

Figure 7.11: Generator architecture

Discriminator

The discriminator's job is to differentiate between real and generated images. It functions as a binary classifier, taking an image as input and outputting the probability that the image is real.

The discriminator comprises a series of downsampling blocks followed by a classification head. The downsampling blocks progressively reduce the spatial dimensions of the input image while extracting its features. The classification head then processes the extracted features to predict the probability that the input image is real.

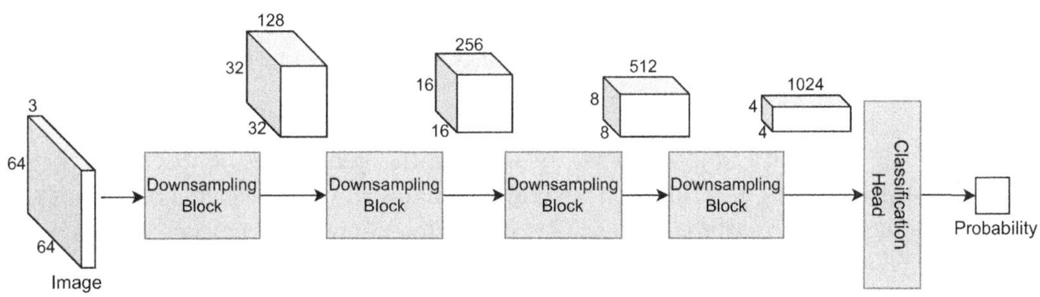

Figure 7.12: Series of downsampling blocks

A downsampling block consists of several convolution operations to progressively decrease the input's spatial dimension. In PyTorch, we typically use a "*Conv2D*" layer with a stride of 2 to halve the spatial dimensions. Like the generator, batch normalization (*BatchNorm2D*) and non-linear activation function (*ReLU*) are used in between convolution layers to enhance training stability and performance.

The classification head includes one or two fully connected layers followed by a *sigmoid* activation function. The sigmoid function ensures the final output ranges between 0 and 1, which is crucial for interpreting the output as a probability.

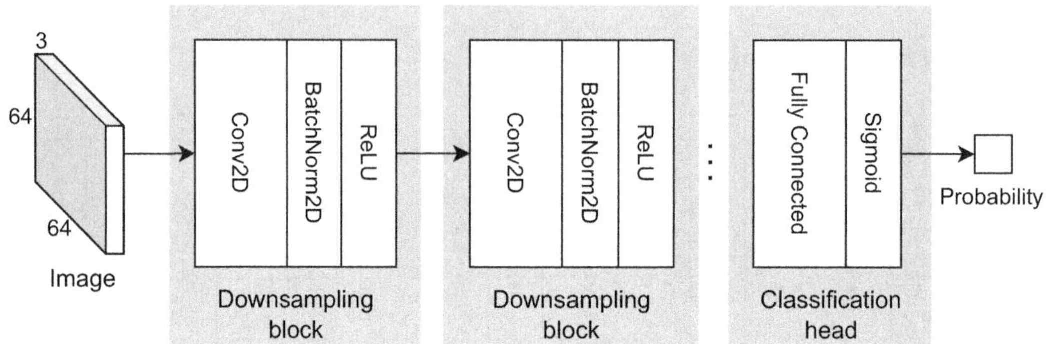

Figure 7.13: Discriminator architecture

Various versions of GANs have been developed over the years to serve different purposes. For instance, StyleGAN [18] modifies the generator's architecture to control attributes of generated faces, such as age, hair color, and facial expression. For more details on the StyleGAN architecture and its key architectural choices, refer to [18].

Training

To produce realistic images, we train the GAN using a unique process called adversarial training. In adversarial training, the generator and the discriminator are trained simultaneously in a game-like scenario. The generator aims to produce images that look real, while the discriminator improves its ability to distinguish between real and generated images. During this adversarial process, the generator learns to produce increasingly more convincing images. At the same time, the discriminator gets better at identifying fake images. This competitive process continues until the generator produces images that the discriminator can no longer detect as fake.

When training GANs, it is important to ensure both the generator and discriminator improve together, avoiding scenarios where one dominates the other. Such a balance is empirically shown to be crucial for successful training. To maintain this balance, it is common to alternate between the following two steps:

1. Train the discriminator for a few iterations while keeping the generator frozen.
2. Train the generator for a few iterations while keeping the discriminator frozen.

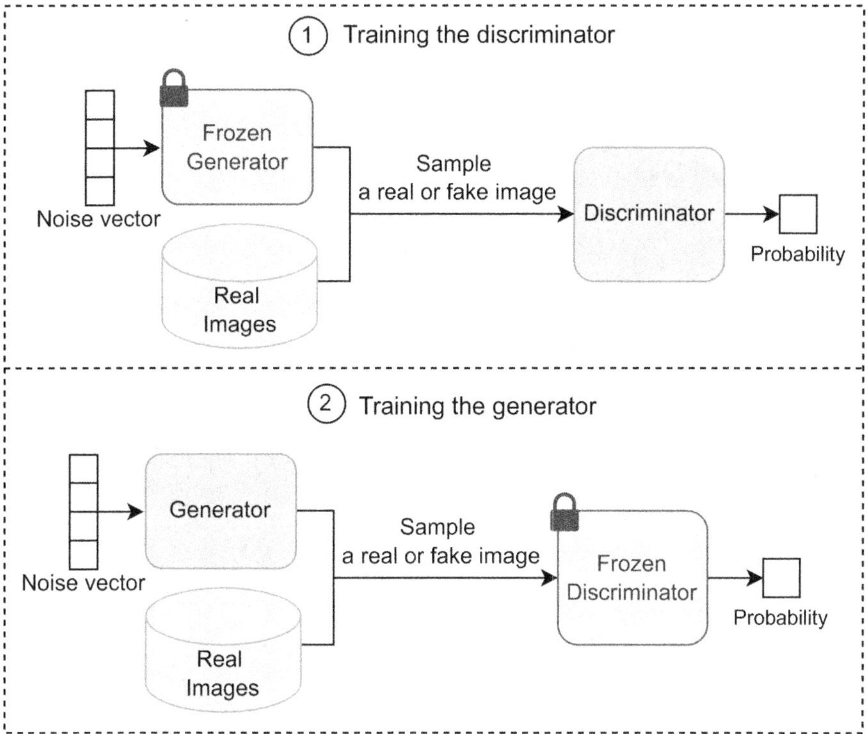

Figure 7.14: Generator and discriminator alternative training

Next, let's examine the ML objective and loss function for training a GAN model.

ML objective and loss function

The generator and discriminator have their own specific, conflicting goals. The discriminator aims to distinguish accurately between real and generated images. The generator aims to produce images that the discriminator cannot distinguish from real ones. We first explore the loss function and ML objective of each component and then combine them into a unified loss function for the GAN.

Discriminator

We employ binary cross-entropy as the loss function for the discriminator, as it is commonly used in binary classification models.

$$L_D = -\overbrace{\frac{1}{m}\sum_{i=1}^{m}\log D\left(\mathbf{x}^{(i)}\right)}^{\text{loss contribution from real images}} - \overbrace{\frac{1}{n}\sum_{j=1}^{n}\log\left(1 - D\left(G\left(\mathbf{z}^{(j)}\right)\right)\right)}^{\text{loss contribution from fake images}}$$

Where:

- $D\left(x^{(i)}\right)$ is the discriminator's predicted probabilities for a real image,
- $G\left(z^{(j)}\right)$ is the generator's output (a fake image) given random noise,
- m is the number of real images,
- n is the number of fake images.

The discriminator's ML objective is to minimize the binary cross-entropy loss function.

Generator

The generator aims to produce realistic images that the discriminator cannot distinguish from real ones. Ideally, the discriminator should predict probabilities close to 1 for images that have been produced by the generator. To achieve this, the ML objective is formulated as maximizing $\log\left(D\left(G\left(z^{(j)}\right)\right)\right)$ for all fake images or, equivalently, minimizing the following loss function:

$$L_G = \frac{1}{n}\sum_{j=1}^{n}\log\left(1 - D\left(G\left(\mathbf{z}^{(j)}\right)\right)\right)$$

GAN's minimax loss

The minimax loss [19], originally used in the GAN paper, unifies the generator's and discriminator's losses into a single function:

$$\text{Minimax loss } = \frac{1}{m}\sum_{i=1}^{m}\log D\left(\mathbf{x}^{(i)}\right) + \frac{1}{n}\sum_{j=1}^{n}\log\left(1 - D\left(G\left(\mathbf{z}^{(j)}\right)\right)\right)$$

The discriminator aims to maximize the loss, while the generator aims to minimize it. Therefore, the overall ML objective is:

$$\min_G \max_D\left(\frac{1}{m}\sum_{i=1}^{m}\log D\left(\mathbf{x}^{(i)}\right) + \frac{1}{n}\sum_{j=1}^{n}\log\left(1 - D\left(G\left(\mathbf{z}^{(j)}\right)\right)\right)\right)$$

Besides the minimax loss, researchers have proposed other loss functions to improve training stability in GANs. To learn more about these loss functions, refer to [20].

Common training challenges in GANs

GANs are difficult to train compared to other generative models such as autoregressive or diffusion models. Discussing these challenges is beneficial in an ML interview. In this section, we discuss three main challenges of training GANs:

- Vanishing gradients
- Mode collapse
- Failure to converge

Vanishing gradients

The vanishing gradient problem [21] occurs when gradients become very small during training. This problem primarily affects the generator. When the discriminator becomes too good at distinguishing between real and fake images, it provides very small gradient values for the generator to update its parameters. This slows down or stops the generator's learning process.

Two common techniques to mitigate the vanishing gradient problem are:

- Modified minimax loss
- Wasserstein loss

Modified minimax loss: The original GAN paper points out that minimizing the original ML objective can cause training to stall. To overcome this, the paper recommends altering the generator's objective to maximize

$$L_G = \frac{1}{n}\sum_{j=1}^{n}\log\left(D\left(G\left(\mathbf{z}^{(j)}\right)\right)\right)$$

This minor adjustment is inspired by formulating the ML objective from a different perspective. With this change, the generator aims to maximize the probability of fake images being identified as real, rather than minimizing the probability of fake images being identified as fake.

Wasserstein loss: This loss function is used in a modified GAN called a "*Wasserstein GAN*" or "*WGAN*." Let's examine the ML objective for a WGAN's discriminator and generator.

- **WGAN's discriminator:** The discriminator for a WGAN, also known as the "critic," differs from the one in a traditional GAN. Instead of classifying images as real or fake, the critic outputs a score representing the "realness" of an image. The critic loss is defined as the difference between the critic's outputs for real images and fake images. Hence, the critic's ML objective is to maximize the critic loss.

  $$\text{Critic loss } = D(x) - D(G(z))$$

- **WGAN's generator:** The ML objective for the generator of a WGAN is to maximize the probability of fake images being identified as real:

  $$\text{Generator loss} : D(G(z))$$

Mode collapse

Ideally, a GAN model should produce different variations of images with different random inputs. Mode collapse refers to situations where the generator produces a limited variety of images. Let's see why this might happen.

During training, the generator might learn to trick the system by finding one image that seems most plausible to the discriminator. Once the generator finds this most plausible image, it may keep producing the same image to fool the discriminator. Hence, the generator never learns to generate other images. This type of failure in a GAN is known as "mode collapse". Two common techniques to mitigate mode collapse are:

- Wasserstein loss
- Unrolled GAN [22]

To learn more about the unrolled GAN and how it mitigates the mode collapse, refer to [4].

Failure to converge

Training GANs is typically challenging and the process is often unstable. This is due to the "failure to converge" problem, a common issue in training GANs. Let's explore why this happens.

As the generator improves during training, the discriminator's performance declines because it becomes increasingly more difficult to distinguish between real and fake images. If the generator reaches a point where it can mimic real data perfectly, the discriminator's accuracy drops to 50 percent; it effectively begins to make random guesses, much like flipping a coin. This decline in discriminator performance hinders GAN convergence since its feedback gradually becomes less and less useful to the generator. When training continues past a certain point, the generator starts training on useless feedback, and its quality may collapse as a result.

There are various approaches to improve the training stability and convergence of GANs:

- **Normalization:** Applying techniques like batch normalization helps stablize training by ensuring consistent distributions across layers.
- **Different learning rates:** Using different learning rates for the generator and discriminator can help balance their progress and avoid instability in training.
- **Regularization:** Employing regularization methods like weight decay prevents overfitting and helps maintain training stability.
- **Adding noise to discriminator inputs:** Injecting noise into the inputs of the discriminator can prevent it from becoming too powerful early on, which helps balance the competition between the generator and the discriminator.

To learn more about the specific details of these approaches, refer to [21] and [23].

Sampling

Sampling is the process of generating new images from a trained GAN model. Before discussing sampling methods, let's first review the concept of latent space in a GAN.

During training, the generator learns to transform various noise vectors into images. This process forms a latent space—a multidimensional space where each point represents a potential noise vector. This latent space is meaningful to the GAN because its generator can map each point to its corresponding image.

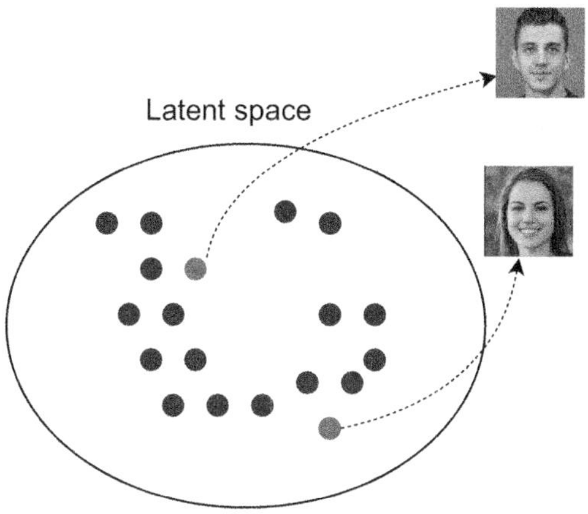

Figure 7.15: Latent space points map to face images

To generate a realistic face image, we sample a point from this latent space, known as a latent vector. The generator then takes this latent vector and transforms it into an image.

There are two methods to sample a latent vector from a learned latent space:

- Random sampling
- Truncated sampling

Random sampling

Random sampling uses a standard Gaussian distribution to draw latent vectors from the latent space. This ensures a diverse selection of latent vectors, leading to the generation of varied images.

Truncated sampling

Truncated sampling restricts the latent vectors to a smaller, high-probability region of the latent space. By truncating the distribution, the method reduces the chance of generating outliers, resulting in higher-quality images. This approach is beneficial when the primary goal is to maintain high realism in the generated faces. If you are interested in learning about the details and implementation of truncated sampling, refer to [24].

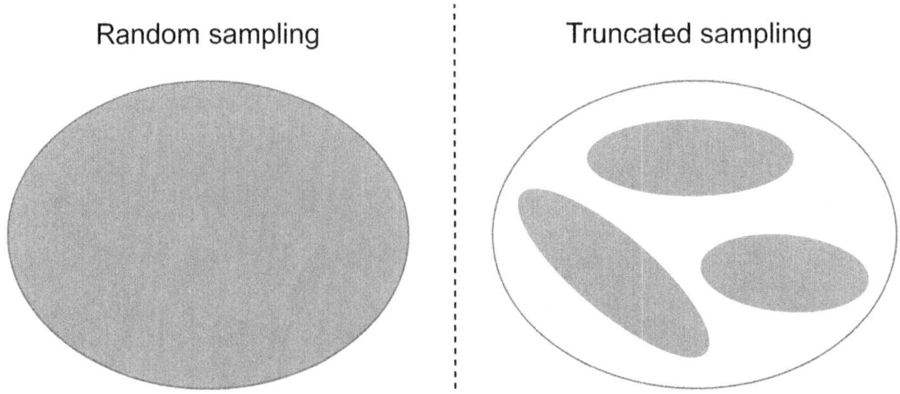

Figure 7.16: Random vs. truncated sampling (Gray regions represent sampling areas)

In summary, random sampling ensures diversity by exploring the entire latent space, while truncated sampling focuses on a high-probability region to enhance realism. For realistic face generation, we utilize random sampling as it leads to diversity and usually works well in practice.

Evaluation

Offline evaluation metrics

Evaluating image generation systems involves assessing both the quality and diversity of the generated images. Several metrics have been developed for this purpose, such as Inception score [25], Fréchet Inception distance (FID) [26], and Kernel Inception distance (KID) [27]. Among these, Inception score and FID are the most widely used. Human evaluation also continues to be an essential method of assessing generative models.

In an ML system design interview, the interviewer's goal is to assess your intuition and practical understanding, rather than test your detailed knowledge of formulas and theories. However, having a broad understanding of some of these metrics can still be helpful. Let's briefly examine the Inception score and FID.

Inception score

The Inception score is a widely used metric to evaluate the quality of generated images in generative models such as GANs. The metric relies on a pretrained image classification model, such as "*Inception v3*" [28], to assess how well the generated images resemble real-world objects.

Here's a step-by-step explanation of how the metric is calculated:

1. **Generating images:** We start by generating a large set of images using the model we want to evaluate.

2. **Computing class probabilities:** For each generated image, the Inception model provides a probability distribution over all of its 1,000 object classes. A high-quality image should lead to a distribution with a peak (i.e., a high probability for one class) indicating that the model recognizes it as a clear instance of a class.
3. **Calculating the marginal distribution:** Marginal distribution refers to the average of the predicted class probabilities across all images. This helps us understand the overall distribution of classes represented in the generated set. If the images are diverse, the marginal distribution will be flat and spread across many classes.
4. **Computing KL divergence:** The KL divergence measures how different the predicted class distribution for each image is from the marginal distribution. High-quality images will have a distribution that is very different from the marginal distribution. This is because a high-quality image is expected to have a peak in its distribution, while the marginal distribution is expected to be close to uniform if the images are diverse.
5. **Calculating the Inception score:** The Inception score is the exponentiated average of the KL divergence across all images. A high Inception score indicates that individual images have been confidently classified into a variety of classes, which means the generated images are both diverse and of high quality.

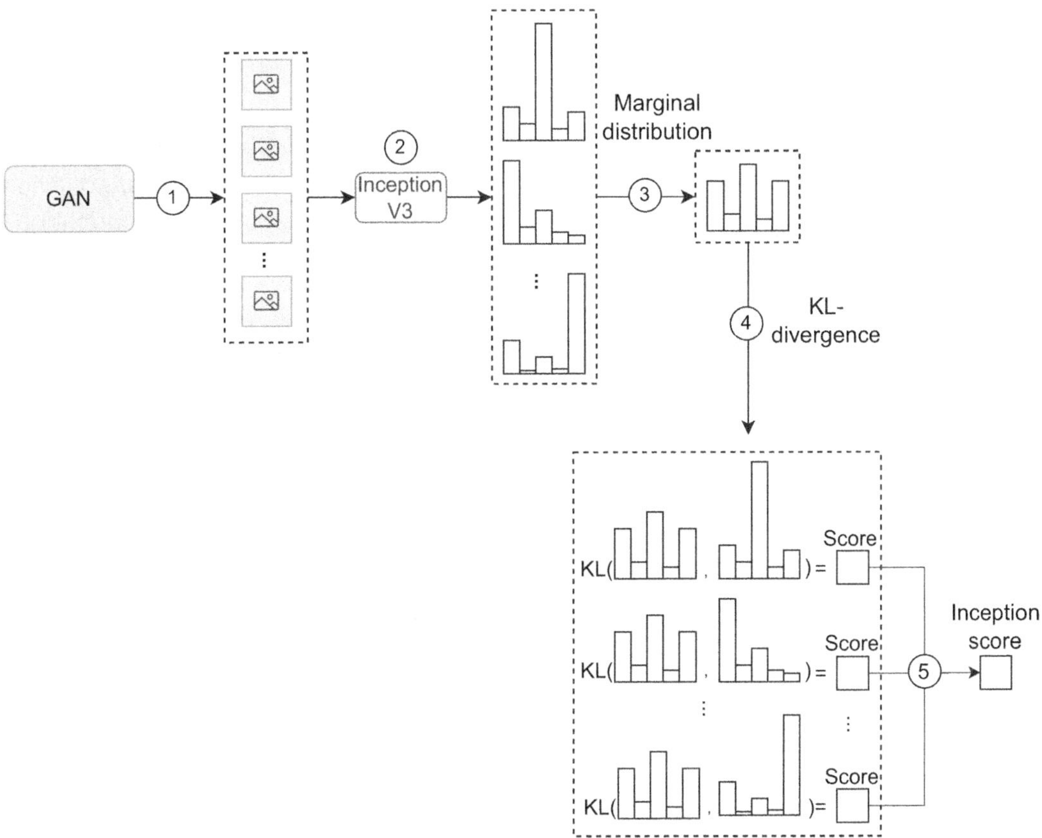

Figure 7.17: Inception score calculation

How does the Inception score measure both diversity and quality?

- **Diversity:** The Inception score evaluates diversity by checking if the generated images result in a nearly uniform marginal distribution across classes, indicating that the images are spread evenly across different classes.
- **Quality:** High-quality images result in a sharp, peaked probability distribution, indicating that the image is clearly recognized as belonging to a particular class. The Inception score compares this distribution with the marginal distribution to assess image quality.

Fréchet inception distance (FID)

FID is another popular metric for evaluating the quality of images produced by generative models. It assesses how similar the distribution of generated images is to the distribution of real images. Unlike the Inception score, which uses class probabilities, FID considers the statistics of the features extracted by a pretrained model such as *Inception v3*. The Inception model is chosen because it is trained on a large and diverse dataset (ImageNet) and can extract meaningful features that represent the content and style of the images.

Here's a step-by-step explanation of how FID is calculated:

1. **Generating images:** We start by generating a large set of images using the model we want to evaluate. These images will be compared to a set of real images to evaluate their quality and diversity.
2. **Extracting features:** We pass each image (both generated and real) through the Inception v3 model and extract features ("activations") from a specific layer, usually one near the end of the network. Features from this deep layer capture high-level information—such as shapes, textures, and objects—which is crucial for assessing the realism of the images.
3. **Calculating mean and covariance:** We calculate the mean and covariance of the extracted features separately for generated and real images. These statistical measures summarize the distributions of features for both sets of images.
4. **Computing Fréchet distance:** We calculate the FID as the Fréchet distance between the mean and covariance of generated and real images. The Fréchet distance measures how close the two distributions are. A lower FID indicates greater similarity between the distributions, meaning the generated images are more realistic and diverse. To learn more about the Fréchet distance and its formula, refer to [29].

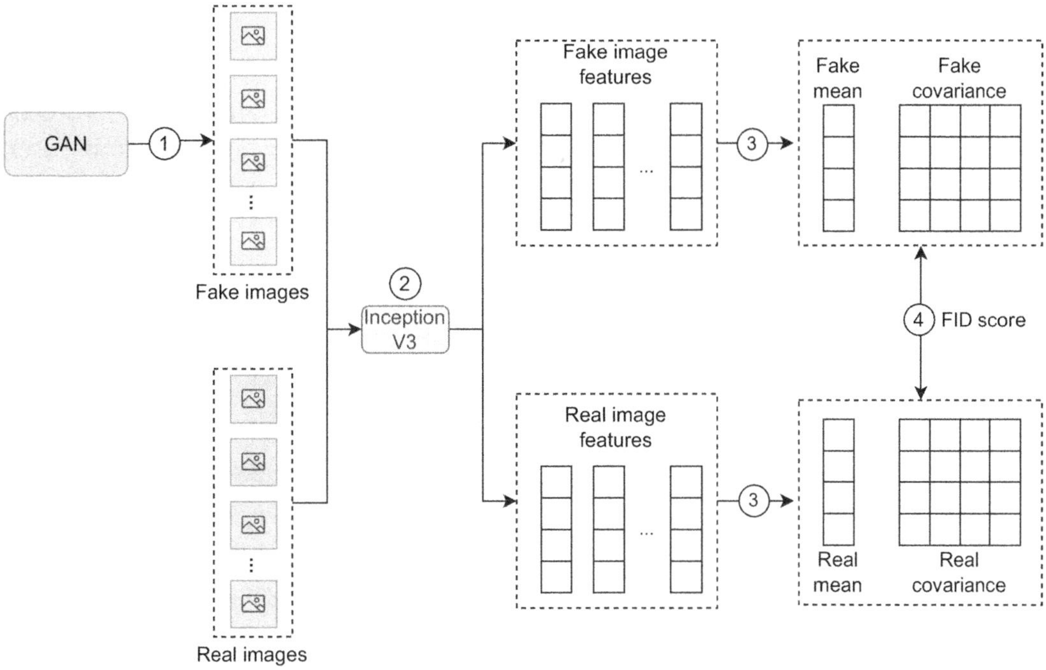

Figure 7.18: FID calculation

How does the FID measure both diversity and quality?

- **Diversity:** The FID considers the covariance of the features, reflecting the spread and variation in the image features. A diverse set of generated images will have a feature distribution similar to that of real images, showing the model's ability to produce a wide range of different images.
- **Quality:** FID ensures the generated images are high-quality by comparing their feature distributions to those of real images. If the mean and covariance of the generated images' features are similar to those of the real images, this indicates that the generated images are likely to be of high quality.

FID and Inception score are useful for assessing the quality and diversity of image generation models, but they don't always align with human judgment. This is mainly because these metrics rely on ImageNet classes, which can introduce artifacts. The authors of [30] suggest that using a non-ImageNet-trained model like CLIP could provide a better alignment with human evaluation.

While CLIP-based metrics show promise in improving alignment with human judgment, they still cannot fully replace the insights gained from direct human feedback. Human evaluation still remains the most reliable method for assessing the quality of generated images, as it captures nuances that automated metrics might miss.

Human evaluation

Human evaluation is crucial for assessing image generation systems since automated metrics can miss subjective qualities such as aesthetic appeal. There are different protocols to perform human evaluation. One protocol, as outlined in [31], involves presenting users with pairs of images generated by different models. The human evaluators are asked to choose which image looks more photorealistic. This approach lets us compare models based on criteria that align more closely with human judgment.

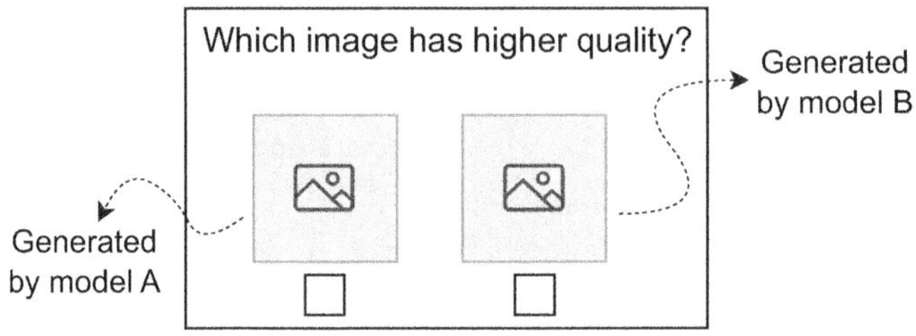

Figure 7.19: Pairwise comparison during human evaluation

Online evaluation metrics

Various metrics are typically monitored in practice to ensure that the image generation system performs well and meets user expectations. Two common metrics are:

- **User feedback:** This metric is vital as it directly reflects users' opinions about the generated images. User feedback can be gathered through surveys, ratings, or direct comments.
- **Latency:** Latency refers to the time it takes from when a request is made until the image is fully generated and delivered to the user. Fast response times are crucial for maintaining a good user experience, especially in interactive applications. Monitoring latency helps identify performance bottlenecks and ensures the system meets user expectations.

Overall ML System Design

In this section, we explore the holistic design of a realistic face generation system. The key components we'll examine are:

- Face generator
- Training service
- Evaluation service
- Deployment service

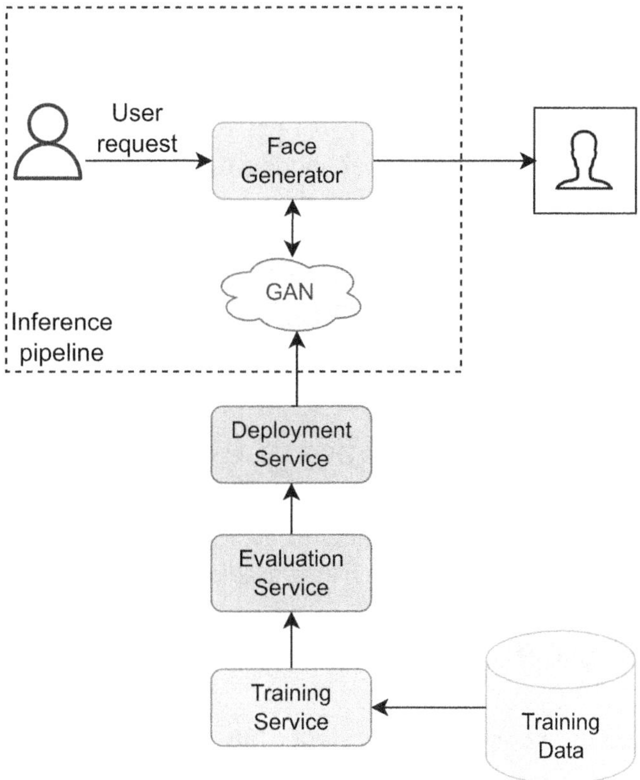

Figure 7.20: Realistic face generation overall design

Face generator

The face generator is the core component responsible for generating realistic faces. It handles user requests and interacts with the trained GAN model to sample high-quality images. Users can optionally specify desired attributes such as age, gender, hairstyle, and expression. The service leverages StyleGAN properties to adjust the noise vector in the latent space based on these attributes.

If you are interested in learning more about the architectural details of attribute control and latent manipulation, read [32, 33].

Training service

The training service continuously improves the GAN model by periodically retraining it with user-approved generated images and new training data.

Evaluation service

The evaluation service automatically evaluates newly trained models. It uses predefined metrics to assess their performance. The evaluation results determine whether the new model meets quality standards and should replace the existing one.

Deployment service

The deployment service deploys improved models to the production environment. It ensures a smooth transition with minimal downtime during updates. The deployment service also monitors the performance of deployed models to ensure they function as expected.

Other Talking Points

In case there's extra time after the interview, you might discuss these further topics:

- Various GAN architectures, such as DCGAN, WGAN, and StyleGAN, and the trade-offs of each architecture [34, 35, 18].
- Techniques for stabilizing GAN training to avoid mode collapse and convergence issues, including the use of Wasserstein loss, gradient penalty, and other robust training methods [36].
- Utilize conditional GANs (cGANs) to generate faces based on specific conditions or inputs [37].
- Evaluation metrics of condition consistency [38, 39].
- Style-mixing in face generation [18].

Summary

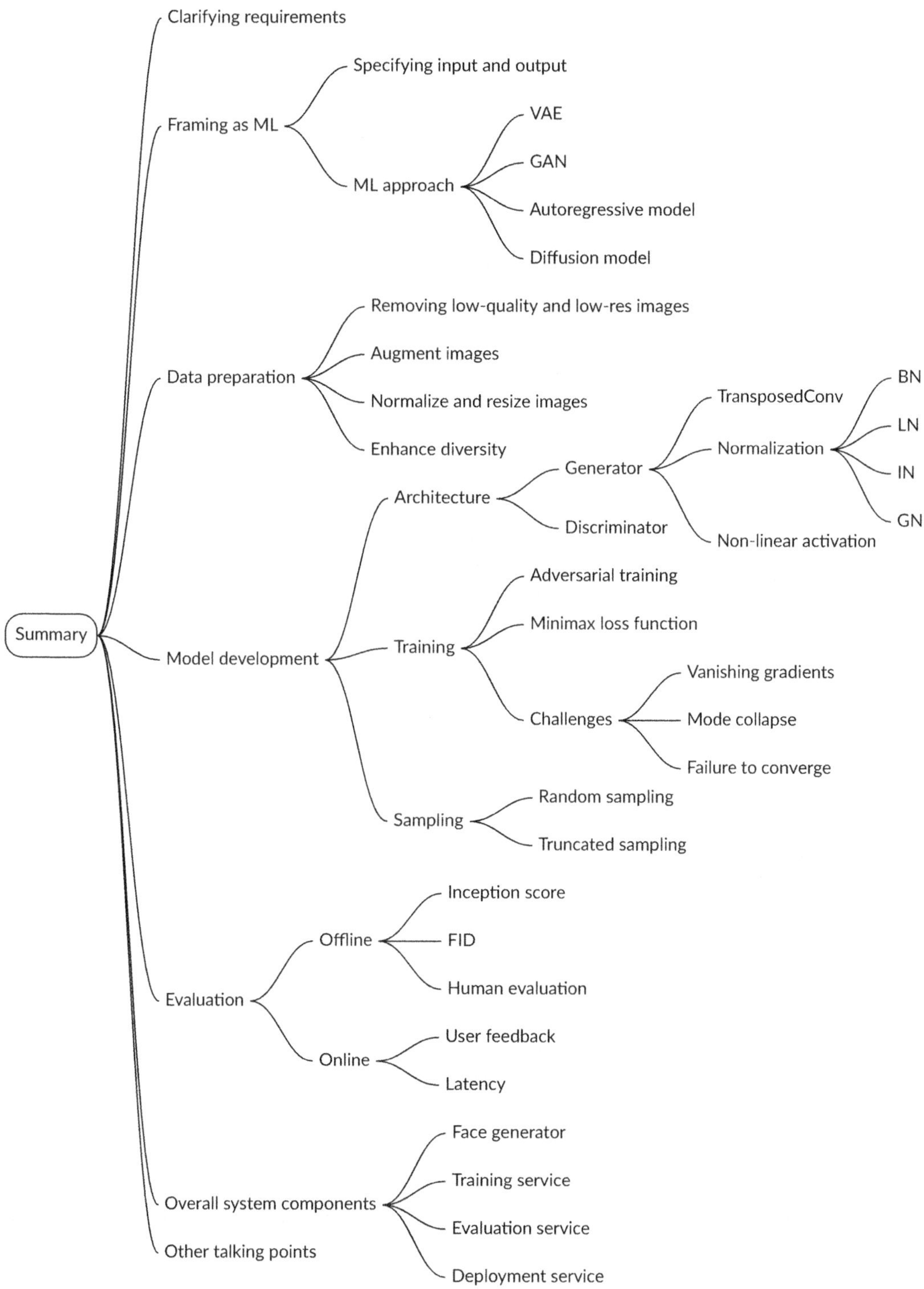
Summary
Clarifying requirements
Framing as ML
Specifying input and output
ML approach
VAE
GAN
Autoregressive model
Diffusion model
Data preparation
Removing low-quality and low-res images
Augment images
Normalize and resize images
Enhance diversity
Model development
Architecture
Generator
TransposedConv
Normalization
BN
LN
IN
GN
Non-linear activation
Discriminator
Training
Adversarial training
Minimax loss function
Challenges
Vanishing gradients
Mode collapse
Failure to converge
Sampling
Random sampling
Truncated sampling
Evaluation
Offline
Inception score
FID
Human evaluation
Online
User feedback
Latency
Overall system components
Face generator
Training service
Evaluation service
Deployment service
Other talking points

Reference Material

[1] StyleGAN2. https://arxiv.org/abs/1912.04958.

[2] Auto-Encoding Variational Bayes. https://arxiv.org/abs/1312.6114.

[3] Generative Adversarial Networks. https://arxiv.org/abs/1406.2661.

[4] Combating Mode Collapse in GAN Training: An Empirical Analysis Using Hessian Eigenvalues. https://arxiv.org/abs/2012.09673.

[5] Google's GAN Course. https://developers.google.com/machine-learning/gan/training.

[6] StackGAN: Text to Photo-Realistic Image Synthesis with Stacked Generative Adversarial Networks. https://arxiv.org/abs/1612.03242.

[7] Zero-Shot Text-to-Image Generation. https://arxiv.org/abs/2102.12092.

[8] Muse: Text-To-Image Generation via Masked Generative Transformers. https://arxiv.org/abs/2301.00704.

[9] DALL·E 3. https://openai.com/index/dall-e-3/.

[10] Attribute-Specific Control Units in StyleGAN for Fine-Grained Image Manipulation. https://arxiv.org/abs/2111.13010.

[11] A Guide to Convolution Arithmetic for Deep Learning. https://arxiv.org/abs/1603.07285.

[12] Batch Normalization: Accelerating Deep Network Training by Reducing Internal Covariate Shift. https://arxiv.org/abs/1502.03167.

[13] Layer Normalization. https://arxiv.org/abs/1607.06450.

[14] Instance Normalization: The Missing Ingredient for Fast Stylization. https://arxiv.org/abs/1607.08022.

[15] Group Normalization. https://arxiv.org/abs/1803.08494.

[16] Deep Learning using Rectified Linear Units (ReLU). https://arxiv.org/abs/1803.08375.

[17] PyTorch's Tanh Layer. https://pytorch.org/docs/stable/generated/torch.nn.Tanh.html.

[18] A Style-Based Generator Architecture for Generative Adversarial Networks. https:

//arxiv.org/abs/1812.04948.

[19] Minimax. https://en.wikipedia.org/wiki/Minimax.

[20] Loss Functions in GANs. https://developers.google.com/machine-learning/gan/lo ss.

[21] Towards Principled Methods for Training Generative Adversarial Networks. https: //arxiv.org/abs/1701.04862.

[22] Unrolled Generative Adversarial Networks. https://arxiv.org/abs/1611.02163.

[23] Stabilizing Training of Generative Adversarial Networks through Regularization. http s://arxiv.org/abs/1705.09367.

[24] Megapixel Size Image Creation using Generative Adversarial Networks. https://arxi v.org/abs/1706.00082v1.

[25] Inception Score. https://en.wikipedia.org/wiki/Inception_score.

[26] GANs Trained by a Two Time-Scale Update Rule Converge to a Local Nash Equilibrium. https://arxiv.org/abs/1706.08500.

[27] Demystifying MMD GANs. https://arxiv.org/abs/1801.01401.

[28] Rethinking the Inception Architecture for Computer Vision. https://arxiv.org/abs/ 1512.00567.

[29] FID Calculation. https://en.wikipedia.org/wiki/Fr%C3%A9chet_inception_distance.

[30] The Role of ImageNet Classes in Fréchet Inception Distance. https://arxiv.org/abs/ 2203.06026.

[31] Hierarchical Text-Conditional Image Generation with CLIP Latents. https://arxiv.or g/abs/2204.06125.

[32] Alias-Free Generative Adversarial Networks. https://arxiv.org/abs/2106.12423.

[33] StyleGAN3. https://nvlabs.github.io/stylegan3/.

[34] Unsupervised Representation Learning with Deep Convolutional Generative Adversarial Networks. https://arxiv.org/abs/1511.06434.

[35] Wasserstein GAN. https://arxiv.org/abs/1701.07875.

[36] Stabilizing Generative Adversarial Networks: A Survey. https://arxiv.org/abs/1910 .00927.

[37] Conditional Generative Adversarial Nets. https://arxiv.org/abs/1411.1784.

[38] CLIPScore: A Reference-free Evaluation Metric for Image Captioning. https://arxiv.org/abs/2104.08718.

[39] DreamBooth: Fine Tuning Text-to-Image Diffusion Models for Subject-Driven Generation. https://arxiv.org/abs/2208.12242.

8

High-Resolution Image Synthesis

Introduction

Generative AI offers a fascinating ability to create highly realistic and diverse images. In this chapter, we explore a technique that enables the generation of detailed and varied images in just seconds.

Figure 8.1: An image generated by VQGAN [1]

Clarifying Requirements

Here is a typical interaction between a candidate and an interviewer:

Candidate: Should the system focus on specific categories of images at the start?
Interviewer: For simplicity, let's begin with natural scenes and urban landscapes. We can explore other categories later.

Candidate: Do we have training data consisting of natural scenes? What's the dataset size?
Interviewer: We have a large dataset with about 5 million high-resolution images of natural scenes and landscapes.

Candidate: Should the system support additional conditioning, such as input text describing the desired image?
Interviewer: Good question. We'll focus on image generation without input conditions. However, the system should be flexible to support input prompts.

Candidate: What resolution range should we aim for when generating the images?
Interviewer: The system should generate images with either 1024×1024 or 2048×2048 pixels, based on user requests.

Candidate: Should the images be generated in real time, or is some delay acceptable?
Interviewer: Real-time generation isn't necessary. However, a reasonable processing time is important. Let's aim for five seconds per image.

Frame the Problem as an ML Task

Specifying the system's input and output

For high-resolution image synthesis, the user simply requests a new image. The output is a high-resolution image.

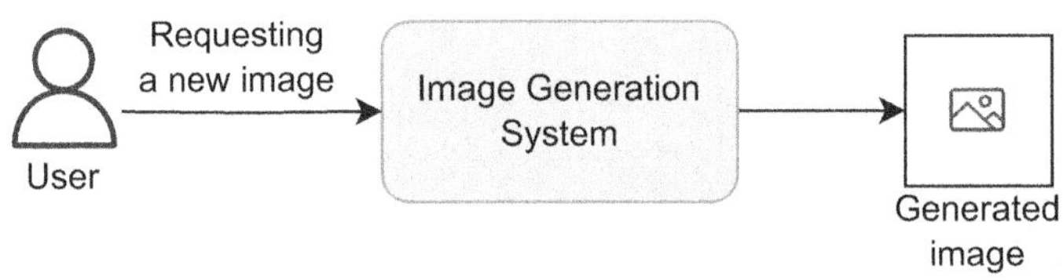

Figure 8.2: Input and output of an image generation system

Choosing a suitable ML approach

As discussed in Chapter 7, there are several approaches to image generation, including VAEs, GANs, autoregressive models, and diffusion models. In this section, we choose the one best suited for the task.

Most variants of VAEs and GANs struggle to generate high-resolution images, such as those with resolutions of 512x512 pixels and above. They face a challenge known as posterior collapse. This occurs because, as the resolution increases, these models require a decoder with a higher capacity to capture additional details. During training, the decoder can become so powerful that it starts to ignore input from the latent space, as it can model the output independently. As a result, the latent variables contribute little to the generation process, reducing the diversity of the images.

While both autoregressive and diffusion models can generate high-resolution images, they differ significantly in complexity and resource requirements. Autoregressive models are often considered slow due to their sequential nature, where each pixel depends on the ones generated before it. This dependency leads to a time complexity that increases linearly with the number of pixels, resulting in an $O(N^2)$ complexity for an image of size $N \times N$, and the process is difficult to parallelize. To address this limitation, autoregressive models generate images chunk by chunk instead of pixel by pixel. For example, generating a 1024×1024 image using chunks of 64×64 pixels requires only 256 steps or tokens, significantly reducing the computational overhead compared to traditional pixel-based methods.

On the other hand, the complexity of diffusion models increases super-linearly with image size, resulting in a computational complexity of $O(TN^2)$, where N is the number of pixels and T represents the number of denoising steps. Larger images often require more refinement steps to maintain quality and coherence, which further escalates computational demand.

In practice, generating a high-resolution image using standard diffusion models can take several minutes[1]. In contrast, Transformer-based autoregressive models can accomplish similar tasks in seconds due to their chunk-based generation approach. For this chapter, we focus on autoregressive models for educational purposes. In Chapter 9, we will cover diffusion models in detail. Let's now delve into autoregressive models and their key components.

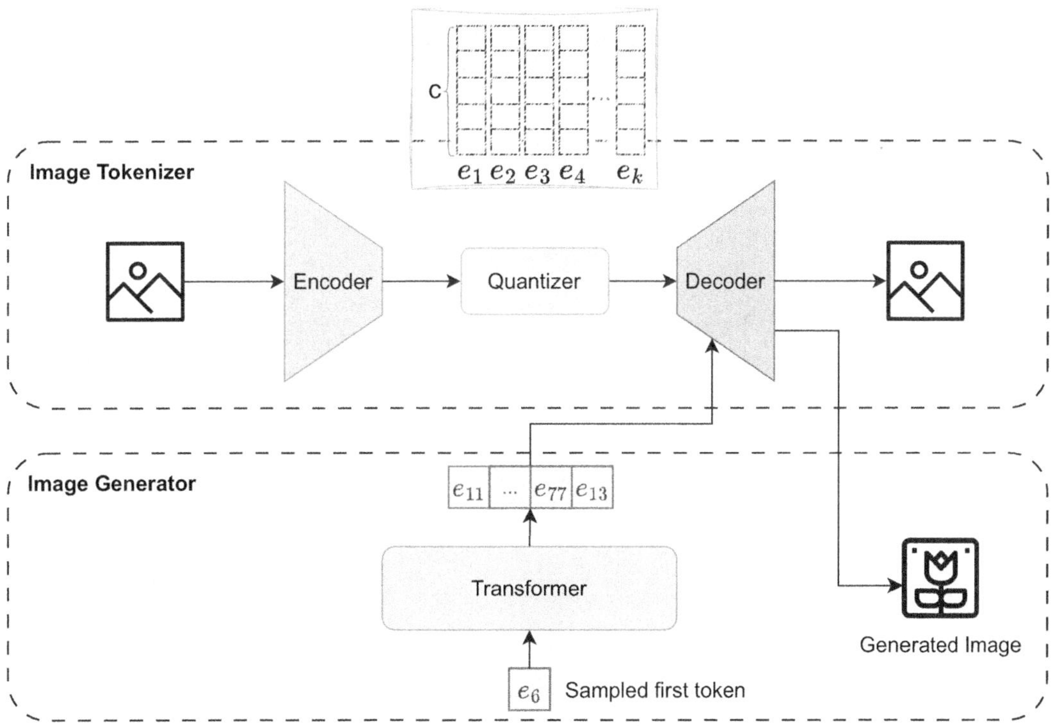

Figure 8.3: Autoregressive image generation

1 Certain optimizations and techniques (e.g., latent diffusion model) can significantly speed up the generation process in diffusion models. These methods are discussed in detail in Chapter 10 and Chapter 11.

Autoregressive models generate images by treating them as a sequence generation task. This approach relies on two primary components:

- Image tokenizer
- Image generator

Image tokenizer

Image tokenization refers to representing an image with a sequence of discrete tokens. This is crucial in autoregressive models, where the image is generated sequentially, chunk by chunk.

The image tokenizer is a separate model, trained independently. Its main functions are to encode an image into a sequence of discrete tokens and decode a sequence of discrete tokens back into an image.

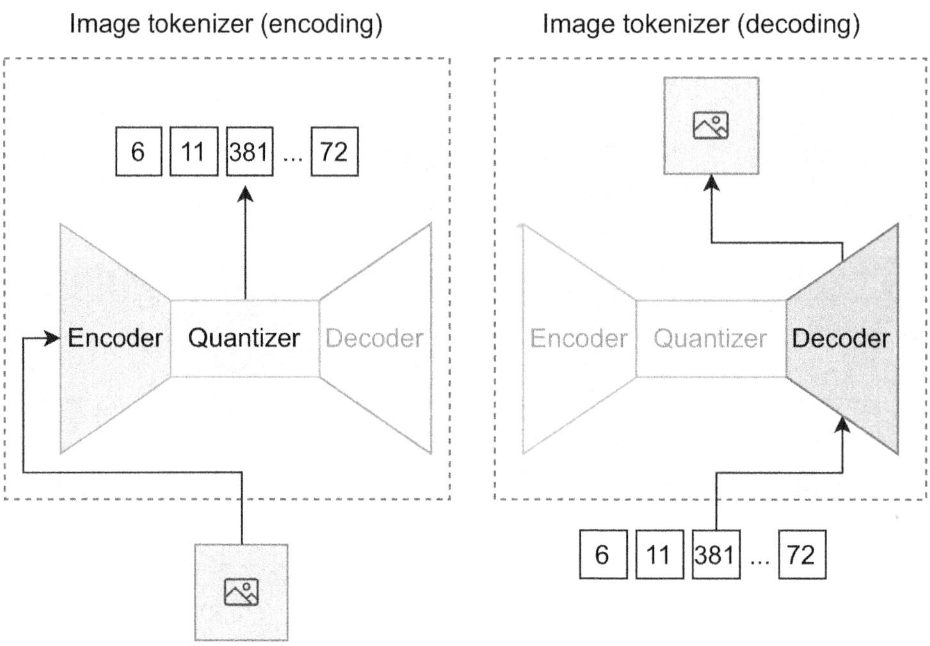

Figure 8.4: Image tokenizer's encoding and decoding

Image generator

The image generator is the primary model for generating images chunk by chunk. While there are various architectures for sequence generation, the decoder-only Transformer is the most effective choice for two reasons. First, the decoder-only Transformer has a flexible architecture that can handle different modalities. In a chatbot, it takes text tokens as input and generates text tokens as output. In image captioning, it takes an image as input and outputs text tokens. For image generation, it generates a sequence of image tokens as output, which are then decoded into an image.

Second, the Transformer architecture is effective at capturing long-range dependencies through its attention mechanism, which is beneficial for generating coherent images.

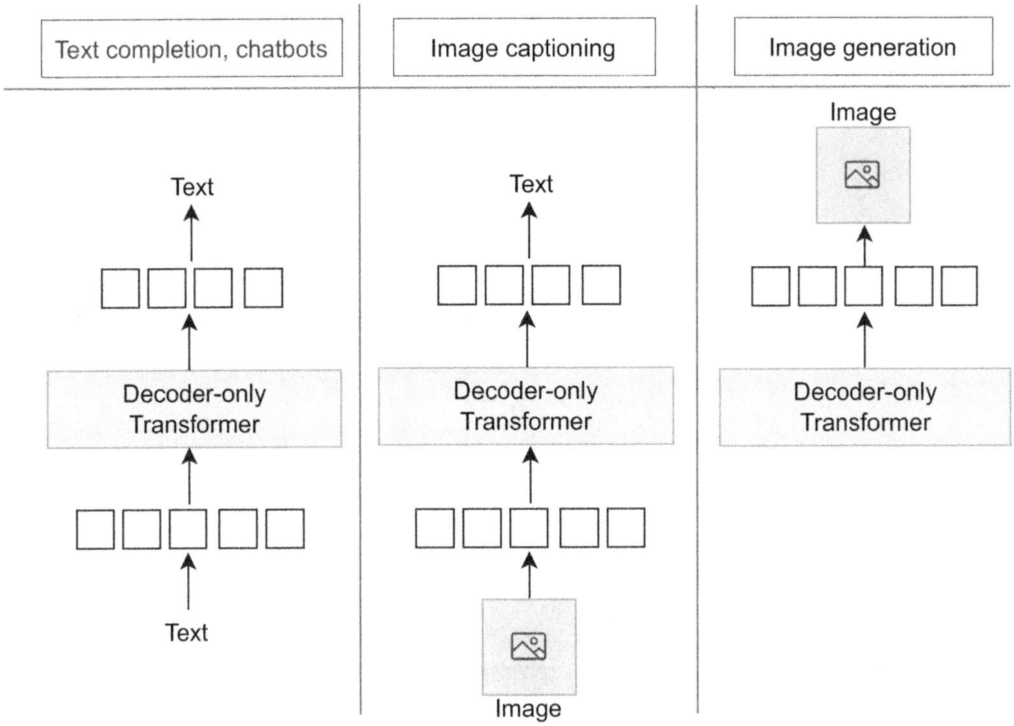

Figure 8.5: Decoder-only Transformer's flexibility in handling various modalities

In summary, we approach image generation with a Transformer-based autoregressive model. First, an image generator (decoder-only Transformer) generates a sequence of discrete tokens. Then, an image tokenizer decodes these tokens into the final image. We will explore the architecture, training, and sampling processes of these components in detail in the model development section.

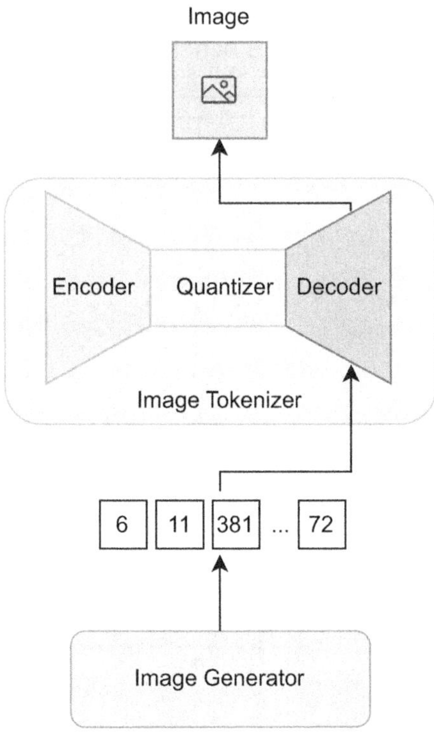

Figure 8.6: Autoregressive image generation

Data Preparation

The data preparation process involves two crucial steps:

- Image cleaning and normalization
- Image tokenization

Image cleaning and normalization

In this step, we remove low-quality images from the training data and ensure the remaining ones are consistent. This is achieved by applying the following operations:

- **Remove low-quality images:** We remove images with low resolution, excessive noise, or irrelevant content. We also ensure the dataset includes a wide range of styles, subjects, and compositions. This step is crucial for the generative model to produce diverse, high-quality images.
- **Normalize images:** Normalization involves scaling pixel values to a range, typically 0 to 1, to stabilize the training process.
- **Resize images:** Images often come in different sizes and aspect ratios. Resizing them to a uniform size ensures the model receives consistent inputs. Based on the inter-

viewer's requirements, we resize all images to 1024×1024.

Image tokenization

The image generator requires images to be represented as a sequence of discrete tokens. To achieve this, after training the image tokenizer, we tokenize all images in our training dataset into discrete tokens. It's important to note that this data preparation step is intended primarily for the image generator, not the image tokenizer.

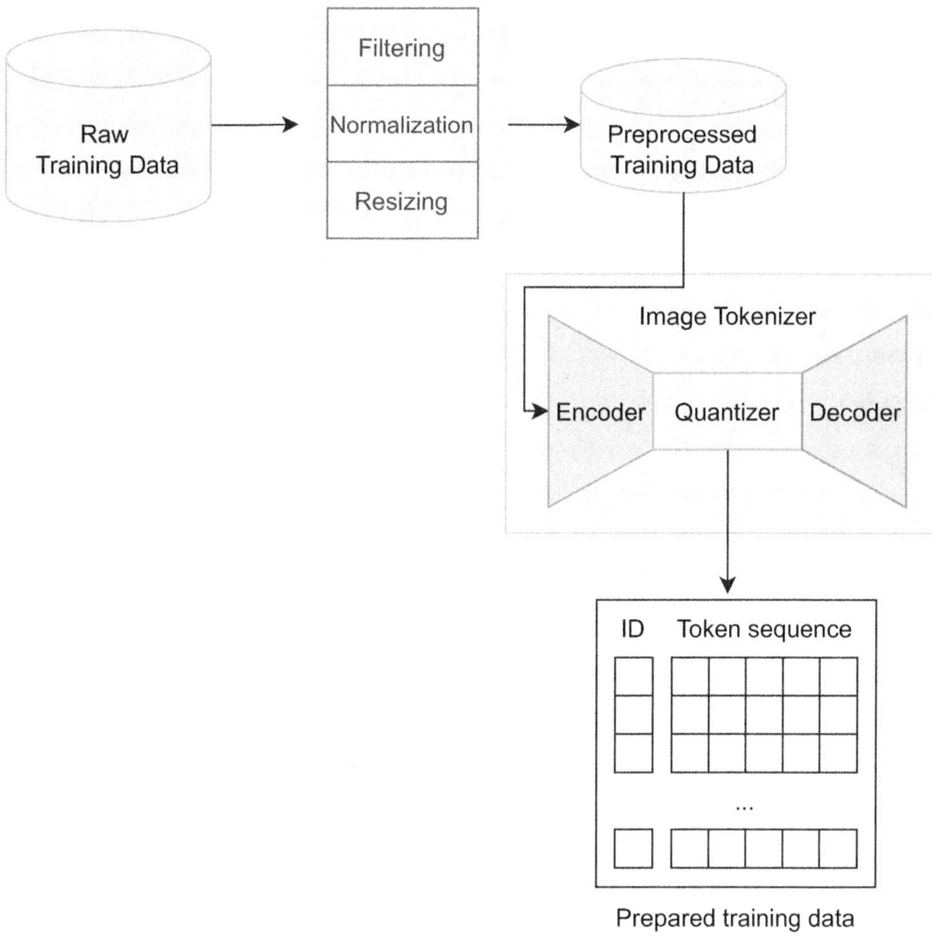

Figure 8.7: Data preparation process

These two steps ensure the training data is high-quality, consistent, and represented as a sequence of numerical inputs.

Model Development

Architecture

In this section, we explore the architecture of both the image tokenizer and the image generator.

Image tokenizer

The image tokenizer model has two functions:

1. Encoding an image into a sequence of discrete tokens
2. Decoding a sequence of discrete tokens back into an image

A common architecture specifically designed for image tokenization is the Vector-Quantized VAE (VQ-VAE) [2], which is a variant of the standard VAE discussed in Chapter 7. The VQ-VAE consists of three components:

- Encoder
- Quantizer
- Decoder

Encoder

The encoder maps the input image into a lower-dimensional latent space. This component encodes important features of the image into an encoded representation.

The encoder's architecture is a deep convolutional neural network (CNN) with several convolution layers, each followed by a *ReLU* [3] activation function. These layers process the input image and extract visual features.

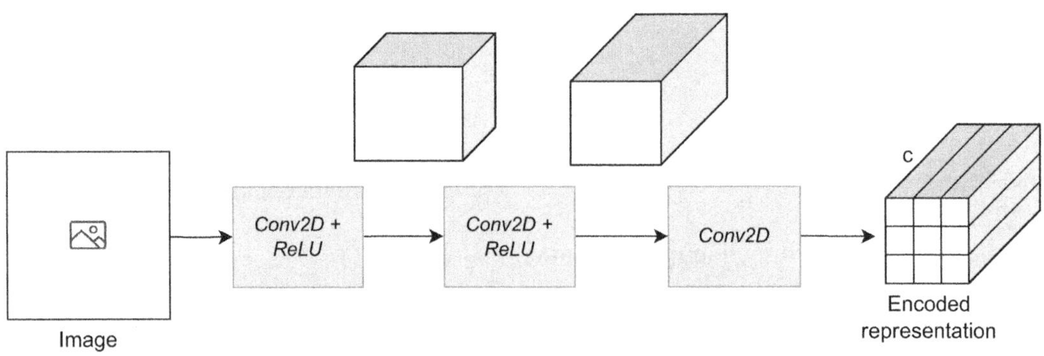

Figure 8.8: The encoder converts an input image into an encoded representation containing 9 features, each with c channels

Quantizer

The quantizer converts continuous latent vectors into discrete tokens. There are two main reasons why VQ-VAE introduces a quantizer component to a standard VAE:

- Avoiding posterior collapse
- Reducing the learning space

Avoiding posterior collapse

Posterior collapse is a common issue in standard VAEs where the latent variables contribute little or are ignored because the decoder generates accurate outputs without using the latent space. The quantization step addresses this by discretizing the latent variables, thus forcing the model to use them during reconstruction. This ensures the decoder doesn't overpower the latent space and keeps the latent variables actively involved in shaping the output.

Reducing the learning space

Continuous vectors are difficult to predict sequentially because they have endless possibilities and small differences. By turning these vectors into discrete tokens, the quantizer simplifies the process by allowing the Transformer to focus on fewer options.

The quantizer uses an internal codebook to convert continuous latent vectors into discrete tokens. This codebook contains learnable embeddings that represent different patterns in the input images. Each embedding acts as a token, represented by an integer from 1 to k. The quantizer replaces each continuous vector with the closest token in the codebook based on Euclidean distance [4].

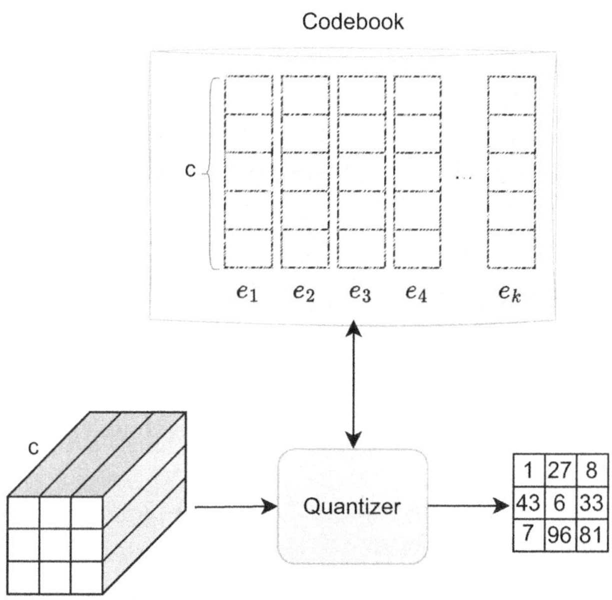

Figure 8.9: Quantization process

Note that the quantizer is an embedding table. Its sole parameter is the codebook, which is learned during training. The quantizer's single responsibility is to map each continuous vector with the closest token in the codebook; therefore, the output is a collection of token IDs.

Decoder

The decoder converts discrete tokens back into the original image. It typically uses a deep CNN with transposed convolutions (ConvTranspose2d) to gradually transform the representation to the original image size. To learn more about convolutions and transposed convolutions, refer to [5].

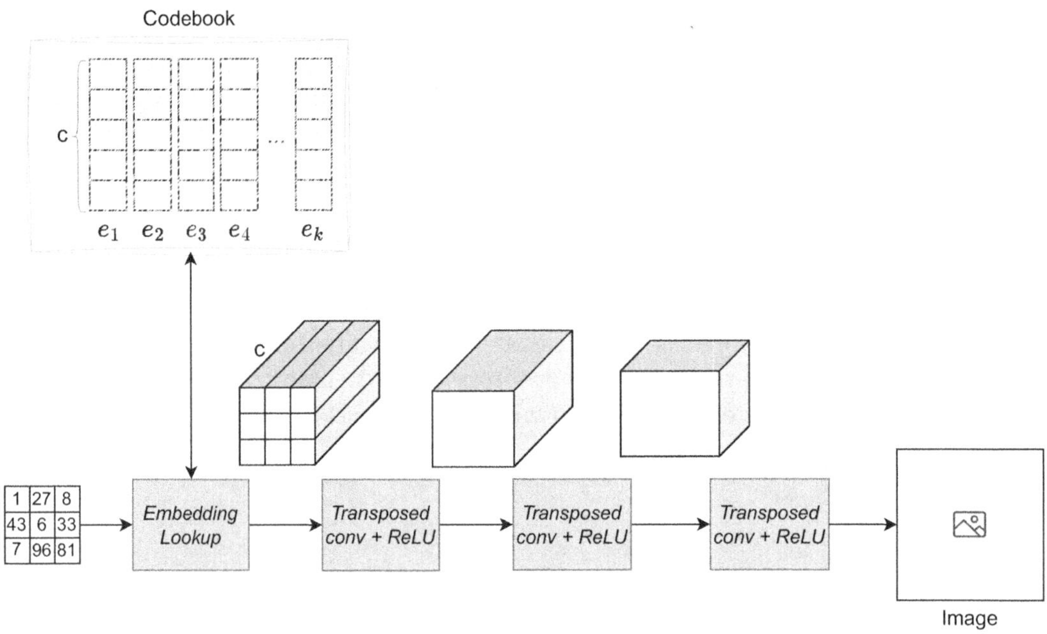

Figure 8.10: Decoding process

Image generator

The image generator generates a sequence of discrete tokens representing an image. As mentioned earlier, a decoder-only Transformer is often used for sequence generation tasks, which includes the following components:

- **Embedding lookup:** Replaces each discrete token with its embedding from the codebook.
- **Projection:** Projects each token embedding into a dimensionality that matches the Transformer's internal representation.
- **Positional encoding:** Adds positional encodings to the sequence to provide spatial information.
- **Transformer:** Processes the input sequence and outputs an updated sequence of vec-

tors.

- **Prediction head:** Utilizes the updated embeddings to predict the next token.

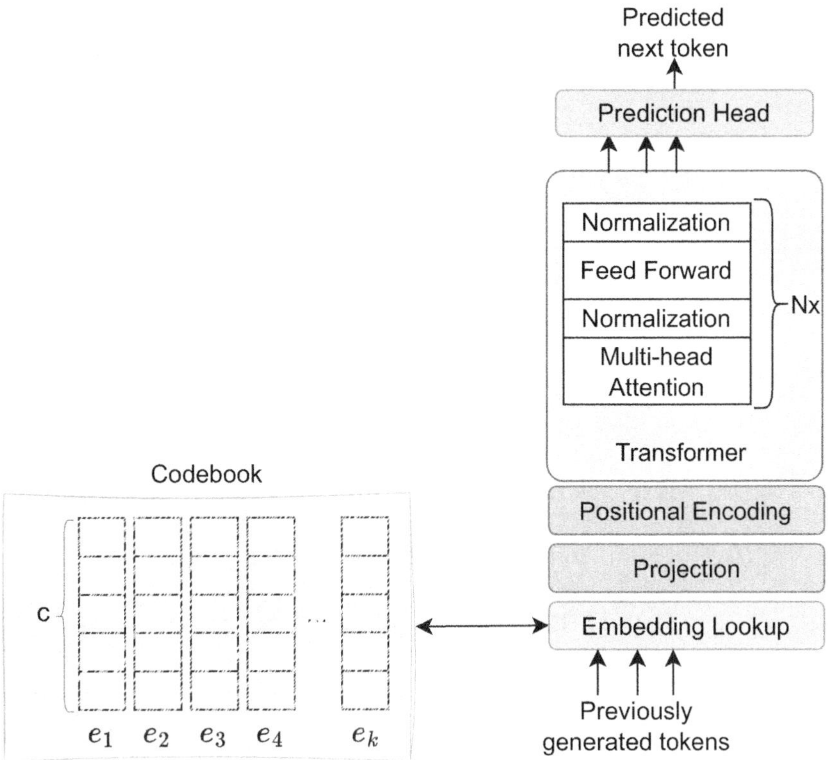

Figure 8.11: Decoder-only Transformer components

Training

In autoregressive image generation, we have two training stages:

- Stage I: Training the image tokenizer
- Stage II: Training the image generator

Stage I: Training the image tokenizer

The training process involves optimizing the encoder, decoder, and codebook so the model can accurately reconstruct the original images. This process can be described in three steps:

1. The encoder processes an input image and converts it into a continuous representation.
2. The quantizer replaces the continuous representation with discrete tokens using its internal codebook.
3. The decoder uses the discrete tokens to reconstruct the original image.

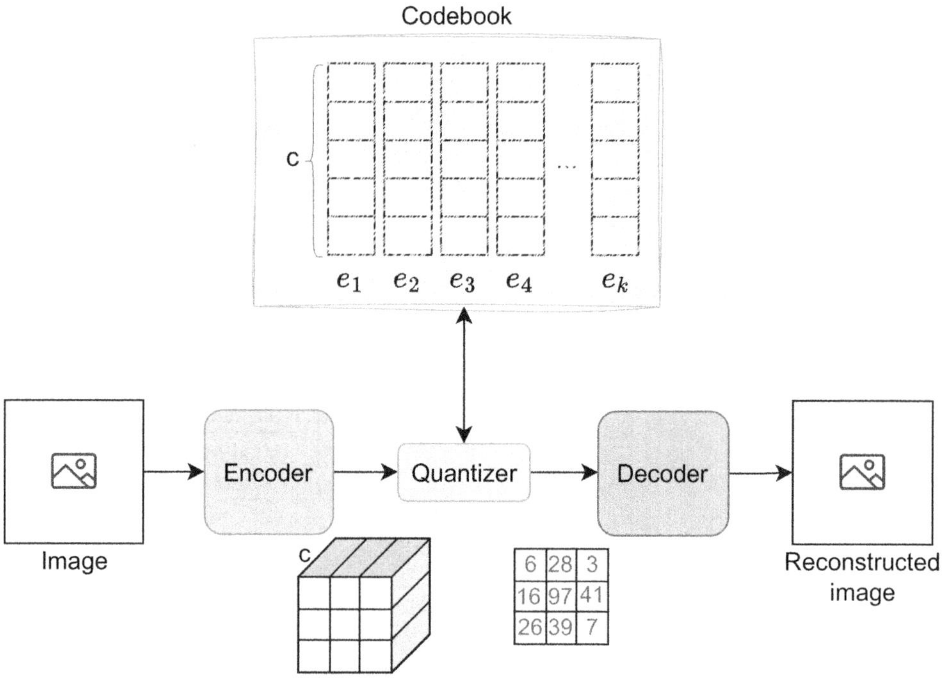

Figure 8.12: Image tokenizer training process

Since the quantizer lookup operation lacks a well-defined gradient for backpropagation, the VQ-VAE paper proposes approximating the gradient by copying it from the decoder input directly to the encoder output. This approach means that only the selected tokens receive gradients from the decoder, while unselected tokens do not receive any gradients.

Training data

We train the image tokenizer with 5 million images. Since the training is self-supervised and doesn't require image labels, we include other publicly available image datasets to enhance the tokenizer's robustness. In particular, we use the LAION-400M dataset [laion], which contains 400 million images. This results in a richer codebook that captures diverse visual patterns.

ML objective and loss function

The ML objective of the image tokenizer is to accurately reconstruct original images from their quantized tokens. To achieve this ML objective, the following loss functions are typically employed during the training process:

- Reconstruction loss
- Quantization loss

Reconstruction loss: The reconstruction loss measures the difference between the original image and its reconstruction from the quantized tokens. It is typically calculated using the mean squared error (MSE) formula:

$$\text{Reconstruction loss} = \frac{1}{n}\sum_{i=1}^{n}(x_i - \hat{x}_i)^2$$

Where:

- x_i is the pixel value of the original image,
- $\hat{x}_i$ is the pixel value of the reconstructed image,
- n is the total number of pixels in the image.

Quantization loss: The quantization loss measures the distance between the encoder's outputs and the nearest embedding in the codebook. This loss encourages the encoder to produce outputs that are closer to the codebook embeddings.

$$\text{Quantization loss} = \left\|\text{sg}[E(x)] - z_q\right\|_2^2 + \left\|\text{sg}\left[z_q\right] - E(x)\right\|_2^2$$

Where:

- $E(x)$ is the continuous latent vector produced by the encoder, E, from the input x,
- z_q is the quantized latent vector selected from the codebook Z,
- $\text{sg}(.)$ represents the stop-gradient operation that blocks the gradients from flowing through the term. It is used here to prevent the codebook from being updated when optimizing the encoder.

For more details on the quantization loss formula, refer to the VQGAN paper [1].

In practice, using both reconstruction loss and quantization loss during training works well for reconstructing low-resolution images. However, for high-resolution images, the model may still produce artifacts. To improve reconstruction quality at high resolutions, two additional loss functions are typically employed:

- Perceptual loss
- Adversarial loss

Perceptual loss: Perceptual loss measures the difference between the features of the original and reconstructed images extracted from a specific layer of a pretrained model such as *VGG* [6]. The formula is:

$$\text{Perceptual loss} = \sum_{l}\|\phi_l(x) - \phi_l(\hat{x})\|_2^2$$

Where:

- ϕ_l denotes the feature map of the layer, l, from a pretrained VGG model,
- x is the original image,
- $\hat{x}$ is the reconstructed image.

The perceptual loss encourages the model to reconstruct images that are perceptually similar to the original images. *VGG* features encode high-level details such as content and style. The perception loss guides the training process so that the model can better preserve these details in the reconstructed images.

Adversarial loss: Adversarial loss is derived from GANs [7], where a discriminator tries to distinguish between real and reconstructed images. This loss is used to measure how well the image reconstructed by the image tokenizer can fool the discriminator. The formula, as we saw in Chapter 7, is:

$$\text{Adversarial loss} = -\log(D(\hat{x}))$$

Where:

- D is the discriminator network,
- $\hat{x}$ is the reconstructed image.

This loss function encourages the model to produce reconstructed images that a trained discriminator cannot distinguish from real images. The *VQGAN* paper introduced a patch-based version of this loss to reduce unnatural artifacts and improve the realism of the reconstructions.

Overall loss: The overall loss function is often a weighted sum of the individual losses described above. The weights (λ_i) are hyperparameters that need tuning based on specific performance goals and experiments.

$$\begin{aligned} \text{Overall loss} = \lambda_{\text{rec}} &\times \text{reconstruction loss} + \\ \lambda_{\text{quant}} &\times \text{quantization loss} + \\ \lambda_{\text{perc}} &\times \text{perceptual loss} + \\ \lambda_{\text{adv}} &\times \text{adversarial loss} \end{aligned}$$

After training the image tokenizer, we convert all 5 million training images into discrete tokens and cache them, as detailed in the data preparation section. This step ensures that all images are represented as a sequence of discrete tokens, which is required for training the image generator.

Stage II: Training the image generator

Training the image generator, which is a decoder-only Transformer, is similar to the process described in earlier chapters. The training data consists of sequences of discrete tokens, and the model learns to predict these tokens sequentially during training.

We employ next-token prediction as our ML objective and cross-entropy as the loss function to measure how accurate the predicted probabilities are compared to the correct visual tokens.

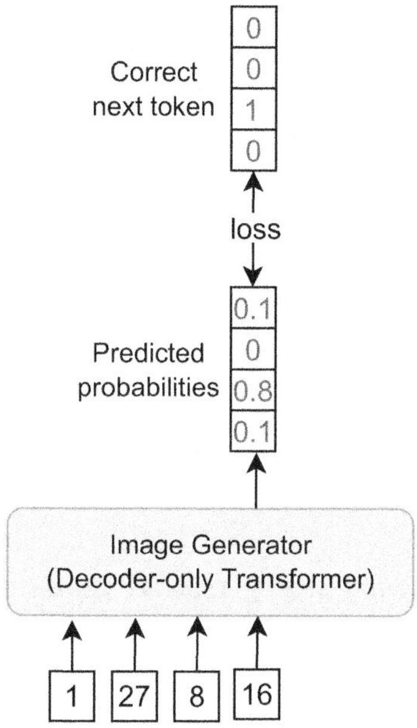

Figure 8.13: Image generator loss calculation

Sampling

In autoregressive models, generating a new image involves two steps:

1. Generating a sequence of discrete tokens
2. Decoding discrete tokens into an image

1. Generating a sequence of discrete tokens

In the first step, the image generator produces a sequence of tokens. The autoregressive nature of the generation ensures that each token is conditioned on preceding tokens, leading to coherent images.

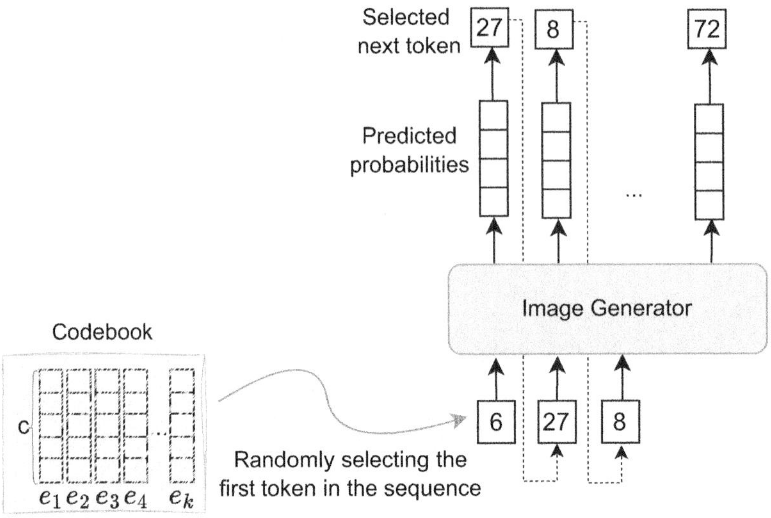

Figure 8.14: Generating a sequence of discrete tokens using the image generator

Here is a step-by-step process to autoregressively generate a sequence of tokens:

1. Randomly select a token from the codebook as the first token. This initial token acts as a seed for the rest of the generation process.
2. Autoregressively generate tokens one by one. This involves:
   a. Passing the current sequence of tokens to the image generator to predict the probability distribution over the codebook
   b. Selecting the next token using a sampling method such as top-p sampling
   c. Appending the chosen token to the current sequence

This process continues until the entire image is generated. The number of iterations depends on the resolution and size of the desired output image. For example, generating an image of 1024×1024 pixels, with each visual token representing a 64×64 pixel block, requires 256 tokens. The process continues until all 256 tokens are generated. Once the sequence of tokens is complete, it is transformed into an actual image, which is the focus of the next step.

2. Decoding discrete tokens into an image

In this step, the sequence of discrete tokens is transformed into an image by using the decoding functionality of the image tokenizer.

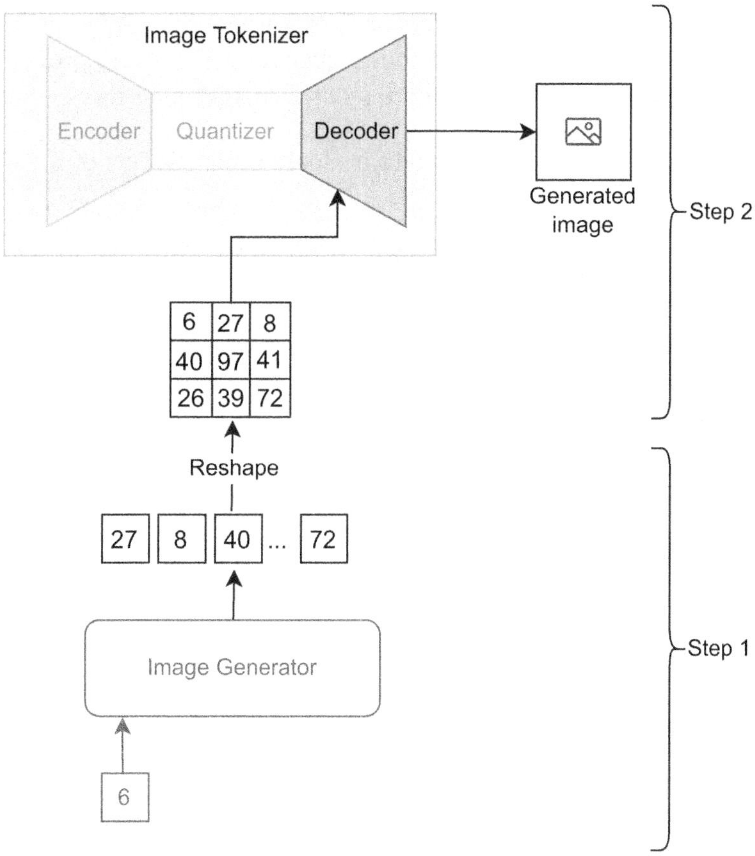

Figure 8.15: Decoding tokens into an image

Evaluation

The evaluation metrics for high-resolution image synthesis are similar to those in Chapter 7. We'll briefly review them in this section without going into detail.

Offline evaluation metrics

The following metrics are typically employed to measure the quality and diversity of the generated images:

- **Inception score:** Measures how similar the generated images are to images of real-world objects by utilizing a pretrained *Inception v3* model. To learn more about the Inception score, refer to [8].
- **Fréchet inception distance (FID):** Compares the distribution of generated images to real images by comparing features extracted from a pretrained *Inception v3* model. This metric measures how similar the statistics of generated and real images are. To learn more about FID, refer to [9].

- **Human evaluation:** Human evaluators are presented with pairs of images and asked to judge their photorealism and aesthetic qualities. The votes provide a statistical measure of which models produce more realistic images over time.

In addition to those metrics, it is common to evaluate other aspects of the model such as latency and cost.

- **Time to generate an image:** Measures the time it takes for the model to generate an image. This metric is important to monitor since users generally expect quick results.
- **Cost per generation:** Calculates the cost to generate an image. This metric depends on factors such as model complexity, resolution, and infrastructure expenses. Monitoring the cost of generation is crucial as it impacts business revenue.

Online evaluation metrics

In practice, companies monitor various metrics to assess the system's real-time quality. Common metrics include:

- **User feedback:** Collects direct feedback from users regarding generated images.
- **Periodic surveys:** Gathers user opinions on the quality and relevance of generated images.
- **Subscription rate:** Measures how often users subscribe to services or features related to image generation.
- **Churn rate:** Measures the rate at which users stop using the service.

Overall ML System Design

Once we are satisfied with the performance of the image generator and image tokenizer models, we can integrate them to construct the image synthesis system. The primary components in a high-resolution image synthesis system are:

- Generation service
- Decoding service
- Super-resolution service

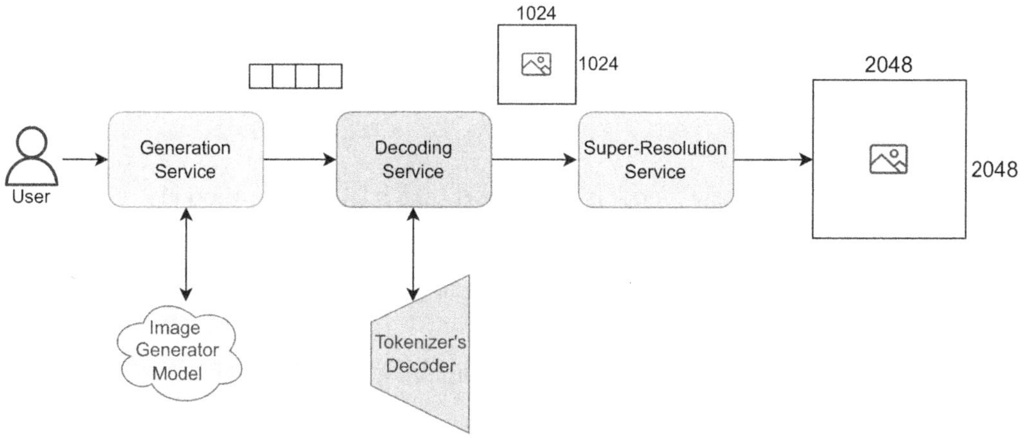

Figure 8.16: High-resolution image synthesis overall ML design

Understanding the purpose of each component and their interactions will provide a holistic view of the system. Let's explore each in more detail.

Generation service

The generation service handles user requests and interacts with the trained image generator model to produce a sequence of visual tokens.

Decoding service

The decoding service interacts with the image tokenizer to convert the generated sequence of visual tokens into an image. Note that when we deploy the model, we don't need the encoder in the image tokenizer – it is only used during training.

Separating generation and decoding services is crucial because the image generator and tokenizer are different models with distinct computational needs and latencies. This approach allows each service to scale independently and manage resources efficiently.

Super-resolution service

Super-resolution service uses a pretrained model to increase the resolution of generated images. For example, if the desired resolution is 2048×2048 but the generator produces only 1024×1024, we use a super-resolution model with a 2x upscale factor.

This service is crucial for applications requiring detailed and realistic visuals, such as medical imaging. There are many established solutions for super-resolution, from CNN-based [10] to GAN-improved [11]. To learn more about recent approaches, refer to [12].

Other Talking Points

If there's time remaining at the end of the interview, you could explore these additional points:

- Extending autoregressive models to support text-based generation [13, 14].
- Support applications such as image completion and image super-resolution [15].
- Balancing diversity vs. fidelity in sampling, using techniques such as temperature scaling [16].
- Enhancing the stability with adversarial training, gradient clipping, and learning rate scheduling [17, 18].
- Using progressive growing and multi-scale architectures to improve image quality and detail [19].
- Creating interactive systems for users to refine and customize generated images [20].

Summary

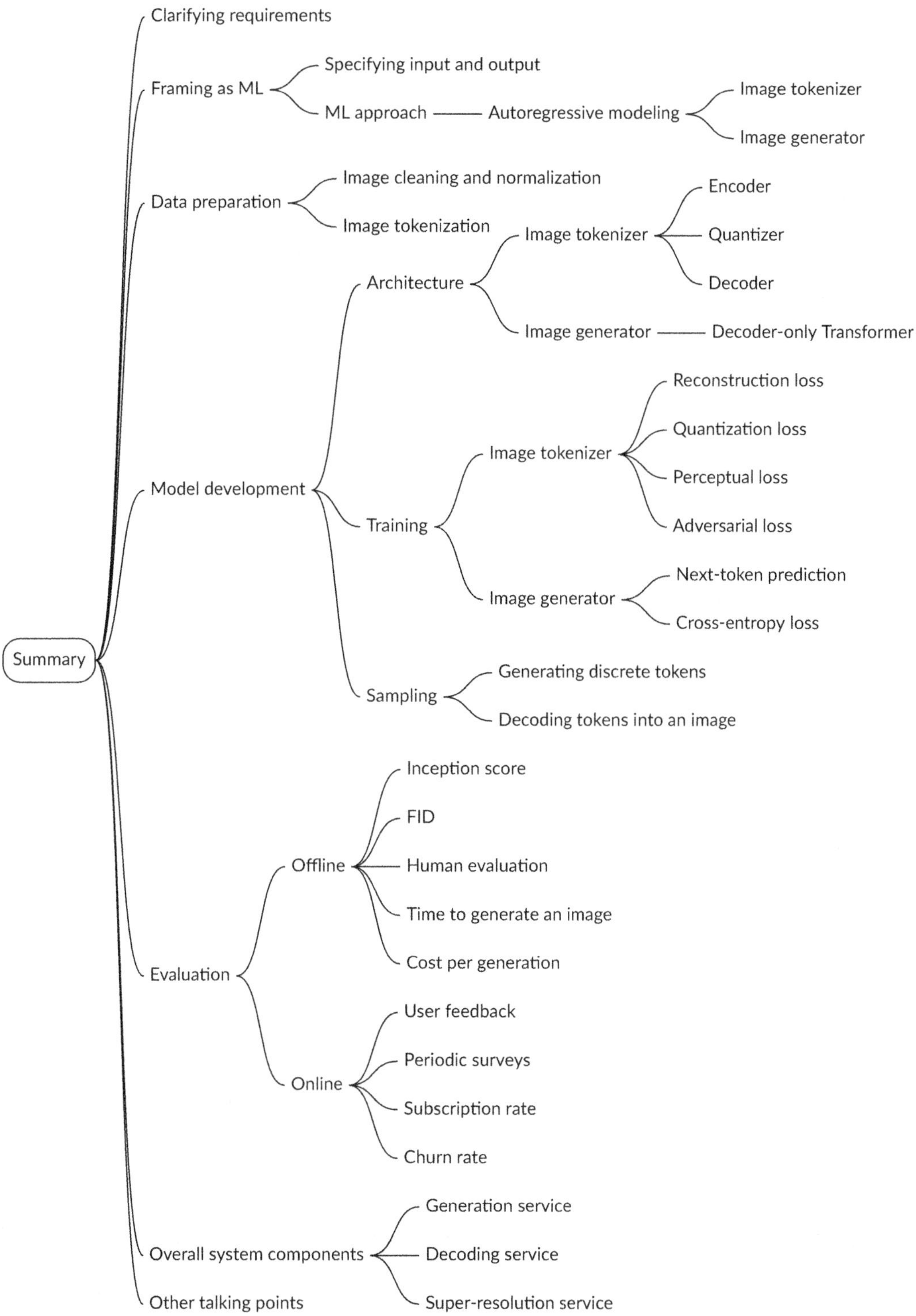
Summary
Clarifying requirements
Framing as ML
Specifying input and output
ML approach
Autoregressive modeling
Image tokenizer
Image generator
Data preparation
Image cleaning and normalization
Image tokenization
Model development
Architecture
Image tokenizer
Encoder
Quantizer
Decoder
Image generator
Decoder-only Transformer
Training
Image tokenizer
Reconstruction loss
Quantization loss
Perceptual loss
Adversarial loss
Image generator
Next-token prediction
Cross-entropy loss
Sampling
Generating discrete tokens
Decoding tokens into an image
Evaluation
Offline
Inception score
FID
Human evaluation
Time to generate an image
Cost per generation
Online
User feedback
Periodic surveys
Subscription rate
Churn rate
Overall system components
Generation service
Decoding service
Super-resolution service
Other talking points

Reference Material

[1] Taming Transformers for High-Resolution Image Synthesis. https://arxiv.org/abs/2012.09841.

[2] Neural Discrete Representation Learning. https://arxiv.org/abs/1711.00937.

[3] Deep Learning using Rectified Linear Units (ReLU). https://arxiv.org/abs/1803.08375.

[4] Euclidean Distance. https://en.wikipedia.org/wiki/Euclidean_distance.

[5] A Guide to Convolution Arithmetic for Deep Learning. https://arxiv.org/abs/1603.07285.

[6] Very Deep Convolutional Networks for Large-Scale Image Recognition. https://arxiv.org/abs/1409.1556.

[7] Generative Adversarial Networks. https://arxiv.org/abs/1406.2661.

[8] Inception Score. https://en.wikipedia.org/wiki/Inception_score.

[9] FID Calculation. https://en.wikipedia.org/wiki/Fr%C3%A9chet_inception_distance.

[10] Image Super-Resolution Using Very Deep Residual Channel Attention Networks. https://arxiv.org/abs/1807.02758.

[11] ESRGAN: Enhanced Super-Resolution Generative Adversarial Networks. https://arxiv.org/abs/1809.00219.

[12] NTIRE 2024 Challenge on Image Super-Resolution (×4): Methods and Results. https://arxiv.org/abs/2404.09790.

[13] Muse: Text-To-Image Generation via Masked Generative Transformers. https://arxiv.org/abs/2301.00704.

[14] VQGAN-CLIP: Open Domain Image Generation and Editing with Natural Language Guidance. https://arxiv.org/abs/2204.08583.

[15] LAR-SR: A Local Autoregressive Model for Image Super-Resolution. https://openaccess.thecvf.com/content/CVPR2022/papers/Guo_LAR-SR_A_Local_Autoregressive_Model_for_Image_Super-Resolution_CVPR_2022_paper.pdf.

[16] Long Horizon Temperature Scaling. https://arxiv.org/abs/2302.03686.

[17] Learning Rate Scheduling. https://d2l.ai/chapter_optimization/lr-scheduler.html.

[18] Adversarial Training. https://adversarial-ml-tutorial.org/adversarial_training/.

[19] Progressive Growing of GANs for Improved Quality, Stability, and Variation. https://arxiv.org/abs/1710.10196.

[20] CogView2: Faster and Better Text-to-Image Generation via Hierarchical Transformers. https://arxiv.org/abs/2204.14217.

9

Text-to-Image Generation

Introduction

In many cases, instead of allowing the model to generate content from random noise (as discussed in Chapters 7 and 8), we want to control the content of the generated image. Text-to-image generation is a fascinating application of generative AI that allows users to enter a text prompt, which the model transforms into a detailed image. Several text-to-image services are commercially available, such as OpenAI's DALL-E 3 [1], Google's Imagen [2], and Adobe's Firefly [3].

Figure 9.1: An example of a prompt and a generated image by OpenAI's DALL-E 3 [1]

Clarifying Requirements

Here is a typical interaction between a candidate and an interviewer:

Candidate: What resolution do we target for generated images?
Interviewer: We aim for high-resolution images, specifically 1024×1024 pixels.

Candidate: Should the system support multiple languages for text input or just English?
Interviewer: We'll focus on English initially, but the system's architecture should be adaptable for other languages later.

Candidate: How large is the dataset for training a text-to-image model?
Interviewer: We have about 500 million images from user assets, most with captions.

Candidate: How detailed and complex can the text prompts be? Is there a limit to their complexity or length?
Interviewer: The system should handle detailed text prompts, with a maximum length of 128 words.

Candidate: What speed should the system achieve for image generation?
Interviewer: The goal is near-real-time generation. Let's aim for 10 seconds per image.

Candidate: What types of images should the system generate? Are we focusing on a specific domain, like landscapes?
Interviewer: The system should be capable of generating, based on text prompts, a wide range of images, including realistic landscapes, portraits, and abstract or conceptual art.

Candidate: It's important to ensure the images aren't biased by age, race, or gender. Can I start by focusing on those three attributes?
Interviewer: Great point. It's crucial to have a fair system. Let's begin by addressing those three attributes.

Candidate: Ethical considerations are crucial. We need filters and checks to avoid generating offensive, inappropriate, or harmful images. Does that sound correct?
Interviewer: Yes, that's correct.

Frame the Problem as an ML Task

Specifying the system's input and output

The input to the system is a text prompt provided by the user that describes the desired image. This prompt usually includes details like scenes, objects, colors, styles, and emotions.

The output is a visually detailed image that adheres to the text prompt. For example, as shown in Figure 9.2, a prompt like "A boat on an ocean" produces an image depicting this scene.

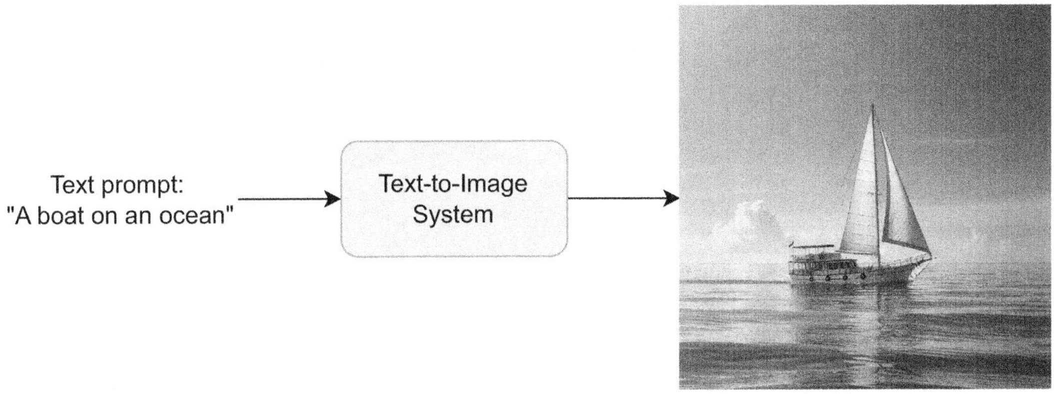

Figure 9.2: Input and output of a text-to-image system (Image credit: [4])

Choosing a suitable ML approach

Text-to-image generation is a multimodal task that involves understanding text and generating a corresponding image. There are two primary approaches for building text-to-image systems:

- Autoregressive models
- Diffusion models

Let's briefly review each and choose the one that best suits our needs.

Autoregressive models

These models treat text-to-image generation as a sequence generation task. A decoder-only Transformer takes a sequence of text tokens as input and outputs a sequence of visual tokens representing an image. An image tokenizer then decodes these visual tokens into the actual image.

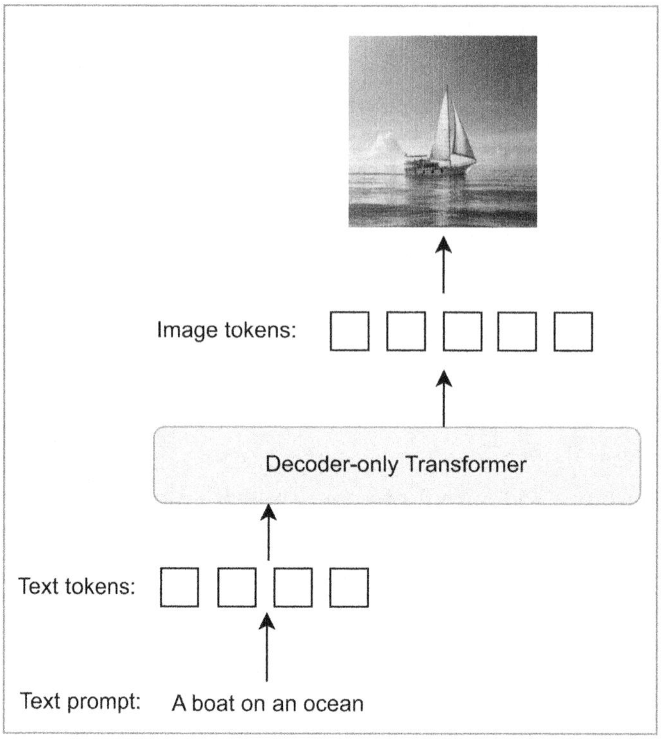

Figure 9.3: Autoregressive text-to-image generation

Several text-to-image models have been developed using this approach, such as OpenAI's DALL-E [5] and Google's Muse [6].

Diffusion models

First introduced in 2019 [7], diffusion models gained mainstream attention about three years later. They use a different approach for text-to-image generation by starting with random noise and gradually transforming it into a clear image based on the text prompt. This process typically involves a text encoder, such as OpenAI's CLIP [8] or Google's T5 [9], which converts the text prompt into an embedding. This embedding captures the meaning of the prompt and guides the diffusion model to generate images that match it.

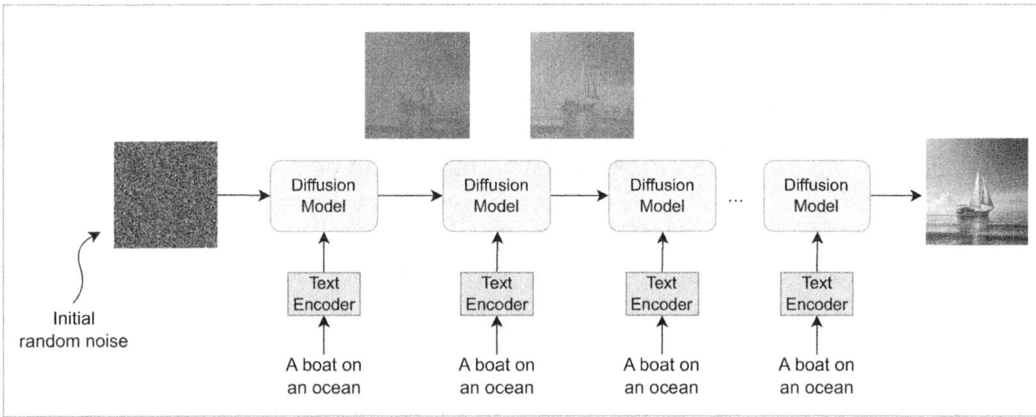

Figure 9.4: Diffusion-based text-to-image generation[1]

Examples of diffusion-based text-to-image models include Google's Imagen 3 [2], OpenAI's DALL-E 2 [10], and Stability AI's Stable Diffusion [11].

Diffusion versus autoregressive models

Autoregressive models frame text-to-image generation as a sequence generation task, while diffusion models approach it as an iterative refinement process. This key difference in modeling impacts their capabilities.

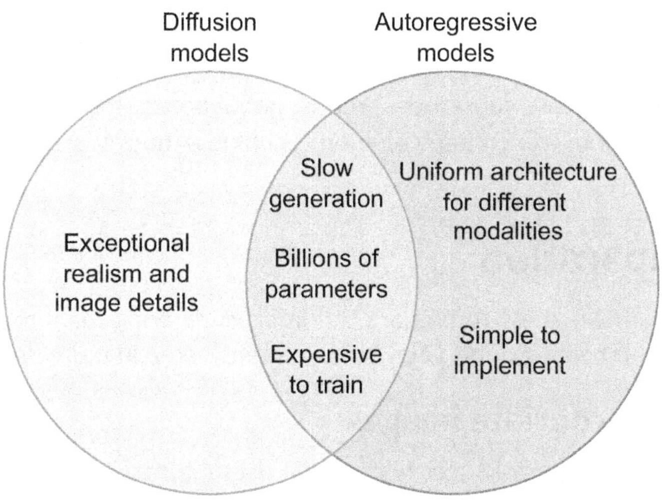

Figure 9.5: Diffusion vs. autoregressive model characteristics

Both diffusion and autoregressive models can produce realistic images, are slow in generation, typically have billions of parameters, and require substantial computational resources for training. Despite these similarities, they differ in three key aspects:

[1] In practice, we provide the diffusion model with additional conditioning inputs, such as the timestep. This will be discussed further in the training section.

1. **Implementation complexity:** Autoregressive models are simpler to implement during both training and inference. During training, they are more statistically efficient because they can obtain useful gradient signals from all steps in a single forward-backward pass. In contrast, diffusion models are less statistically efficient, requiring sampling of different noise levels for each training example. At inference time, once the Transformer in an autoregressive model generates the sequence of visual tokens, these tokens form the final image. Diffusion models, however, refine the image over many steps, adding complexity to the implementation.
2. **Image quality:** Diffusion models have shown better performance in generating highly detailed and realistic images. Their iterative process allows the model to continuously refine and enhance fine details, leading to superior overall realism in the generated images.
3. **Flexibility in sampling:** Diffusion models are more flexible in trading off sampling speed and image quality. They can easily adjust the number of sampling steps—more steps usually lead to higher-quality images but take more time. Once trained, an autoregressive model cannot easily make such adjustments.

In this chapter, we choose diffusion models to prioritize exceptional image quality. In the model development section, we explore the architecture, training methods, and sampling techniques of diffusion models.

Data Preparation

Our dataset consists of approximately 500 million image–caption pairs. However, large-scale datasets often require substantial preprocessing before they can be used for model training. In this section, we explore common techniques to prepare images and captions for diffusion training.

Image preparation

We focus on two main steps to prepare the images: filtering inappropriate images and standardizing the remaining ones. Let's delve into each step in more detail.

Filtering inappropriate images

In large-scale datasets, many images may not be useful for training. It's crucial to remove these to ensure the model learns only from high-quality and safe data. To achieve this, we perform the following steps:

- **Remove small images:** We discard image–caption pairs where the image size is smaller than a certain threshold, for example, 64×64 pixels. Small images are often of poor quality and may not provide valuable information for training.
- **Deduplicate images:** We use deduplication methods, such as [12], to remove identical or perceptually similar images. This prevents the model from being biased toward

certain images that appear more frequently.

- **Remove inappropriate images:** We employ harm detection and NSFW (Not Safe For Work) detection models to filter out harmful content such as violence or nudity. This ensures the model doesn't learn to generate inappropriate images.
- **Remove low-aesthetic images:** We use specialized ML models to eliminate images that aren't aesthetically pleasing. This helps the model focus on high-quality images during training.

Standardizing images

- **Adjust image dimensions:** The diffusion model requires inputs of specific dimensions. Therefore, it's crucial to have training data of similar sizes. For example, if the expected model input is 128×128, we first resize the images so that the smaller dimension is 128, preserving the aspect ratio. Then, we center-crop them to achieve the final size of 128×128.
- **Normalize images:** We normalize pixel values to a standard range such as [0, 1] or [-1, 1] for more stable training.

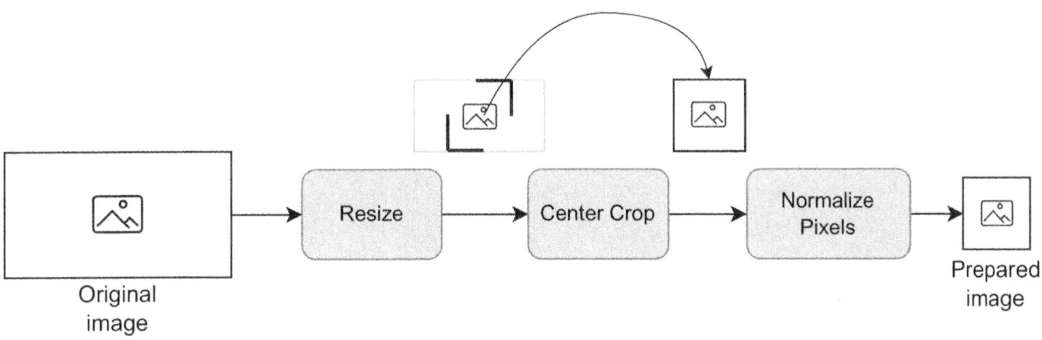

Figure 9.6: Image preparation steps

Caption preparation

In addition to images, captions are often irrelevant or missing. Here are common steps to ensure captions are consistent and of high quality:

- **Handle missing or non-English captions:** For images without captions or with captions in another language, we use an image captioning model such as BLIP-3 [13] to automatically generate descriptive captions. If you would like to build an image captioning system from scratch, refer to Chapter 5.
- **Enhance captions:** We use a pretrained model such as CLIP [8] to score the relevance of each image–caption pair. For pairs scoring below a threshold, we replace the original caption with an auto-generated one using the BLIP-3 model.
- **Remove poorly matched pairs:** After enhancing captions, we remove image–caption pairs with CLIP similarity scores below a threshold. This step ensures that the model

is exposed only to pairs whose captions accurately describe the images.

Model Development

Architecture

A diffusion model, as previously explained, progressively denoises a noisy image through multiple steps until it becomes clear. In each step, as illustrated in Figure 9.7, the model takes a noisy image as input and predicts the noise to be removed. Two common architectures are typically used for this purpose:

- U-Net
- Diffusion Transformer (DiT)

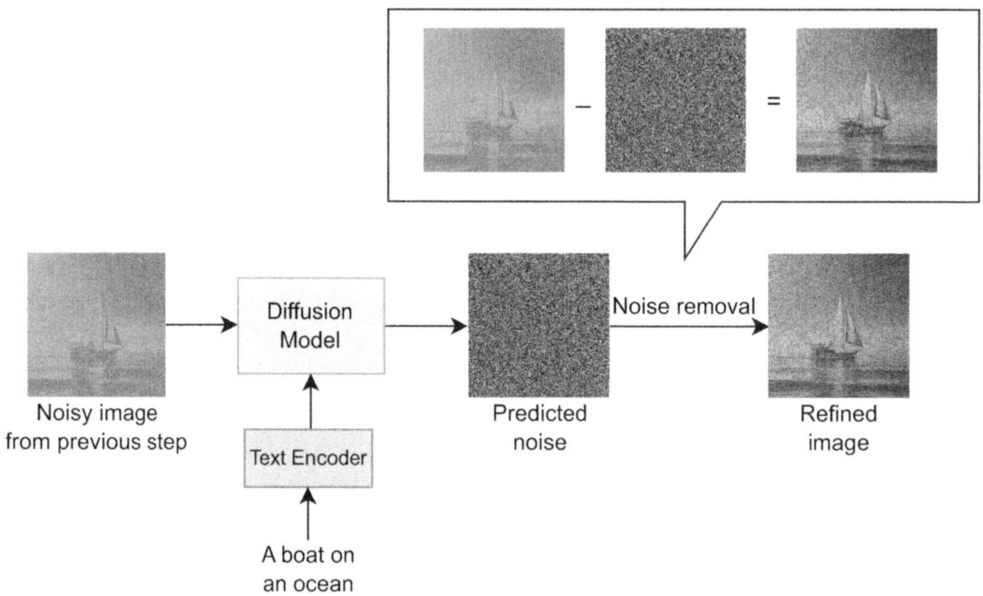

Figure 9.7: Input and output of the diffusion model in a single step[2]

U-Net

U-Net [14] is a convolutional neural network (CNN) architecture originally developed for biomedical image segmentation. It consists of a series of downsampling blocks followed by upsampling blocks, as shown in Figure 9.8.

[2] For simplicity, we omitted the timestep input to the diffusion model. This will be covered in more detail in the training section.

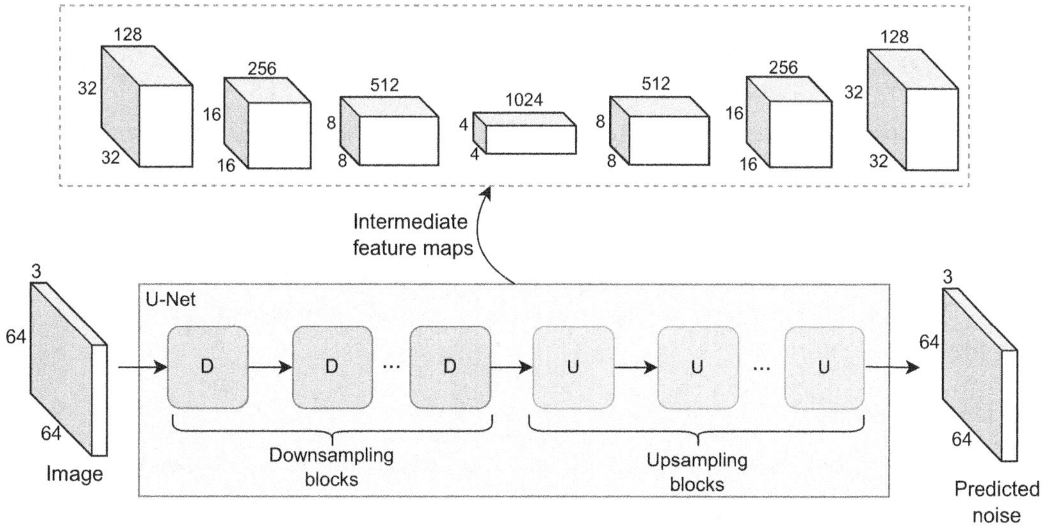

Figure 9.8: U-Net downsampling and upsampling blocks

Downsampling blocks

The downsampling blocks progressively reduce spatial dimensions (height and width) while increasing depth (number of channels), leading to a compressed representation of the input. Each downsampling block typically consists of the following:

- **Convolution operation:** Extracts visual features from the input.
- **Batch normalization:** Normalizes feature maps to stabilize training.
- **Non-linear activation:** Introduces non-linearity to learn complex patterns.
- **Max-pooling:** Reduces the feature map dimensions.
- **Cross-attention:** Cross-attends to additional conditions, such as text prompt tokens. This is necessary to ensure the text prompt influences the predicted noise.

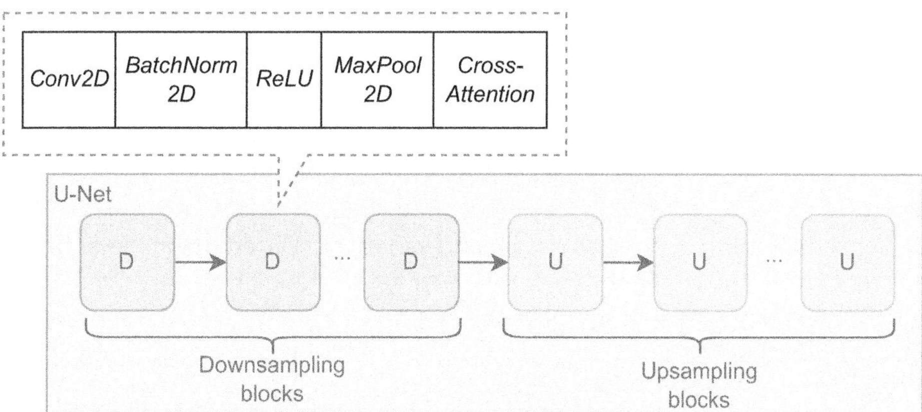

Figure 9.9: Typical layers in a downsampling block

Let's explore the cross-attention layer in more detail, as this is the first instance where we're applying cross-attention between different modalities—image and text inputs. The text prompt is processed by a text encoder, such as a Transformer-based model, which converts words or tokens into a sequence of continuous embeddings. These embeddings capture the semantic meaning of the text. During each denoising step of the diffusion process, the model receives a noisy image as input and processes it through layers like *Conv2D* and *BatchNorm2D* to extract visual features. In the cross-attention layer, the queries are derived from the image features, while the keys and values come from the text embeddings. This enables the model to align and integrate information effectively from the text into the image features.

Upsampling blocks

The upsampling blocks symmetrically increase spatial dimensions and decrease feature map depth. The final output matches the original input size, which, in this case, is the predicted noise. Each upsampling block consists of the following:

- **Transposed convolution:** Uses operations like PyTorch's *ConvTranspose2D* to process and increase the feature map's dimensions.
- **Batch normalization:** Normalizes feature maps to stabilize training.
- **Non-linear activation:** Introduces non-linearity to learn complex patterns.
- **Cross-attention:** Maintains the influence of additional conditions during upsampling.

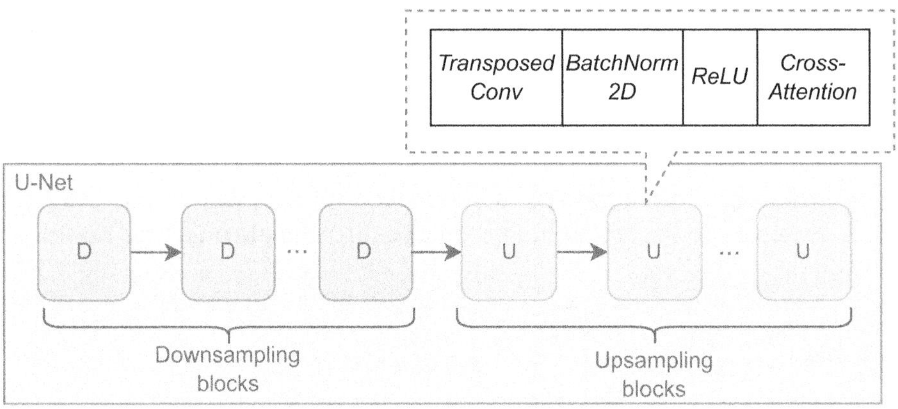

Figure 9.10: Typical layers in an upsampling block

The U-Net architecture has various details and variations. Different implementations may use different layers and configurations. However, understanding the key components and structure is generally sufficient for most ML system design interviews. For more in-depth information, refer to [14].

DiT

DiT [15] is another popular architecture in diffusion models. Unlike U-Net, which uses a series of downsampling and upsampling layers, DiT primarily relies on a Transformer architecture to process the noisy input image and predict the noise.

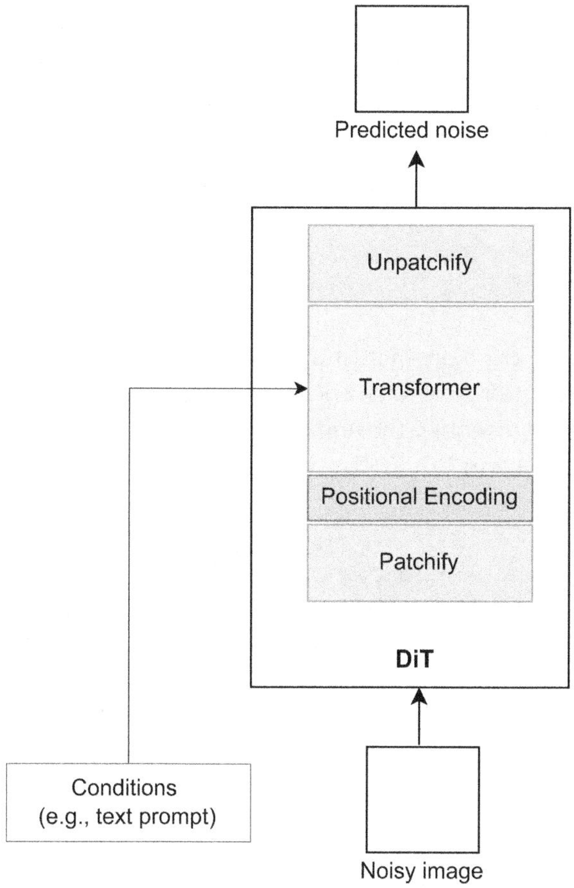

Figure 9.11: DiT components

DiT is primarily inspired by the Vision Transformer (ViT) [16] architecture discussed in Chapter 5. DiT components are:

- **Patchify:** Converts the input image into a sequence of patch embeddings.
- **Positional encoding:** Attaches position information to each patch embedding to indicate its location in the original image.
- **Transformer:** Processes the sequence of embeddings and other conditioning signals, such as the text prompt, to predict the noise for each patch.
- **Unpatchify:** Converts the sequence of predicted noise vectors into an image with the same dimension as the original input image.

In summary, both U-Net and DiT architectures perform well in practice. U-Net was originally used in several text-to-image models such as Google's Imagen [17] and Stability AI's Stable Diffusion [11]. Recently, the DiT architecture has shown great promise for text-to-image generation. For educational purposes, we use the U-Net architecture in this chapter. Chapter 11 explores the DiT architecture in more detail.

Training

A diffusion model is trained by employing the diffusion process. The diffusion process has two phases:

- Forward process
- Backward process

Forward process

In the forward process, also known as the **noising process**, noise is gradually added to an image over multiple steps (denoted as t or timesteps) until the image becomes completely noisy. The value of t, representing the number of steps, is typically chosen randomly from a range, usually between 1 and 1,000. The forward process does not involve any ML models or parameter updates.

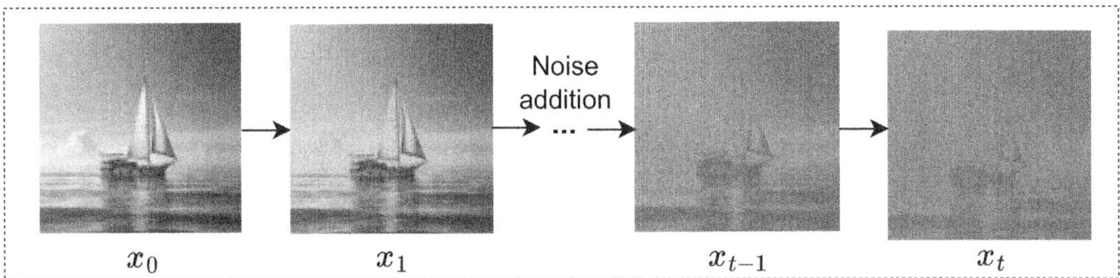

Figure 9.12: Forward diffusion process

Backward process

In the backward process, also known as the **denoising process**, an ML model learns to reverse the forward process. At each step, the model predicts the noise in the noisy image. This predicted noise is then used to reduce the noise in the input image. As shown in Figure 9.13, this process is repeated until the image becomes clear.

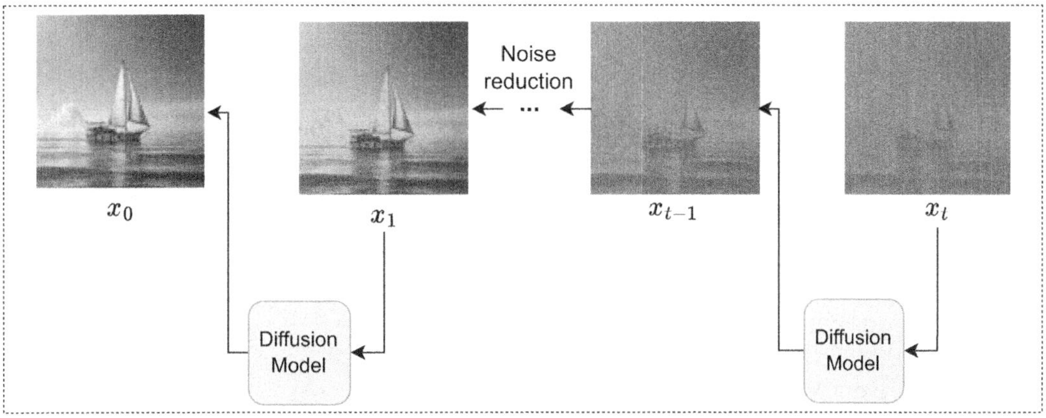

Figure 9.13: Backward diffusion process

With an understanding of both the forward and backward processes, we can now explore how they are applied during the diffusion training process.

Diffusion training process

During training, we introduce noise to the original image by simulating the forward process, then ask the model to predict this noise. This process involves four key steps:

1. Noise addition
2. Preparation of conditioning signals
3. Noise prediction
4. ML objective and loss calculation

This section includes some math for those who are interested, but the details do not affect the design of the ML system.

1. Noise addition

The first step is to simulate the forward diffusion process by adding noise to the original image over multiple timesteps. At each timestep, we corrupt the image slightly by adding Gaussian noise. This gradual addition of noise transforms the image into pure noise over time.

The amount of noise added at each timestep is controlled by a noise schedule. The noise schedule is defined by a set of variance parameters, $\beta_1, \beta_2, \dots, \beta_T$, where T is the total number of timesteps. Each $\beta_t \in (0, 1)$ controls the amount of noise added at timestep t.

The noise schedule typically increases the values of β incrementally:

$$\beta_1 < \beta_2 < \dots < \beta_T$$

Thus, smaller amounts of noise are added in the early steps, preserving more of the original image, and larger amounts of noise are added in the later steps, accelerating the diffusion process.

With the noise schedule defined, we can express the noisy data at timestep t using the noise addition formula:

$$x_t = \sqrt{(1-\beta_t)}x_{t-1} + \sqrt{\beta_t}\epsilon$$

where:

- x_t is the noisy image at timestep t,
- x_{t-1} is the noisy image at timestep $t-1$,
- ϵ is the Gaussian noise sampled from the standard normal distribution $N(0, I)$,
- β_t is the variance schedule parameter at timestep t, controlling the amount of noise added.

Iteratively adding noise over many steps can be time-consuming. Instead, it can be shown that the noisy data at timestep t can be directly derived from the original data, x_0:

$$\begin{aligned}
x_t &= \sqrt{\alpha_t}x_{t-1} + \sqrt{1-\alpha_t}\epsilon_{t-1} \\
&= \sqrt{\alpha_t}\left(\sqrt{\alpha_{t-1}}x_{t-2} + \sqrt{1-\alpha_{t-1}}\epsilon_{t-2}\right) + \sqrt{1-\alpha_t}\epsilon_{t-1} \\
&= \sqrt{\alpha_t\alpha_{t-1}}x_{t-2} + \sqrt{1-\alpha_t\alpha_{t-1}}\epsilon'_{t-2} \\
&= \dots \\
&= \sqrt{\alpha'_t}x_0 + \sqrt{1-\alpha'_t}\epsilon
\end{aligned}$$

where:

- x_t is the noisy image at timestep t,
- $\alpha_t = 1 - \beta_t$ and $\alpha'_t = \prod_{i=1}^{t}\alpha_i$ are reparameterizations of β_t,
- ϵ is the Gaussian noise sampled from the standard normal distribution $N(0, I)$.

In summary, during noise addition, we randomly sample t and compute x_t directly from x_0, without the need to iteratively add noise at each timestep, using the following formula:

$$x_t = \sqrt{\alpha'_t}x_0 + \sqrt{1-\alpha'_t}\epsilon$$

2. Preparation of conditioning signals

To predict the added noise, the model typically expects two additional pieces of information: the image caption and the sampled timestep, t, which indicates the noise level. We use separate encoders (see Figure 9.14) to prepare each of these conditioning signals to be processed by the model.

3. Noise prediction

The primary goal of training a diffusion model is to learn how to reverse the forward diffusion process-that is, to reconstruct the original data, x_0, from its noisy version, x_t. It has been shown that directly predicting x_0 is not as effective. Instead, training the model to predict the noise, ϵ, added during the forward process simplifies the task and improves performance. Therefore, in this step, the model predicts the noise, ϵ, given the noisy input, x_t, and the timestep, t.[3]

4. ML objective and loss calculation

The ML objective is to minimize the difference between the true noise, ϵ, and the model's prediction. The loss function used is the mean squared error (MSE) between the true noise and the predicted noise:

$$L = E_{t,x_0,\epsilon}\left(\|\epsilon - \epsilon_\theta\left(x_t, t\right)\|^2\right)$$

where:

- t is a timestep sampled uniformly from $\{1, 2, \ldots, T\}$,
- $\epsilon \sim N(0, I)$ is the Gaussian noise used in the forward process,
- x_t is the noisy data at timestep t, computed using the noise addition formula,
- $\epsilon_\theta\left(x_t, t\right)$ is the prediction of the neural network model (U-Net or DiT).

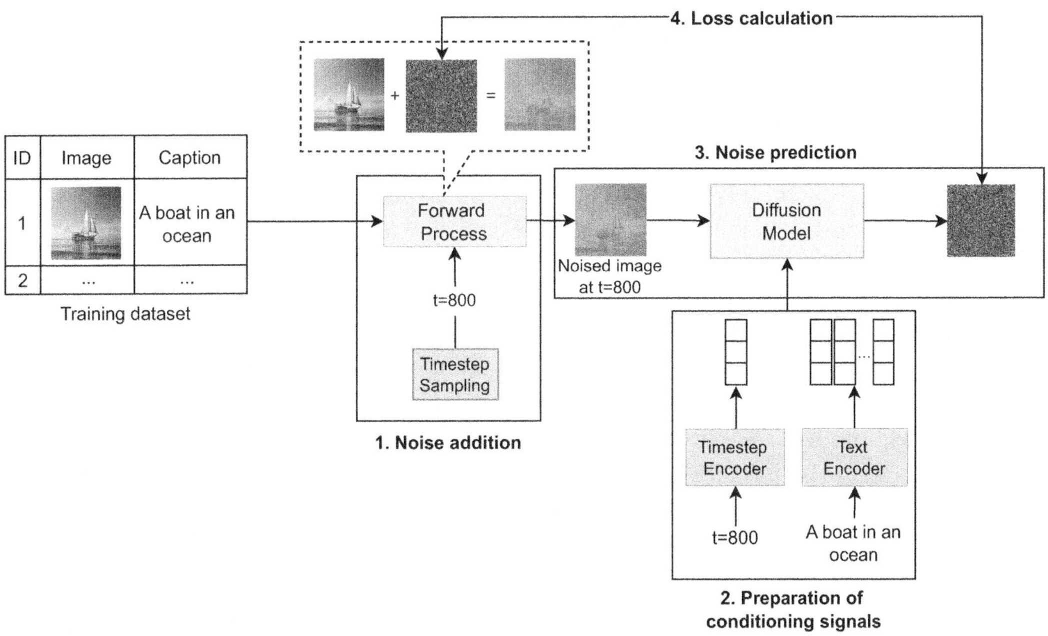

Figure 9.14: A single iteration in diffusion training

To enhance the reading experience, we have omitted the mathematical details, such as

[3] For simplicity, we include only the noisy image, x_t, and the timestep, t, as the input. As mentioned earlier, conditioning signals can also be included as inputs.

the derivation of the tractable mean and the loss simplification. For more information on diffusion training, refer to [18].

Sampling

Sampling refers to generating a new image from a trained diffusion model. In this section, we'll explore how sampling works in diffusion models and how noises are transformed into coherent images guided by the text prompt.

The sampling process starts with an image of random pixels, typically drawn from a Gaussian distribution. The model then gradually refines this image step by step. At each step, the diffusion model predicts the noise present in the current image and uses this prediction to adjust the image slightly in the right direction. This gradual refinement continues, each step producing a clearer image until a clear and detailed image is achieved.

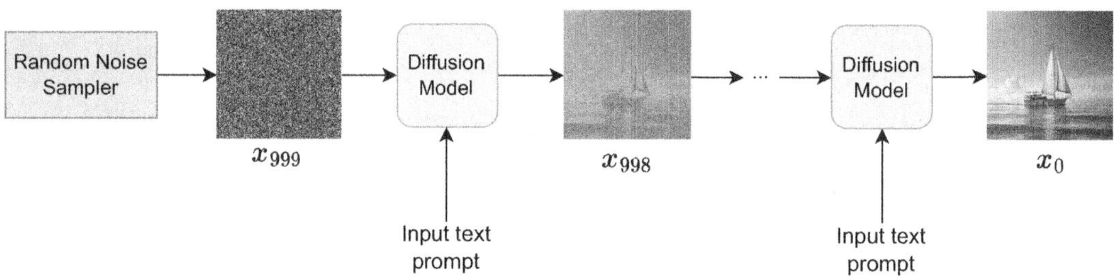

Figure 9.15: Sampling process

The basic sampling process described above has two drawbacks. First, it often fails to generate images that accurately match the text prompt. Second, it is slow, because generating each sample requires many iterative steps. The following two techniques are commonly employed in practice to mitigate the issues described above:

- **Classifier-free guidance (CFG):** CFG [19] improves the alignment between images and text prompts in diffusion models. During training, the model learns to generate images with and without the text prompt. During sampling, CFG adjusts the balance between these two modes. CFG ensures the generated images closely match the text prompts by increasing the influence of the conditioned (text prompt) mode and reducing the unconditioned (no text prompt) mode. This adjustment guides the diffusion process to produce more accurate results. To learn more about CFG, refer to [19].
- **Reduction of diffusion steps:** Sampling algorithms such as DDIM [20] reduce the number of diffusion steps from the standard 1,000 to as few as 20. This significantly speeds up the generation process while maintaining image quality. To learn more about DDIM, refer to [20].

In most ML system design interviews, the focus is on high-level concepts and how components work together, not on the intricate details. If you are interested in exploring diffusion models in more depth, refer to [21, 19, 20].

Challenges in text-to-image diffusion models

Diffusion models are typically very large. For example, DALLE-2 has 3.5 billion parameters [10]. This capacity is necessary since these models have to learn diverse concepts, shapes, and styles.

Training such large models poses several challenges during both training and sampling. The most common ones include:

- Resource-intensive model training
- Slow image generation

Resource-intensive model training

Training diffusion models is computationally intensive, requiring significant processing power. It also requires substantial GPU memory due to the size of the model and the high-dimensional nature of the generated images. Most modern GPUs may not have sufficient memory to fit model parameters, activations, and gradients during training. The following strategies are commonly employed to overcome these challenges:

- **Mixed precision training:** This technique uses both 16-bit and 32-bit floating-point types to reduce memory usage and increase computational efficiency. To learn more, refer to [22].
- **Model and data parallelism:** These methods distribute training across multiple devices. Most distributed training frameworks, such as FSDP [23] and DeepSpeed [24], support various parallelism techniques.
- **Latent diffusion models:** These models operate in a lower-dimensional space instead of pixel space, significantly speeding up training and inference. Chapter 11 examines this approach in more detail.

Slow image generation

Generating images from text in diffusion models is slow for two main reasons. First, due to the sequential nature of the diffusion sampling process, multiple steps are needed to refine the image. Second, as diffusion models have billions of parameters, significant computations occur at each step.

Common strategies to mitigate this challenge include:

- **Parallel sampling:** Implementing parallel processing during sampling reduces the time needed to generate images [25].
- **Model distillation:** A distilled model improves generation speed because of its reduced size, but it retains the behavior and performance of the original model. To learn more about model distillation in diffusion models, refer to [26].
- **Model quantization:** This technique reduces the precision of the model's weights, which decreases memory usage and speeds up generation.

Evaluation

Offline evaluation metrics

A consistent and reliable benchmark is key to evaluating text-to-image models. DrawBench [17] serves this purpose by providing a curated set of prompts that test various aspects of image generation such as object composition, interaction, and context understanding. These prompts, ranging from simple to complex, help to assess how accurately the model generates images from text. Due to its comprehensiveness, we use DrawBench to evaluate our text-to-image model. Let's examine both automated metrics and human evaluation to assess three key areas of the model's ability to generate images:

- Image quality
- Image diversity
- Image–text alignment

As discussed in previous chapters, Inception score (IS) [27] and Fréchet Inception distance (FID) [28] are two common metrics for evaluating quality and diversity in image generation systems. In this section, we focus primarily on image–text alignment.

Image–text alignment

Image–text alignment refers to how accurately the generated images match the text prompts. Measuring this alignment is important because it ensures the generated images are faithful to the user's input. A common metric for assessing this is CLIPScore [29], which evaluates the degree of alignment. Before diving into CLIPScore, let's briefly review CLIP.

CLIP

CLIP [8] is a model developed by OpenAI that has been trained to match images with their corresponding descriptions. It consists of two encoders: one for text and one for images. The text encoder converts input text into a text embedding; the image encoder converts the image into an image embedding.

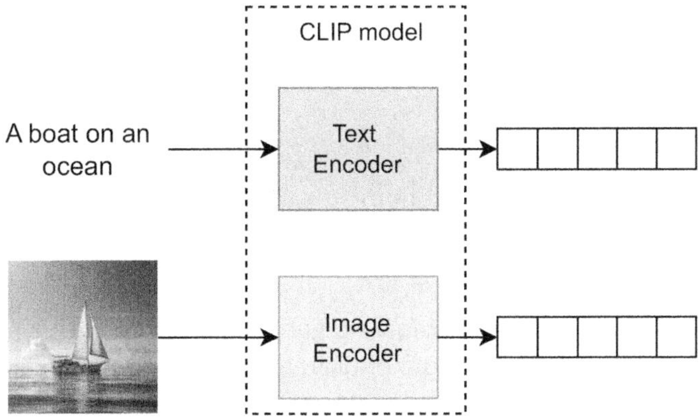

Figure 9.16: CLIP encoders

During training, CLIP learns to align embeddings by bringing related text and image embeddings closer together and pushing unrelated ones apart. This helps CLIP develop a shared embedding space where both an image and its associated text will map into the same space.

After training, similar text descriptions map close to each other in the embedding space, and images map near their relevant descriptions.

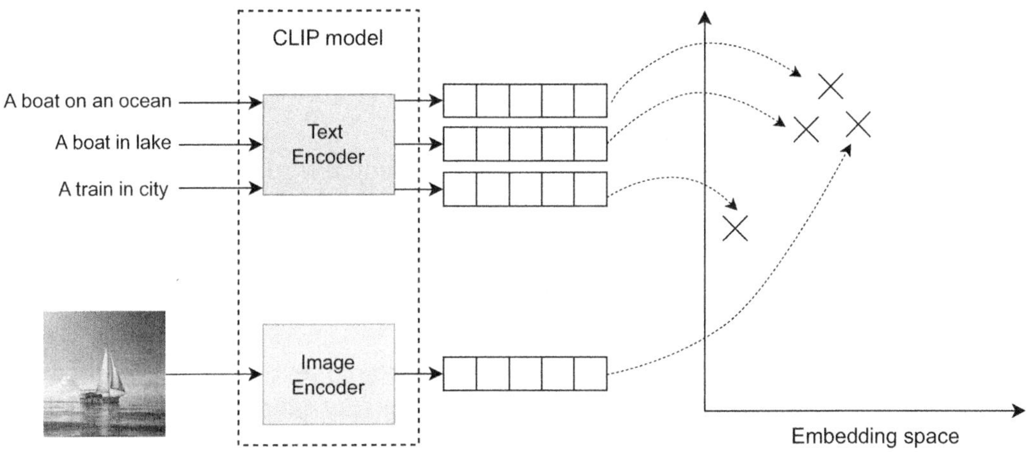

Figure 9.17: Text and image feature vectors mapped to the CLIP embedding space[4]

With an understanding of the CLIP model, we can now easily explore CLIPScore as a metric for evaluating image-text alignment.

CLIPScore

The CLIPScore measures the cosine similarity between the CLIP embeddings of a text

[4] For simplicity, the embedding space is visualized in 2D. In reality, it is a d-dimensional space, where d represents the embedding size.

description and an image. It shows how closely the image matches the text in the high-dimensional embedding space. A higher score indicates better alignment between an image and a description.

Human evaluation

Human evaluation complements the automated metrics by assessing both image quality and text alignment using the following approach:

- **Image quality:** Human raters compare a generated image with a reference image by judging which of the images is more photorealistic. Image quality is determined by the percentage of times the generated image is chosen over the reference image.
- **Text alignment:** Human raters are shown an image and its caption and then asked, "*Does the caption accurately describe the above image?*" The responses "yes," "somewhat," and "no" are scored as 100, 50, and 0, respectively. These scores are averaged separately for generated images and reference images to measure text alignment.

Online evaluation metrics

Online metrics measure how the model works in production. Common metrics to evaluate our text-to-image model include:

- **Click-through rate (CTR):** The percentage of users who click on the generated images. A high CTR indicates that users find the generated images useful.
- **Time spent on page:** The average time users spend with the service. Longer viewing times indicate higher user engagement.
- **User feedback:** Direct feedback from users is collected through feedback. Positive feedback indicates satisfaction with the image quality and text alignment.
- **Conversion rate:** The percentage of users who take a desired action (e.g., purchase, sign up) after interacting with generated images. A high conversion rate indicates satisfaction with the model's performance.
- **Latency:** The time it takes to generate an image from a text prompt. Lower latency indicates faster performance, which is important for user satisfaction.
- **Throughput:** The number of image generations the model can handle per second. High throughput ensures the service can serve more users.
- **Resource utilization:** The computational resources (e.g., CPU, GPU, memory) used to run the model and serve users. Efficient resource utilization is key to reducing costs.
- **Average cost per user per month:** Generating images with models that have billions of parameters is costly. If users are unhappy with the images, they might repeatedly generate new ones using the same prompt but different seeds, hoping for better results. This behavior increases our expenses. By monitoring this metric, we can ensure that costs remain justifiable.

Overall ML System Design

While the diffusion model is at the core of a text-to-image generation system, several other pipelines are crucial for ensuring efficiency, safety, and quality. In this section, we delve into the holistic design of a text-to-image generation system by examining the following pipelines:

- Data pipeline
- Training pipeline
- Model optimization pipeline
- Inference pipeline

Data pipeline

The data pipeline prepares data for training by removing inappropriate images, standardizing the rest, and storing them. It ensures captions are present and relevant and uses a pretrained model such as Google's T5 [9] to pre-compute and cache caption embeddings. This caching reduces computation during training.

In addition to preparing text–image pairs from the training data, the pipeline also collects and processes newly generated data such as user prompts, generated images, and user feedback. This new data is added to the training set for future use.

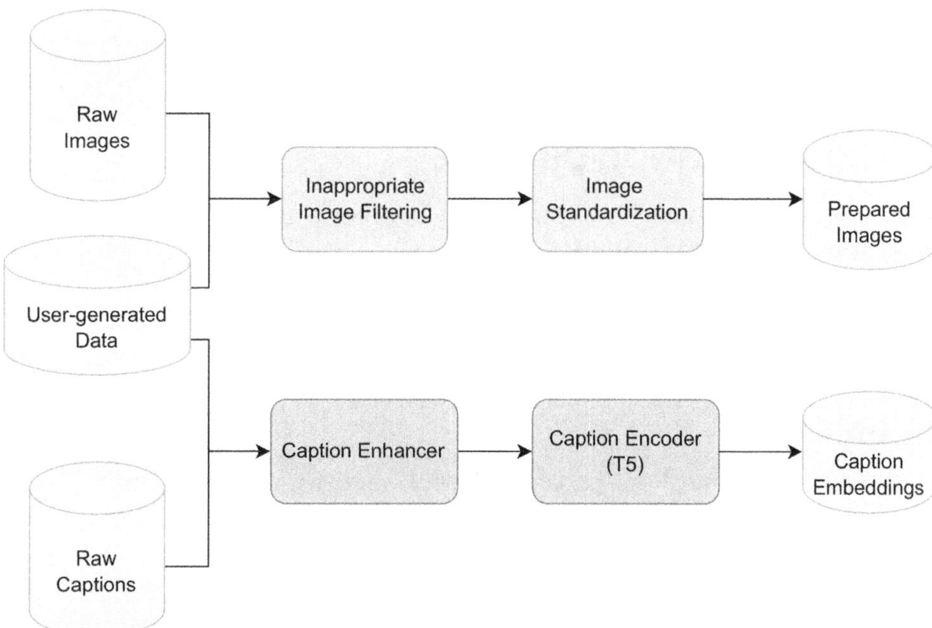

Figure 9.18: Data pipeline

Training pipeline

The training pipeline trains a model using the latest training data collected by the data pipeline.

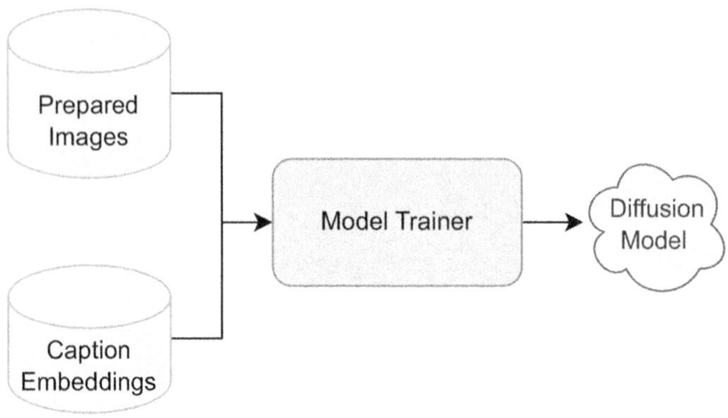

Figure 9.19: Training pipeline

The training pipeline ensures that the model adapts to recent user prompts and is trained on higher-quality generated images.

Evaluation pipeline

The evaluation pipeline assesses newly trained models using predefined automated metrics to determine whether or not they meet performance and quality standards for deployment.

Model optimization pipeline

The model optimization pipeline is responsible for enhancing the efficiency of the model. There are several methods to optimize models:

- **Model compression:** Use techniques such as quantization and pruning to reduce model size and generation time.
- **Model distillation:** Distill the model into a smaller one to reduce the model size and generation time.
- **Optimized algorithms:** Replace sampling with more efficient algorithms for faster generation.

Once the model optimization is completed, the optimized model can replace the existing model in production.

Inference pipeline

The inference pipeline handles user requests and generates images based on text prompts. It comprises several components, each playing an important role in ensuring the system's quality and safety. In this section, we will examine the key components:

- Prompt auto-complete
- Prompt safety service
- Prompt enhancement
- Image generation
- Harm detection
- Super-resolution service

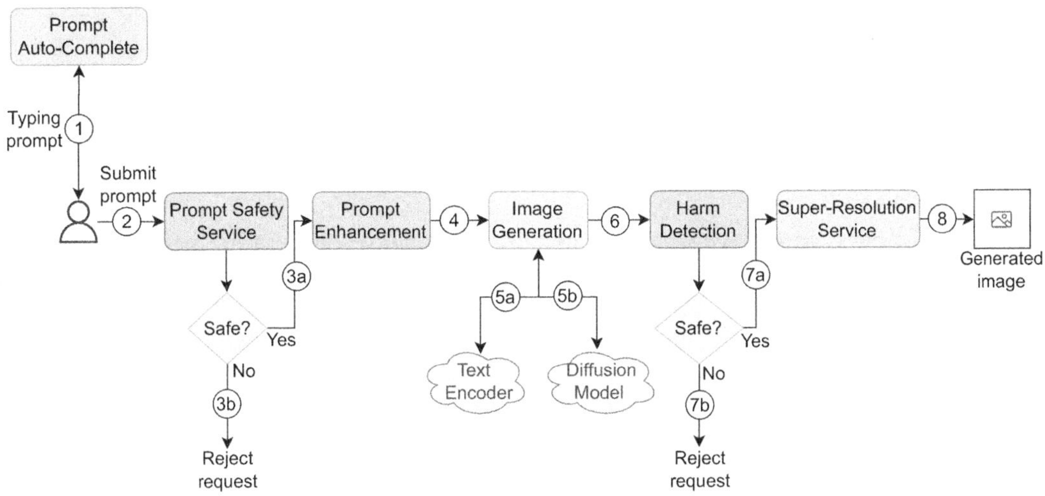

Figure 9.20: Inference pipeline

Prompt auto-complete

The prompt auto-complete component uses a specialized model to suggest possible next words or phrases in real-time as the user types their prompt. This enhances user experience by providing potential completions.

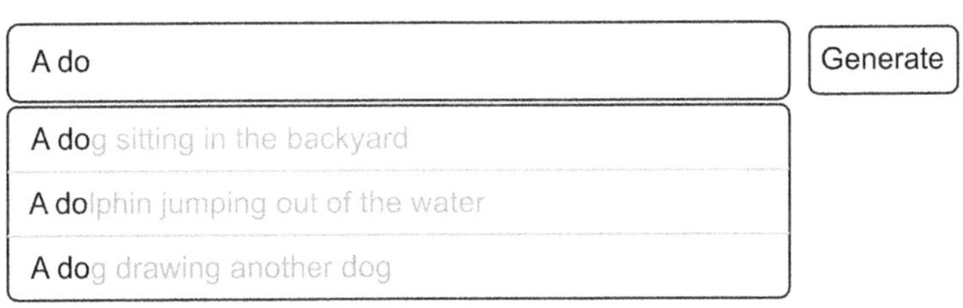

Figure 9.21: Suggested phrases by the auto-complete

Prompt safety service

This service uses a text classification model to process user prompts and reject those that violate our usage policies, for example, requests for violence, hateful imagery, or nudity.

This service ensures that the system adheres to safety standards and prevents the generation of inappropriate images.

Prompt enhancement

The prompt enhancement component refines user prompts to improve their clarity, coherence, and details.

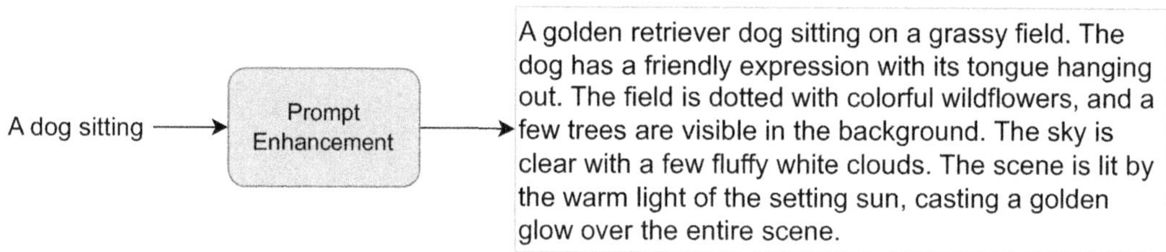

Figure 9.22: An example of prompt enhancement

This component is widely used in advanced image and video generation systems [30], as it effectively helps the model produce better outputs. It improves the quality of generated images by offering the model a more coherent and detailed prompt.

Image generation

The image generation component is the core of the inference pipeline. It interacts with the T5 text encoder to encode the enhanced text prompt into a sequence of tokens. These tokens are passed to the diffusion model to generate one or multiple images for each prompt.

Harm detection

This component ensures that generated images are safe for users. If an image still contains violence or nudity despite previous safeguards, the component flags it and blocks it from being shown.

Super-resolution service

The super-resolution service increases the resolution of the generated images. This step ensures that the final output is visually appealing and meets resolution requirements.

In practice, text-to-image systems often use at least one super-resolution model because diffusion models typically cannot generate high-resolution images directly. Instead, the diffusion model is trained at a lower resolution, and specialized super-resolution models enhance the resolution. For example, the base model might generate a 64x64 image, which a first super-resolution model increases to 256×256, followed by a second model that boosts it to 1024×1024. Google's *Imagen Video* [31] follows this approach to achieve the desired resolution.

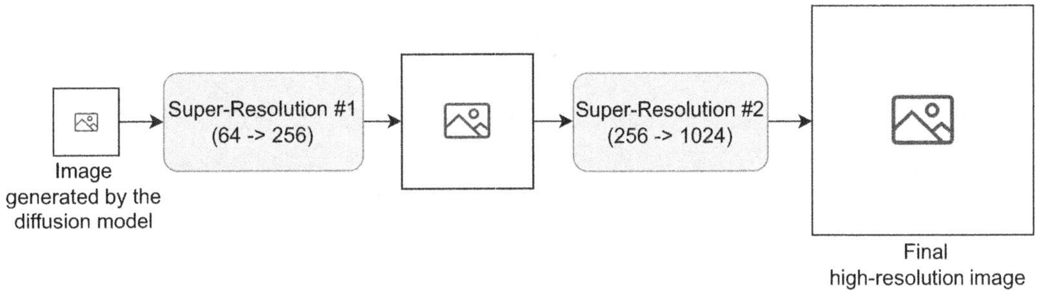

Figure 9.23: A cascade of super-resolution models

In summary, various pipelines work together to ensure that a text-to-image system is reliable, high-quality, and safe. The data pipeline provides the foundation for continuous improvement, while the training and model optimization pipelines enhance the model's performance. The inference pipeline ensures safe, efficient, and high-quality image generation. These pipelines create a system ready for real-world challenges.

Other Talking Points

If time permits at the end of the interview, consider discussing these additional topics:

- Using consistency models for faster image generation [26].
- Employing RLHF for quality improvement [32].
- Extending the text-to-image model to support inpainting and outpainting applications [33].
- Personalizing the text-to-image model to a particular concept (Chapter 10).
- Details of different scheduling techniques [34].
- Details of DDPM and DDIM, including their theoretical foundations [20, 18].
- Supporting multiple aspect ratios and resolutions using techniques such as Patch n' Pack [35].
- Details of developing a re-captioning model [36, 37, 13].
- Improving the diversity–fidelity trade-off with guidance [19].
- More advanced controls over the generated images using techniques like ControlNet [38].
- Controlling the style of the generated images [39].

Summary

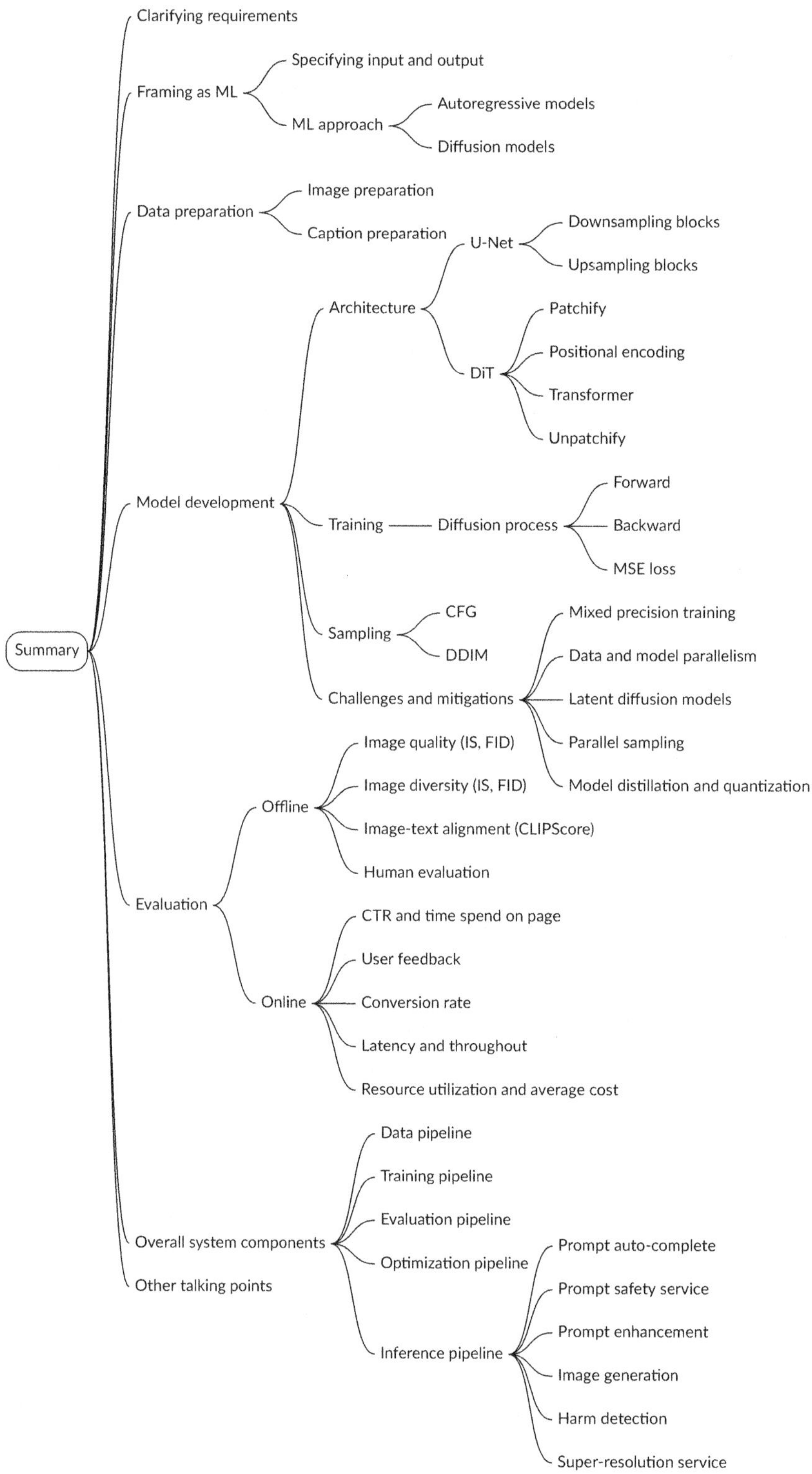
Summary
Clarifying requirements
Framing as ML
Specifying input and output
ML approach
Autoregressive models
Diffusion models
Data preparation
Image preparation
Caption preparation
Model development
Architecture
U-Net
Downsampling blocks
Upsampling blocks
DiT
Patchify
Positional encoding
Transformer
Unpatchify
Training
Diffusion process
Forward
Backward
MSE loss
Sampling
CFG
DDIM
Challenges and mitigations
Mixed precision training
Data and model parallelism
Latent diffusion models
Parallel sampling
Model distillation and quantization
Evaluation
Offline
Image quality (IS, FID)
Image diversity (IS, FID)
Image-text alignment (CLIPScore)
Human evaluation
Online
CTR and time spend on page
User feedback
Conversion rate
Latency and throughout
Resource utilization and average cost
Overall system components
Data pipeline
Training pipeline
Evaluation pipeline
Optimization pipeline
Inference pipeline
Prompt auto-complete
Prompt safety service
Prompt enhancement
Image generation
Harm detection
Super-resolution service
Other talking points

Reference Material

[1] OpenAI's DALL-E 3. https://openai.com/index/dall-e-3/.

[2] Imagen 3. https://arxiv.org/abs/2408.07009.

[3] Adobe's Firefly. https://www.adobe.com/products/firefly.html.

[4] Introducing ChatGPT. https://openai.com/index/chatgpt/.

[5] Zero-Shot Text-to-Image Generation. https://arxiv.org/abs/2102.12092.

[6] Muse: Text-To-Image Generation via Masked Generative Transformers. https://arxiv.org/abs/2301.00704.

[7] Generative Modeling by Estimating Gradients of the Data Distribution. https://arxiv.org/abs/1907.05600.

[8] Learning Transferable Visual Models From Natural Language Supervision. https://arxiv.org/abs/2103.00020.

[9] Exploring the Limits of Transfer Learning with a Unified Text-to-Text Transformer. https://arxiv.org/abs/1910.10683.

[10] Hierarchical Text-Conditional Image Generation with CLIP Latents. https://arxiv.org/abs/2204.06125.

[11] High-Resolution Image Synthesis with Latent Diffusion Models. https://arxiv.org/abs/2112.10752.

[12] On the De-duplication of LAION-2B. https://arxiv.org/abs/2303.12733.

[13] xGen-MM (BLIP-3): A Family of Open Large Multimodal Models. https://www.arxiv.org/abs/2408.08872.

[14] U-Net: Convolutional Networks for Biomedical Image Segmentation. https://arxiv.org/abs/1505.04597.

[15] Scalable Diffusion Models with Transformers. https://arxiv.org/abs/2212.09748.

[16] An Image is Worth 16x16 Words: Transformers for Image Recognition at Scale. https://arxiv.org/abs/2010.11929.

[17] Photorealistic Text-to-Image Diffusion Models with Deep Language Understanding. https://arxiv.org/abs/2205.11487.

[18] Denoising Diffusion Probabilistic Models. https://arxiv.org/abs/2006.11239.

[19] Classifier-Free Diffusion Guidance. https://arxiv.org/abs/2207.12598.

[20] Denoising Diffusion Implicit Models. https://arxiv.org/abs/2010.02502.

[21] Introduction to Diffusion Models. https://lilianweng.github.io/posts/2021-07-11-diffusion-models/.

[22] Mixed Precision Training. https://arxiv.org/abs/1710.03740.

[23] FSDP tutorial. https://pytorch.org/tutorials/intermediate/FSDP_tutorial.html.

[24] DeepSpeed. https://github.com/microsoft/DeepSpeed.

[25] Parallel Sampling of Diffusion Models. https://arxiv.org/abs/2305.16317.

[26] Consistency Models. https://arxiv.org/abs/2303.01469.

[27] Inception score. https://en.wikipedia.org/wiki/Inception_score.

[28] FID calculation. https://en.wikipedia.org/wiki/Fr%C3%A9chet_inception_distance.

[29] CLIPScore: A Reference-free Evaluation Metric for Image Captioning. https://arxiv.org/abs/2104.08718.

[30] Sora overview. https://openai.com/index/video-generation-models-as-world-simulators/.

[31] Imagen Video: High Definition Video Generation with Diffusion Models. https://arxiv.org/abs/2210.02303.

[32] Finetune Stable Diffusion Models with DDPO via TRL. https://huggingface.co/blog/trl-ddpo.

[33] Kandinsky: an Improved Text-to-Image Synthesis with Image Prior and Latent Diffusion. https://arxiv.org/abs/2310.03502.

[34] On the Importance of Noise Scheduling for Diffusion Models. https://arxiv.org/abs/2301.10972.

[35] Patch n' Pack: NaViT, a Vision Transformer for any Aspect Ratio and Resolution. https://arxiv.org/abs/2307.06304.

[36] InternVL: Scaling up Vision Foundation Models and Aligning for Generic Visual-Linguistic Tasks. https://arxiv.org/abs/2312.14238.

[37] BLIP-2: Bootstrapping Language-Image Pre-training with Frozen Image Encoders and Large Language Models. https://arxiv.org/abs/2301.12597.

[38] Adding Conditional Control to Text-to-Image Diffusion Models. https://arxiv.org/abs/2302.05543.

[39] StyleDrop: Text-to-image generation in any style. https://research.google/blog/styledrop-text-to-image-generation-in-any-style/.

10

Personalized Headshot Generation

Introduction

Personalized text-to-image (T2I) models are one of the emerging applications of generative AI. Imagine asking a T2I model to generate an image of your friend John with the prompt "John sitting on a chair while reading a book." While the model will likely produce an image of a person sitting and reading, it probably won't depict "John." To do that, we need to personalize a T2I model by having it learn the subject of interest (i.e., John).

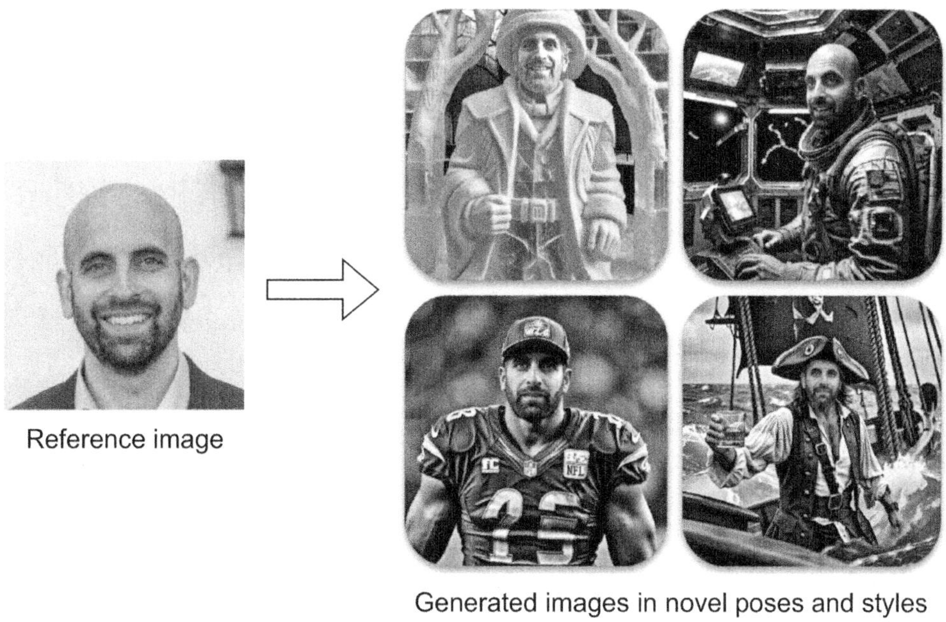

Figure 10.1: Personalized T2I model generating identity variations (Images taken from [1])

In this chapter, we explore how to develop a personalized T2I model capable of generating professional-quality headshots of specific individuals.

Clarifying Requirements

Here is a typical interaction between a candidate and an interviewer:

Candidate: Are the generated headshots primarily intended for business profiles, such as LinkedIn?
Interviewer: Correct.

Candidate: I assume users will provide several images of themselves in different variations – pose, angle – with their faces visible. Is that correct? How many images will we ask them to upload?
Interviewer: Yes, that's correct. Let's assume between 10 to 20 images.

Candidate: What if some images are not suitable, like if they're too dark or the face isn't visible?
Interviewer: We need to detect those and notify the user to provide better images.

Candidate: Should users be able to specify features such as hairstyle in the generated images?
Interviewer: For simplicity, let's assume attribute control isn't required.

Candidate: What resolution is required for the headshots?
Interviewer: The system should support 1024x1024 outputs.

Candidate: Can I assume we can start from a pretrained generic T2I model?
Interviewer: Yes.

Candidate: Should users be able to provide text prompts to control the generated headshots?
Interviewer: We prefer to keep it simple, so assume users won't provide text prompts.

Candidate: How many headshot images should the system generate?
Interviewer: 50 images.

Candidate: What is the expected latency?
Interviewer: The user provides the images, and we notify them by email when the images are ready. The overall process should take less than an hour.

Frame the Problem as an ML Task

In this section, we use headshot generation as a case study to explore an important aspect of image generation: personalization. This process involves adapting a pretrained T2I model to learn a new subject, in this case, the user's face.

Specifying the system's input and output

The input includes several images of the user's face, taken from different angles and in different poses. The output consists of professional headshots of the individual. These headshots are high-quality and diverse, and they preserve the person's identity.

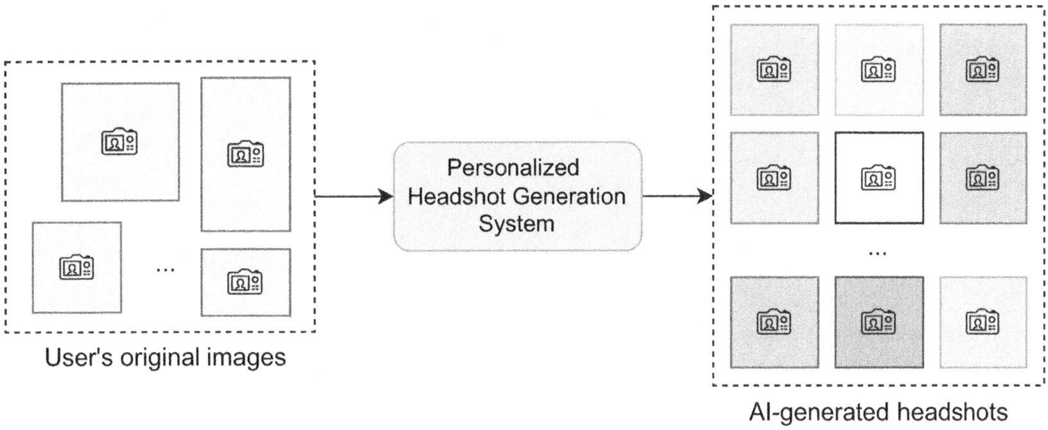

Figure 10.2: Input and output of a headshot generation system

Choosing a suitable ML approach

Diffusion models work exceptionally well at generating very detailed and realistic images. A common practice for personalization is to start with a T2I model pretrained on a broad range of images as a base model.

There are two primary approaches to personalizing a pretrained T2I model: tuning-based and tuning-free.

Tuning-based methods finetune the T2I model on a set of reference images for each identity. This approach integrates the new identity into the model, allowing it to generate a variety of images while preserving the identity.

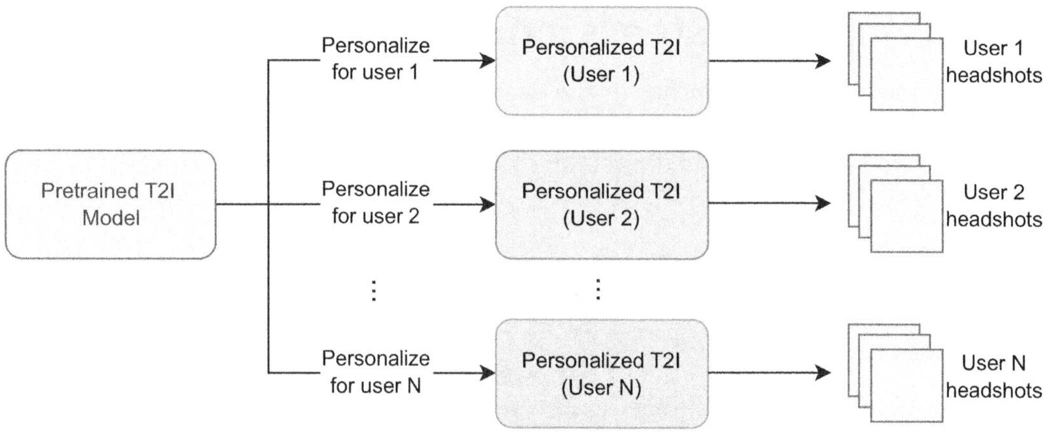

Figure 10.3: Tuning-based approach for T2I personalization

On the other hand, tuning-free methods bypass the need for finetuning the T2I model for each new identity. Instead, they finetune the pretrained T2I model along with a visual encoder once. After this training, the visual encoder extracts features from a new reference image and injects them into the T2I model. This allows the model to generate personalized images without adjusting its internal weights for each identity.

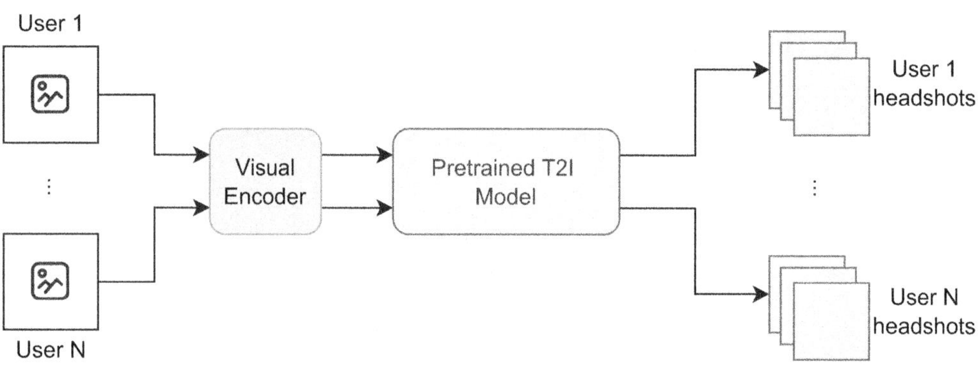

Figure 10.4: Tuning-free approach for T2I personalization

Tuning-free methods, such as Meta's Imagine Yourself [1], are simpler because they only require training once. A single model should be deployed, and only one reference image is needed, allowing the same T2I model to generate personalized images for multiple identities. However, these methods often rely on a single reference image to capture facial features, which may not capture all the details from different angles or expressions. Additionally, they require special adjustments tailored to the subject. For instance, [1] uses specific encoders and proposes a technique for generating synthetic paired data.

On the other hand, tuning-based methods tend to capture more detailed features of the subject. They are also more versatile, handling a wider range of subjects beyond human faces. Given these advantages, we focus on tuning-based methods in the rest of this chapter. If you are interested in learning more about tuning-free methods, refer to [2, 3, 1].

Several tuning-based methods can be used to achieve personalization, each offering unique advantages and disadvantages. Three of the most common ones are:

- Textual inversion
- DreamBooth
- Low-rank adaptation (LoRA)

Textual inversion

Textual inversion [4] personalizes a T2I model by introducing a new special token that represents the subject and learning its embedding. During finetuning, the model updates the special token's embedding, while the diffusion model, text encoder, and other token embeddings remain unchanged.

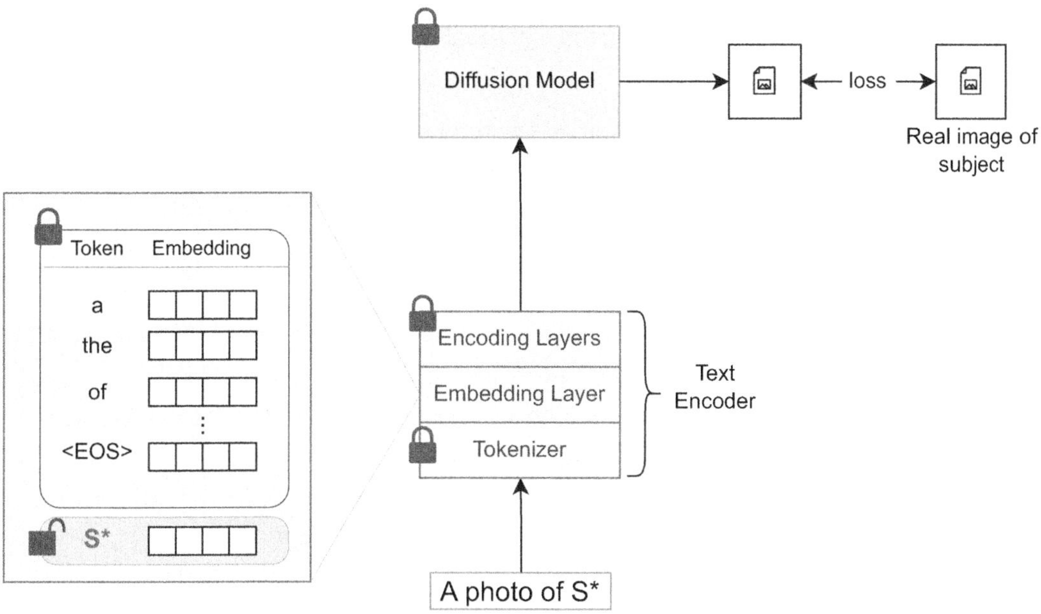

Figure 10.5: Textual inversion updating only the special token embedding

After finetuning, the model generates images of the new subject when prompted with the special token.

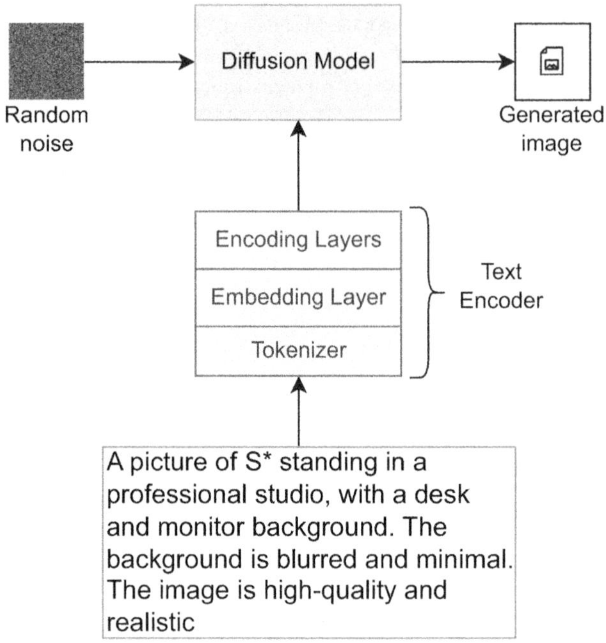

Figure 10.6: Generating an image of the subject of interest

Let's review the pros and cons of textual inversion.

Pros:

- **Efficiency:** Textual inversion training involves learning only a new token embedding, making it a lightweight and efficient process.
- **Preservation of original model capabilities:** The diffusion model's capabilities are maintained since its parameters remain unchanged.
- **Minimal storage requirements:** Minimal storage is required because only the special token embedding needs to be stored for each personalized model.

Cons:

- **Difficulty in learning subject details:** Textual inversion often struggles to learn new subject details accurately due to its limited capacity to encode these details. This limitation arises because the new subject is represented by a single token embedding.

In summary, while textual inversion is an efficient method for personalizing a T2I model, it often struggles to capture and preserve all the details of the new subject.

DreamBooth

DreamBooth [5] is a popular personalization method that was introduced by Google in 2023. It finetunes a pretrained diffusion model using images of the subject of interest. Unlike textual inversion, DreamBooth updates all the diffusion model's parameters during finetuning. This allows the model to capture the new subject's details more effectively.

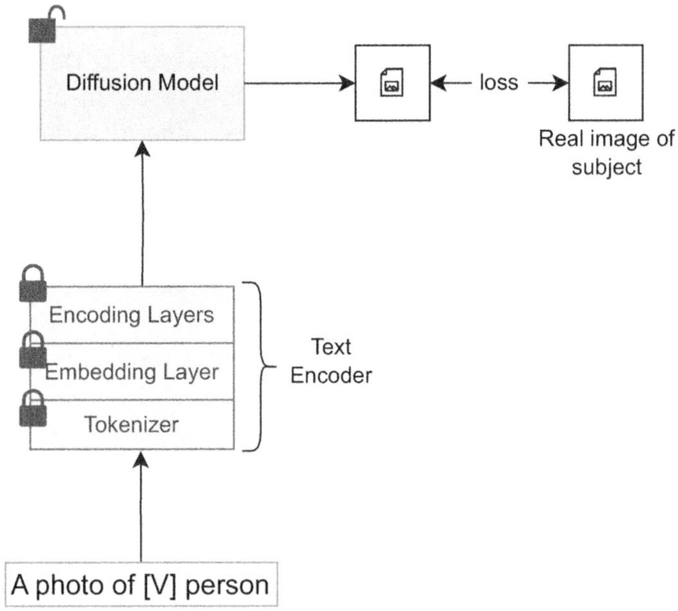

Figure 10.7: DreamBooth method updating the entire diffusion model

DreamBooth relies primarily on two techniques for successful finetuning:

- Rare-token identifier
- Class-specific prior preservation loss

Rare-token identifier

Most personalization methods select an identifier to represent the subject of interest. While textual inversion creates a new token for this purpose, DreamBooth selects an identifier using the existing vocabulary of tokens. The authors have found that simply choosing any existing token won't work well in practice. Let's explore why simple approaches such as selecting a common or random identifier won't work, and why the rare-token identifier is preferred.

Challenges with common or random token identifier

A simple way to represent the subject of interest is to choose a common English word such as "unique" or "special". This approach is problematic because the token usually has an established meaning. For example, if we choose "special" to refer to the subject of interest using a prompt like "a special person sitting", the model might struggle because "special" already has a broad, established meaning in the context of language. The model has to separate this token from its original meaning and then learn a new meaning for it that references the new subject.

Another way to represent the subject is to randomly combine characters. This approach also poses issues because the tokenizer might treat each character separately, leading to strong prior associations for these characters. For example, if we choose "xxy5syt00" to represent the subject, the tokenizer might break it down into individual characters, each of which could have pre-existing associations within the model. This fragmentation can cause the model to generate outputs that are influenced by the meanings or patterns associated with those individual characters or sub-units, rather than treating the identifier as a unique and cohesive entity.

How the rare-token identifier works

DreamBooth resolves these problems by selecting rare tokens—those that appear infrequently in the training data. Representing the subject of interest with these tokens strikes a balance: they're distinct enough to avoid strong prior associations but still cohesive so that tokenizers treat them as a single unit.

Here is the step-by-step process to form an identifier:

1. **Identifying a few rare tokens in the vocabulary:** The model's vocabulary contains a large set of tokens, each with a unique ID. A "rare token" is one that appears infrequently in the training data. Such rare tokens are identified by assessing token frequency distribution.
2. **Generating a sequence of rare tokens:** Once we have identified the rare tokens, we generate a sequence using some of these tokens.
3. **Forming the identifier:** The tokenizer converts the sequence of token IDs back into their corresponding text form. This forms an identifier to represent the subject. "XyZ", "SKS", and "[V]" are possible examples of an identifier.

Class-specific prior preservation loss

DreamBooth finetunes all layers of the diffusion model. While this enhances the quality of generated images, it can lead to overfitting, where the model loses diversity in its outputs. For example, training the model on images of a specific dog might make it struggle to generate images of other dogs.

To address this problem, DreamBooth uses class-specific prior preservation loss to maintain general class characteristics. This prevents the model from overfitting to the specific examples and losing its ability to generate diverse images that belong to the broader class. We will examine DreamBooth's loss function in the training section.

DreamBooth has several pros and cons.

Pros:

- **Effective at learning subject details:** Updating more parameters allows the model to learn the details of the subject more accurately.
- **Fewer images required:** Because the entire diffusion model is updated, a smaller image

set is needed to learn the subject.

Cons:

- **High storage requirement:** After finetuning for each subject, the entire diffusion model has to be stored for future use. This can require several gigabytes per subject, which is costly and not scalable.
- **Resource-intensive:** Updating the entire diffusion model demands more GPU memory during training.

In summary, DreamBooth learns subject details effectively but is costly to train and store. In contrast, textual inversion is efficient and compact, but less effective. Next, we'll explore LoRA, which offers a balanced approach.

LoRA

LoRA, introduced by Microsoft [6], is a powerful method for efficiently finetuning very large models. This method was originally developed for adapting large language models (LLMs) to specific tasks but was later adopted for other tasks including T2I personalization.

The key motivation behind LoRA is that finetuning all parameters of large pretrained models, such as GPT-3 [7], is time-consuming and costly. Instead, LoRA adapts a large model to a new task by introducing a small set of parameters and updating only those, thus significantly reducing computational costs.

Due to its importance, let's examine in detail the mathematical foundations of LoRA.

The mathematics of LoRA

In a typical neural network layer, a weight matrix, $W \in \mathbb{R}^{d_{\text{out}} \times d_{\text{in}}}$, transforms the input vector, $x \in \mathbb{R}^{d_{in}}$, into the output vector $y \in \mathbb{R}^{d_{\text{out}}}$.

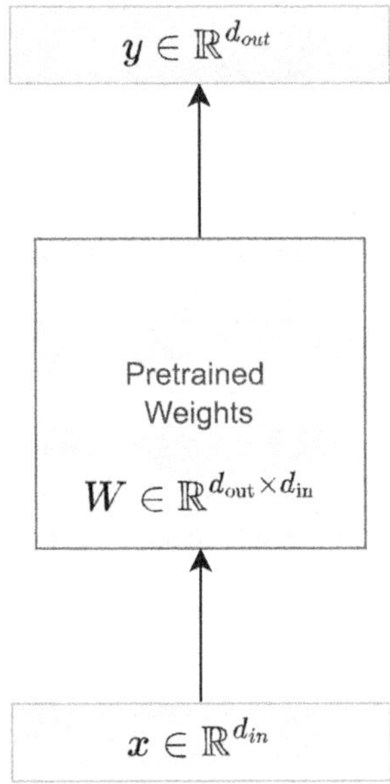

Figure 10.8: A fully connected neural network layer

The goal of finetuning is to adjust weight parameters, W, to improve the performance of the specific task. Instead of modifying W directly, LoRA modifies the weights by introducing an additional low-rank component, ΔW, which can be expressed as a product of two learnable lowrank matrices:

$$\Delta W = AB$$

where:

- $A \in \mathbb{R}^{d_{\text{out}} \times d_r}$,
- $B \in \mathbb{R}^{d_r \times d_{\text{in}}}$,
- d_{in} and d_{out} represent input and output dimensions,
- r is a small integer representing the rank, typically much smaller than d_{in} and d_{out}.

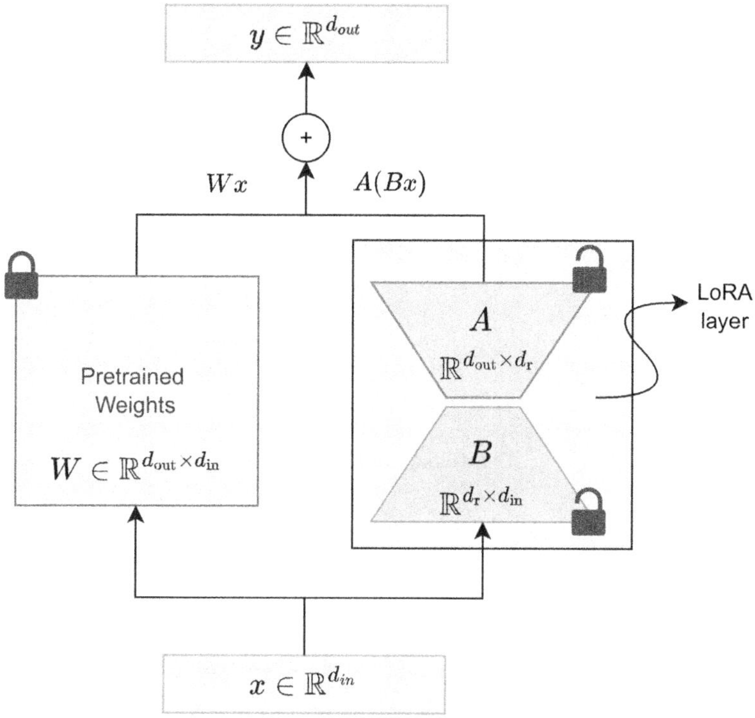

Figure 10.9: Injection of low-rank matrices

Learning the new parameters introduced by LoRA is more efficient than finetuning the full matrix. Specifically, the original matrix, W, has $d_{\text{out}} \times d_{\text{in}}$ parameters, while the low-rank approximation introduces only $r \times (d_{\text{in}} + d_{\text{out}})$ parameters. For small values of r, this can lead to significant savings in both storage and computation.

LoRA for T2I personalization

To apply LoRA, we inject trainable parameters into the diffusion model and update only those parameters during finetuning to learn the new identity. This method requires training of only a fraction of the model's parameters, which is much faster and more memory-efficient.

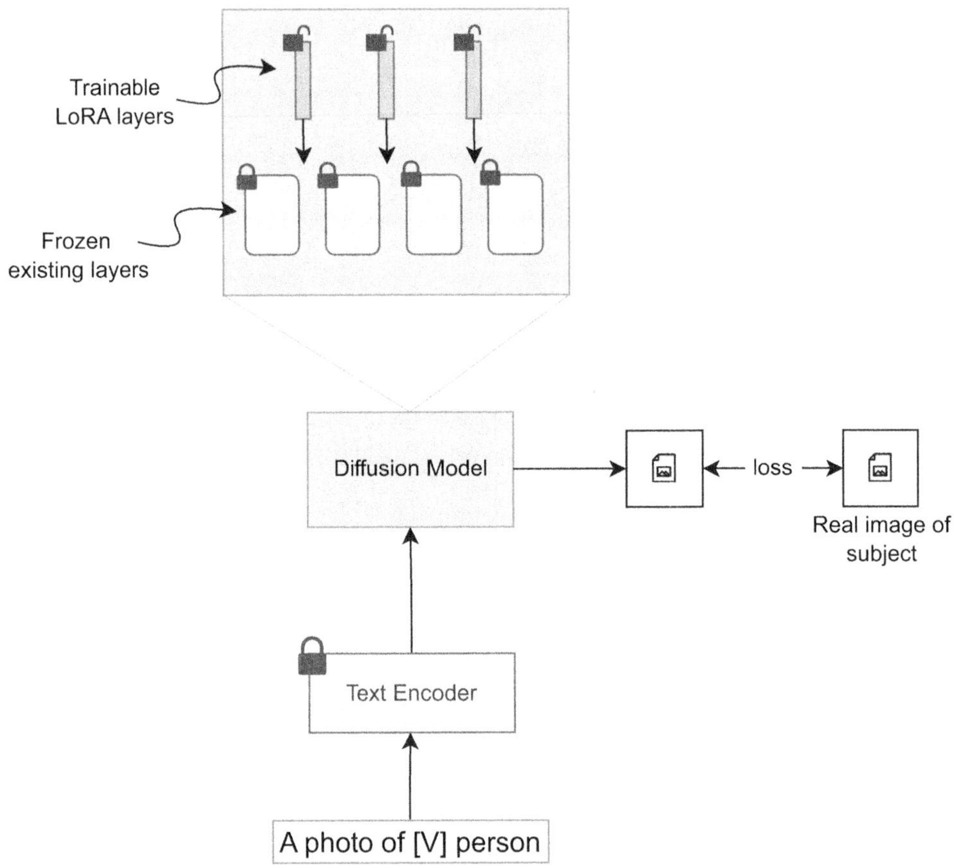

Figure 10.10: LoRA method injecting and learning new parameters in the diffusion model

Pros:

- **Preserves original model capabilities:** LoRA preserves the T2I's capabilities by freezing the original model parameters.
- **Reduces memory and computational needs:** LoRA updates only a small fraction of the model's parameters, making it more efficient than DreamBooth.
- **Minimizes storage requirements:** Since the original model remains unchanged, only the LoRA layers are stored. This typically means just a few megabytes per personalized model, which is cost-efficient and scalable.

Cons:

- **Less effective learning:** LoRA is less effective than DreamBooth because it finetunes only a small number of parameters, thus limiting its capacity to learn the new subject.
- **Slight increase in inference time:** LoRA slightly increases inference time due to additional parameters and computations. However, this is often negligible compared to the overall benefits of reduced storage requirements and faster adaptation times.

Table 10.1 provides a comparison of the three tuning-based personalization methods.

	Textual Inversion	LoRA	DreamBooth
Learning effectiveness	Low	Moderate	High
Required storage	Low	Moderate	High
Required training resources	Low	Moderate	High
Maintaining the original model's capabilities	Yes	Yes	No

Table 10.1: Comparison of popular tuning-based personalization methods

Which method is more suitable for headshot generation?

The suitability of these methods depends on the use case and the system requirements. For headshot generation, we choose DreamBooth for three main reasons:

1. **Better identity preservation:** DreamBooth is most effective at preserving details of the subject, leading to better identity preservation.
2. **Acceptable training time:** According to [5], it takes around 15 minutes to finetune a diffusion model using DreamBooth. This training time is acceptable given that we are required to share the generated images with the user within an hour.
3. **No need for storage:** We don't need to save personalized models after generating the headshots, so storage concerns with the DreamBooth approach are not relevant.

Data Preparation

The number of images needed varies depending on the method. Tuning-free methods generally require just one image, whereas tuning-based methods such as DreamBooth need around 10–20 images.

Since we are using DreamBooth, users are asked to upload 10–20 images. These images may come in different resolutions and aspect ratios. To prepare them for training, we follow these steps:

- Image resizing
- Image augmentation
- Generic face data addition

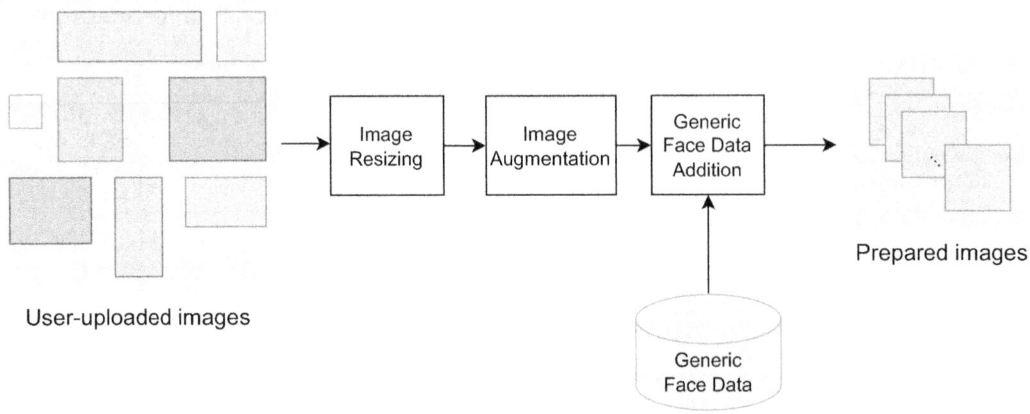

Figure 10.11: Preparing data for training

Image resizing

Diffusion models typically require fixed input dimensions, but user-uploaded images often vary in dimensions. We resize the images to uniform dimensions suitable for the diffusion model.

Image augmentation

T2I models require lots of images to learn concepts such as objects, identities, and scenes. However, for personalization, we often lack a large dataset. We use image augmentation techniques such as mirroring, slight rotations, and scaling to artificially expand the dataset. This step is essential when only a small number of images is available for training.

Generic face data addition

Training only on the provided images may cause the model to overfit to a specific identity and forget previously learned knowledge. To prevent this, we combine user-uploaded images with a larger, generic dataset of faces. We generate these images using a pretrained diffusion model with prompts such as "an image of a person."

Model Development

Architecture

The DreamBooth method finetunes a pretrained diffusion model. We use a model with a U-Net architecture, pretrained to output 1024×1024 images, similar to what we covered in Chapter 9. The architecture remains unchanged: a series of downsampling blocks followed by a series of upsampling blocks.

Training

To finetune a pretrained diffusion model, we follow the same process as training a diffusion model from scratch:

- **Noise addition:** Noise is added to an image based on a randomly selected timestep.
- **Conditioning signals preparation:** Separate encoders prepare the image caption and timestep as conditioning signals for the model to predict noise.
- **Noise prediction:** The model predicts the noise to be removed from the noisy image using the conditioning signals.

Training data

The training data consists of user-uploaded images and generic face images added during data preparation. User-uploaded images are labeled as "An image of a [V] person," while generic face images are labeled as "An image of a person."

ML objective and loss function

The key challenge in personalization is to ensure the model can generate both general categories (e.g., human faces) and specific instances within those categories (e.g., a unique individual). To address this, we use two loss functions:

- Reconstruction loss
- Class-specific prior preservation loss

Reconstruction loss

This loss function measures the differences between the reconstructed image and the actual images of the specific subject. It helps the model preserve the subject's identity.

Class-specific prior preservation loss

This loss function measures the difference between the generated images and actual images of generic faces. It ensures the model maintains the characteristics of the human class and avoids overfitting to specific identities.

Overall loss

The overall loss function is a weighted combination of the reconstruction loss and the class-specific prior preservation loss. The formula for the overall loss can be expressed as:

$$\text{Overall loss} = \alpha \times \text{reconstruction loss} + \beta \times \text{class-specific prior preservation loss}$$

α and β are hyperparameters that control the trade-off between maintaining a specific identity and preserving human characteristics. The ML objective is to minimize the overall loss, which allows the model to generate images of unique identities while retaining its ability to produce generic human face images.

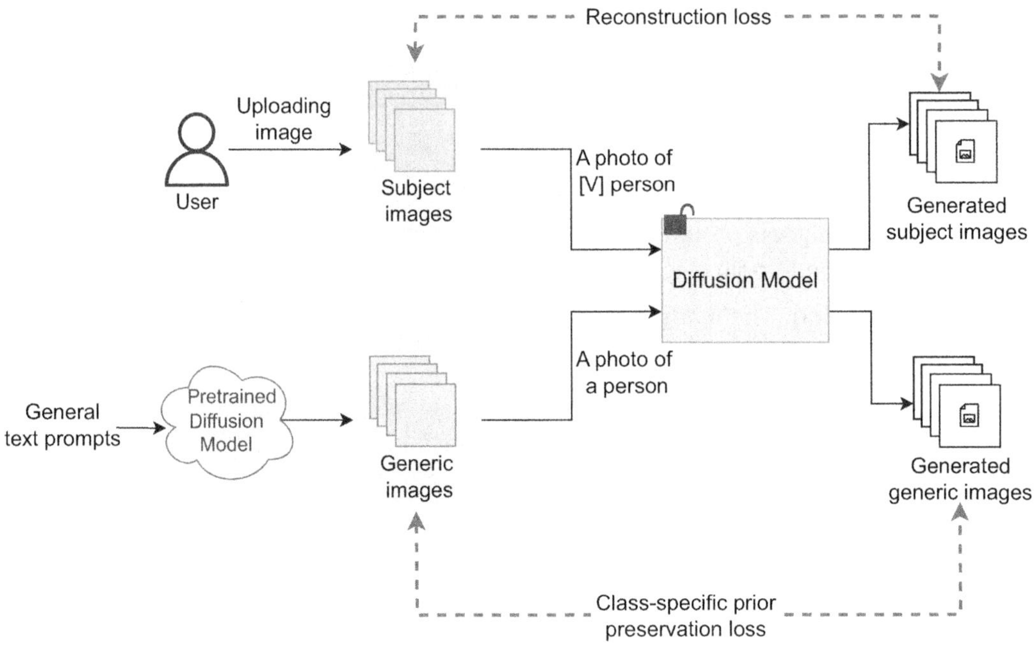

Figure 10.12: Overall loss calculation

Sampling

The sampling process for headshot generation is similar to the T2I generation discussed in Chapter 9, as both use diffusion models. However, a key difference lies in how we provide text prompts. In Chapter 9, the user provided the text prompt. For example, a user might input "a cat sitting on a chair," and the diffusion model would generate an image reflecting that text.

In headshot generation, the users don't provide prompts. Instead, we create a set of hand-engineered prompts. These prompts represent various professional settings and include the identifier used during training to ensure the generated images reflect the user's identity. Some examples include:

- "A professional headshot of [V] smiling in front of a plain white background."
- "A close-up of [V] with a neutral expression, wearing formal attire."
- "A headshot of [V] with soft lighting, looking slightly to the left."
- "A profile shot of [V] against a blurred outdoor background."
- "A professional headshot of [V] wearing a business suit, with a confident expression."

After creating the prompts, we sample one image per prompt from the diffusion model. We follow the standard diffusion process sampling steps:

1. Generate initial random noise.

2. Iteratively denoise the input through multiple steps, using Classifier-free guidance (CFG) [8] during each step to reduce noise and refine image details. To review CFG, refer to [8] or Chapter 9.

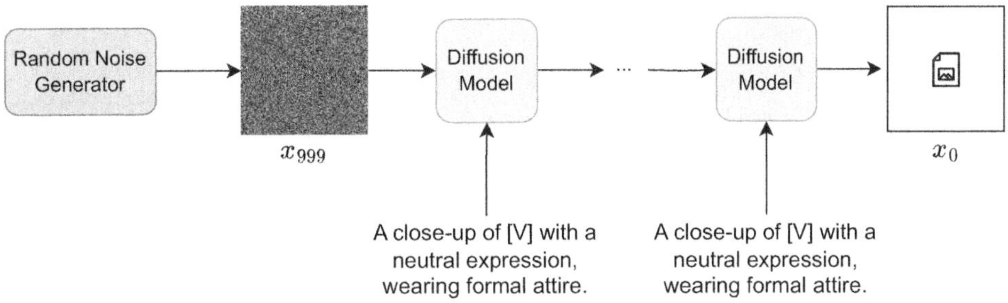

Figure 10.13: Sampling a headshot image

Evaluation

Offline evaluation metrics

It is important to evaluate personalized diffusion models to ensure our model is capable of preserving the user's identity in the generated images. We assess the performance of a personalized diffusion model by focusing on three main aspects:

- Text alignment
- Image quality
- Image alignment

Text alignment

Text alignment refers to how closely generated images match text prompts. A common metric for measuring this is the CLIPSocre [9], which ensures the images are not only high quality but also relevant to the input text.

Image quality

As we explored in previous chapters, we employ common metrics such as FID [10] and Inception score [11] to measure the quality of the generated images.

Image alignment

Image alignment, particularly relevant to personalized text-to-image models, refers to assessing the visual similarity between generated images and the subject of interest. For instance, if the model is tasked with generating an image of a specific backpack, image alignment measures how closely the generated image resembles that backpack.

Commonly used metrics for measuring the visual similarity between the generated and original subject are:

- CLIP score
- DINO score
- Facial similarity score

CLIP score

CLIP model [12] uses two encoders—one for images and one for text. These encoders are trained to ensure that the image and text embeddings of a relevant image-text pair are close in the embedding space.

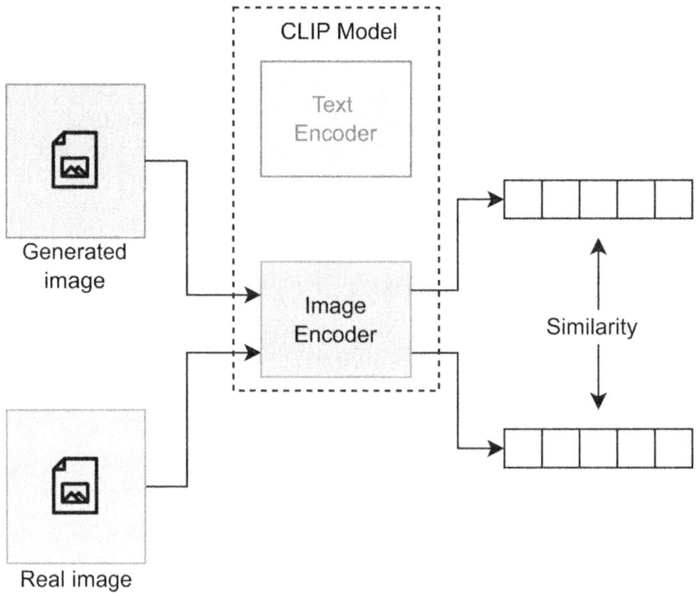

Figure 10.14: Image alignment calculation with CLIP

To measure image alignment using CLIP, we discard the text encoder and use the image encoder to generate embeddings for both the generated and real images. We then calculate the cosine similarity between these embeddings to assess their similarity. Higher scores indicate that the personalized diffusion model creates images that are more visually similar to real images.

DINO score

DINO [13] is a self-supervised learning method developed by Meta. DINO learns visual representations of images without the need for labeled data. In particular, it uses a method called contrastive learning [14], whereby the model learns to distinguish between similar and dissimilar images by organizing them in an embedding space—similar images are placed closer together, and dissimilar ones are positioned farther apart.

DINO, along with its more recent variations like DINOv2 [15], is particularly good at capturing similarities between images because it is trained to recognize subtle differences.

This makes DINO particularly effective for measuring image alignment. By comparing the embeddings of a generated image with a real one, DINO can evaluate how well the generated image matches the real one.

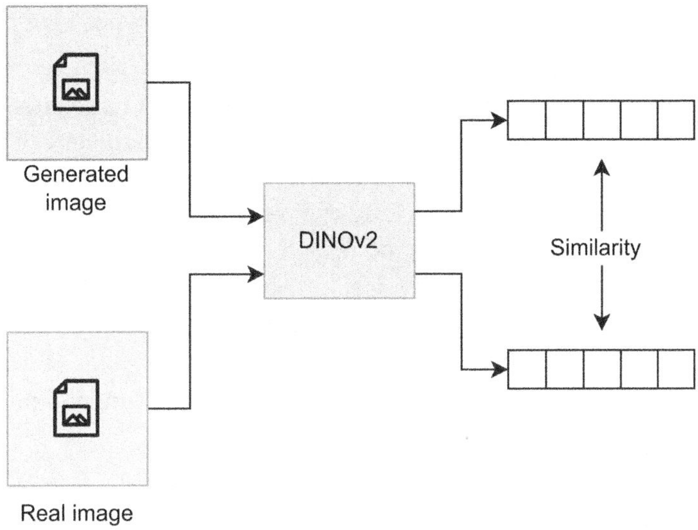

Figure 10.15: Image alignment calculation with DINOv2 [15]

DINO versus CLIP

DINO is preferred for comparing images because it is trained to capture detailed visual features. For example, two images, one with a yellow jacket and another with a red jacket, might have a low DINO score due to the color difference. On the other hand, CLIP is better for comparing images with text, as it is trained to match descriptions with visuals. The same images with different jacket colors might have a high CLIP score if both reflect a person wearing a jacket.

Facial similarity score

While CLIP and DINO measure visual similarity between generated and real images, they aren't designed to assess identity preservation. For example, two face images might show different individuals, but CLIP and DINO could still give a high similarity score. To address this, we use a face recognition model to compare generated and real images. These models specialize in identifying and measuring facial similarity, which is a crucial requirement in a personalized headshot generation system.

Combining DINO, CLIP, and facial similarity scores provides a comprehensive evaluation of image alignment in the personalized diffusion model.

Online evaluation metrics

Online evaluation is crucial in headshot generation. It measures user satisfaction directly, which is vital when users pay for the service, as higher satisfaction often leads to increased revenue. We focus on two primary metrics:

- **User feedback:** This metric directly reflects user satisfaction. After receiving their generated headshots, users rate their satisfaction on a scale from 1 to 5. High ratings indicate that the headshots meet or exceed expectations, while lower scores highlight improvements are needed.
- **Conversion rate to paid service:** This metric measures the percentage of users who move from showing interest to becoming new paying customers. It is calculated by dividing the number of new paying customers by the total number of users who engaged with the service—such as visiting the website, signing up for a trial, or making inquiries—within a specific time period.

Overall ML System Design

Generating professional headshots requires more than just a diffusion model. In this section, we examine three key pipelines:

- Data pipeline
- Training pipeline
- Inference pipeline

Data pipeline

This pipeline has two responsibilities:

- Preparing images with the subject of interest
- Preparing images of generic human faces

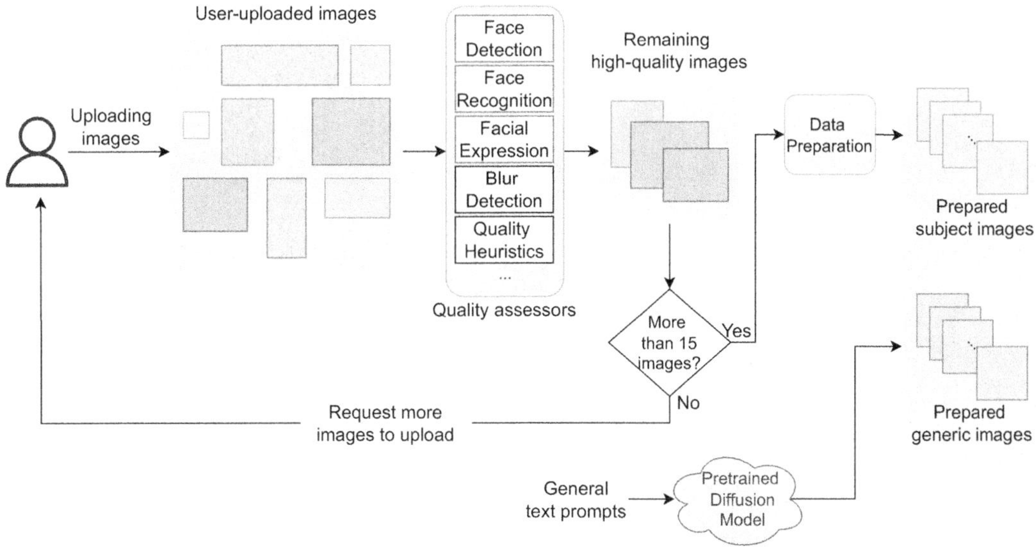

Figure 10.16: Data pipeline components

Preparing images with the subject of interest

This process evaluates user-uploaded images to ensure they meet predefined standards and prepares them for training.

Specifically, it verifies that the images are diverse and contain only a single object of interest: the user's face. To achieve this, we use various heuristics and ML models to analyze the images, checking factors such as clarity, diverse angles, expressions, and the presence of the user's face. If any images fail to meet these criteria, they are rejected, and the user is asked to upload more. This ensures that only high-quality images are used to finetune the diffusion model.

Preparing images of generic human faces

This step involves preparing images with generic faces to prevent the model from overfitting to the subject of interest. We use the pretrained T2I model to generate these images with prompts like "a person sitting on a chair."

Training pipeline

This pipeline is responsible for personalizing the pretrained diffusion model.

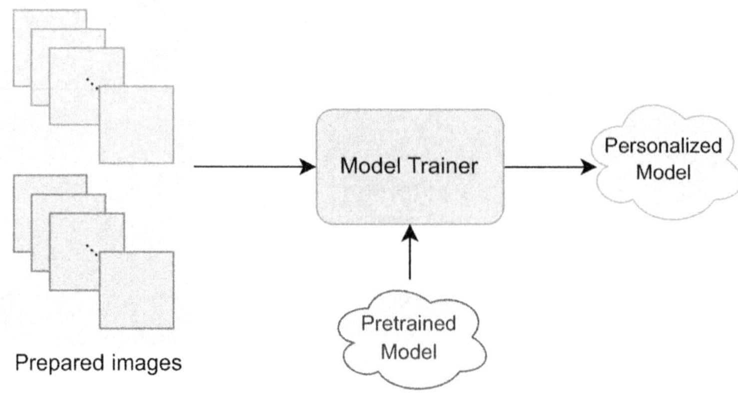

Figure 10.17: Finetuning a pretrained diffusion model

Inference pipeline

The inference pipeline is responsible for generating the headshots of the user using a personalized T2I model. Three main components in the inference pipeline are:

- Image generator
- Quality assessment service
- Uploader service

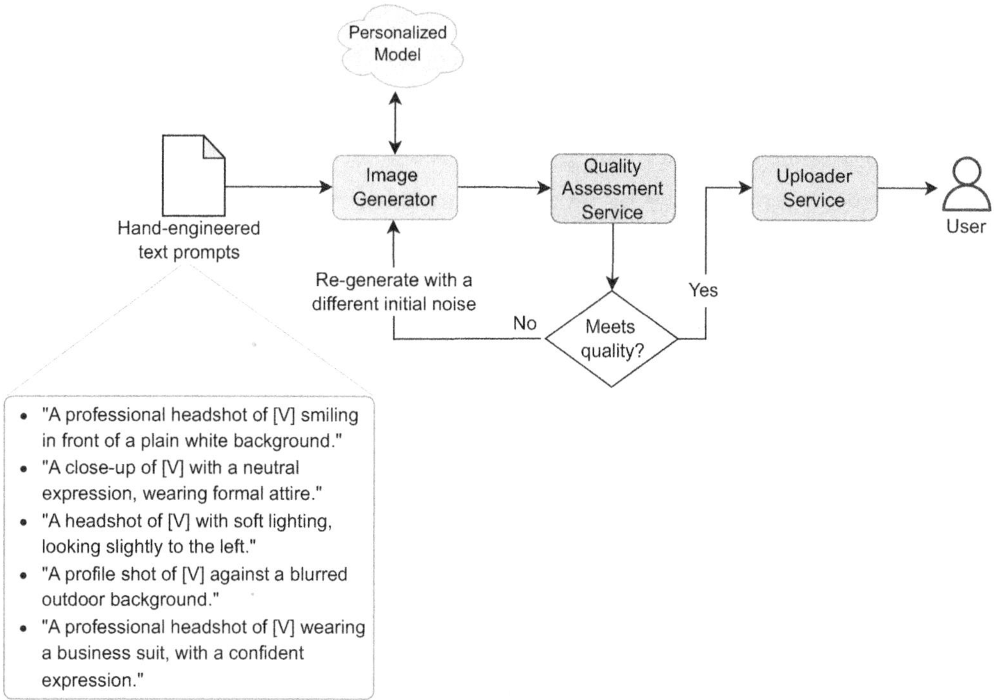

Figure 10.18: Inference pipeline components

Image generator

The image generator utilizes the personalized T2I model and hand-engineered text prompts to generate one image per prompt.

Quality assessment service

This service ensures the generated images meet identity preservation standards. This service uses a pretrained face recognition model to compare the generated headshot with the user's real images. If the generated image fails to preserve the user's identity, the service rejects it and requests that the image generator produce a new image using the same text prompt but with a different initial noise.

Uploader service

The uploader service manages the delivery of generated images to the user. It uploads the images to cloud storage so users can download their headshots.

Other Talking Points

If there is extra time at the end of the interview, here are some additional talking points:

- Preventing catastrophic forgetting during the finetuning [16].
- The details of choosing a rare token for the new subject, and its importance [5].

- Details of class-specific prior preservation loss [5].
- Addressing the issue of reduced output diversity after finetuning [5].
- Supporting multiple sizes and aspect ratios in generated images [17].
- Details of tuning-free methods such as Meta's Imagine Yourself [1].
- Mitigating the risks and ethical concerns around deepfake generation and detection [18].
- ML techniques to handle personally identifiable information (PII) securely while ensuring data privacy [19, 20].

Summary

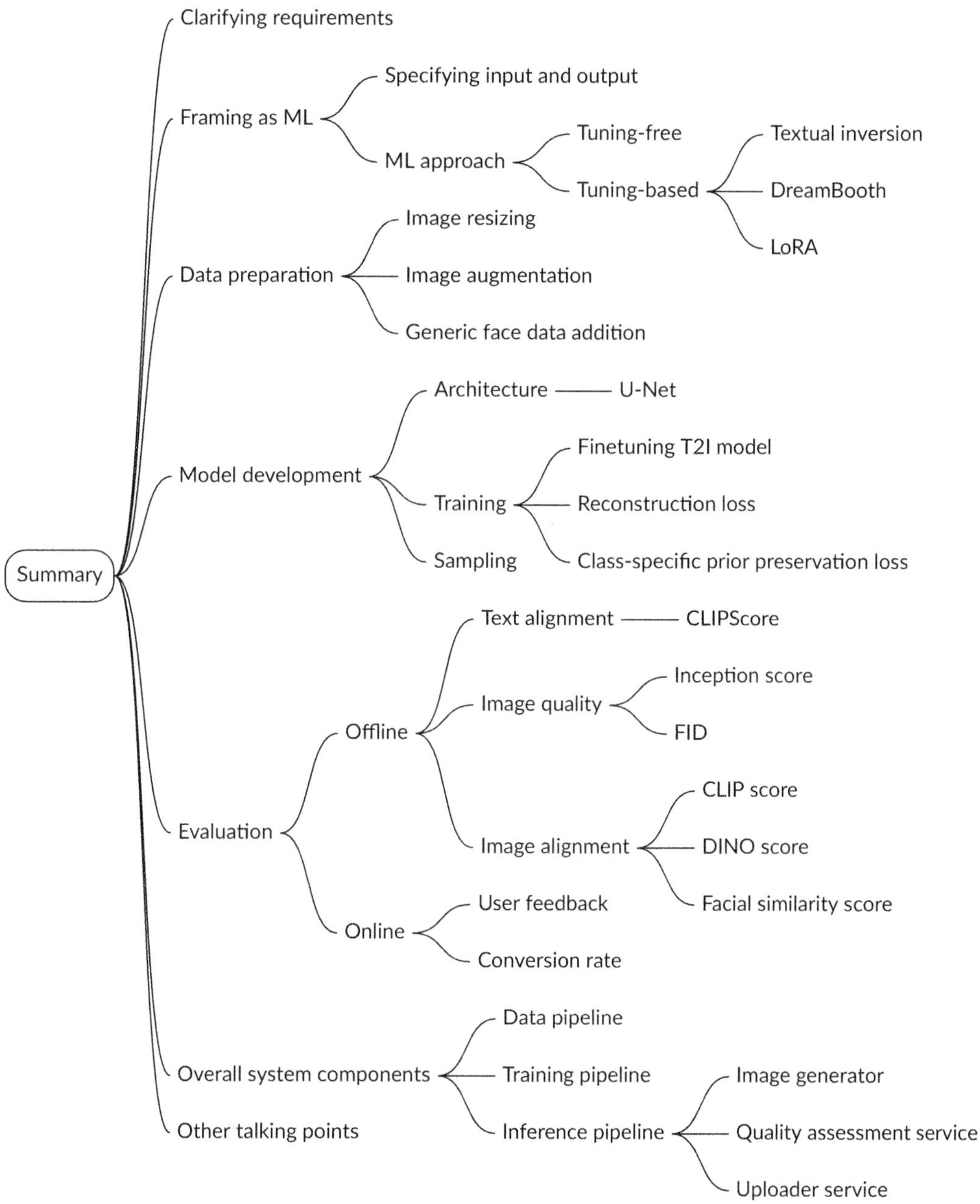
Summary
Clarifying requirements
Framing as ML
Specifying input and output
ML approach
Tuning-free
Tuning-based
Textual inversion
DreamBooth
LoRA
Data preparation
Image resizing
Image augmentation
Generic face data addition
Model development
Architecture
U-Net
Training
Finetuning T2I model
Reconstruction loss
Class-specific prior preservation loss
Sampling
Evaluation
Offline
Text alignment
CLIPScore
Image quality
Inception score
FID
Image alignment
CLIP score
DINO score
Facial similarity score
Online
User feedback
Conversion rate
Overall system components
Data pipeline
Training pipeline
Inference pipeline
Image generator
Quality assessment service
Uploader service
Other talking points

Reference Material

[1] Imagine yourself: Tuning-Free Personalized Image Generation. https://ai.meta.com/research/publications/imagine-yourself-tuning-free-personalized-image-generation/.

[2] MoA: Mixture-of-Attention for Subject-Context Disentanglement in Personalized Image Generation. https://arxiv.org/abs/2404.11565.

[3] InstantID: Zero-shot Identity-Preserving Generation in Seconds. https://arxiv.org/abs/2401.07519.

[4] An Image is Worth One Word: Personalizing Text-to-Image Generation using Textual Inversion. https://textual-inversion.github.io/.

[5] DreamBooth: Fine Tuning Text-to-Image Diffusion Models for Subject-Driven Generation. https://arxiv.org/abs/2208.12242.

[6] LoRA: Low-Rank Adaptation of Large Language Models. https://arxiv.org/abs/2106.09685.

[7] Language Models are Few-Shot Learners. https://arxiv.org/abs/2005.14165.

[8] Classifier-Free Diffusion Guidance. https://arxiv.org/abs/2207.12598.

[9] CLIPScore: A Reference-free Evaluation Metric for Image Captioning. https://arxiv.org/abs/2104.08718.

[10] FID calculation. https://en.wikipedia.org/wiki/Fr%C3%A9chet_inception_distance.

[11] Inception score. https://en.wikipedia.org/wiki/Inception_score.

[12] Learning Transferable Visual Models From Natural Language Supervision. https://arxiv.org/abs/2103.00020.

[13] Emerging Properties in Self-Supervised Vision Transformers. https://arxiv.org/abs/2104.14294.

[14] Contrastive Representation Learning. https://lilianweng.github.io/posts/2021-05-31-contrastive/.

[15] DINOv2: Learning Robust Visual Features without Supervision. https://arxiv.org/abs/2304.07193.

[16] An Empirical Study of Catastrophic Forgetting in Large Language Models During Continual Fine-tuning. https://arxiv.org/abs/2308.08747.

[17] SDXL: Improving Latent Diffusion Models for High-Resolution Image Synthesis. https://arxiv.org/abs/2307.01952.

[18] Deepfakes, Misinformation, and Disinformation in the Era of Frontier AI, Generative AI, and Large AI Models. https://arxiv.org/abs/2311.17394.

[19] Privacy-Preserving Personal Identifiable Information (PII) Label Detection Using Machine Learning. https://ieeexplore.ieee.org/document/10307924.

[20] Does fine-tuning GPT-3 with the OpenAI API leak personally-identifiable information? https://arxiv.org/abs/2307.16382.

11

Text-to-Video Generation

Introduction

Text-to-video generation is a key application of generative AI, enabling the generation of videos from textual descriptions. This chapter delves into the crucial components required to build a text-to-video model.

Prompt: A stylish woman walks down a Tokyo street filled with warm glowing neon and animated city signage. She wears a black leather jacket, a long red dress, and black boots, and carries a black purse. She wears sunglasses and red lipstick. She walks confidently and casually. The street is damp and reflective, creating a mirror effect of the colorful lights. Many pedestrians walk about.

Figure 11.1: An example of a generated video by OpenAI's Sora model [1]

Clarifying Requirements

Here is a typical interaction between a candidate and an interviewer:

Candidate: What is the expected length of the generated videos?
Interviewer: Let's aim for five-second-long videos.

Candidate: What video resolution are we targeting?
Interviewer: We should aim for high-definition quality to ensure the videos suit a wide range of modern platforms and devices. Let's aim for 720p resolution.

Candidate: Is 24 frames per second (FPS) the desired rate for the generated video?
Interviewer: Yes.

Candidate: What is the expected latency for generating a video?
Interviewer: Video generation is computationally expensive. For the start, a few minutes of processing time will be acceptable. In future iterations, we will optimize for efficiency and speed.

Candidate: Should we focus on a specific video category?
Interviewer: No, the system should generate videos across various genres and subjects.

Candidate: Should the system support multiple languages for text input, or are we starting with English only?
Interviewer: Let's start with English.

Candidate: Should the generated videos include audio output?
Interviewer: Let's focus on silent videos for now. Audio could be considered for an enhancement for future iterations, but it's not a priority at this stage.

Candidate: What is the approximate size of our training data?
Interviewer: We have a large video dataset, around 100 million diverse videos with captions. Some captions might be noisy or non-English.

Candidate: A common approach to building a text-to-video model is to extend a pretrained text-to-image model to handle videos. Do we have a pretrained text-to-image model?
Interviewer: Yes, that is a fair assumption.

Candidate: Considering the high computational demands of video generation, what is our compute budget?
Interviewer: Training a video generation system requires significant computational resources. We have over 6,000 H100 [2] GPUs available for text-to-video training.

Candidate: Shall we ensure the system has safeguards to prevent generating offensive or harmful videos is crucial?
Interviewer: Great point. Yes, we need to ensure our proposed system is safe for users.

Frame the Problem as an ML Task

This section frames the text-to-video generation problem as an ML task and highlights the necessary considerations beyond those used in Chapter 9 for text-to-image generation.

Specifying the system's input and output

The input is a descriptive text outlining a scene, action, or narrative. The output is a five-second 720p (1280×720) video that visually and temporally aligns with the given text prompt.

For example, given a text input like "A dog playing fetch in a park on a sunny day," the system should generate a video depicting this scene, capturing the dog's movement, the park's environment, and the ambiance of a sunny day.

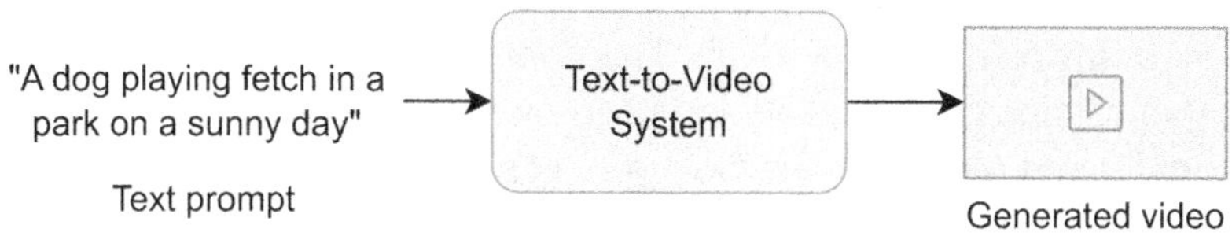

Figure 11.2: Input and output of a text-to-video system

Choosing a suitable ML approach

Text-to-video generation is similar in nature to text-to-image generation. Both generate visuals from textual descriptions. Techniques such as autoregressive modeling and diffusion models that are popular in text-to-image generation are also effective for text-to-video generation. As we saw previously, diffusion models have demonstrated strong performance in producing detailed and realistic visuals. Therefore, we choose a diffusion model to develop our text-to-video generation system.

There is, however, a crucial difference between image and video generation. For video generation, the model must process and generate a sequence of frames rather than a single image. This significantly increases the computational load. For instance, generating a five-second video at 24 FPS means the model must produce 120 frames. A 512×512 image might take around 1 second to generate on a high-end GPU such as the NVIDIA's H100, but scaling this to a five-second 720p video would require much more time, as each 720p frame has about 3.6 times more pixels. As a result, generating a five-second 720p video could take around seven minutes.

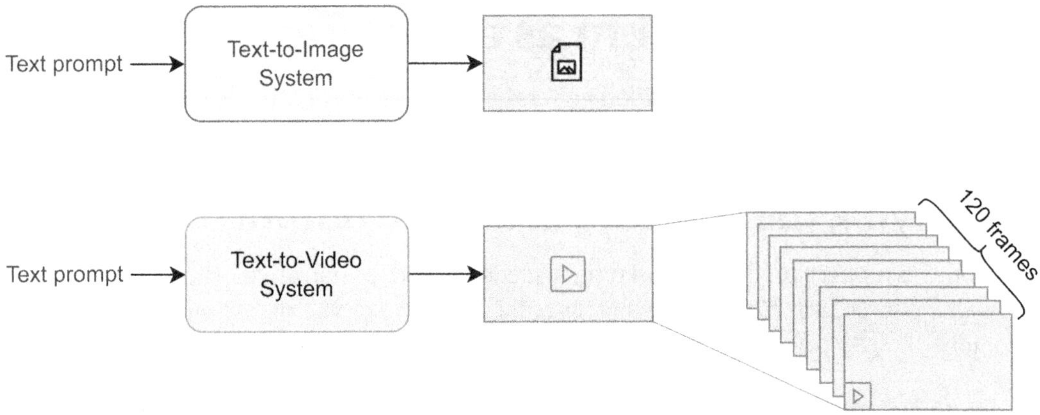

Figure 11.3: Text-to-video generating a sequence of frames

To address the complexity and computational cost of video generation, we employ the popular latent diffusion model approach. This approach was first popularized by the Stable Diffusion paper [3] and later applied and used by most video generation models, such as OpenAI's Sora [1] and Meta's Movie Gen [4]. Let's explore this approach further.

Latent diffusion model (LDM)

The core idea behind LDM is to have a diffusion model operate in a lower-dimensional latent space rather than directly in the pixel space. The diffusion model learns to denoise these lower-dimensional latent representations rather than the original video pixels in the training dataset.

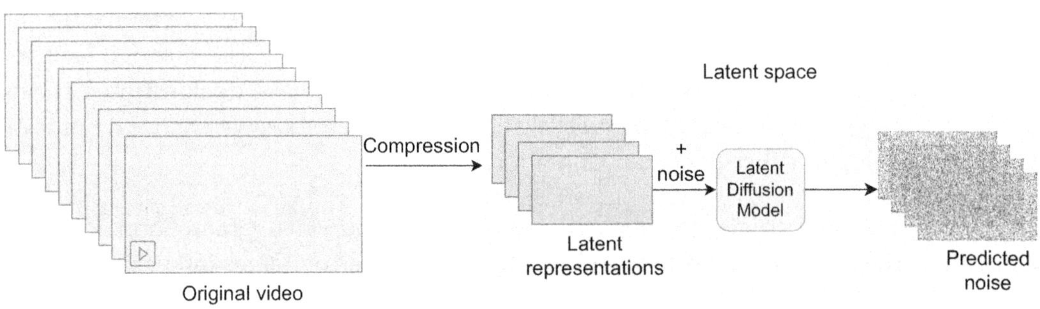

Figure 11.4: Diffusion model operating in a lower-dimensional latent space

LDM relies primarily on a compression network to compress video pixels into a latent representation. Let's examine the compression network in more detail.

Compression network

The compression network is a neural network that maps video pixels to a latent space. It takes raw video as input and outputs a compressed latent representation, reducing both its frame count (temporal dimension) and its resolution (spatial dimensions).

The compression network is usually based on a Variational Autoencoder (VAE) [5] model that is trained separately from the diffusion model. The VAE's visual encoder transforms the input video into a latent representation, while its visual decoder reconstructs the original video frames from this latent space.

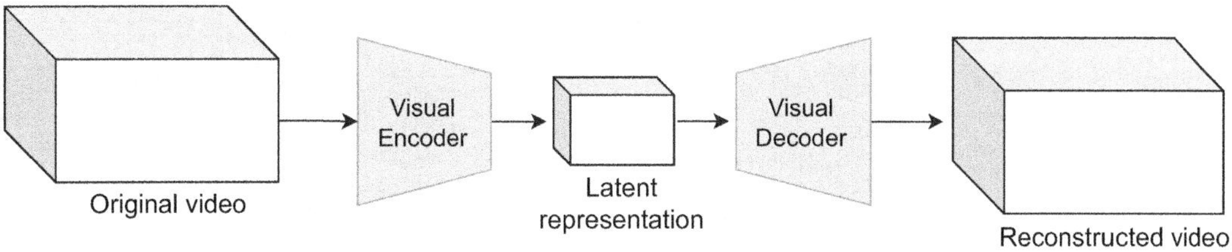

Figure 11.5: Compression network consisting of visual encoder and decoder

How does LDM address computational complexity?

LDMs require less computing power than standard diffusions because processing compressed representations is cheaper than handling high-dimensional pixels. To understand the impact of this compression, let's walk through an example.

Imagine we need a video with 24 FPS, a duration of five seconds, and a resolution of 720p. This means 120 frames, each with 1280×720 pixels—a substantial amount of data to process. If we use a compression network similar to [4] that reduces both the temporal and spatial resolution by a factor of 8, the video's spatial dimension becomes 160x90 pixels, and its temporal dimension shrinks to 15 frames.

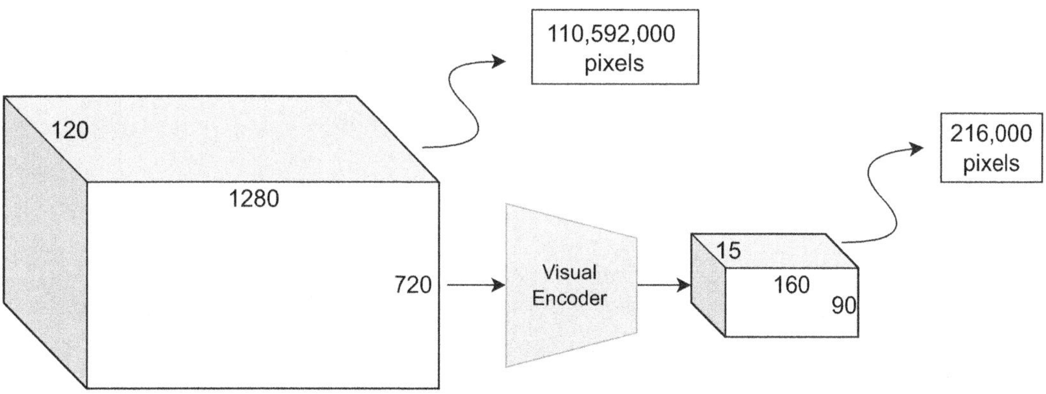

Figure 11.6: Impact of compression on data volume

This compressed representation is 512 times smaller than its pixel-space equivalent, making LDM training 512 times more efficient. This efficiency results in faster generation times and reduced resource consumption, which is especially valuable when handling high-resolution video data.

How to generate a video using a trained LDM

To generate a video using a trained LDM, we start with pure noise in the latent space. The LDM gradually refines it into a denoised latent representation. The visual decoder then converts this latent representation back into pixel space to produce the final video.

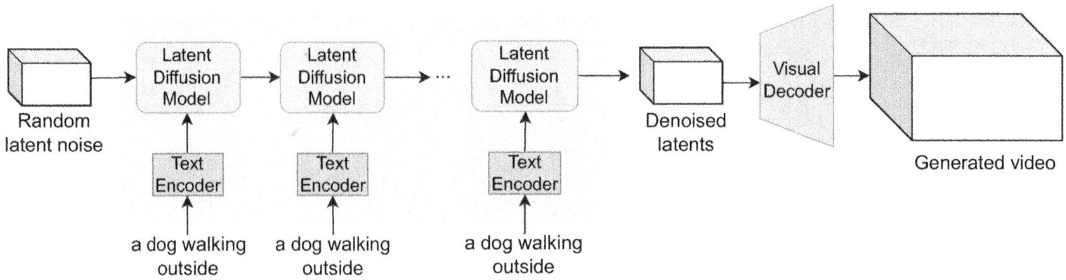

Figure 11.7: Video generation using a trained LDM

For this chapter, we choose an LDM approach to develop our text-to-video generation system because it's efficient and it reduces computational load. To learn more about LDM, refer to [6].

Data Preparation

The dataset for text-to-video generation includes 100 million pairs of textual descriptions and their corresponding videos. These pairs cover various subjects and actions, allowing the model to learn from diverse videos. In this section, we prepare the videos and captions for training our LDM.

Video preparation

We focus on three key steps in preparing videos for training:

1. Filter inappropriate videos
2. Standardize videos
3. Precompute video representations in the latent space

Filter inappropriate videos

Large datasets often contain unwanted content. This step removes inappropriate videos to ensure the model learns only from high-quality ones. Common steps include:

- **Remove low-quality or short videos:** We follow Movie Gen [4] and remove low-resolution, short, slow motion, or distorted videos with compression artifacts.
- **Remove duplicated videos (deduplication):** We use a deduplication method such as [7] to eliminate identical videos. This ensures training data is diverse and the model will not be exposed to certain videos more than others.
- **Remove harmful videos:** We use harm-detection models to identify and remove videos

with explicit content. This step is vital to ensure our text-to-video model will not generate harmful videos.

Standardize videos

- **Adjust video length:** We split longer videos into five-second clips to ensure training data consists only of videos of the same length.
- **Standardize frame rate:** We re-encode the videos with higher frame rates to 24FPS to ensure all the videos have the same frame rates.
- **Adjust video dimensions:** We resize and crop videos to a standard size, for example, 1280x720 pixels.

Precompute video representations in the latent space

As the LDM operates in the latent space, it needs only latent representations as input. Thus, each training iteration normally requires the following steps:

1. Extract frames from a video in the training data.
2. Pass these frames through a pretrained compression network to obtain latent representations.
3. Use the latent representations to continue training the diffusion model.

However, those steps are inefficient. Extracting frames and compressing them for millions of videos each time we train a new model slows diffusion training. Computing latent representations on the fly is resource-intensive and time-consuming.

To optimize the process, we precompute the latent representations for all videos and cache them in storage. During training, the diffusion model directly accesses the precomputed latent representations without waiting for frame extraction or compression processes. This approach significantly speeds up the diffusion training process, while keeping the storage cost manageable. Let's run a quick calculation to understand the storage need.

Back-of-the-envelope calculation: Assume that each video frame, when compressed into a latent representation, reduces in size by a factor of 512. So, if a video with 1,000 frames takes up about 1,000 MB, its latent representation would only take around 2 MB. If we cache latent representations for 100 million videos, the total storage required would be around 200 TB. Given modern storage capabilities, this is relatively manageable, especially compared to the significant time saved during training.

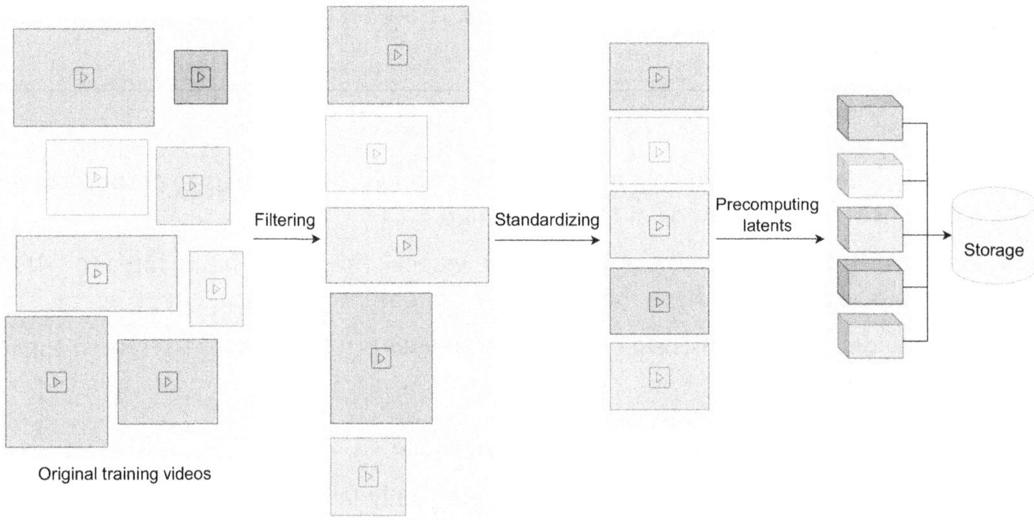

Figure 11.8: Video data preparation

Caption preparation

It's important to have high-quality, consistent captions. Some captions are likely to be missing or irrelevant. Common steps for preparing captions are:

- **Handle missing or non-English captions:** For videos without captions or with captions in another language, we use models such as LLaMa3-Video [8] or LLaVA [9] to automatically generate descriptive captions.
- **Re-captioning:** We improve existing captions using pretrained video captioning models such as LLaMa3-Video or LLaVA to generate longer, more detailed versions. The Sora team [1] has shown that this process is essential for enhancing quality and text alignment.
- **Precomputing caption embeddings:** Diffusion model training requires caption embeddings for conditioning. We use the text encoder to precompute caption embeddings, speeding up LDM training.

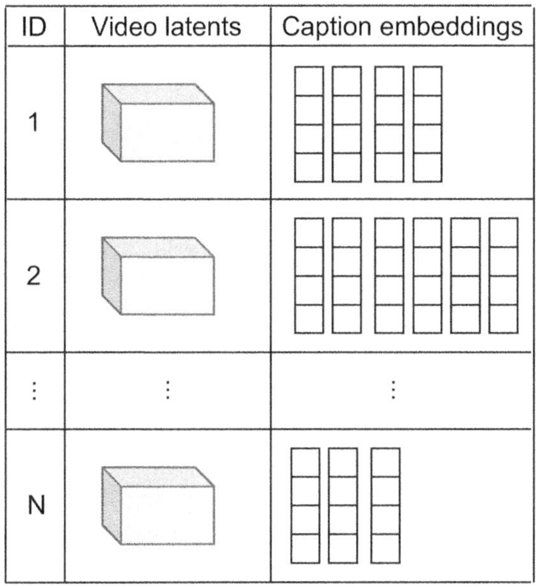

Figure 11.9: Prepared video-caption data for training

Model Development

Architecture

When selecting the architecture for a text-to-video diffusion model, we have two main options: U-Net and DiT. We'll examine each and determine the additional layers required to extend them to handle videos.

U-Net for videos

Let's briefly review the U-Net architecture before extending it to process videos. As we explored in Chapter 9, the U-Net architecture consists of a series of downsampling blocks followed by a series of upsampling blocks. Each downsampling block includes 2D convolutions to process and update image features and a cross-attention layer to update features by attending to the text prompt.

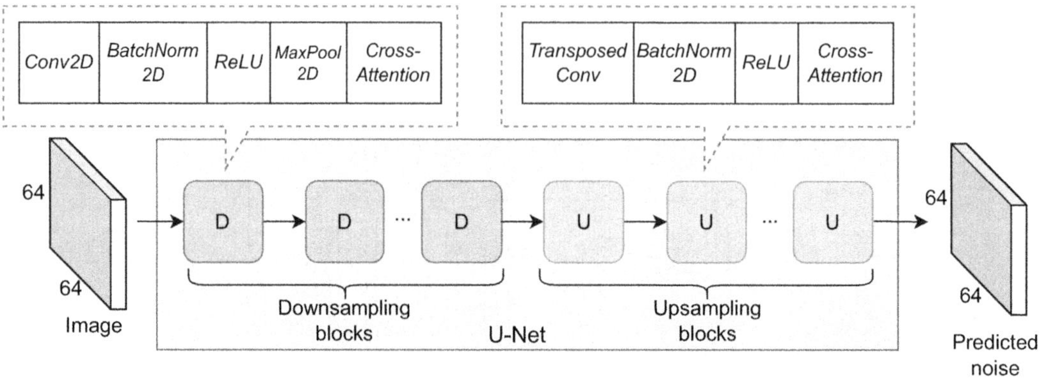

Figure 11.10: U-Net architecture for image generation

However, these layers mainly focus on capturing the relationships between pixels within a single image. This design presents a challenge for videos, where maintaining temporal consistency is crucial for smooth motion and continuity across frames. Current layers, however, operate spatially within individual frames rather than across frames.

To address this shortcoming, we modify the U-Net architecture to understand relationships across frames. In particular, we inject two commonly used temporal layers:

- Temporal attention
- Temporal convolution

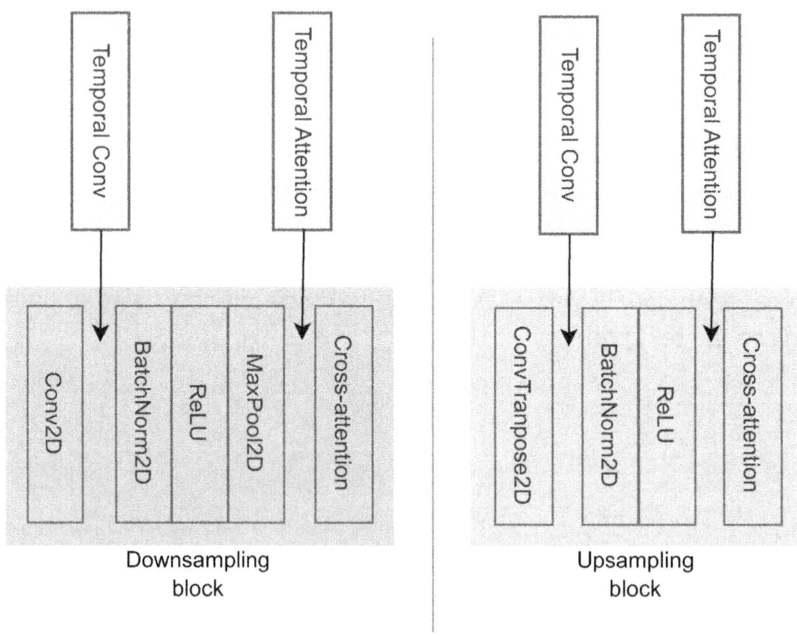

Figure 11.11: Injecting temporal layers into the U-Net's downsampling and upsampling blocks

Let's briefly review each layer.

Temporal attention: Temporal attention utilizes the attention mechanism across frames. Each feature is updated by attending to relevant features across other frames. Figure 11.12 shows how a certain feature in frame 2 is updated by attending to the features in the other frames.

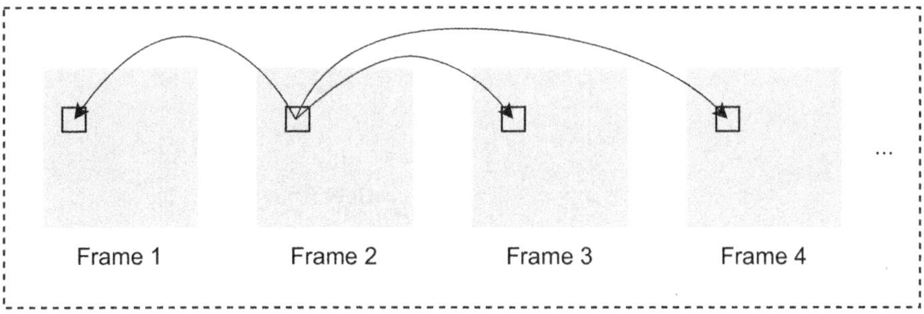

Figure 11.12: Temporal attention updating features by looking across frames

Temporal convolution: Temporal convolution refers to applying a convolution operator to a 3D segment of data, to capture the temporal dimension. Figure 11.13 illustrates 2D and 3D temporal convolutions.

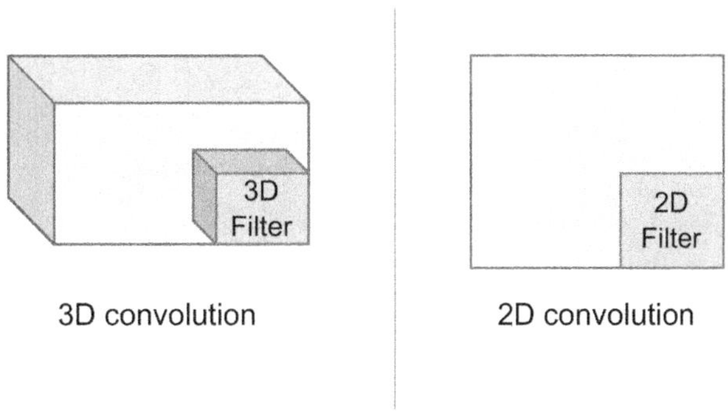

Figure 11.13: 2D convolution vs. 3D convolutions

In summary, to extend a U-Net architecture to process videos, we can interleave temporal convolution and temporal attention layers in each downsampling and upsampling block. These layers allow the U-Net architecture to model the motion in input videos and generate a sequence of frames that are temporally consistent. To learn more about how these layers can be interleaved, refer to [10].

DiT for videos

Unlike U-Net, which is based mainly on convolutions, DiT relies primarily on the Transformer architecture. As shown in Figure 11.14, DiT consists of four main components:

- Patchify

- Positional encoding
- Transformer
- Unpatchify

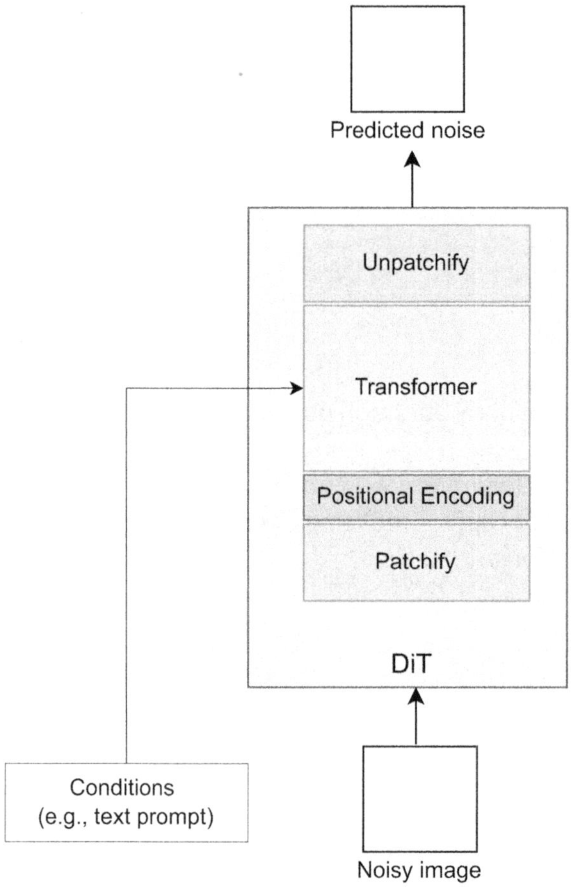

Figure 11.14: DiT components

Let's examine each component and understand its purpose.

Patchify

This component converts the input to a sequence of embedding vectors. It first divides the input into smaller, fixed-size patches. Each patch is then flattened to form a sequence of vectors. The flattened patches are finally transformed into patch embeddings using a projection layer. This step is crucial to align the embedding size of each flattened patch with the Transformer's hidden size.

The patchify process is similar for both image and video inputs. For images, it divides the input into fixed-size 2D patches. For videos, the video is divided into 3D patches.

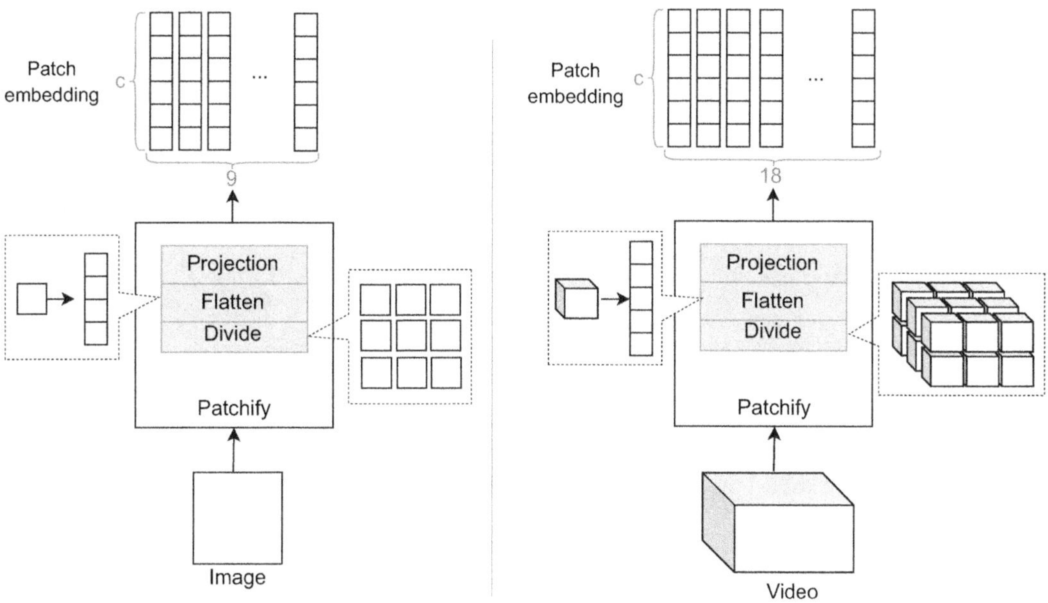

Figure 11.15: Patchify for image vs. video

Positional encoding

The positional encoding component produces an embedding for each position in the original sequence. These embeddings provide the Transformer with information about the location of each patch in the original input.

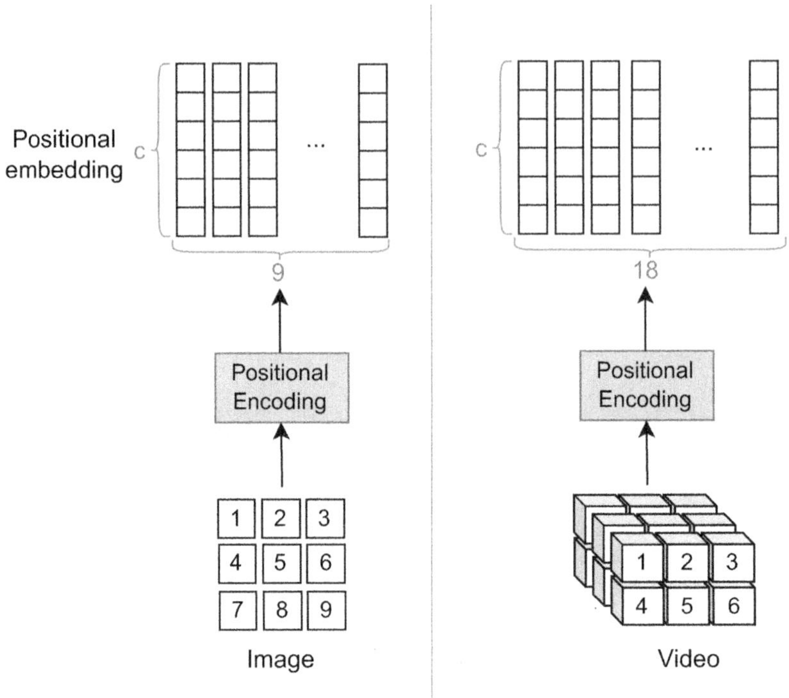

Figure 11.16: 1D positional encoding for image vs. video

As we saw in Chapter 2, there are different ways to encode positions: Some methods use fixed positional encoding during training, while other methods make the positional encoding learnable. There are also different ways to assign positions to each patch. For example, we can give each patch a single number to show its place in a sequence or use 3D coordinates (2D for images) to show where each patch is in space and time.

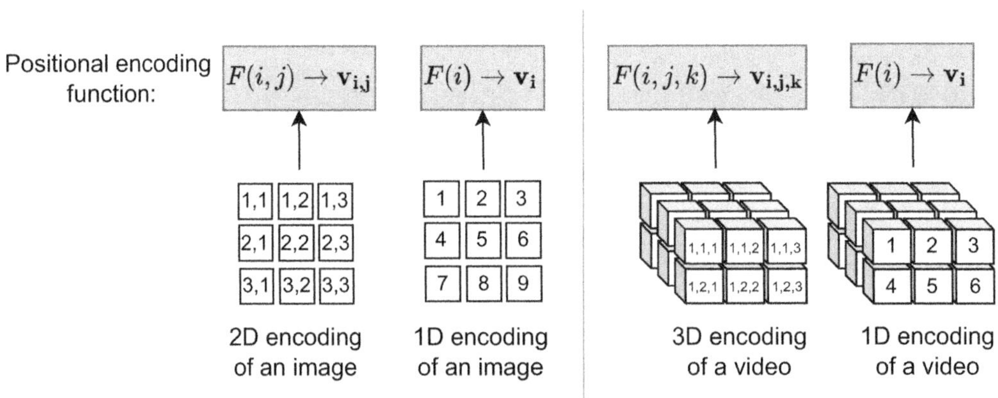

Figure 11.17: 1D, 2D, and 3D positional encoding

There is not one best way to do positional encoding. We often need to run experiments to find the approach that will be most effective for the data and task. In this chapter, we follow OpenSora [11] and use RoPE [12] positional encoding. To learn more about positional encoding in text-to-video models, refer to [4].

Transformer

The Transformer processes the sequence of embeddings and other conditioning signals, such as the text prompt, to predict noise for each patch.

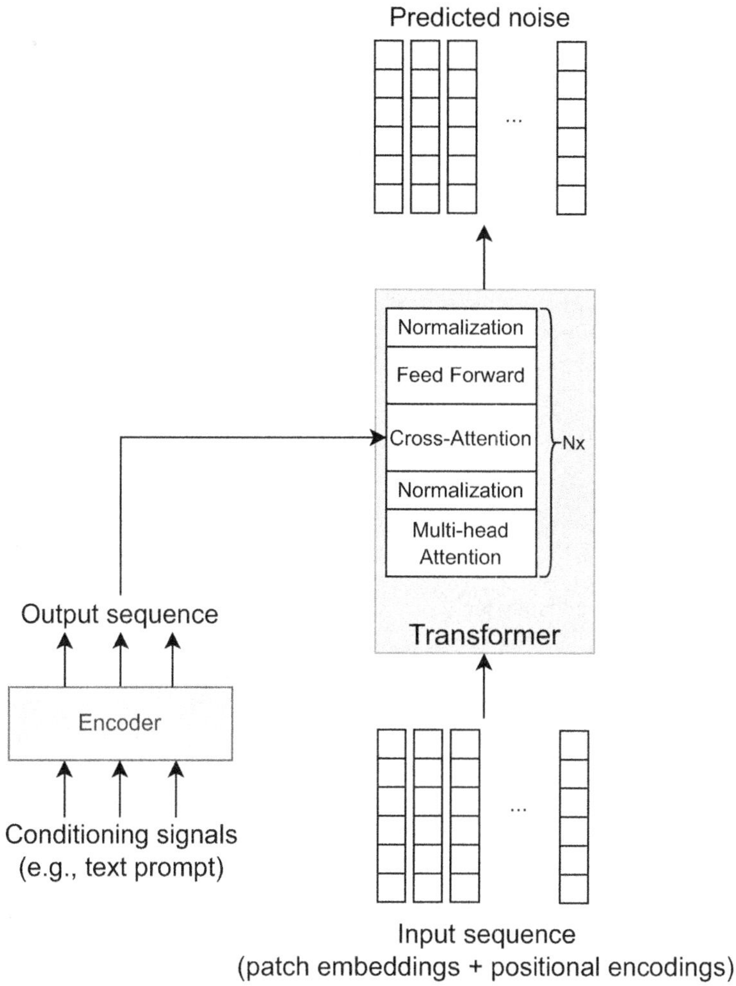

Figure 11.18: Transformer component

Unpatchify

Unpatchify converts the predicted noise vectors back to the original input dimensions. It includes a *LayerNorm* for normalization, a linear layer to adjust vector length, and a reshape operation to form the final output.

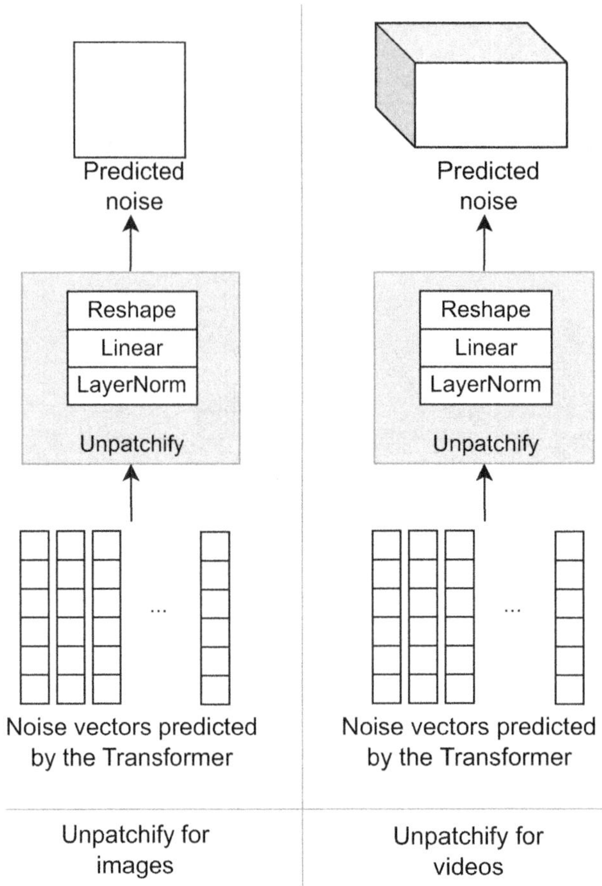

Figure 11.19: Unpatchify component

U-Net vs. DiT

Both U-Net and DiT architectures are proven to be effective for text-to-video generation. The U-Net architecture has been around for longer and has been extensively tested. Popular U-Net-based text-to-video models include Stable Video Diffusion [13] by Stability AI and EMU video [14] by Meta.

The DiT architecture is more recent and has shown great promise, with superior results. DiT performs better with increased data and computational resources due to the scalable nature of Transformers. In addition, it has a flexible architecture, making it easier to adapt to videos and other input modalities. Meta's Movie Gen and OpenAI's Sora is a popular model based on the DiT architecture.

In this chapter, we follow Sora and choose the DiT architecture.

Training

Training a video diffusion model is very similar to training an image diffusion model. During training, we add noise to the original video by simulating the forward process and train the model to predict the added noise. The three concrete steps involved in one iteration of training are:

1. **Noise addition:** A timestep is randomly sampled to determine the level of noise addition. The sampled timestep is used to add noise to the input video.
2. **Noise prediction:** The DiT model receives the noisy video as input and predicts the added noise based on conditioning signals such as text prompt and the sampled timestep.
3. **Loss calculation:** The loss is measured by comparing the predicted noise to the actual noise.

To review diffusion training in more detail, refer to Chapter 9.

ML objective and loss function

The primary loss function is the reconstruction loss, calculated using the mean squared error (MSE) formula. This loss measures the difference between the predicted noise and the actual noise, encouraging the model to accurately predict the added noise. The ML objective is to minimize the reconstruction loss, leading to accurate video reconstruction.

Researchers have experimented with utilizing other loss functions to enhance text-to-video performance. To learn more, refer to [4].

Challenges in training video diffusion models

Training a DiT model for text-to-video generation involves several challenges and design decisions. This section explores two important challenges:

- Lack of large-scale video–text data
- Computational cost of high-resolution video generation

Lack of large-scale video–text training data

Training large models requires lots of data. As opposed to training text-to-image models, where a huge amount of image–text paired data is available, paired video–text data is scarce. This scarcity presents a challenge in training effective video generation models.

There are two common strategies for addressing the lack of large-scale data:

1. **Train the DiT model on both image and video data:** This strategy treats each image as a single-frame video, thus allowing the model to train on both image–text and video–text data.
2. **Pretrain the DiT model on image data:** This strategy first pretrains the DiT model on image–text pairs to leverage extensive image data and build a strong visual foundation.

The pretrained model is then finetuned on video-text pairs for video generation.

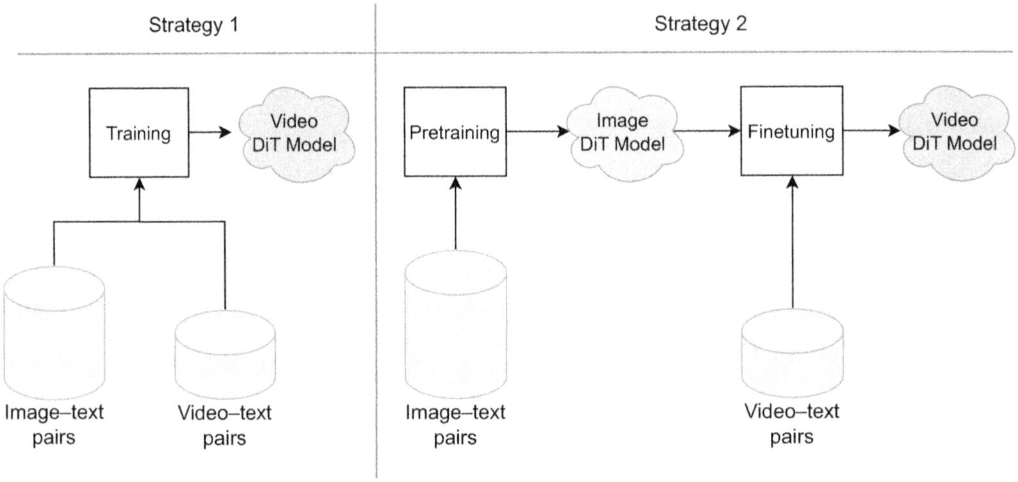

Figure 11.20: Two strategies to utilize image-text training data

Both strategies leverage hundreds of millions of image-text data in training, allowing the DiT model to learn from both images and videos. For simplicity, we choose the first strategy, as it requires only one stage of training. However, both strategies can be effective in practice.

Computational cost of high-resolution video generation

As discussed earlier, processing and generating videos is more expensive than images. This is primarily because videos generally contain hundreds of frames, making the process slower and more costly. Generating high-resolution videos, such as 720p or 1080p, adds to the challenge.

Here are a few common strategies to reduce the computational cost of training high-resolution video generation models:

- **Employ an LDM-based approach:** Instead of training the DiT model directly in pixel space, we use a compression network to convert videos from pixel space into a lower-dimensional latent space. Training the diffusion model in this latent space reduces the computational load.
- **Precompute video representations:** By precomputing video representations in the latent space before training, we avoid repetitive computations during training. Utilizing this cached data speeds up the training process.
- **Utilize a spatial super-resolution model:** As proposed by Google's *Imagen Video* [15], we use a separately trained model to upscale the resolution of generated videos. The DiT model generates videos at a lower resolution that are then enhanced to the desired resolution by a spatial super-resolution model. For example, the DiT model can generate videos at 720p, and a spatial super-resolution model can then upscale them

to 1080p or 4K.

- **Utilize a temporal super-resolution model:** As proposed by [15], we employ a model to increase the temporal resolution by interpolating between frames. For instance, if a video should be five seconds at 24 FPS (i.e., 120 frames total), the DiT model can generate it at 12 FPS (60 frames), and a temporal super-resolution model can then interpolate to achieve 24 FPS.
- **Use more efficient architectures:** We can adopt an efficient implementation of the attention mechanism [16] to reduce the computational load during training. Additionally, techniques like Mixture of Experts (MoE) [17] can be used to accelerate the training process.
- **Use distributed training:** We use distributed training techniques, such as tensor parallelism, to parallelize training across multiple devices. By splitting the model, data, or both across different devices, we can significantly speed up training and handle larger video datasets more efficiently. This approach is particularly useful for high-resolution video generation, where memory and computational demands are substantial. For an overview of distributed training, refer to Chapter 1.

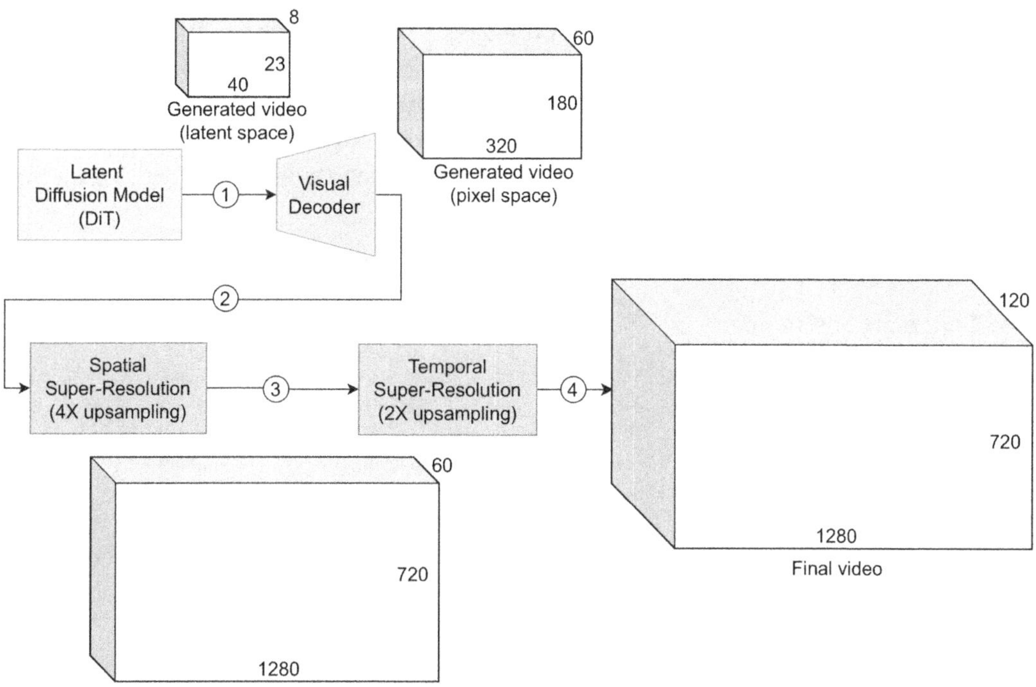

Figure 11.21: Efficient text-to-video pipeline

Sampling

The sampling process in diffusion models starts with random noise, and the model iteratively denoises the sample until a fully denoised video representation in the latent space is obtained. For more details on sampling in diffusion models, refer to Chapter 9.

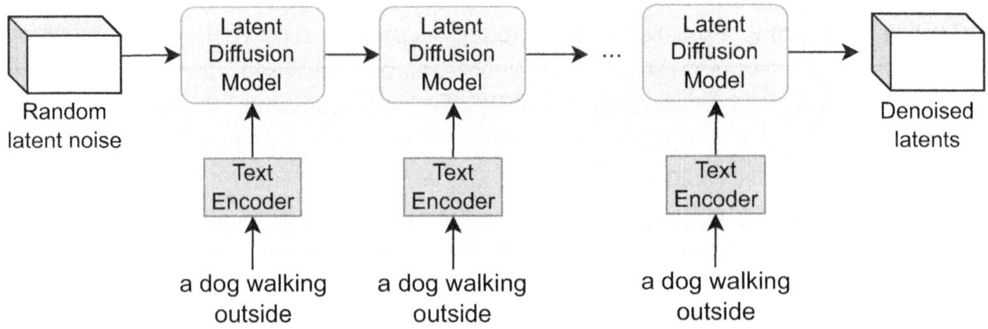

Figure 11.22: Sampling process from a trained LDM

Evaluation

Offline evaluation metrics

A consistent benchmark is crucial for evaluating video generation models. *VBench* [18] and *Movie Gen Bench* [19] offer this by providing a curated set of prompts designed to test various aspects of video generation such as motion coherence, temporal consistency, and scene complexity. We can use these benchmarks to measure how well the model creates realistic and smooth videos, focusing on video quality, motion accuracy, and scene transitions. Let's explore both automated metrics and human evaluation, focusing on three key areas:

- Frame quality
- Temporal consistency
- Video–text alignment

Frame quality

Frame quality refers to measuring the quality of each frame independently. To measure this quality we employ FID [20] and Inception score (IS) [21], both of which are commonly used for images. The overall quality is calculated by averaging the IS and FID scores of all frames. Other metrics such as LPIPS [22] and KID [23] can also be used.

While FID and IS measure the quality of individual frames, they don't account for the temporal consistency in generated videos. For instance, a video might have high-quality frames but lack smooth transitions, resulting in a high FID score without visual coherence. Let's explore temporal consistency and the common metrics used to measure it.

Temporal consistency

Temporal consistency refers to how smoothly visual content transitions from one frame to the next. Evaluating temporal consistency is important to ensure the generated video flows naturally. A common metric for measuring temporal consistency is the Fréchet Video

Distance (FVD).

FVD

FVD [24], which is an extension of FID, evaluates both the visual quality and temporal consistency of videos. It compares the statistical distribution of generated videos to real videos in an embedded space.

Here's a step-by-step guide to calculating the FVD score:

1. **Generating videos:** We start by generating a large set of videos using the model we want to evaluate. These videos will be compared against a set of real videos to evaluate their quality and consistency.
2. **Extracting features:** We pass each video (both generated and real) through a pretrained I3D model [25] and extract features from a specific layer. The I3D model extends the Inception v3 [26] architecture to sequential data by training it for action recognition.
3. **Calculating mean and covariance:** We calculate the mean and covariance of the extracted features separately for generated and real videos. These statistical measures summarize the distribution of features for both sets of videos.
4. **Computing Fréchet distance:** We calculate the FVD score as the Fréchet distance between the mean and covariance of generated and real videos. The Fréchet distance measures how close the two distributions are.

A lower FVD score indicates greater similarity between the distributions, meaning the generated videos are more realistic and temporally consistent.

Video–text alignment

Video–text alignment refers to how accurately the generated video reflects the textual description on which it was conditioned.

A commonly used metric to measure video–text alignment is the CLIP similarity score, calculated as follows:

1. **Extracting frame-level features:** We pass each video frame through a pretrained CLIP image encoder to get visual features. The text is encoded using the text encoder to obtain textual features.
2. **Calculating similarities:** For each frame, we compute the cosine similarity between its visual features and the textual features. This score indicates how well the frame content aligns with the text.
3. **Aggregating per-frame similarities:** We aggregate these similarity scores to get a single score representing the overall video–text alignment. Aggregation can be done by averaging, taking the maximum score, or using other statistical methods.

A high CLIP similarity score indicates that generated videos are aligned with their corresponding text.

Human evaluation

Alongside the described automated metrics, human evaluation is still vital for assessing generative models, as it provides a subjective assessment that complements automated measures.

For human evaluation, we generate videos from test prompts using two different models. We then present pairs of videos, one from each model, to human annotators. They choose the better video based on assessing video–text alignment, video quality, and temporal consistency. This process allows us to compare two models to see which one performs better.

Online evaluation metrics

Online evaluation metrics for text-to-video models are similar to those for text-to-image models. Important metrics include:

- Click-through rate
- Time spent on the page
- User feedback
- Conversion rate

These metrics help gauge user engagement, satisfaction, and overall model performance in production.

Overall ML System Design

In this section, we dive into the holistic design of a text-to-video generation system. In particular, we examine the following pipelines:

- Data pipeline
- Training pipeline
- Inference pipeline

Data pipeline

The data pipeline prepares training data by filtering unsuitable images and videos, standardizing them, and precomputing and storing latent representations. It ensures captions are relevant and detailed by re-captioning and using a pretrained text encoder to precompute and store caption embeddings.

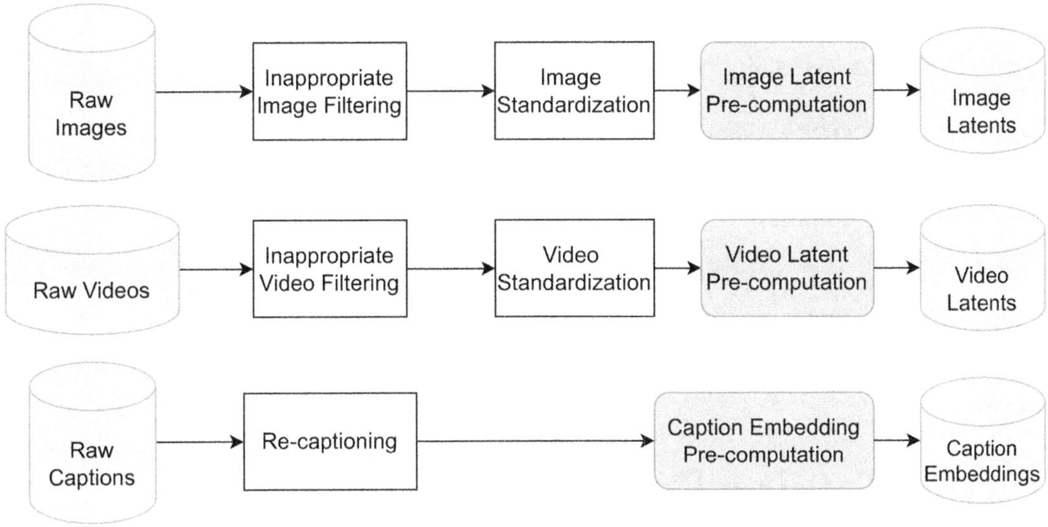

Figure 11.23: Data pipeline

Training pipeline

The training pipeline trains the model using the training data prepared by the data pipeline.

Inference pipeline

The inference pipeline processes real-time user requests to generate videos from text prompts. As shown in Figure 11.24, it has several crucial components that ensure system quality and safety.

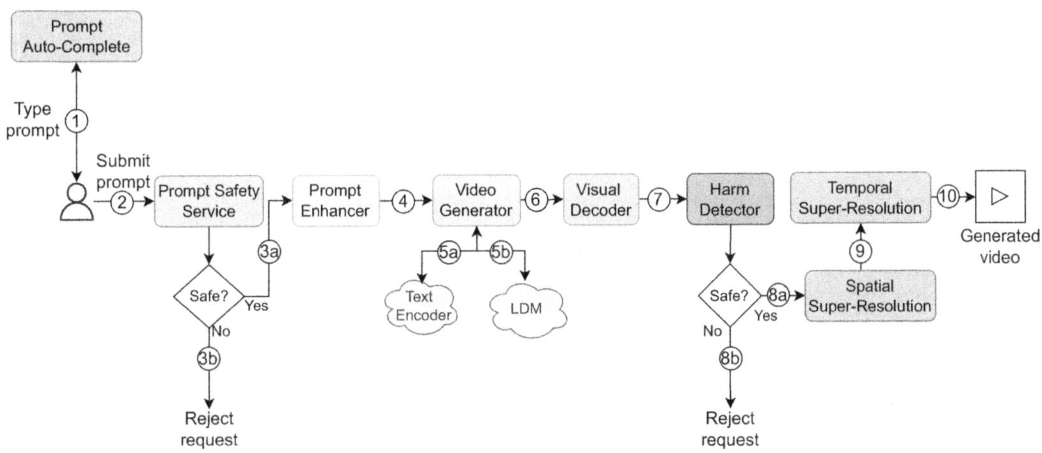

Figure 11.24: Inference pipeline components

Most of the components are similar to those explored in Chapter 9 for text-to-image generation. The unique components for text-to-video generation are:

- Visual decoder
- Temporal super-resolution

Visual decoder

The LDM generates output in the latent space, not the pixel space. The visual decoder then uses the compression network to convert this latent representation back into the pixel space.

Temporal super-resolution

This component interpolates between the generated frames, leading to smoother motion in videos.

Other Talking Points

In case there's extra time at the end of the interview, you might discuss these further topics:

- Ensuring sampling flexibility for variable durations, resolutions, and aspect ratios [1].
- Extending the text-to-video model to downstream applications such as inpainting, outputpainting, video-to-video stylization, frame interpolation, super-resolution, and animating images (image-to-video) [10].
- Support for controlling the generated videos such as the level of desired motion and the type of motion (camera vs. object motion) [27].
- Using progressive distillation techniques to reduce the computational demands of training [28].
- Details of spatial and temporal super-resolution models [15].
- Details of re-captioning model [9, 8].
- Different noise schedulers [29].
- Noise conditioning augmentation techniques [30].
- Personalizing a text-to-video model to a particular subject [31].
- ControlNet for text-to-video models [32].
- Details of Stable Cascade method [33].
- Details of visual compression network [13].

Summary

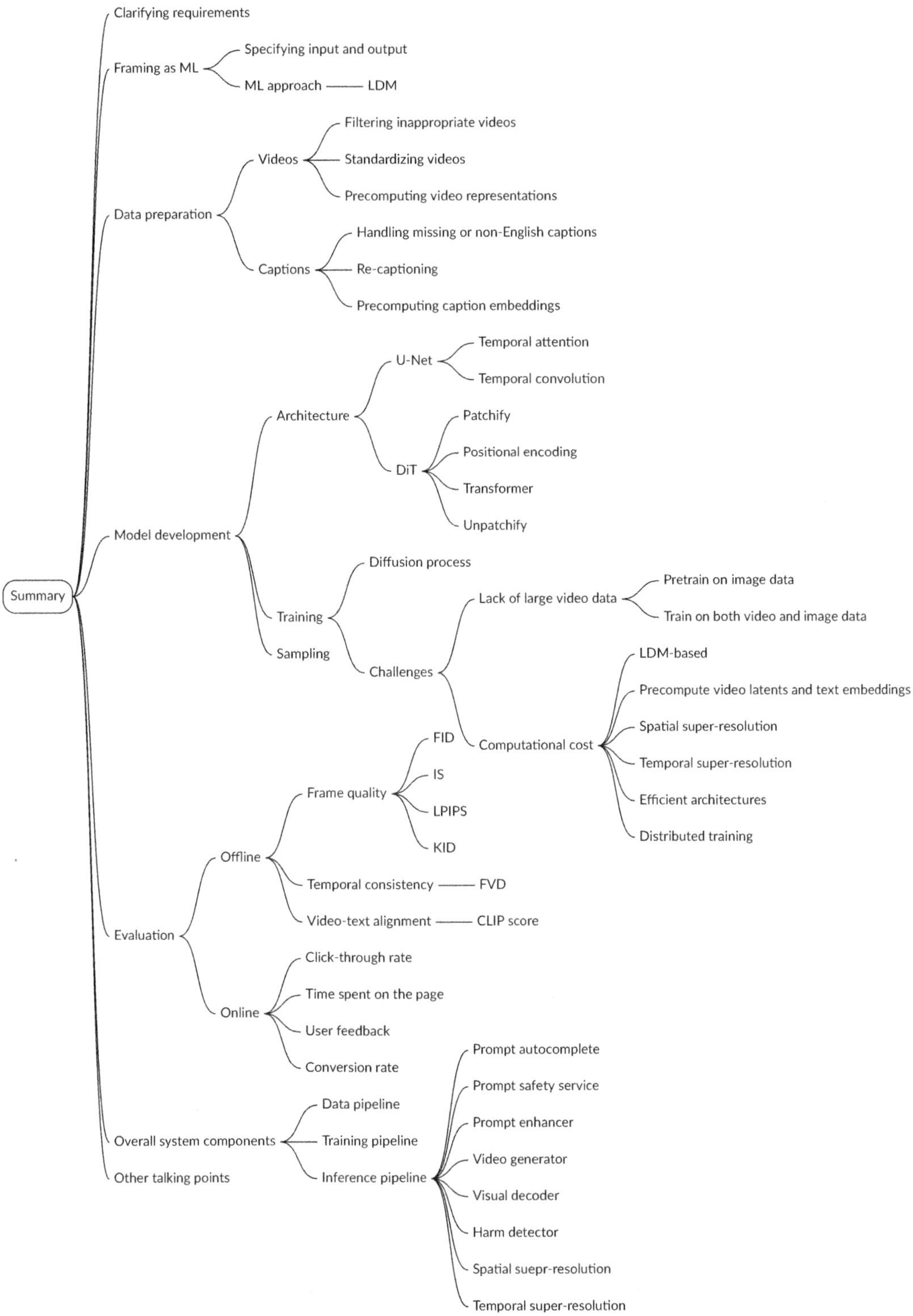

Summary
Clarifying requirements
Framing as ML
Specifying input and output
ML approach
LDM
Data preparation
Videos
Filtering inappropriate videos
Standardizing videos
Precomputing video representations
Captions
Handling missing or non-English captions
Re-captioning
Precomputing caption embeddings
Model development
Architecture
U-Net
Temporal attention
Temporal convolution
DiT
Patchify
Positional encoding
Transformer
Unpatchify
Training
Diffusion process
Challenges
Lack of large video data
Pretrain on image data
Train on both video and image data
Computational cost
LDM-based
Precompute video latents and text embeddings
Spatial super-resolution
Temporal super-resolution
Efficient architectures
Distributed training
Sampling
Evaluation
Offline
Frame quality
FID
IS
LPIPS
KID
Temporal consistency
FVD
Video-text alignment
CLIP score
Online
Click-through rate
Time spent on the page
User feedback
Conversion rate
Overall system components
Data pipeline
Training pipeline
Inference pipeline
Prompt autocomplete
Prompt safety service
Prompt enhancer
Video generator
Visual decoder
Harm detector
Spatial suepr-resolution
Temporal super-resolution
Other talking points

Reference Material

[1] Video generation models as world simulators. https://openai.com/index/video-generation-models-as-world-simulators/.

[2] H100 Tensor Core GPU. https://www.nvidia.com/en-us/data-center/h100/.

[3] High-Resolution Image Synthesis with Latent Diffusion Models. https://arxiv.org/abs/2112.10752.

[4] Meta Movie Gen. https://ai.meta.com/research/movie-gen/.

[5] Auto-Encoding Variational Bayes. https://arxiv.org/abs/1312.6114.

[6] The Illustrated Stable Diffusion. https://jalammar.github.io/illustrated-stable-diffusion/.

[7] On the De-duplication of LAION-2B. https://arxiv.org/abs/2303.12733.

[8] The Llama 3 Herd of Models. https://arxiv.org/abs/2407.21783.

[9] LLaVA-NeXT: A Strong Zero-shot Video Understanding Model. https://llava-vl.github.io/blog/2024-04-30-llava-next-video/.

[10] Lumiere: A Space-Time Diffusion Model for Video Generation. https://arxiv.org/abs/2401.12945.

[11] OpenSora Technical Report. https://github.com/hpcaitech/Open-Sora/blob/main/docs/report_02.md.

[12] RoFormer: Enhanced Transformer with Rotary Position Embedding. https://arxiv.org/abs/2104.09864.

[13] Stable Video Diffusion: Scaling Latent Video Diffusion Models to Large Datasets. https://arxiv.org/abs/2311.15127.

[14] Emu Video: Factorizing Text-to-Video Generation by Explicit Image Conditioning. https://arxiv.org/abs/2311.10709.

[15] Imagen Video: High Definition Video Generation with Diffusion Models. https://arxiv.org/abs/2210.02303.

[16] HyperAttention: Long-context Attention in Near-Linear Time. https://arxiv.org/abs/2310.05869.

[17] Mixture of Experts Explained. https://huggingface.co/blog/moe.

[18] VBench: Comprehensive Benchmark Suite for Video Generative Models. https://vchitect.github.io/VBench-project/.

[19] Movie Gen Bench. https://github.com/facebookresearch/MovieGenBench.

[20] FID calculation. https://en.wikipedia.org/wiki/Fr%C3%A9chet_inception_distance.

[21] Inception score. https://en.wikipedia.org/wiki/Inception_score.

[22] The Unreasonable Effectiveness of Deep Features as a Perceptual Metric. https://arxiv.org/abs/1801.03924.

[23] Demystifying MMD GANs. https://arxiv.org/abs/1801.01401.

[24] Towards Accurate Generative Models of Video: A New Metric & Challenges. https://arxiv.org/abs/1812.01717.

[25] Quo Vadis, Action Recognition? A New Model and the Kinetics Dataset. https://arxiv.org/abs/1705.07750.

[26] Rethinking the Inception Architecture for Computer Vision. https://arxiv.org/abs/1512.00567.

[27] Moonshot: Towards Controllable Video Generation and Editing with Multimodal Conditions. https://arxiv.org/abs/2401.01827.

[28] Progressive Distillation for Fast Sampling of Diffusion Models. https://arxiv.org/abs/2202.00512.

[29] Schedulers. https://huggingface.co/docs/diffusers/v0.9.0/en/api/schedulers.

[30] Photorealistic Text-to-Image Diffusion Models with Deep Language Understanding. https://arxiv.org/abs/2205.11487.

[31] CustomVideo: Customizing Text-to-Video Generation with Multiple Subjects. https://arxiv.org/abs/2401.09962.

[32] Control-A-Video: Controllable Text-to-Video Generation with Diffusion Models. https://controlavideo.github.io/.

[33] Introducing Stable Cascade. https://stability.ai/news/introducing-stable-cascade.

Afterword

Congratulations! You've completed this interview guide, gaining crucial skills and knowledge to design complex GenAI systems. Not everyone has the discipline or persistence to achieve what you've accomplished. Take a moment to pat yourself on the back. Your hard work will pay off.

Securing your dream role in this fast-evolving field is a journey that requires continuous learning and practice. The more you refine your skills, the more confident you'll become. Keep practicing, and best of luck on your path ahead!

Thank you for buying and reading this book. Without readers like you, our work would not be possible. We hope you have enjoyed the book!

If you have comments or questions about this book, feel free to contact us at hi@bytebytego.com. If you notice any errors, please let us know so we can make corrections for the next edition. Thank you!

Printed in Dunstable, United Kingdom

77939206R00212